The Letters of
Baron Friedrich von Hügel
and
Professor Norman Kemp Smith

THE LETTERS OF
BARON
FRIEDRICH VON HÜGEL
AND
PROFESSOR
NORMAN KEMP SMITH

Edited by

LAWRENCE F. BARMANN

New York
FORDHAM UNIVERSITY PRESS
1981

Printed in the United States of America

For
JAMES LEONARD MARSH
JOHN JOSEPH O'BRIEN
VINCENT CHRISTOPHER PUNZO
supportive friends
and
stimulating colleagues

What a pleasure it is to have friends whom one can admire, nothing surely makes one grow like that.

FRIEDRICH VON HÜGEL to NORMAN KEMP SMITH
1 April 1924

CONTENTS

The Letters of
Baron Friedrich von Hügel
and
Professor Norman Kemp Smith

Baron
FRIEDRICH VON HÜGEL
ca. 1921

Professor
NORMAN KEMP SMITH
in the early 1920s

INTRODUCTION

Whatever else might be said of the personal letters of men now dead, certainly they are autobiographical materials of the first importance. The 130 letters and cards which passed between Baron Friedrich von Hügel and Professor Norman Kemp Smith from 1918 until 1925 are no exception. This correspondence offers a unique insight into the thought and lives of both men, and supplies a touchstone which any interpretation of either man representing itself as true can ignore only at grave risk. The fact that both von Hügel and Kemp Smith kept almost every piece of written communication which passed between them indicates, as well, something of the value which each placed on the other and on their relationship.

Philosophers, not unlike novelists, have their cycles of influence and popularity. The ideas which influence one generation may have to wait a century or more before they are developed or renewed by another. Academic philosophers of the late-twentieth century are mostly concerned with the one-dimensional issues of linguistic analysis, and they have for the moment lost interest in the epistemological problems and the historical method which engaged von Hügel and Kemp Smith more than half a century ago. Nevertheless, the thought of these two men is intricately connected with some of the main strands of the Western intellectual tradition, and unless Western society totally repudiates its past, von Hügel's and Kemp Smith's ideas will in some future time again interest and influence even the academic philosophers.

But even now von Hügel and Kemp Smith are read, and they still have their influence—if not so much on academic philosophers, at least on educated individuals interested in religious thought and in the history of ideas generally. Both Kemp Smith and von Hügel approached philosophical problems historically, and this shared methodology and interest were both a strong bond of their friendship and one important reason why their thought will endure. The letters which passed between the two men are not philosophical disquisitions. They are not even developed commentary on men and theories, although sometimes they are interesting and partially formulated insights on them. They are simply letters between two outstanding men who happened to share, at a certain period in history, a common interest in the epistemological question and its relationship to religion. Moreover,

1

the correspondence turns out to reveal less of specific, let alone detailed, philosophical positions held by either man and more of the growth of a friendship. And so these letters are mainly autobiographical, almost in a homely way, of Kemp Smith at the very zenith of his career, and of von Hügel in his final, declining years. The letters are full of family events, personal concerns, daily happenings, and observations on the passing scene. This does not mean that the letters are of no value for understanding these men as thinkers. They are immensely important in that regard, because before one can know a thinker well, he must know him as a man and in the milieu in which he thought. Ideas are separated from history only at the risk of misunderstanding both. A careful use of the von Hügel — Kemp Smith correspondence reveals attitudes and character traits in both men which can make their published work more fully understood in the light of the nuanced individuality which produced it.

Friedrich von Hügel and Norman Kemp Smith were separated in age by exactly twenty years. Both were born on May 5th: the former in 1852, the latter in 1872. Von Hügel was the son of a German diplomat in Austrian service and of a Scottish mother, born in Florence and raised there and in Brussels. His education was private, and after his father's death in 1870, he settled permanently in England with his mother and brother and sister. In 1873 he married Lady Mary Catherine Herbert, daughter of Lord and Lady Sidney Herbert of Lea, and sister to the thirteenth and fourteenth Earls of Pembroke. They made London their home (first in Hampstead and then in Kensington), and the Baron embarked on a lifetime study of Biblical criticism and religious philosophy. Von Hügel's special intellectual interests and pursuits were in areas in which general Roman Catholic scholarship was especially deficient, and these led him into close association with scholars and thinkers whose research and conclusions (especially in Biblical criticism and its implications for Church doctrine) were often far in advance of any officially accepted Catholic position of the time. The result was a crisis in which the Church authorities who were bent on conservation put a muzzle on the modernists who were bent on new growth. Most of von Hügel's closest friends and associates were driven from the Church, and he himself avoided a confrontation through prudent (some have said timid) avoidance of further conflict and a retreat into silence and the quiet pursuit of religious philosophy. As early as 1908 he had published, at the very peak of the ecclesiastical controversy, his two-volume study of *The Mystical Element of Religion as*

Studied in Saint Catherine of Genoa and Her Friends; and this would be followed in future years by other books. But his occasional essays, reviews, and addresses best represent, perhaps, the special problems and quality of his later work. One collection of these was published in 1921, and is the partial concern of several letters between von Hügel and Kemp Smith. The manuscript which he tentatively titled in 1920 "The Reality of God: A Study of Its Self-Manifestations" was published in its incomplete state posthumously. That manuscript's gradual development and the question of its becoming the Gifford Lectures at Edinburgh in 1924–1925 are the partial subject matters for numerous letters in this collection, which in turn form an important aid for understanding the posthumous book.

Kemp Smith, on the other hand, was born in Dundee, the sixth and last child of a cabinetmaker. Although he was christened Norman Duncan Smith, he never used his middle name (which had been his mother's maiden name), and in 1910 upon his marriage to Amy Kemp assumed her maiden name in its place and as part of his surname. In 1888 he matriculated at St. Andrews University, where he was subsequently influenced by Professors Andrew Seth (later Pringle-Pattison), John Burnet, and Henry (later Sir Henry) Jones. He took his degree with first-class honors in 1893, spent some time studying further at the Universities of Jena, Zürich, Berlin, and Paris, and then began a teaching career in philosophy at the University of Glasgow, first under Sir Henry Jones and later under Professor Robert Adamson. It was Adamson's influence which led to his later interest in Kant. In 1902 he published *Studies in the Cartesian Philosophy*, which won for him in the following year the doctor's degree from St. Andrews. In 1906, after being interviewed by Woodrow Wilson in Edinburgh, he sailed for America to take up a teaching position at Princeton University where the connection with the Scottish universities was still very strong. By 1913 Kemp Smith had become Chairman of the Department of Philosophy and Psychology there, and in 1914 he became the McCosh Professor of Philosophy. Kemp Smith's approach to philosophy was historical rather than systematic, which is to say that he pursued philosophical problems by thoroughly studying them in the thought of the great thinkers of the past rather than in the construction of a philosophical system of his own. He very strongly insisted that philosophical problems could not be successfully treated in isolation, either from the historical milieux which had produced them and the thinkers who had reflected on them or from other ultimate questions of a philosophic nature. In the course of his career, Kemp Smith managed to get into the minds and thought of Descartes, Hume, and Kant, with a subtlety and perception which has not been surpassed, and his studies of these three thinkers are, perhaps, his greatest contributions to general philosophy.

After the outbreak of the First World War Kemp Smith obtained an academic leave from Princeton and sailed in March 1916 for Britain in the hope of serving his country's cause. How that academic leave from Princeton lasted for the rest of his life as a result of his being offered the Chair of Metaphysics at Edinburgh is interestingly chronicled in this volume's letters. Too old for active military duty, he obtained a civilian position in the Intelligence Section of the Ministry of Munitions in London, though he was soon transferred to the Department of Information of the War Office and Admiralty. During these war years Kemp Smith was putting the finishing touches on his *A Commentary to Kant's Critique of Pure Reason*, which he had begun in 1912 and which would be published in the summer of 1918, and also looking out for opportunities in the London area which might hold some interest for him philosophically. One such opportunity was the night of 29 November 1917, when von Hügel addressed The Quest Society at the Kensington Town Hall on the topic of "Religion and Illusion." He spoke for about fifty minutes, and this was followed by nearly an hour's questions. Von Hügel estimated that about 150 persons were present, among whom, although unknown to him at the time, was Norman Kemp Smith. Apparently the address stimulated Kemp Smith to look into the Baron's published works and, in the spring, to seek an opportunity to call upon him. The opportunity came in the form of pre-publication copies of his *Commentary*, one of which Kemp Smith posted to von Hügel. On May 8 von Hügel sent Kemp Smith a letter of thanks for the book and an invitation to call upon him. Kemp Smith responded with the letter which is the first in this volume's collection. The meeting took place at von Hügel's home in Kensington on May 24, with the resulting relationship documented by the 130 communications published here.

That Kemp Smith should first have seen and heard von Hügel at a lecture in which the latter was speaking of "Religion and Illusion" is not without significance. Although he wrote very little directly on the subject, as a mature philosopher Kemp Smith was consistently concerned both professionally and personally with the ultimate question of spiritual values. He referred to his own philosophic position as that of an *idealist,* although his meaning for the term differed radically from that of his contemporaries and of almost everyone else who has ever used it. And in the only systematic work he ever wrote, *Prolegomena to an Idealist Theory of Knowledge,* he defined his idealism as a philosophy which maintained "that spiritual values have a determining voice in the ordering of the Universe." Kemp Smith was looking for something as a philosopher and as a man, and his letters to von Hügel indicate that he felt von Hügel had some insight into what it was he was seeking. Throughout their correspondence, Kemp Smith repeatedly told von Hügel how much he had learned and was learning from the latter's books and conversations. As early as June 1918, shortly after their first meeting and conversation, Kemp Smith told von Hügel that he was reading the latter's *Mystical Element of Religion* "slowly, at intervals, & am gaining more from it than from any philosophical work I have read in the past few years." A year later, after delivering a paper on "The Spiritual Value of Fear" before the London Society for the Study of Religion, Kemp Smith told von Hügel that "It especially delights me that my paper has been liked by you. In a paper of this kind I would rather have your approval than that of anyone else that I have the privilege of knowing. It represents positions to which I have been feeling my way for some years, & largely in reaction against earlier, and, as I now recognise, more superficial ways of thinking." Later that month von Hügel sent to Kemp Smith a copy of l'abbé Henri Huvelin's *Quelques Directeurs d'âmes,* and Kemp Smith responded: "I am only half way through it, reading in it, or rather, to use your phrase, browsing in it, at leisure; but already I can see how much I am to get from it. It is very beautiful, full of true wisdom and insight. You have placed me under a great debt— one more in the many I owe to you." At the end of 1919, Kemp Smith told von Hügel that a passage in the Inaugural Address which he had just given on assuming the Edinburgh Chair was the result of von Hügel's influence: "My insistence upon the importance for Idealism of maintaining the genuineness of knowledge & the absoluteness of the logical criteria, it will interest you to know, is the direct outcome of a passage of your own—in, I think, your 'Eternal Life': I have been trying to locate the passage this evening, but without success—I read it, I know, in some work of yours while in London some 12 months ago. It has been in my mind ever since, & what I say on pp. 18–19 is the result thereof." In March of 1920, after beginning a study of H. J. Holtzmann's on the New Testament at von Hügel's suggestion, he wrote: "As I am finding, I can always rely with confidence on your recommendations of books as not only justified by their intrinsic merits but as certain to prove helpful in my own personal difficulties & needs —an immense boon for which I cannot sufficiently thank you." Two years later, after the publication of von Hügel's first series of *Essays and Addresses*, Kemp Smith told von Hügel that his *Essays* "are much in my mind as I write my concluding lectures, for my advanced class —concluding a course semi-historical in which the nature & function of reason has been the main connecting theme. If you saw the lecture I gave today on what I call the historical or *institutional* view of reason (as ags the 18th Cent. 'natural reason') you would recognise many points as showing the influence of your book." In March 1924 Kemp Smith's own *Prolegomena to an Idealist Theory of Knowledge* was published, and when sending a copy to von Hügel, he told the Baron he was sending it "not that you may read it [because von Hügel was seriously ill], but that you may glance at my Preface in which I am glad to be able to make acknowledgement of my debt to you." In the Preface Kemp Smith had written: "Since 1912, however, my views have undergone very radical alteration, though still in the direction of realism and without departure from the idealist standpoint. In this recasting of my views I have been greatly aided by the study of the works of Baron von Hügel." Then, less than two weeks after sending the book, and after having visited von Hügel in person in Kensington, Kemp Smith wrote: "I cannot properly tell you how great a pleasure it has been to me to have seen you again. I always feel, however, that I do not manage to convey to you how great I feel my debt to you both for the inspiration of your writings & for what I value so greatly the high privilege of the friendship you so richly extend to me in my un- worthiness—unworthy save perhaps in my knowledge of its value & of my own undesert." Back in Edinburgh and well into the new aca- demic term, Kemp Smith wrote: "The Term's work, too, is in full swing. Last week I was reading the essays of my 3 best advanced stu- dents—in competition for a £20 prize that has the dignified title of 'Bruce of Grangehill & Falkland's Prize,' in memory of an 18th Cen- tury holder of my Chair—& *two* out of the three quote from your 'Essays & Addresses'. So my teaching must carry *some* measure of genuine guidance to the springs of truth—would you not agree?" And again two months later in the same lighthearted vein: "A very de- lightful Indian student of mine, of Brahmin caste from Madras, has carried off my copy of your 'Mystical Element in Religion' to read during his vacation. But I fear he has too much of the Gandhi – Tagore (of whom he is a pupil) – Rolland simplicity & sentimentality of mind to profit fully: however Providence through me is giving him his chance."

Von Hügel died on 27 January 1925, and on the following day Kemp Smith's obituary of him appeared in *The Scotsman*. In it he publicly, though less personally, made some of the points which he had made earlier about von Hügel in the letters, and he further remarked of the Baron that "his ardour of spirit, his force of character and great powers of mind have enabled him to make contributions to philosophical and theological literature that are of the very first importance, and that will very generally be regarded as justifying the declaration made by Dean Inge in one of his *Outspoken Essays* that Baron von Hügel is 'the deepest thinker, perhaps, of all living theologians in this country'."

These remarks and others which Kemp Smith made in the letters clearly indicate that he felt von Hügel was helping him to clarify something, and clearly the something had to do with the epistemological probems underlying ultimate religious issues and specifically the question of divine existence. What *exactly* the something was, and *precisely* how von Hügel had helped, has yet to some extent to be refined. But if these are not fully answered questions about the influence of the older man upon the younger, there is no doubt whatsoever that the issue had nothing to do with ecclesiastical proselytism. Kemp Smith was a quiet and reserved man. Those who knew him as teacher and friend respected the quality of his thought and life, and saw in his openness to transcendental reality without commitment to any specific religious group a further mark of his intellectual integrity. Von Hügel, on the other hand, was wholeheartedly committed to Roman Catholicism, and precisely because of this commitment felt free to criticize, challenge, and attempt to reform the Roman institution, as well as to share insights which he had gleaned from it with others outside. These letters clearly show the two men within these two frameworks, and the depth of their affection for one another and the openness of their sharing in no way committed either of them to the faith dimension of the other. To worry that it might is to miss the point of this relationship. Immediately after Kemp Smith was appointed to the Chair of Metaphysics at Edinburgh, von Hügel wrote to tell him that he wished Kemp Smith could see his way to committing himself to membership in some historical church. His reason for the suggestion was that he felt convinced that such church membership was a unique means of drawing on a type of experience which would enhance Kemp Smith's qualities precisely as a philosopher. Kemp Smith responded with gratitude for von Hügel's concern and care, but he also gave a straightforward explanation of why church membership was not in conscience possible for him just then. In fact, throughout his life Kemp Smith remained unattached to any formal church structure, although, as the letters indicate, he entertained a special sympathy for Presbyterianism because it was the religion of his youth and of his native Scotland.

The type of experience which von Hügel was hoping Kemp Smith might find in seriously practiced church membership was a growth in the sense of his own *creatureliness*. This sense of creatureliness seemed to von Hügel to be absolutely essential for any man, however brilliant or however ordinary, who seriously set out in search of God or even grappled philosophically with the question of divine existence. In his *Mystical Element of Religion* von Hügel had made the point that for the religious dimension of the human person to be full and balanced it had to consist of three intertwined and interacting aspects. These were the intellectual, mystical, and institutional elements of religion— all essential for full religion. In his letter to Kemp Smith about church membership, von Hügel was reminding the Edinburgh scholar that the institutional element can be ignored only at the risk of unbalance and a certain superficiality in the development even of the intellectual element. He is certainly not telling him that he must become a mindless sheep to be led with docility by any shepherd–cleric who might happen to hold a position of ecclesiastical authority—he could hardly have instanced Troeltsch (as he did in the letter) as a "splendid illustration" of what he meant had this been so. Rather, he was making a point about intellectuals which he himself had been experiencing and living for most of his adult life: that God is best approached through intellectual activity in conjunction with the cultivation of a sense of one's own creatureliness. And this sense of creatureliness can be very effectively, perhaps most effectively, cultivated through the trials and tribulations ("frictions" and "costingness") of practiced membership in an historical church. Von Hügel did not maintain in his letter to Kemp Smith, nor did he ever maintain, that church membership was essential for attaining and keeping the creaturely mentality. What he did maintain was that a sense of creatureliness was essential for anyone who would grow in true religious sensitivity and insight; that church membership could be helpful—indeed was one of the most obvious means—for developing this sense of creatureliness; but that this sense could also be developed in a multitude of other ways, and often was. When von Hügel's favorite daughter had temporarily ceased to practice her religion in the 1890s, he told her that he could live with that fact as long as she maintained her sense of creatureliness and nurtured it by other means.

It is not insignificant that in Kemp Smith's posthumously published paper "Is Divine Existence Credible?"—a paper given before the British Academy in 1931—he concluded that such existence is credible, not through any of the traditional and rationalistic "proofs," but through the immediate experience of one's own creatureliness and of God as non-creaturely, and he concluded the address by quoting a relevant saying of von Hügel's. The Baron's ideas on mysticism and the importance of the sense of creatureliness in the genuinely searching man seem to have influenced Kemp Smith in his pursuit of ultimate spiritual issues, but they in no way committed him to von Hügel's Roman Catholicism or to membership in any other religious institution.

If the fact of von Hügel's influence on Kemp Smith is quite clear from the letters, while the *exact* form of this influence is somewhat less so, there can be no doubt at all about either the fact or the form of Kemp Smith's influence on von Hügel. The relationship between the two men covered the last six-and-one-half years of von Hügel's life, years of failing health and other serious frustrations. He needed support, inspiration, and stimulus to persevere in the intellectual work which had been the main thrust of his whole life. And this was what Kemp Smith supplied in an extraordinarily generous manner. Von Hügel realized and remarked that in having a sympathetic friend with such potential and, indeed, with such achievement already realized, as Kemp Smith had, he would be able to extend through his younger friend the ideals and intellectual values which meant so much to him far beyond what he himself had or could achieve alone. That theme was expressed in various of von Hügel's letters to Kemp Smith.

Another aspect of the friendship which was important to von Hügel was the dimension of almost unqualified sharing of nearly everything, large and small, and the mental and emotional support which he gained from this. Late in November 1919 von Hügel told Kemp Smith: "I am fast coming to feel what has happened to me repeatedly—that just because I have a practically unlimited range of convictions, interests, hopes and fears in common with you (I mean, in a degree and way that has not occurred, with living men, more than,—say, a dozen times, or even less, in my long life)—I put off and off writing to you, since there forms in my head and heart a whole mass of things to say—a mass too large to unpack and sort out into a letter." And five months later von Hügel told Kemp Smith that he thanked "God every day for the most solid, precious Friend He has deigned to give me in you." In January 1921 von Hügel wrote Kemp Smith: "I am a bit late with my New Year's wishes and yet, even so, this is only the 3rd real letter I write so far in 1921. First to Troeltsch, then to Loisy, now to you. And indeed, as far as union of convictions and bracing influence go, you come immediately after Troeltsch, my poor friend L. remaining sadly negative and purely immanental." And in the last letter he wrote in 1921 von Hügel told Kemp Smith that he wondered "whether you at all realise how much, how rarely much, your kind support and sympathy are to me."

In 1922 the University of Edinburgh appointed von Hügel Gifford Lecturer for 1924–1925 and 1925–1926. Although he initially accepted the appointment, his health declined in the course of the year and he resigned the appointment in November. The remaining two years of his life were spent in increasingly bad health, but also in spurts of intellectual activity up to within a very few months of his death. In March 1924 von Hügel suffered a collapse which must have impressed Kemp Smith with the nearness of the approaching end. For the remaining nine months of the Baron's life, Kemp Smith wrote him almost weekly charming, lighthearted, sharing sorts of letters which meant more to the dying man than almost anything else during that time. About two months before his death, von Hügel tried to tell his friend how grateful he really was: "I wonder whether you realize what you are doing for me. These letters of yours coming in so regularly once a week telling me so unforcedly exactly what I so much care to know with their gentle simplicity, entire spontaneity, kindliness & yet discrimination, they remind me of nothing so much as of the healing waters of Wildbad in the Schwarz Wald, where after you had got into the water, you would in some minutes feel all sorts of usually quite unperceived aches & pains & then this same water would brace them away."

The von Hügel – Kemp Smith correspondence is, of course, not merely the chronicle of a relationship and its development. It is also an account, disconnected and spotty as letter accounts inevitably are, of the intellectual and social milieux in which both men moved. Most of the British, and many American, academic philosophers are commented on; and glimpses into the world of the British universities of this period are frequent. Observations about world events and internationally known figures were regular aspects of the two men's communications. Significant as these letters are for understanding the thought of the two men who wrote them and for grasping their criticisms of other thinkers, this correspondence is much more than philosophical footnotes. It is a cultural barometer of the times. And those times were so different from this far end of the twentieth century that contemporary men who wish now to understand the years following the Great War need to study such barometers carefully, if they really care to know that era in its own terms. Here in these letters, for instance, are two men who stand well above the petty emotional tyranny of aggressive nationalism recounting their experiences of such tyranny operating in the British universities through an anti-German animus which refused to acknowledge the merits of Ernst Troeltsch in one instance and of Otto Schlapp in another. Here the reader finds an invaluable introduction to William James's *Varieties of Religious Experience* in an estimate of that book's values and pitfalls from two men far better equipped than most to make such judgments. Or, again, here one catches just a fleeting glimpse of the Greek Prime Minister Eleutherios Venizelos, not in his later struggles for his country's well-being, but in his youthful days as a highway robber in Crete! In 1922, long before Albert Einstein's name became a household word throughout the world, von Hügel remarked to Kemp Smith: "I have read, as you suggested Einstein's own accounts of his Theory. I understand all pretty well—except where he *would* be 'clear' and give me fearsome algebraic formulae. That man is no quack, and he may turn out right ere we are, say, 5 years older. Do, please, put some note or other—something—into your 'Commentary' about this. I simply cannot I find treat Space and Time as certainly infinite. I never, somehow, could believe in that infinitude, and now E. comes along apparently on the point of demonstrating that they are not infinite. — I delight in E.'s *Realism*—it shows everywhere; and I feel that somehow the finitude point will not really weaken Realism—if we somehow manage well.—" Von Hügel and Kemp Smith were both so sensitively alive to a multitude of dimensions in the world about them that a correspondence between the two is bound to reflect this. And so a reader of this volume will discover.

A word, at last, needs to be said about the manner in which these letters have been prepared for publication. In his will von Hügel left his extensive library to St. Andrews University in gratitude for its having been the first to recognize him with an honorary doctor's degree. His executors also gave the various collections of letters which von Hügel had received and preserved through the years to the University, and one such collection was the Kemp Smith letters. Von Hügel's letters to Kemp Smith remained in the latter's hands until his death in 1958, and then passed to his literary executors. In the late 1960s these letters too finally joined their counterparts in this correspondence in the von Hügel manuscripts collection at St. Andrews. This edition of the letters, then, includes in their entirety all the von Hügel – Kemp Smith letters at St. Andrews, and three brief communications from von Hügel to Kemp Smith (13 December 1919, 2 February 1920, and 9 February 1920) which are now in the University Library at Edinburgh. From von Hügel's *Diaries*, which generally record letters received and sent, and from the internal evidence of the letters themselves, it seems unlikely that any other significant piece of correspondence between the two men exists beyond those published here. The letters produced here have been transcribed exactly as they were written—including misspellings, faulty grammar, and inconsistent punctuation. Only about a dozen very minor exceptions to this rule were made, and these only to avoid unnecessary confusion. Footnotes have been used only to clarify a reference in the letters which is not immediately evident to contemporary readers, and to identify most of the individuals mentioned by either writer. A very few such individuals were either unidentifiable by the editor or were considered of insufficient significance from the point of view of this correspondence to warrant identification, and some seemed too obvious for a footnote. Opinions will clearly differ on this last point, since all might agree that Kant, Condorcet, and Jane Austen need no identification, whereas many might think that Fustel de Coulanges or Otto von Gierke do! The footnotes attempt primarily to identify the contemporaries of both men who are mentioned in the letters and who might not be readily identifiable by present-day readers of these letters. The length of the identification in no way implies anything about the relative importance of the one identified. On the contrary, more obscure individuals are often more fully identified than those with whom the reader might be expected to be familiar. In no sense are the footnotes an analysis or commentary on the two correspondents' ideas. Several appendices have been added to the volume in order to make available to the reader documents of some length about which the letters speak in detail, and which are especially significant for understanding these latter. The handwriting of both men is atrocious from the point of view of legibility, and sometimes only after a word or phrase has been stared at for weeks, in different lights and in different mental attitudes, have their strange characters yielded intelligibility. To have these letters in a readable and usable form should be an advantage to many.

Because they would not have reached this form without the permission, encouragement, interest, and help of others, acknowledgment of these others is an obligation which the editor here happily fulfills. These include Professor Kemp Smith's daughter, Janet, Mrs. Martin Ludlam, without whose consent this volume would never have been published; Kemp Smith's literary executors and former students, Professor A. J. D. Porteous, Dr. George E. Davie of the University of Edinburgh, and the late Professor R. D. Maclennan—Dr. Davie especially has been extraordinarily gracious in sharing of information and offering a critique for parts of the manuscript as well as in arranging for use of the photograph of Kemp Smith, and all three of whom have made the editor's task lighter through their helpful Introductions to the volume of Kemp Smith's posthumous papers published in 1967 by Macmillan of London as *The Credibility of Divine Existence*; the Librarian, St. Andrews University, who at the outset of this project was Mr. D. MacArthur, but since Mr. MacArthur's retirement in 1976 has been Mr. A. Graham Mackenzie; Mr. Robert N. Smart, Keeper of Manuscripts at St. Andrews University Library, whose help over the years and especially whose patience in answering bothersome questions and providing photocopies of various documents in his care have been crucial to whatever merits this volume has; Edinburgh University Library which allowed the publication of the three von Hügel manuscripts in its collection; Dr. J. T. D. Hall, Keeper of Special Collections, Edinburgh University Library; The American Philosophical Society of Philadelphia which in the summer of 1971 awarded the editor a substantial grant from its Johnson Fund, enabling him to complete basic work on the manuscripts at St. Andrews; Dr. David G. Schultenover, S.J., of Creighton University, Omaha, Nebraska, whose English rendering in footnotes of the lengthy German quotations from Troeltsch and the briefer ones from von Ranke in several of von Hügel's letters will make these readily accessible to the reader without German; James Thin Ltd for permission to republish Kemp Smith's Inaugural

Address which they originally published in 1919; and, finally, Dr. Rita Adams whose careful and patient preparation of the typescript for all the letters and their annotations was an invaluable contribution to this book's completion. Their contributions have all been positive; any deficiencies in this volume are the sole responsibility of the editor.

Saint Louis University   LAWRENCE F. BARMANN

The
Letters

May 21. 1918   Ministry of Information
                                      Norfolk Street,
                                         Strand,
                                    London, W. C. 2

To Baron von Hügel.

Dear Sir,

Many thanks for your very kind letter. As Mr Herbert[1] is not
free in the afternoons, I should like, if I may, to call upon you
by myself. May I come on Friday afternoon next (the 24th),[2] or
should that not be convenient, on the following Tuesday afternoon (the 28th)? I can come anytime that suits you best between
2.30 & 5.30. Yes, I am myself Scotch, having been born in For-
farshire. I taught in Glasgow University, before crossing to
Princeton University in 1906. You know, I think, my friend W. E.
Hocking[3] of Harvard.

                        With kind greetings,
                          Sincerely Yours,
                          NORMAN KEMP SMITH.

[1] The certain identity of this Herbert is possibly now beyond recovery. It might refer to Sidney Herbert (1890–1939), von Hügel's nephew, who served in the War and in 1919–1920 acted as private secretary to the British Secretary of State for War. Possibly it could refer to a J. A. Herbert, who was a colleague of von Hügel's in the London Society for the Study of Religion (LSSR).

[2] Baron von Hügel's manuscript *Diary* for 24 May 1918 notes: "In aft., *Professor Norman Kemp Smith came—1st sight of him.* Is married to an English woman (attracted alternately to Quakers and Catholics), and has one child—a lit-

tle girl. Talked abt his 'Commentary.' Found he knows my books well—hence sent me *his* book.—Lent him Troeltsch's 'die geschichtlichkeit Jesu'." These *Diaries* are now part of the permanent collection of von Hügel manuscripts at St. Andrews University Library, Scotland, and in further notes will be identified simply as *Diaries*, with appropriate dates.

[3] William Ernest Hocking (1873–1966), American idealist philosopher, emphasizing in his writings the religious dimensions of philosophy; educated at Harvard University, and Professor of Philosophy there from 1914 until he retired in 1943.

Ministry of Information,
Norfolk Street
W. C. 2.

Dear Baron von Hügel,[4]

Very many thanks for so kindly sending me your two articles from the Constructive Review.[5] I have been studying them with the greatest interest, & am taking some notes of the first article before returning it to you. Troeltsch[6] is quite a new discovery to me, & I am indebted to you for drawing my attention to him. There are several points in these articles that I should like to discuss with you.

Your second card has just reached me. Monday afternoon will suit me excellently. I shall call at 3 p.m.

You asked me last week to mention any passages in my Commentary[7] that are likely to have special interest for you. In the main those sections which are italicised in the Table of Contents give my broader discussions of Kant's general positions; but I may refer you, in addition to the sections in my Introduction, to pp. 33–43 on Kant's own Introduction; pp. 117–120 on Kant's attitude to the problems of modern geometry; pp. 270–284 on Phenomenalism & Subjectivism, & pp. 372–4; p. 291 ff. on Inner Sense; p. 312 ff. on Kant's Refutation of Idealism; pp. 414–417 on Kant's method of distinguishing between Phenomena & Noumena; pp. 425–31 in Introduction to the Dialectic; & the other italicised sections in the remainder of Table of Contents. My Index gives the relevant pages on all the main points. I am very

---

[4] This letter is undated, but had to be written between May 25 and June 1, 1918. Baron von Hügel's *Diary* indicates that he sent Kemp Smith the two articles mentioned in this letter on May 25; the *Diary* also indicates that on June 1 he wrote the note to which Kemp Smith responded on June 3.

[5] "On the Specific Genius and Capacities of Christianity, Studied in Connection With the Works of Professor Ernst Troeltsch," *The Constructive Quarterly*, 2, No. 5 (March 1914), 68–98; and ibid., No. 8 (December 1914), 673–701.

[6] Ernst Troeltsch (1865–1923), German liberal Protestant theologian and intellectual historian; Professor of Theology at Heidelberg University, 1894–1914, and Professor of Philosophy as well, 1910–1914; Professor of Philosophy at the University of Berlin, 1915–1923. His best-known work was *Die Soziallehren der christlichen Kirchen und Gruppen* (1912). See the excellent account of von Hügel's relationship with Troeltsch in Hans Rollmann, "Troeltsch, von Hügel and Modernism," *The Downside Review*, 96, No. 322 (January 1978), 35–60.

[7] *A Commentary to Kant's 'Critique of Pure Reason'* (London: Macmillan, 1918).

well aware how confusing a book, written thus as a Commentary, can be; & have sought to connect up its parts by occasional systematic discussions, & by frequent cross-references.

I agree very heartily in your insistence upon the indispensableness of the historical & contingent in all philosophical speculation, & also in your opposition to subjectivism, tho' I was surprised to find in your "Mystical Element of Religion"[8] that you consider Volkelt's[9] position as successfully avoiding the subjectivist bog. I also find difficulty in accepting your Leibnitzian view of the subconscious (as I indicate on p. 273 of my Commentary). I tend to picture the subconscious—the subconscious that really counts in religious & other experience—as modification & growth in mental powers (of insight & feeling), not as the retention of specific experiences, important as the latter may occasionally be. But these matters can best be discussed by word of mouth. I look forward very greatly to my visit on Monday.

Yours very gratefully,
NORMAN KEMP SMITH.

June 3. 1918.   Ministry of Information.
                                 Norfolk Street,
                                 Strand,
                                 London, W. C. 2

Dear Baron von Hügel,

I am extremely sorry to hear that your health is causing you trouble, & that you have to undergo an operation.[10] But I shall at least, I trust, have the pleasure of seeing you tomorrow eve-

[8] The Mystical Element of Religion as Studied in Saint Catherine of Genoa and Her Friends, 2 vols. (London: Dent, 1908).

[9] Johannes Immanuel Volkelt (1848–1930), German philosopher and writer on aesthetics.

[10] According to von Hügel's Diary he was in a nursing home from the 9th to the 13th of June, and on the 10th had removed from his right nostril three "polypuses (a biggish, a very big and a little one)."

ning.[11] Yesterday I spent a very happy morning reading in your 'Mystical Element of Religion' the section on Quietism. Your book has been a constant standbye to me for many months past. I am reading it slowly, at intervals, & am gaining more from it than from any philosophical work I have read in the past few years.

The two pamphlets—your article & Troeltsch's own—I shall return by post within a day or two.

With kind greetings,
Yours ever gratefully,
NORMAN KEMP SMITH.

June 10. 1918.   Ministry of Information.
                                  Norfolk Str.
                                  W. C. 2

Dear Baron von Hügel,

I am returning, under separate cover, your article & the Troeltsch pamphlet which you have so kindly lent me. Both of them have interested me profoundly, & of your article I have made extensive notes. As soon as opportunity offers, I shall obtain Troeltsch's chief works, & make a thorough study of them. Philosophy at present—I mean that of the professional philosophers —sadly needs to be fructified by close contact with the realities it professes to study. Dialectic, that is, logical analysis & abstract

---

[11] The LSSR met at Caxton Hall, Westminster, on the evening of Tuesday, June 4, to hear and discuss a paper delivered by the Rev. Edward Mewburn Walker (1857–1941), Fellow and Tutor of Queen's College, Oxford, on "Democracy from a Christian Standpoint." Kemp Smith had been invited to attend as a guest of von Hügel, who himself was one of the founding members of the LSSR in 1904. Both men attended the meeting; and von Hügel noted that his deafness prevented his catching more than half the spoken address. He found what he heard "lucid; interesting, but not, I thought, sufficiently busy w[ith] the rel[igious] side, and hardly very rich or very deep." Von Hügel himself spoke for nearly fifteen minutes in comment on the paper, mentioning "the Jewish-Xtian Apocalyptic outlook & its likeness & unlikeness to contemp[orary] visionary Democracy." *Diaries*, 4 June 1918.

ratiocination, often seem to me to be the curse of philosophy. I have immense respect for the part which the abstract has played in the history of human thought, but an equally strong consciousness of its delusive powers. I have the ambition to attempt a history of philosophy, in which the historical, contingent, & personal factors would receive a larger share of attention than they usually do.

I enjoyed the meeting last Tuesday. The argument of the address, tho' I sympathised with the speaker's emphasis on the defects & dangers of present day democracy—seemed to me very unsatisfactory. After defining democracy as a form of government, he proceeded to argue against it regarded as a way of salvation. An attack on secularism is hardly sufficient when put forward as an estimate of the significance of the democratic ideal. Also, he seemed to ignore the profound truth of de Tocqueville's remark that democracy is the most difficult of all forms of government, because it demands for its possibility higher moral standards in the individual citizens. The eschatological character of the early Christian beliefs, upon which you dwelt, I am only beginning to appreciate.

I trust the doctor is better pleased with your condition, & that after your operation, & before many months have passed I may again have the privilege of calling upon you.

With renewed & grateful thanks.

Yours sincerely,
Norman Kemp Smith.

March 15. 1919.   16 Corrennie Gardens,
                                            Edinburgh.

Dear Baron von Hügel,

Many thanks for your most kind letter. Unfortunately I am now at Windermere, & next week am proceeding to Edinburgh, with little likelihood of being in London before returning to America in September.[12] I am delighted to hear that your health now improves, & trust your working powers will soon be restored to you. I look back upon my visit to you with the greatest pleasure, & shall always esteem it a great privilege to have met you in person.

Now that my Commentary is off my hands & I have entire leisure until September I am rejoicing in the return to philosophy, & planning further work. Your recommendation of Troeltsch has greatly profited me. His 'Soziallehren' I have run through rapidly, with immense interest, & hope to make a more thorough study of it when I can secure a copy of my own, on the happy establishment of peace. The other volume of his collected writings contains much valuable matter. He is quite a new discovery to me. Maitland's translation of Gierke, & his own brilliant introduction I have also been reading—led thereto by your reference to him in one of your prefaces.

Your own studies in Mysticism keep recurring to my mind, in many diverse connections, as I work—a sure sign that they are helping me to clearness in several of my chief difficulties.

Mr Bevan[13] wrote some little time ago asking me to read a paper to your 'Society for the Study of Religion.' Had I been in London I should have welcomed the opportunity of having a paper discussed by the Society, & should, I think, have spoken on a subject which I find very fruitful—especially in the light of the present state of Europe—the doctrine of original sin. Doubtless the honour of the invitation has been due to your kindly mediation.

---

[12] At this date Kemp Smith anticipated returning to Princeton University in September 1919 to resume his duties there as McCosh Professor of Philosophy, duties which had been interrupted by the First World War and his return to Britain to work in his country's cause.

[13] Edwyn Robert Bevan (1870–1943), British historian and philosopher, influenced by von Hügel and through him brought into the LSSR. The manuscript Minutes of the LSSR for 4 February 1919

note: "The Secretary was instructed to write to Professor Kemp Smith, to invite him to address the Society or read a paper on April 1, on which date the Society would hold an extraordinary meeting should Prof. Kemp Smith accept." But the Minutes for March 4 note: "The Secretary read a letter from Professor Kemp Smith regretting his inability to attend a meeting of the Society in April." MSS Minutes of LSSR, Vol. I, #WL80, OD.17 (Dr. Williams's Library, London).

If I am in London at any time I shall look forward to the privilege of again calling upon you.

Yours ever gratefully,

NORMAN KEMP SMITH.

This letter is *strictly confidential*,   19th April 1919
as concerns the A. & R. Committee.[14]   13, Vicarage Gate,
H.   Kensington,
London,   W. 8.

Dear Professor Kemp Smith,

Altho' it was already a month ago that I received your letter, written from Windermere, I still am full of delight and of profound consolation concerning its contents—your frame of mind and plans of work. You see—here am I, to be fully 67 in another fortnight or so; and still so weak as sometimes seriously to fear that I shall never be able to resume my dearly loved work. And there are you—still with mounting strength and the presumption of some 30, 40 years of strenuous, most fruitful labour before you. What a joy then, if I can feel fully sure that your general orientation and your fundamental positions are deeply right, are essentially fruitful and admirably supplementary, indeed corrective, of the outlook now so curiously dominant among the younger school of Christian thinkers—at least in Great Britain.

[14] The Army and Religion Committee, of which von Hügel speaks at length in this letter, grew out of a desire on the part of a British worker with the Y.M.C.A. among the British troops in France, and others concerned about the religious dimension of the British soldiers in the First World War, "to consider and interpret what was being revealed under War conditions as to the religious life of the nation, and to bring the result before the Churches." The Committee was chaired by the Anglican Bishop of Winchester, Dr. Edward Stuart Talbot, and its final report published as *The Army and Religion: An Enquiry and its Bearing upon the Religious Life of the Nation* (London: Macmillan, 1919). See also von Hügel's *Diaries*, 30 June, 2, 14, 16, 31 July, 1, 2, 3, 10, 11 August, 10, 11 December 1917; 10 May, 2 July 1918; 8 February, 28 April 1919.

—Please note, too, that this fact—this outlook—has been brought home to me—I mean, its prevalence, and its tenacious ingrainedness—by my service on that 'Army and Religion' Committee. I found myself there, tho' *most* kindly treated, yet quite obviously only one of 3 or 4 members out of the total of 22 who held that Preliminary Pessimism, that conviction as to the *abiding* costliness of our little earthly life, which I had expected (vainly, it turned out) to underlie the thought of, and to be deliberately accepted by, at least all my Presbyterian colleagues. But—not a bit of it. Both the Presbyterians and the Anglicans—indeed the other bodies as well—were in the large majority of their members, definitely hostile to all such abiding limitations and difficulties in our earthly lot. Any and every doctrine of original sin was sensitively traced and scouted in even the most moderate positions and forms. Nothing but the strongly accentuated possibility of our being able, by our best, conjointed efforts, to bring about, *hic et nunc*, perfection, sheer, full perfection, upon this our earth; and a doctrine (insofar as the other life retained any definite function and outlines at all) of the Apokatastasis—taken as a final, full beatitude of all human souls: nothing but these two positions was congenial to this majority. And it greatly interested me to find for myself, gradually, how the one religious argument which at first appeared to me to be strong in their case for the first position, really crumbled away, upon closer consideration. I mean the *Parousia* conviction, as it underlies the earliest utterances and documents of the Christian outlook. It was this proximateness, this suddenness of the *Parousia*, of the New Heaven and the New Earth, which these friends thought themselves to be quite simply reaffirming. Yet this their thinking is demonstrably mistaken—they do *not* reproduce that primitive Christian mentality at all. The Parousia was indeed, between say A.D. 30 and A.D. 90, conceived as proximate and sudden; and men were indeed appealed to most strongly with regard to it, in this its proximateness and suddenness. But stronger again, was the conviction and teaching, that the Parousia itself, that this new order of things, was not the work of men, whether slow and gradual, or quick and *hic et nunc*; but that it was the pure work, the sheer gift, of God. Men could not produce it, work they never so hard; they could not even hasten this work of God's event. Men could only prepare themselves to be awake and not unworthy of it, whensoever it might come. —Thus it is a profound travesty of the Parousia doctrine and temper, to take the element of proximity and suddenness, and to use this element as part of a scheme of human effort and human productivity, in lieu of the original scheme of divine action and human passivity. The original scheme is profoundly pessimistic in its man-ward side; this other scheme is enthusiastically optimistic (i.e. shallow) in its man-ward side. The original scheme is deeply religious; the new scheme is a sort of fanatical moralism.

I am confident that much of this, to me very strange, position springs from very excessive reaction against Calvinism. And it pleases me very specially to find a man like yourself, still young and a most careful, most competent scholar and thinker, and one doubtless sprung from a Presbyterian stock, not thus reacting, but, on the contrary, keeping crisply and firmly what that position held and holds of profound truth.

May I [be] permitted to see you more and more established and developed along these deep, great lines! And, if I am taken soon, may you live to do far better, far more influential, work than I have done, or could still hope to do!—

Now I want you kindly to consider, very carefully, whether you cannot do me, and (I am sure) many others, a great service, a deep delight. I fully understand that you cannot possibly speak (on Original Sin—bravo!)—speak before our *LSSR*—in November next. But do, *pray*, see whether you could not get them at Princeton University to so arrange for you that you could speak before us in London on *October 7th*. On my part, I herewith undertake to arrange for that 1st Tuesday in October, and for you to have an excellent—a most attentive and very competent audience. I need not know your decision till *May 24th*, so that you have time to communicate with your authorities before settling. I would myself study your Paper most carefully, in hopes of being fit to come and join in the discussion. Do, do not say 'No'; but do your level best to come, and—a month hence,—let me have 'Yes' from you![15]

Please remember [me] very kindly and gratefully to Professor Pringle Pattison.[16] I had been studying his 'Idea of God' very carefully, just before I broke down last summer.[17] If I live with renewed strength, I hope to study in print that fine book with the most attentive interest. His positions as to Epistemology delighted me more than ever. The semi-Pantheism of the second half of the book I must not pretend to have found satisfactory.[18]

Yours v. sincerely
F. v. HÜGEL.

April 28. 1919.   16, Corrennie Gardens,
                                   Edinburgh.

Dear Baron von Hügel,

Your letter has given me great pleasure. For some years I have been ambitious to write upon what I should describe as 'traditional views of human nature'—meaning the Christian doctrine

---

[15] Von Hügel's *Diary* for 19 April 1919 notes: "*Long, important letter to Prof. N. Kemp Smith*, Edinburgh, on Xtian optimism, and pressing him to arrange for an address on 'Original Sin' (his own choice) to our LSSR on Oct. 7 next."

[16] Andrew Seth Pringle-Pattison (1856–1931), Scottish philosopher who held chairs in philosophy at University College, Cardiff, 1883–1887, and St. Andrews University, 1887–1891; he held the Chair of Logic and Metaphysics at the University of Edinburgh from 1891 until his retirement in 1919.

[17] *The Idea of God in the Light of Recent Philosophy* (Oxford: Clarendon, 1917). Von Hügel's copy of the book is in the von Hügel collection at St. Andrews University Library, and is heavily annotated inside the covers and in the margins of pages.

[18] In the summer of 1918 von Hügel gave an address in Oxford on "The Idea of God," in preparation for which he read, among other things, Pringle-Pattison's volume. While perusing this book, von Hügel noted in his *Diary* that he had "discovered sadly that he [Pringle-Pattison] explicitly denies ontological distinctness from man of God." *Diaries*, 6 July 1918.

of original sin & the Enlightenment (or Pelagian) doctrine of human perfectibility—on the lines of a plea for the better understanding of the former view. You greatly confirm me in this project, & I find new & helpful your suggestions as to the attitude of the primitive Christian communities. But I am a slow worker, & though the matter has long been in my mind, as I have indicated in articles in the Hibbert Journal in 1914 & 1915, I don't yet see my way to an effective method of treatment.[19] My all too slender knowledge of Church History etc. is a further obstacle. When I get my ideas in order, I shall look forward to submitting the result to you.

Reaction from Calvin partly accounts, no doubt, for the strange attitude which the Clergy in Scotland as elsewhere have been taking up to these questions; but more is due, I believe, to the continuing influence of Enlightenment teaching, so wide-spread in secular literature & in general thought, and by its plausibility easily capturing those who are already, for other reasons, fundamentally confused as to the traditions they are supposed to represent.

I should indeed have welcomed the opportunity of speaking before your Society, & I am very grateful for your second invitation; but as I have been absent from Princeton for three years, I feel that I ought not in fairness to the University to ask for further favours. The Term opens about September 23rd & I must sail about the beginning of the month. Frequently, however, I shall think with regret of the invaluable assistance I should have obtained from the criticisms. The sincere reactions of those to whom the subject is a constant subject of reflection must prove more helpful than much solitary reflection upon what I can discover in books however wise. The doctrines demand restatement to meet our present needs. So I put away the invitation only with the deepest regret.

[19] "The Middle Ages, the Renaissance, and the Modern Mind," *The Hibbert Journal*, 12 (1914), 537–56; and "The Moral Sanction of Force," ibid., 13 (1915), 717–30. Both articles have been reprinted in *The Credibility of Divine Existence: The Collected Papers of Norman Kemp Smith*, edd. A. J. D. Porteous, R. D. Maclennan, and G. E. Davie (London: Macmillan, 1967), pp. 196–225.

I expect to be seeing Professor Pringle-Pattison in a few days, & shall convey your message to him.

It is my earnest hope that your health will steadily strengthen, & that your powers of work will be fully renewed.

Meantime, with kindest greetings and thanks, I am,

Yours ever gratefully,

NORMAN KEMP SMITH.

May 27. 1919.   Eira,

Rhoscolyn,

Holyhead, N. Wales.

Dear Baron von Hügel,

Please pardon my delay in again writing you. I have been moving around a great deal, & also, for a reason I shall explain immediately, have had all my plans of quiet study upset during the past fortnight.

I shall arrive on Monday, June 2nd, about 6 p.m. in London, & shall come straight from the Station to Vicarage Gate. I very gratefully accept your hospitality for the nights of the 2nd & 3rd.[20] On the morning of the 4th I proceed to Gloucester, to visit a friend, returning from there to Holyhead.

A fortnight ago Prof. Pringle-Pattison announced his resigna-

---

[20] Although the letters seem to have been lost, von Hügel's *Diary* indicates that an exchange of letters took place between those of Kemp Smith to the Baron on April 28 and May 27. On May 1 von Hügel learned that the speakers who were supposed to be procured for the LSSR meeting on June 3 were both unavailable. On May 3 he wrote Kemp Smith, urging him to give the Society his "Original Sin" address in June, since he would be unavailable in the autumn, and also urging him to spend several days in London as a guest of the Baron and his wife. On May 12 he received Kemp Smith's answer accepting both offers, but then finding it necessary to change the topic of the address because Original Sin had been discussed at a recent LSSR meeting. *Diaries*, 1, 3, 12 May 1919.

tion of the Chair of Logic & Metaphysics in Edinburgh University. After consulting with my friends in Scotland, I have decided to become a candidate. This involved a great deal of correspondence, & some interviewing, which quite prevented my getting at my paper. However I got South last Saturday, & have made good headway in getting my ideas on to paper. It is delightful, though a little difficult, to turn thus from the disagreeables of candidacy to the pleasant labours of writing. But I shall not be able to finish the paper before Monday, & must therefore content myself with placing it in your hands on arrival. You may perhaps be able to glance through some of it before the meeting; & to have my main thesis before you. I'll also try to prepare a synopsis, & forward it towards end of week.[21]

My chief opponent for the Logic Chair, as the situation appears at present, will be J. B. Baillie,[22] Prof. of Moral Philosophy in Aberdeen University. A. E. Taylor[23] is not, it seems, likely to be a candidate.

I have been wondering whether Dean Inge[24] is a member of

---

[21] Ordinarily the papers to be read before the LSSR were given to von Hügel a day or so before the meetings. In this way he could read them carefully and prepare his own comments for the discussion with the assurance that he had grasped the intent of the speaker. His deafness generally prevented his hearing an address completely on first delivery.

[22] Sir James Black Baillie (1872–1940), Scottish philosopher, who held the Chair of Moral Philosophy at Aberdeen University, 1902–1924, and was Vice-Chancellor of Leeds University, 1924–1938; he was knighted in 1931. In his *Diary* for 31 May 1918 von Hügel noted: "Letters from J. B. Baillie (wants me to write him testimonial for his candidature of the Chair of Logic & Metaphysic, Edinburgh Univ.). . . ." Five years earlier Baillie had called on von Hügel in London, where the two had discussed various contemporary thinkers, and the Baron had judged Baillie "a very winning, quite simple man." *Diaries*, 16 September 1913. Baillie is best known today, perhaps, for his translation, with an introduction and

notes, of G. W. F. Hegel's *The Phenomenology of Mind*, which he first published in London in 1910, and revised in 1931.

[23] Alfred Edward Taylor (1869–1945), British philosopher, international authority on Plato, and Fellow of the British Academy. He was a Fellow of Merton College, Oxford, 1891–1898; lectured in philosophy and Greek literature at Owens College, Manchester, 1896–1903; taught philosophy at McGill University, Montreal, 1903–1908; and was Professor of Moral Philosophy at St. Andrews University, 1908–1924; and Professor of Moral Philosophy at the University of Edinburgh, 1924–1941.

[24] William Ralph Inge (1860–1954), Dean of St. Paul's, and prolific lecturer and essayist on philosophical and theological topics. Among other things, he delivered the Bampton Lectures at Oxford in 1899 on *The Philosophy of Plotinus*, and the Hulsean Lectures at Cambridge in 1925–1926 on *The Platonic Tradition in English Thought*. For a sympathetic account of his life and ideas, see Adam Fox, *Dean Inge* (London: Murray, 1960).

your Society. Recently I read his 'Plotinus' with the greatest interest & enjoyment.

The enclosed is the only reproduction I have been able to secure of the Reid[25] portrait. I got it from Messrs Annan, Glasgow, the official photographers of the National Gallery. Does it meet your desires?

With kind greetings, Yours ever sincerely,

NORMAN KEMP SMITH.

13 Vicarage Gate, Kensington, W. 8.
29 May 1919.

Dear Professor Kemp Smith,—

Altho' we are to have the great pleasure of welcoming you here on Monday next, I yet want just to say shortly 3 things in connexion with your kind letter just received. (1) I am delighted you are standing for the succession to Prof. Pringle Pattison in Edinburgh, and for the (doubtless good) chance that we may thus have you permanently in Gt Britain. True, Prof. Baillie is also a good friend of mine—a fine man who has worked at, and has taught, these great subjects for certainly more years than you have. Yet we over here have him anyhow in Scotland. And then, much [as] I respect also his philosophical convictions (as far as I can understand them), I never feel sure I have really caught his ultimate positions. I always only follow his immediate points. (2) The Photo is delightful—most grateful thanks. (3) Am de-

---

[25] Thomas Reid (1710–1796), Scottish philosopher, whose education and early teaching career centered in Aberdeen until 1764, when he was appointed Professor of Moral Philosophy in Glasgow. He was the leading exponent of the so-called Scottish school of common sense philosophy, holding against Hume's skepticism that an external world was indeed intuitively or immediately known by men. Baron von Hügel had long been interested in Reid, and even noted in his Diary that while in St. Andrews to receive the honorary LL.D. degree he read Campbell Fraser's Thomas Reid. See Diaries, 10 July 1914.

lighted with subject of your LSSR Paper.[26] May the Abstract reach me on Saturday! Yrs cordially,

F. V. HÜGEL.

June 7. 1919.

Eira,
Rhoscolyn,
Holyhead, N. Wales.

My dear Baron von Hügel,

I found awaiting me on my arrival here on the 5th a letter from Pringle-Pattison saying that the Curators of the Edinburgh Logic Chair have decided not to advertise the Chair, but to proceed by enquiry, & that the Principal, Sir Alfred Ewing,[27] asks him to request Baillie & myself to make formal application, stating positions held, publications etc., & to call upon the Electors individually between June 10th & 20th. Pringle-Pattison also considers that we shall have to submit testimonials at the earliest possible date.

The change in the situation has necessitated the writing of some 20 or 30 notes to friends who have promised testimonials, & to others, & I am only at last free to write more congenial letters.

I gather that the choice lies between Baillie & myself, tho' of course it is always possible that other candidates might at the last be invited as the result of the enquiries.

[26] The *Minutes* of the LSSR for 3 June 1919 note: "Professor Norman Kemp Smith was the guest of the evening. . . . Professor N. Kemp Smith then read the society a paper on 'The Spiritual Value of Fear,' which was followed by a discussion, opened, as formerly, by Baron von Hügel." A re-written version of this paper was published in *Credibility of Divine Existence*, pp. 417–38.

[27] Sir James Alfred Ewing (1855–1935), Scottish engineer, educated in Dundee and at the University of Edinburgh; professor of engineering and applied mechanics in Tokyo, Dundee, and Cambridge, 1878–1903; director of naval education, 1903–1916; Principal and Vice-Chancellor of the University of Edinburgh, 1916–1929. He invented instruments for measuring and recording earthquakes, and during the First World War supervised the deciphering of intercepted German wireless messages. He was a Fellow of the Royal Society, and in 1932 became President of the British Association.

The Principal, I am told, has already written asking Ward,[28] Sorley,[29] Stout,[30] Haldane,[31] Sir Henry Jones[32] & Latta[33] for their *private* opinion of the respective claims of Baillie & myself. Several of the other electors are also writing to those whose judgment they value. Should you be appealed to in this confidential manner, I trust that you will not feel that you need refuse to express yourself.[34]

I am glad that the pace is being accelerated. A candidature is very disturbing to work & quiet of mind; & I shall rejoice when it is over. The election may now take place before the end of June. But now let me turn to happier themes.

How can I sufficiently thank you for those two days which the Baroness, your daughter, & yourself made so delightful, stimulat-

---

[28] James Ward (1843–1925), British philosopher and psychologist; abandoned studies for Congregationalist ministry and therewith conventional Christianity as well; studied philosophy, natural science, and psychology; Professor of Mental Philosophy and Logic at Cambridge University, 1897–1925. He delivered the Gifford Lectures at Aberdeen, 1895–1898, on *Naturalism and Agnosticism*, and the Gifford Lectures at St. Andrews, 1907–1910, on *The Realm of Ends, or Pluralism and Theism*. He and von Hügel had occasionally corresponded for years, and had met for discussions when the Baron was in Cambridge to visit relatives.

[29] William Ritchie Sorley (1855–1935), British philosopher, educated at Edinburgh and Cambridge Universities. He held chairs in philosophy at Cardiff, 1888–1894, Aberdeen, 1894–1900, and Cambridge, 1900–1933.

[30] George Frederick Stout (1860–1944), British philosopher, educated at St. John's College, Cambridge; lectured at Cambridge, 1894–1896, Aberdeen, 1896–1898, and Oxford, 1898–1903; Professor of Logic and Metaphysics at St. Andrews University, 1903–1936. He was editor of *Mind*, 1891–1920, the author of many books, and a Fellow of the British Academy.

[31] Richard Burdon Haldane, Viscount Haldane (1856–1928), British statesman, lawyer, and philosopher, educated at the Universities of Göttingen and Edinburgh,

and at Lincoln's Inn; Liberal Member of Parliament for East Lothian, 1885–1911; created viscount, 1911; Lord Chancellor, 1912–1915; and after estrangement from Liberal Party became Lord Chancellor in Labour administration, 1924. He initiated army reform prior to the First World War, interested himself in higher education, and wrote philosophical books.

[32] Sir Henry Jones (1852–1922), Welsh philosopher, educated at Glasgow University. He held chairs in philosophy at University College of North Wales, Bangor, 1884–1891, St. Andrews University, 1891–1894, and Glasgow University, 1894–1922. He became a Fellow of the British Academy in 1904, and was knighted in 1912. Kemp Smith had been his pupil in St. Andrews, and held his first teaching post under him in Glasgow.

[33] Robert Latta (1865–1932), Scottish philosopher, educated at the University of Edinburgh; taught philosophy at University College, Dundee, St. Andrews University, and the University of Aberdeen, before becoming Professor of Logic and Rhetoric in the University of Glasgow, 1902–1925.

[34] On June 9 von Hügel "wrote to Prof. J. B. Baillie—my regret at inability to give him testimonal—bec[ause] of N. K. Smith, whom I want to see Prof. in Europe & have decided to give testimonials neither to him nor to S." *Diaries*, 9 June 1919.

ing & helpful to me! I shall always retain them as among my happiest memories.[35]

It especially delights me that my paper has been liked by you. In a paper of this kind I would rather have your approval than that of anyone else that I have the privilege of knowing. It represents positions to which I have been feeling my way for some years, & largely in reaction against earlier, and, as I now recognise, more superficial ways of thinking. In getting the paper incorporated into the larger discussion which I contemplate of 'traditional views of human nature', I shall constantly have in mind, as my standard of excellence, the writing of something that you can regard as showing true insight, however inadequate & incomplete be my expression of it. I have already profited so greatly by the Troeltsch & the Gierke (including Maitland's Introduction), that without your advice I might well never have known of, that I look forward eagerly to a thorough study, at the earliest opportunity, of Holtzmann,[36] Lagarde,[37] Wellhausen[38] & the Handbuch der Kirchengeschichte. In the avalanche of worthless books that have to be waded through in the search for the really helpful, nothing can be more valuable than the guidance you give me.

[35] Kemp Smith's letter of gratitude to von Hügel's wife, Lady Mary Catherine Herbert von Hügel, can be found in Appendix I. Although Kemp Smith refers to Lady Mary as Baroness (as some people did), her correct title was indeed Lady Mary, because her title in her own right, as daughter of Lord and Lady Herbert of Lea, was considered, in England at least, to be of greater significance than her title as the wife of a foreign baron of the Holy Roman Empire.

[36] Heinrich Julius Holtzmann (1832–1910), German theologian and New Testament critic; son of Adolf Holtzmann (1810–1870), the well-known philologist. Heinrich Holtzmann's Lehrbuch der Neutestamentlichen Theologie (1897) greatly influenced von Hügel, who frequently urged its reading on Kemp Smith in these letters. For a full treatment of von Hügel's relationship with Holtzmann, based on their correspondence, see Hans Rollmann's "Holtzmann, von Hügel and Mod-

ernism," The Downside Review, 97, No. 327 (April 1979), 128–42, and ibid., No. 328 (July 1979), 221–44.

[37] Paul Anton de Lagarde (1827–1891), German Biblical scholar and Orientalist whose real name was Bötticher, though he used his mother's name of Lagarde. He studied in Berlin, Halle, London, and Paris; and he edited numerous Biblical manuscripts in Syriac, Aramaic, Arabic, and Coptic.

[38] Julius Wellhausen (1844–1918), German Biblical scholar, who held professorships at Greifswald (1872), Halle (1882), Marburg (1885), and Göttingen (1892). His source criticism of the Pentateuch and his studies in Old Testament history, especially his Prolegomena zur Geschichte Israels (1883), greatly influenced von Hügel. For von Hügel's evaluation of Wellhausen, see his "Julius Wellhausen," The Times Literary Supplement, No. 842, 7 March 1918, p. 117.

I remember now that a friend, H. R. Mackintosh of the Free Church College in Edinburgh,[39] placed the Holtzmann in my hands some weeks ago, with the remark that it was the best work on its subject; but I fear I would not have followed up his recommendation, as I was taking the book as being largely technical discussion of philological & other similar questions that are outside my field of competent study.

I forgot to ask you, before leaving, for the book you kindly said you would lend me. If you feel you can entrust it to the post, I shall take good care of it, & return it at some early date.

Your friends must eagerly hope for an early and complete restoration of your working powers. I really think that the outlook for philosophy was never more inspiriting. We may surely have confidence that the Enlightenment, humanitarian, teaching will soon yield, even in the most popular writing, to a more satisfying interpretation of human life.

Yours ever most gratefully,
NORMAN KEMP SMITH.

11th June 1919
Clonboy,
Englefield Green,
Surrey.

My dear Professor,

This is no answer, in detail, of your most kind letter, so full of information and of cheering convictions, but only—from a tired man—three small business points. (1) I can, and I will, answer confidentially any confidential enquiry addressed to me, as above, concerning your fitness for the Edinburgh Professorship. (2) My daughter, on reaching Vicarage Gate, for 2 nights to-morrow,

---

[39] Hugh Ross Mackintosh (1870–1936), Scottish theologian, educated in Edinburgh and Germany, and ordained to the Free Church ministry in 1897; Professor of Systematic Theology at New College, Edinburgh, 1904–1936.

will look out and will post to you, my great Abbé Huvelin's[40] 'Quelques Directeurs d'Ames'. I shd. love you to browse prayerfully thro' these pages—the ripe fruit of endlessly heroic life and love. I do not want it back till Sept. 1st—at Vicarage Gate. (3) My Wife and Daughter and I will be only too glad and proud, if you will henceforth look upon 13 V. G., whilst it is ours, as your *pièd-à-terre*, whenever you are in London for 3/4 days. We will most gladly know—we look forward to knowing your Wife and little girl. We dare not offer to take them *in* too, merely because of insufficient accommodation.

Yrs cordially,

F. V. HÜGEL.

18 St. Clair Terrace
Edinburgh.

June 25, 1919

My dear Baron von Hügel,

I must not delay longer to acknowledge receipt of l'Abbé Huvelin's "Quelques Directeurs d'Ames". It has been the best possible companion to me in the restless week of interviewing Electors here in Edinburgh. I am only half way through it, reading in it, or rather, to use your phrase, browsing in it, at leisure; but already I can see how much I am to get from it. It is very beautiful, full of true wisdom & insight. You have placed me under a great debt—one more in the many I owe to you.

This evening I have received word of my election to the Logic Chair. Baillie & I were the only candidates invited to make application. The great bulk of the philosophical support came to

---

[40] L'Abbé Henri Huvelin (1838–1910), extraordinarily successful French spiritual director who had a great personal influence on von Hügel when the latter was a young man. For a statement of the von Hügel–Huvelin relationship, see Lawrence F. Barmann, *Baron Friedrich von Hügel and the Modernist Crisis in England* (Cambridge: Cambridge University Press, 1972), pp. 2–3. The book which von Hügel sent was Huvelin's *Quelques Directeurs d'âmes* (Paris: Gabalda, 1912), a collection of brief addresses given by the Parisian priest and published after his death from the notes of some of his hearers.

me, & it was fairly clear, for some little time, that I should be appointed. But it is none the less satisfactory that it is now definitely settled. Life in Edinburgh will be very congenial to my wife & myself; & I am sure I shall be very happy in the work of the Chair. It is, however, my own short-comings that are most vividly present to me these days. I shall at least spare no effort to prove worthy of the trust.

Your health, I trust, continues to improve. Please convey the very kind greetings of my wife and myself to the Baroness von Hügel and to your daughter. I shall write again, in a time of greater quiet. I am, dear Baron von Hügel,

Yours ever gratefully,
NORMAN KEMP SMITH.

P.S. I do not know whether you were finally appealed to for a confidential opinion upon the candidates. In any case your approval of my work is a very great encouragement to me.

1st July 1919
Clonboy,
Englefield Green,
Surrey.

My very dear Professor,

White nights have prevented me from the joy of at once telling you my delight at your great news—so kindly imparted as soon as ever you knew of the great fact yourself. I weigh my words when I say that this fact ranks with hardly a dozen as pure and as full joys granted me during my now long life. You will do good, much good; you will get good, much good in Edinburgh—in that truly illustrious Chair. —No questions were put to me about you —I took this to be one more sign how secure your prospects were. But I wish I had the health just now to write out, just for your own and your fine wife's eyes, exactly why I am so delighted —exactly why I build such great expectations upon you. Instead of such a study—(unnecessary, surely, at least since our LSSR meeting,) I will venture upon 2 or 3 sentences, which you will forgive—won't you?—if they are too private and in any way tactless! You see, I have got so much money upon this N. K. S. horse: naturally then, I am perhaps over fussily anxious to help its training and grooming to be as complete and as perfect as possible. I venture then to beg you to keep and to develope as much as ever you conscientiously can—or to gain or to regain it, in your own best manner and degree—a definite Church membership, a clearly avowed and regularly practised traditional, institutional, religion. For myself such definite appurtenance has cost me much, all my life. Yet I am more than ever penetrated by the simply *immense* debt I owe (I mean, also just *qua* philosopher of religion) to such appurtenance. Of course, I believe the Roman Catholic Church, to be the deepest, most comprehensive, and the most probing, of these great, irreplaceable training-schools. Yet, equally of course, I know that that great Church is not the only one of such profound aids; and that, as to yourself, *your* home is, presumably, in the Presbyterian, possibly in the Episcopalian, Church. I only want—for this just once—when a man twenty years my junior, is starting his life afresh, to produce so much more than ever I can hope to do: I want to plunge, as it were, the most delicate of thermometers into his heart—for him to read upon it how far he is already quite humble, quite creaturely, quite drawing all that rich religious experience, without which he will never possess completely the full, clear subject-matter for his deepest philosophizings; and without which, again, his motives and his emotions will remain less precise, vivid and virile than they otherwise would be. Troeltsch is a splendid illustration, as well as teacher, of the great truth I mean.

To the man, the Friend, I may say, mayn't I?, that he is now well within my poor prayers; and that I love to think of him as learning with me from that M. Huvelin, who suffered, who willed, who loved, who was and who learnt, so much to the very end.

With our united delighted congratulations also to your wife,

Yr aff. Friend
F. v. Hügel.

P.S. I shall love someday to show you a selection from Abbé Huvelin's private advice to myself—the help which gave me the light and strength to weather—oh, such storms within me and without me.

H.

Clonboy, Englefield Green, Surrey, Aug. 5 1919.
Pray excuse P. C. It is only that I continue to feel interiorly pressed to present you with some memorial of yr appointment and of all it has meant to me. So please tell me, by a P. C., whether you have as yet ordered the big Troeltsch (the 'Sozial-lehren'); or (if so), Holtzmann's 'N. T. Theologie'. If both have been ordered, let me give you Gierke—the 3rd (quite self-complete) vol. of his great 'Genossenschaftsrecht'. (Maitland has only given *one* out of its, I think, ten chapters.) An excellent holiday for you three! Yrs ever

F. v. HÜGEL.

The Whins,

Aug. 11. 1919. Windermere.

My dear Baron von Hügel,

How frequently I have had it in mind to answer your letter, and again—alas!—how I have ever delayed until I could answer it in a mood sufficiently worthy and alert! For I have seldom spent a more unsettled, and in some ways more uncomfortable time than during the past six weeks. First I had a chill which confined me to bed for a week—throwing everything into arrears. I count the chill as my reacclimatisation to these Northern parts. Then my wife & I had to change all our previous arrangements and substitute others, & lastly we had some weeks tramping the historic city & its suburbs to find a house. When we settled on one, it was only to discover that after all the lady owning it had herself failed to secure another, & so was remaining. We started in again, & this time found with much searching a house in Regent Terrace, with a glorious outlook over Holyrood to Arthurs Seat, & near congenial colleagues. How delighted were [*sic*] were! Could anything be more fortunate! But it would have required, as we found on further investigation, much reconstruction, with little prospect of getting the work people therefore. So we were baffled again. All the houses too, that are vacant, are to sell only, never to let. However we now find ourselves landed proprietors, being the owners of 14 Lennox Street—a quiet street, just across the Dean Bridge, at the west end of Princes Street, & with access to the Dean Gardens. It will serve very well for two or three years until we can find the house we can regard as a permanency. As we have got it at a reasonable price, probably we shall be able to sell without serious loss. Mrs Kemp Smith is still in Edinburgh, arranging with painters etc who get entry into the house in the beginning of September.

Unless my Princeton colleague Bowman,[41] as seems unlikely now, sees prospect of sailing this month, my wife will have to cross to America, to arrange for the closing of our house, auctioning most of our furniture, & shipping the rest. It will be a heavy task, & I wish I could have taken her place, or gone with her, but my necessary preparations for the winter's work forbid that. She has taken passage on the Mauretania, due to sail on the 23rd.

Your letter has been the source of very great happiness to me. That my appointment should be greeted by you in this warm & personal manner is a profound encouragement to do my utmost to deserve your trust and goodwill, but also makes me very keenly aware how far I may fall short. Certainly I shall have one added motive for sincere & honest work, & that will be the earning of your continued sympathy & support. Philosophy is a heart-

---

[41] Archibald Allan Bowman (1883–1936), Scottish philosopher, educated at the University of Glasgow; lectured at Queen Margaret College, Glasgow, and at Princeton University, before becoming Professor of Logic at Glasgow in 1926, and then Professor of Moral Philosophy there from 1927 until his death.

breaking subject at times; but as you would assure me, I know, that only means that it is well worth breaking one's heart over. And it has great privileges—not least I value the constant contact with young & eager minds. I know I shall be happier and more energetic immediately the work of the session starts.

What you say as to forming definite Church connections, I shall consider very carefully, & with deep gratitude to you for the friendship that inspires your wise & kindly advice. I move slowly, & I see difficulties. My views have changed very radically in the past ten years, & I feel have deepened in insight beyond anything I had before—becoming at once more definite & more satisfying. And the change has also been entirely in the direction of the religious view of life. Further, I recognise that it is a duty to further religion on its institutional side. For, need I say?, I have no belief in individualism in this field. If I join any Church, it will be the Presbyterian. I am still too sceptical of the conflicting Institutional claims of the various Churches to feel justified in breaking, though aesthetic & some other deeper preferences might be thereby satisfied, with the Church I was born into, & to which my Country is committed. I believe, too, that so long as it can conscientiously be done, more good can be achieved by the individual in cooperation with the general sympathies of the community within which he finds himself, than by his seeking to influence it from without. But that is entirely in line with the spirit of your own advice; & believe me I shall not allow your appeal to be fruitless from any lack of earnest pondering upon it. My wife too joins me in grateful thanks. She is very much in the same position as I am mentally, in this great matter.

Now this morning comes your postcard, to heap coals of fire upon my head for my delay in writing. I should indeed be honoured & delighted to have from you such a memento of my appointment or rather of your splendid and generous interest therein, as you suggest. During the war I tried but failed to obtain Troeltsch's 'Soziallehren' in a copy of my own; & now that German books are again procurable I had not ordered them, as I was awaiting until we had a fixed address and were out of our trunks. Either the Troeltsch or the Holtzmann, as you may care to decide, I should value. So please, dear Baron, make the choice for me; & please inscribe your name that it may be the more closely associated with you.

My photo you honoured me by asking for. I shall send it when my belongings arrive from Princeton: I have a number lying there.

I am still browsing at times, with great profit, in Abbé Huvelin, & should indeed be interested in any selection you feel you could show me of his private writing.

I shall be here until 23rd August, then a week in the hills somewhere, & from Sept. 1st to 30th at c/o Ainley, 30 Alva Street, Edinburgh. But *The University, Edinburgh* is also an address that will always find me. At present I am enjoying hospitality at this cottage which belongs to my sister-in-law—she is looking after our little daughter. By & bye I must summon up energy to start on the writing of the Address that has to be given as an Inaugural at the beginning of Session. Meantime I am resting more or less, have stopped smoking (but do so for a month only: I miss it sadly), & have secured a cycle for exercise.

The sojourn in the country is very greatly benefiting your health, I trust, & adding to your strength. May you soon be restored to working vigour! My wife, were she with me, would join in kindest greetings to the Baronness and to yourself.

I am, my dear Baron
    Yours ever most sincerely & most gratefully,
        NORMAN KEMP SMITH.

Sept. 14. 1919   c/o Ainley
                                    30 Alva Street,
                                      Edinburgh.

My dear Baron von Hügel,
I am returning under separate cover the volume you so kindly lent me. I have found it both helpful & illuminating. The 'Port-Royal' group I have long studied; & I gained much by the fine &

delicate representation of the counter, or perhaps I may say, the supplementary ideals. Very many thanks for directing my attention to it. I am finding that any volume you recommend is a book not to be missed.

You have, I trust, greatly profited by your sojourn in the country; & will be abler for work in the coming winter.

Mrs Kemp Smith was at last able to sail on Sept. 6th, & should be arriving in New York yesterday or today. She will have no easy task in disposing of our numerous belongings in these unsettled times, but in Princeton will have many friends to lend her a helping hand.

I have more or less finished my Inaugural—on 'The Present Situation in Philosophy'—& am turning my mind to the arrangement of my courses, so far as that can be done before my library's coming to me: it is still on the way, & I fear may not yet be out of the Cunard's American storage. My induction is at a Senatus' meeting on Oct 2nd, & classes start in the middle of the month. Meantime most of the University people are out of town. With Pringle-Pattison I shall be spending two or three days at The Haining[42] next week.

In looking into Figgis' 'From Gerson to Grotius' I note that he is a pupil of your friend, the late F. W. Maitland. With kindest greetings to the Baroness, to your daughter, & to yourself

Yours ever sincerely,

NORMAN KEMP SMITH.

39 Melville Street

Oct. 6. 1919   Edinburgh

My dear Baron von Hügel,

I have only just received at the University the photo that you have so kindly sent me. It is splendid, & I shall value it all the more highly for the inscription you have placed upon it. It is now adorning my mantelpiece, & helps give a more home-like look

---

[42] The Haining was Professor Pringle–Pattison's country estate.

to these rooms that I am tenanting until our house is ready. My own photos I expect to be arriving with my library. It reached Glasgow just before the strike, & now that the strike is fortunately over, should come through in a few days.

The strike has also stopped all mail from America, & I have not heard from my wife since her arrival in Princeton. Probably she will be returning before the end of this month.

Save for two days with the Pringle-Pattisons at the Haining, I have been spending a very quiet month in Edinburgh. Now, however, the University people are reassembling, & I shall gladly resume the old philosophical routine that has been unhappily broken for the past five years. My Inaugural Lecture is fixed for the 16th; & I meet my first class the following day. Following the usual custom in Scotland, I am printing my Inaugural, & shall send you a copy. It is designed for a very mixed audience.

Just these days I am rereading some Plato, to renew my impressions & prepare for my teaching.

You are very happily settled; I trust, and have renewed energies for the winter. Any time that you feel able to write, a letter will be a most welcome honour to me.

With kindest greetings to the Baroness & to your daughter & to yourself, & again very many thanks for the photograph—it will be one of my treasured possessions.

Yours ever sincerely,
NORMAN KEMP SMITH.

13th–18th Nov. 1919.
13, Vicarage Gate,
Kensington,
W. 8.

My dear Friend,

(I hope I may now call you so—it is so much more confiding a word than is 'Professor', fine as the latter title can be made!).

I am fast coming to feel what has happened to me repeatedly

—that just because I have a practically unlimited range of convictions, interests, hopes and fears in common with you (I mean, in a degree and way that has not occurred, with living men, more than,—say, a dozen times, or even less, in my long life)—I put off and off writing to you, since there forms in my head and heart a whole mass of things to say—a mass too large to unpack and sort out into a letter. Then, too, I have had to go to Birmingham, to deliver an address which cost me a delightful, but very hard fortnight's work.[43] And now, on last Monday, I started studying up—filling in the gaps in my previous readings—for the book I hope to be allowed to write. I am finding two hours a morning of this, quite within my powers. But so far I have used the afternoons for walk and letters.—

First, then, your *Inaugural.* I have read most of it 3, 4, 5 times, and all of it very carefully. I am delighted with it—especially with your tone—with the fine, difficult and rare combination of deliberate personal conviction and perfect fairness, indeed generosity, to the rival positions. (A. E. Taylor, I find, pretty often fails in this). —Then the points you bring out are, I think, admirably chosen and you put them in a very interesting—in places in a delightfully humorous—way. Let me state what are the turns in the road which I am so deeply glad you take; then, where it is that I have learnt from you; and finally, what I should have liked to be somewhat different.[44]

Your introductory remarks about Pringle Pattison are finely respectful, true, and free from the least touch of exaggeration.— I am very glad of the little sentence, top of p. 6, 'Idealism now— of men': doubtless a fact, but one that as certainly requires, now again, to be clearly brought out. —Top of p. 8: 'So that while each main type—any period in the past'. This is very striking, put thus, and leads over excellently to all that follows. —Top of

[43] In late October, at the invitation of the Anglican Bishop of Birmingham, von Hügel had addressed for fifty minutes the Birmingham Clerical Society on "The Apocalyptic Element in the Teaching of Jesus: Its Ultimate Significance and Its Abiding Function." *Diaries,* 27–28 October 1919.

[44] In order for the reader to make sense of von Hügel's detailed comments on Kemp Smith's Inaugural Lecture, the entire Lecture is reprinted in Appendix II with the pagination and line-count exactly as von Hügel read it and thus referred to it.

p. 9 'Though speaking—human activities': this is a most wisely
generous bit, and ought to win you many young minds. So also
the middle § of p. 9. —Bottom of p. 9 'When through the miscarriage' to 'lives only to condemn' top of p. 10. Yes, like Père
Alfred Lapôtre, a most learned French Jesuit, an authority on
the Pseudo-Isidorian (Papal) Decretals, the bad Popes etc.:
Duchesne used to call him 'spécialiste en matières scabreuses'!
—Page 10, near middle: 'The history of philosophy—sceptical
thinkers'. What a noble saying! And the Greek Chorus comparison is most telling! —Near bottom of p. 10 'The better understanding' to l. 6 of p. 11 'unknowable': a most true §. Then the
account and analysis of Animism, and of the sceptical utter
contempt for it, pp. 11–13 is delightful in its freshness and force.
On p. 14, ll. 5–7, and on p. 16, bottom § 'Even of—their
place' are, conjointly, sadly precise renderings of what this Neo-
Naturalistic School does say and think: my dear *Loisy*,[45] poor
man, is thus painted quite exactly—at least as to what he thinks
he thinks. Altogether p. 16 is a grandly generous description. On
pp. 18, 19, § 'To these questions—own foundations': how right,
splendid! Somehow even Pringle Pattison, admirable though he
is on Agnosticism as really hostile to faith does not quite say as
much or as well as this. It reads to me rather like unto *Aliotta*[46]
at his best—Aliotta, my respect for whose position so amusingly
riles J. A. Smith.[47] And this position I have come to believe most
important for religion: poor Loisy's now equal hostility to certi-

[45] Alfred Firmin Loisy (1857–1940),
French Biblical scholar; Professor of
Scripture at the Institut Catholique (Paris), 1881–1903; Professor of the History
of Religion in the Collège de France,
1909–1932; friend of von Hügel's from
the 1890s, whom von Hügel supported in
the face of ecclesiastical harassment and
eventual condemnation. For the most balanced appraisal to date of the still controversial Loisy, see Ronald Burke's "Loisy's
Faith: Landshift in Catholic Thought,"
The Journal of Religion, 60, No. 2 (April
1980), 138–64.
[46] Antonio Aliotta (1881–1964), Italian philosopher who moved from studies
in experimental psychology into critical

analyses of contemporary philosophy. He
opposed the Idealism of Croce and Gentile, and in his later years was sympathetic
to the Pragmatism represented by James
and Mead. At the time of this letter, von
Hügel could have read his *La misura in
psicologia sperimentale, La reazione idea-
listica contro la scienza*, and *La guerra
eterna e il dramma dell'esistenza*.
[47] John Alexander Smith (1863–1939),
British philosopher and classical scholar,
educated at the University of Edinburgh
and Balliol College, Oxford; Waynflete
Professor of Moral and Metaphysical Philosophy at Oxford, 1910–1936; joint-editor of the Oxford translation of Aristotle,
1908–1912.

tude in religion and certitude in science confirms me as to the interconnection of the two certitudes.—

Middle of p. 20 '. . . so far are the dualisms—rightly understood.' This is admirable indeed! Bravissimo! and so is the whole middle of p. 21 'with animism is bound up—developed experience'. Oh, fine! The argument from 'Present-day naturalism' middle of p. 23 to 'the facts to be accounted for', bottom of p. 27 is finely knit and presses home grandly. Again it proves that L. is right in refusing (*qua* sceptic) to allow that the intellect can reach reality in any subject-matter whatsoever!—

Very satisfactory and useful is all from 'the most important' top of p. 28, up to 'never be detected', top of p. 29.

And your penultimate §, pp. 30, 31 is noble, vibratingly true.

What in this *Inaugural* has been really new to me is your account of the most recent expositions of Naturalism—as holding the logical criteria to have absolute validity etc. pp. 17, 18. This explains to me why L. writes to me so little hopefully as to gaining adhesion to his scepticism with regard to *both* science and religion. When you write, kindly give me the names of the chief of these thinkers.—

My dissatisfactions are, as to *the form* that, whilst your whole language, and the single sentences, indeed the entire paragraphs, are all most appropriate and as easy to follow as the subject-matter permits: the order of the paragraphs somehow disturbs and confuses me. I have found it difficult to make any quite luminous and balanced scheme of your for me too zig-zaggy, too much getting-on and then harking-back way.

Then *as to your formulations*, I am not somehow fully helped or entirely reassured by two passages. The first, is as to the unsatisfactoriness of agnosticism—top of p. 11. Pringle Pattison somehow I feel to emphasize more precisely the week spot of agnosticism, in that it overlooks the very certain fact of the human mind being part and parcel of the real world, and the *position*— the situation of *possession*—which results thence for the validity of such mind's information. Am putting it very badly, but something like that somehow comes home to me more conclusively than do the two arguments given by you. But perhaps you have primarily been after what is now more frequently admitted by others, and not after the most cogent of the insights attained.—

And the second dissatisfaction as to formulations concerns the two paragraphs 'According to Naturalism', 'Idealism on the other hand'—bottom of p. 21, top of p. 22—down to 'standards and values'. I do wish this did not read so confoundedly pantheistically. For years now I have found more and more how catchy —what a very lobster-pot for the unwary mind—is 'The Whole' —if and where the mind is after *God*. I know of course, that, God secured, the religious mind requires a certain order and interconnection in and of the universe which He originates and sustains and even (in *its very real evil*) allows. But the universe is not God, and never can become God, and must not even preliminarily and hypothetically be assumed to be God, or (if it is not God), then to exhaust Reality. I feel here, like Pattison and other solid thinkers (solid at least as to the nature of thought) feel concerning the Cartesian *'Cogito ergo sum'*—that such a demonstrably incomplete *status quaestionis* can never issue in ought but subjectivism. So here we are imprisoned in Pantheism. I know, of course, that Philosophy is not Theology, is not even, directly, Religious Faith. Still, I should like it, if it *must* begin from the 'Whole' point, to accompany such beginning by a warning that even this its starting-point may have, at the end of Philosophy, to be shifted, or to be completed—in a way superceded —because of deeper evidences. But this seems a complicated, rather messy, procedure. Could not another difference be insisted upon, at and for the first? To train minds to be pantheists *qua* philosophers—is *that* necessary?

Will you be so kind as to send copies of this Inaugural (with 'at Baron v. Hügel's suggestion', or the like?) to:

(1) Claude G. Montefiore Esq.
     74 Campden Hill Road
                London, W. 8.
(2) The Rev. M. C. D'Arcy, S.J.
     Ore Place, Hastings.
(3) Evelyn Viscountess de Vesci,
          Abbey Leix, Ireland

(4) Mrs Cecil Chapman,
      The Cottage, Roehampton,
      London, S.W. 15.
(5) Don Antonio Cojazzi
      Valsalice 39, Torino
      Italy.

All these have had you preached to, and will push the *Inaugural*. As to other matters, pray excuse the following hotch-potch.

(1) I quite understood what you wrote as to *appurtenance to a particular religious body*; and very certainly I was not thinking of Rome for you. But I notice, from your answer, that not only you think, but that really you are, not yet ripe for such a step. I mean that I feel you do not yet realise—at least not sufficiently for such action—the great utility—in a sense the real need—of such appurtenance for *yourself*, for your attaining of the maximum insight into religion. I fully perceive with you—I am sure, more keenly, because experimentally than yourself—the difficulties, burthens etc. of any and all such appurtenance; and this, so much so, that only if and when the sense of its necessity for your own soul and its growth comes, would I be happy at your moving, since only this sense, and its assuagement in a religious institution, could make you bear the friction and weight of all such institutions.

(2) I have now secured *one* of the two *Troeltsch* volumes you are to have from me, in memory of your call to Edinburgh—that collection of grand essays. But the book has turned up unbound, and I am waiting for the 'Soziallehren' volume, to have the one, or both, bound alike. With all this post-war delay and muddle, I am still left uncertain whether, and when, I am to have the 'Soziallehren'. But the delay will not prevent your certainly receiving whatever may be procurable.—

(3) Will you kindly tell me, whether you have studied *Vahinger's* [sic] 'Philosophie des Als Ob',[48] and what you think of its power (as a destructive analysis). I have now begun my readings

[48] Hans Vaihinger (1852–1933), German philosopher; founder of the Kant Society, 1904, and co-founder, 1919, as well as editor, 1919–1929, of the *Annalen der Philosophie*.

for my book on God, and want to face quietly the best that has been written *against*. If you possess the book, and have no present need for it, I would greatly esteem its loan—for 2 months, say— but after Xtmas!—

(4) Dr *Theodore Merz*[49] is about to publish 'A Fragment on the Human Mind', which I take will be a most impressive *swan's song*. I should like to think of you as one of its reviewers.

(5) I have, for the moment, mislaid those *talks of M. Huvelin* to myself, for my spiritual life. I will send them later on. What splendour and steadiness of spiritual insight was there! Happy will be philosophy if, without itself getting so far, it will never and nowhere bar the way to such glorious penetration and power!

I do trust your fine, plucky wife is with you now; and that all with you, and her, and the little one, is going on grandly.

My wife and daughter join in very kind regards to yourself.

Yours, with deep, most living interest in your work and outlook, and in all the good they will bring to countless minds,

very sincerely—if I may say so—
affectionately yours
F. VON HÜGEL.

14 Lennox Street
Edinburgh

Dec. 7. 1919

My dear Baron von Hügel,

You must not judge of the pleasure your letter has given me by my delay in acknowledging it. On the contrary, I have wished to wait until I had sufficient freedom of mind to send you my grateful thanks in more fitting manner. That my Inaugural has in the main met with your approval is a high satisfaction to me.

---

[49] John Theodore Merz (1840–1922), educated at the Universities of Giessen, Göttingen, Heidelberg, and Bonn. Although he was director of several large British corporations, he is best known for his multi-volume *History of European Thought in the Nineteenth Century* (1896–1914).

Indeed frequently while writing it, I caught myself wondering how far the views would approve themselves to your judgment, & earnestly hoping that they might—in expression as well as in substance. Even in the two respects in which you criticise I can myself agree. First as regards style, I was more or less aware of trying to say too many things too quickly, & thereby sacrificing effectiveness & unity. I tried to make the sequence better, but could find no way out. My only excuse is that I desired to guard against misunderstanding, & could only do so by digressions & by returning on my own steps. Your other criticism, upon my method of distinguishing between naturalism & idealism, I feel the full force of. Whether I could have succeeded in modifying my statements, guarding against Pantheism, with which I really have no personal sympathy, without having to desert my method of exposition, I am not certain. But probably my main point would still stand, that the differentia of naturalism is its attempt to solve the problems of life from a merely planetary & human stand-point.

As to the third criticism, which you make earlier in your letter, regarding my method of refuting agnosticism, again I should cordially agree. The points I emphasised were mainly dictated by the requirements of my further arguments.

My insistence upon the importance for Idealism of maintaining the genuineness of knowledge & the absoluteness of the logical criteria, it will interest you to know, is the direct outcome of a passage of your own—in, I think, your 'Eternal Life': I have been trying to locate the passage this evening, but without success —I read it, I know, in some work of yours while in London some 12 months ago. It has been in my mind ever since, & what I say on pp. 18–19 is the result thereof.

The naturalistic writers who adopt this absolutist view of knowledge are—all of them so-called "realists"—S. Alexander,[50]

[50] Samuel Alexander (1854–1938), Jewish philosopher, born in Sydney, Australia, and educated at Melbourne University and Balliol College, Oxford; the first professing Jew to receive a fellowship at either Oxford or Cambridge; Professor of Philosophy at Manchester, 1893–1924, where he lived until his death.

B. Russell[51] (at least in his main published works: he is now rather drifting in other directions, I should say), G. E. Moore,[52] Percy Nunn,[53] and the American "Neo-realists", such as Ralph Barton Perry.[54] Alexander's Gifford Lectures should be published very shortly. He wrote me, in acknowledging the Inaugural, that he regards my argument from absoluteness in knowledge to absoluteness in other spheres as *the* fundamental fallacy of idealism. This I rather take as being, from my point of view, an opponent's admission that my argument deals with the fundamentals of the issue. Percy Nunn also writes me that my classing (by implication) the realists with naturalism surprised him as he had thought that realism had got beyond the antithesis between naturalism & idealism, & had come out on the further side of the opposition. He must have had in mind merely the epistemological opposition; but probably, as he is a naturalist of the ultra-humanitarian type (modernised education being his sheet-anchor!), he counts his ethics as having likewise transcended the opposition, by a higher synthesis. However he owns to an occasional twinge of doubt in the reading of my Address—a hopeful sign of grace.

Now my very hearty thanks, dear Baron, for your most generous expression of sympathy & appreciation. They will not lead me to relax in my efforts; quite the reverse, I shall have to en-

---

[51] Bertrand Arthur William Russell, Earl Russell (1872–1970), British philosopher, educated at Trinity College, Cambridge; elected Fellow of Trinity College, 1895 and 1944; held lectureships at Trinity College, the University of California, and Barnes Foundation (Philadelphia); wrote prolifically; received Nobel Prize for Literature, 1950.

[52] George Edward Moore (1873–1958), British philosopher, educated at Trinity College, Cambridge; University Lecturer in Moral Science at Cambridge, 1911–1925; Professor of Philosophy at Cambridge, 1925–1939; editor of *Mind*, 1921–1947; visiting professor at various American colleges and universities, 1940–1944. Moore's major published studies were *Principia Ethica* (1903), *Ethics* (1912), *Philosophical Studies* (1922), and *Some*

Main Problems of Philosophy (1953). The most recent study of Moore is that of Paul Levy, *Moore: G. E. Moore and the Cambridge Apostles* (London: Weidenfeld & Nicolson, 1979).

[53] Sir Percy Nunn (1870–1944), British educator; Master in various secondary schools; examiner in education, philosophy, and psychology in various universities; Director of the University of London Institute of Education, 1922–1936; President of the Aristotelian Society, 1923–1924; knighted in 1930.

[54] Ralph Barton Perry (1876–1957), American philosopher, educated at Princeton and Harvard Universities; after teaching at Williams College, Smith College, and Harvard University, he held a professorship at Harvard from 1913 to 1946.

deavour to live up to them, & to justify them by ever better work. And for that, such encouragement is very helpful in those hopeless intermediate stages when words & thinking seem hopelessly recalcitrant, & insight all to seek. As a friend of mine remarks, it is so hard often to know, when work is not progressing, whether it is because we have not squeezed our heads hard enough, or because the ideas are not there to squeeze out. The assurance from others that past labours have not been altogether unsuccessful is, in such cases, the best inspiration to carry on, & not to despair. A mathematician in Princeton assures me that the difference between those who do independent work in mathematics & the men (with equal power) who don't is mainly a matter of "guts", meaning e.g., of courage in attacking what is difficult & tenacity in holding out until the resistance gives way. My courage is strengthened by your kindly & generous sympathy.

I have been very glad to send copies to those you mention, & have had pleasant acknowledgments from Montefiore[55] & D'Arcy.[56] I could not make out the letters you placed after the latter's name; were they S(ociety of) J(esus)?

Under separate cover I send Vaihinger's 'Als Ob'. On looking into it in Princeton I was greatly disappointed. It is not of the quality of his Kantian work, & of course suffers from being edited in its incomplete & immature stage of elaboration. But perhaps you may find it serviceable for your purposes. I shall not be needing it, so please keep it as long as you have use for it.

Merz I have hitherto found more interesting in his historical than in his constructive work. But the latter I know very imperfectly.

A *quite excellent* book on Nietzsche appeared in 1917 by

[55] Claude Joseph Goldsmid Montefiore (1858–1938), Jewish Biblical scholar and philanthropist; joint-editor of The Jewish Quarterly Review, 1888–1908; President of University College, Southampton, 1915–1934; with von Hügel one of the founding members of the LSSR, 1904.

[56] Martin C. D'Arcy (1888–1977), English Jesuit philosopher, educated at Campion Hall, Oxford; author of several popular philosophical studies, and lecturer in Britain and America. His letters from von Hügel were published by Joseph P. Whelan, "Friedrich von Hügel's Letters to Martin D'Arcy," The Month, N.S. 42, Nos. 1–3 (July–August 1969), 23–26.

W. M. Salter[57] (a brother-in-law of Wm James), entitled "Nietzsche the Thinker—A Study", published by Henry Holt. I think you ought to take account of it. Most valuable, it appears to me, is Nietzsche's attempt (& failure) to satisfy his genuinely religious spirit by naturalistic fare, & also his criticism of sentimental humanitarianism. (Cf his saying: "We thirst for great & deep souls, & discover at best a social animal". Or again his remark regarding the "little good perfect things", occasionally to be met with in life, that "their golden ripeness heals the heart", & that their perfection "teaches hope".) It is some time since I have seen a new book that seemed to me so genuine a piece of work, maintaining a high level of insight from start to finish. Salter sent me the book some months ago. He has a very beautiful nature, & is sorely handicapped by extreme deafness. His home is in Boston. Large part of his partial sympathy with Nietzsche is due, probably, to the very general absence in America of those aristocratic standards of excellence upon which Nietzsche is so insistent.

My wife reached Liverpool almost a fortnight ago, after an excellent sunny & calm voyage, but had to go direct to London for a week where a sister of hers was having an operation the following day. Now, however, our little family is complete again, & we shall settle down rapidly.

Work proceeds very happily, & I am thoroughly enjoying it. The students are very keen & serious in their work, & make a very inspiring audience. We are at full pressure, but lectures stop at end of this coming week, & after a week of examinations the Christmas vacation starts. I shall take advantage of the leisure to write you again.

My kindest greetings to the Baroness & to your daughter, & believe me

Yours ever gratefully & affectionately

NORMAN KEMP SMITH.

[57] William Mackintire Salter (1853–1931), American writer and lecturer, educated at Knox College (Illinois), Yale Divinity School, and Harvard University.

13 Vicarage Gate, London, W. 8.
13th Dec. 1919.

At the end of my week's toil, I want to thank you, most warmly, for your grand 12 pp. letter, so full of interest and encouragement; and for Vaihinger's 'Als Ob' book, which arrived this morning. I had hoped (from the apparently excessive laudations it received, to find it equal, say, to Feuerbach's 'W. des Xtenthums', from which I learnt so much). But in any case, it will teach me what those praisers considered so powerful. I shall have first to do my Introduction and Part I, rearrange Part II, before tackling it. Only in Part III do I plan to consider the unbelievers. I hope to write properly in another week or two. Yrs ever

F. v. HÜGEL

Very happy Xtmas to you three!

13 Vicarage Gate, London, W. 8.
Febr. 2, 1920

My dear Professor and much cared for Friend,

Your long letter at Xtmastide was a most substantial gift— I have been ruminating various points of it ever since. This, tho' so late, is still not an answer—no real letter at all, altho' I have just *loads* to tell and to ask you. It is only a note, forced out of me *hic et nunc* by the standing of my now 16 years long friend, *Dr Angelo Crespi of Milan*,[58] for the Italian Lectureship, now vacant in Edinburgh University. I have just written off my testimonial for him to the Electors; but I want, quite confidentially, to put in, to you, the little shadows and limits, since I hope you

[58] Angelo Crespi was an Italian intellectual who was influenced by the Italian Catholic modernists and probably through them introduced to von Hügel. He first met von Hügel in London on 3 July 1907. He was in close touch with the Baron from their first meeting until von Hügel's death, and translated some of the latter's essays into Italian for publication in Italian journals. For a very brief statement on Crespi's thought, see Maurice Nedoncelle, "Dr. Angelo Crespi," *The Dublin Review*, 224, No. 447 (January 1950), 106–108.

will be able to help in the matter, and may be better armed in his defence if you know the few week places about him. He looks then somewhat peculiar—has a bad cast in one of his eyes; and his utterance of English is, at first, rather difficult to follow. (As to this latter point, if it were thought necessary, I could perhaps determine him to go thro' that splendid course of Phonetics at King's College, London). He used, in his early twenties, to be a militant secularist socialist. But he has, now during some 12 or more years, grown out of that into very rich, mellow and balanced social and religious convictions. I should love to have him at Edinburgh, teaching much and learning more amongst all that world, and especially with a certain Norman Kemp Smith! —The Troeltsch 'Gesammelte Schriften', vol. I is now at last getting bound for you; I hope to send it to you in another 16 days. —My mornings are most happily given to my book. I love so to realise as I toil at it all the grand common ground we share together.

Aff. Friend
F. VON HÜGEL.

14 Lennox Street,
Edinburgh

Feb. 4. 1920

My dear Baron von Hügel,

I did not fulfil my promise of writing again just after my last letter. Procrastination, & some tiredness—& no real excuse! In the Christmas holidays I had a few days in St Andrews with friends from Edinburgh, & some golf. The Moderator of the Church of Scotland, our Professor of Divinity here, W. P. Paterson,[59] joined us the last two days. He is very attractive, & a very real force for good in Scotland. Two of his sons he lost in the war, & that has aged him considerably, but he is very young in spirit.

[59] William Paterson Paterson (1860–1939), Scottish theologian and ordained minister of the Church of Scotland, educated at the University of Edinburgh and in Germany; professor of divinity at Edinburgh, 1903–1934, and Dean of the Faculty of Divinity, 1912–1928; Moderator of the General Assembly of the Church of Scotland, 1919.

Just before College reopened the Scots Philosophical Club (consisting of all those teaching philosophy in Scotland) met in Edinburgh—for a dinner one evening, followed by a forenoon's discussion next day, the subject being my Inaugural lecture. A. J. Balfour[60] & Lord Haldane, the two Honorary Members of the Club, were present. The former I heard speaking of you very warmly. He took little part in the discussion. Haldane made his usual speech, that I have heard now some four times, on orders of reality & the categories appropriate to each! As is usual in large companies the discussion did not amount to very much.

The Senatus & Court have approved the changes I have proposed in my classes—including change of title of my degree class from 'Logic and Philosophical Introduction' to 'Philosophy' simply—a title I much prefer. It is a very satisfactory class this year. The students are so eager & keen & hardworking—as I hear they are in all the classes—that I feel I ought to be giving them better than my best. Philosophy is very delightful to teach, but heartbreaking when, as I so often have to, I feel the shortcomings & thinness of the very best, with all my efforts, that I can give.

I am sending you a copy of my friend Bowman's—he was a pupil of mine in Glasgow & then a colleague in Princeton—Sonnets. You will appreciate the fine spirit they reveal. I miss his company greatly.

Your friend, should he be coming North to see the Electors, will, I hope, call upon me. I shall indeed be delighted to help him, if I find I can, though I fear my influence in such an appointment will not count for much. Still I can doubtless help him with introductions & some knowledge as to who count in deciding the election. If I hear anything of value in regard to it, I shall let you know. The principle now very generally favoured is to appoint

[60] Arthur James Balfour, first Earl of Balfour (1848–1930), British philosopher and statesman, educated at Eton and Trinity College, Cambridge; diverted from his philosophic studies to politics by his uncle, the third Marquess of Salisbury; from the time he entered Parliament in 1874 until his death he held numerous cabinet and other positions, including that of Prime Minister, 1902–1905. With von Hügel he was one of the original members of the Synthetic Society, 1896–1910. The most significant study of Balfour as a man of ideas is John David Root's "The Philosophical and Religious Thought of Arthur James Balfour (1848–1930)," *The Journal of British Studies*, 19, No. 2 (Spring 1980), 120–41.

an Englishman, if such can be found adequately equipped, in preference to a native of the country represented.

Your portrait I have got framed & it adorns my mantelpiece in my study. When I get discouraged I look up to it, & take new heart. Your sympathy & more than kindly judging of me lay upon me, I feel, a heavy responsibility that I may not disappoint you. My experience in life has all along been that I never succeed in anything until it seems impossible that I can do anything but fail; and now—in consequence—my knowledge of that is at times my best encourager. It lends me the necessary courage. My abilities are such that I can never achieve anything without the hardest of work, & anything that I write is always in its first drafts very repulsive & uncouth.

Holtzmann's two volumes that you recommended I have procured, & of late have been reading a little in, but so far only 100 pp. & hardly sufficient yet to show how far I shall profit. W. James's 'Varieties of Religious Experience' I read again last week. Some parts I found very suggestive & helpful, especially in Lecs. XIV & XV on the Value of Saintliness. The newness of the work here leaves me little time for fresh reading or for outside writing.

It is splendid to hear that you are able to keep steadily in the mornings at your new book. Good progress to it!

The photo that I hope to send you I have not secured yet: perhaps it may arrive among the baggage now overdue from Princeton.

W^m McDougall[61] of Oxford has been appointed Professor of Psychology at Harvard in succession to Münsterberg.[62]

A number of us are fighting hard to secure the new Professorship of German here for Otto Schlapp[63] who has been the Lec-

---

[61] William McDougall (1871–1938), British psychologist, educated at Owens College, Manchester, St. John's College, Cambridge, and St. Thomas Hospital; taught at Oxford, 1903–1920, Harvard, 1920–1927, and Duke Universities, 1927–1938; elected Fellow of the Royal Society in 1912.

[62] Hugo Münsterberg (1836–1916), German psychologist, educated at Leipzig and Heidelberg; taught at University of Freiburg, 1887–1891, and at Harvard, 1892–1916; editor of Harvard Psychological Studies from 1903 until his death.

[63] Otto Schlapp (1859–1939), born in Germany and educated in modern languages and philosophy at the Universities of Jena, Edinburgh, Berlin, Leipzig, and Strasburg; Lecturer in German at the University of Edinburgh, 1894–1920, Reader, 1920–1926, Professor, 1926–1929.

turer for the past 25 years. There is a great deal of ungenerous & narrowminded opposition on account of his German birth. He is a splendid teacher & a very fine man, & highly popular with his students. A majority of the Senate too have signed our memorial in his support. So I think we shall succeed & save the fair name of the University.

My wife & daughter are both well. The latter I took to the Zoo the other afternoon. She can now knit while I read her stories. Please convey my very kind greetings to the Baroness & to your daughter.

Yours very gratefully & affectionately,
NORMAN KEMP SMITH

13 Vicarage Gate, London, W., 9th Febr. 1920
My dear Friend,

I write thus promptly again, still not to answer you properly —now also this second fine long letter—but because I have just had Dr Crespi with me, and because he has begged me to write and tell you that he begs you kindly to let him know direct (Dr Angelo Crespi, 13 Callow Street, Chelsea, London, S.W. 3) as to when he had better appear in Edinburgh to see the Electors etc. He could leave London any time from next Sunday, 15th Febr. onwards, but he is afraid to appear perhaps too early on the scene —to seem too pushing etc. So he will not move, till you fix him, by post-card or wire, the best date for appearing. He will, whenever he reaches Edinburgh, first call upon you for hints as to his plan of campaign. So far he believes himself the best equipped of the Italian candidates.

Yrs affectionately
F. v. HÜGEL.

14 Lennox Street

Feb. 12. 1920   Edinburgh.

Dear Baron von Hügel,

I have written Dr Angelo Crespi. The election cannot be before the meeting of the University Court on March 15th, so he had best defer his coming until near that date. I am making all possible enquiries, & shall keep him informed of anything serviceable that I hear.

The enclosed is *not* the photo that I hoped would come with my papers from Princeton. However I send you this in lieu of a better, as I don't know when I shall again be having my photo taken. This one is about eleven or twelve years back.

I have undertaken to give a public lecture to the Edinburgh branch of the Workers Educational Association in the beginning of May, & am choosing as my subject: "Traditional Views of Human Nature." Any suggestions that occur to you will be very welcome. I wish to dwell on the deficiencies of the Enlightenment views, & have a gorgeous passage (p. 91) from your friend Spiller's 'Education(!) of the Child'.[64]

With kindest greetings.

Yours ever affectionately

NORMAN KEMP SMITH

[64] Kemp Smith is probably referring to a publication entitled *The Training of the Child* which Spiller himself refers to as a "popular manual." See Gustav Spiller, *The Origin and Nature of Man: An Enquiry into Fundamentals, Reconciling Man's Proud Achievements with Man's Humble Descent* (London: Williams and Norgate, 1935), p. 286*n*2. On the matter of "the deficiencies of the Enlightenment views," one of Kemp Smith's former students and literary executors has commented to the editor: "The significant change however was that instead of doing what he mentioned to the Baron as a project—writing a book on the shallowness of the Enlightenment—he instead published in the '30s two books which are still very much alive—his *Philosophy of David Hume* and his remarkable edition of Hume's *Dialogues* of which the message in both cases was that the Enlighten-ment—at least in so far as Hume embodied it—was far more complex and profound in its attitude to religion and metaphysics than the Baron had thought. I seem to remember that the publication of the fragment of the Baron's intended Gifford Lectures had proved a disappointment to Kemp Smith. Indeed one might say that the point of Kemp Smith's *Philosophy of David Hume* was explicitly to refute the short way of dismissing Hume as atomistic which characterises the Baron's treatment of Hume. This latter atomistic interpretation of Hume by the way —what Kemp Smith called the Reid–Green interpretation—was embodied in the Baron's sources especially Pringle–Pattison, Kemp Smith's predecessor against whom Kemp Smith reacted very strongly." George Davie to Lawrence Barmann, 23 November 1978.

P.S. Do you know Lord Charnwood's 'Abraham Lincoln'[65]—an excellent book. I have just finished it.

16th–19th Febr. 1920
13, Vicarage Gate,
Kensington,
W. 8.

My dear Kind Friend,

At last I will really try and answer, and thank you for, all your three letters and notes and your most welcome gift. My mornings carry away with them my best strength, and then in the afternoons I become flat and weary—eschewing all longer writing of letters etc. I will take your communications in reversed order; and will end with certain happenings and occupations of my own.—

Your last note, then, of Febr. 12, accompanied your photograph. I am very glad to have this picture of you, still so unmistakeably like. It shall look at me every morning before I start work. True, I would probably have liked the more recent one even better. If it, this later one, does still turn up, I might perhaps have that one too? My other close friends are all represented by at least 2 photoes in my gallery!—

As to Dr Crespi, I am most grateful for your valuable zeal—your long letter to himself and your hints in his interest to myself. I very sincerely think you would find him a very instructive companion on your walks, if he ends up by getting this post. And he could greatly help in getting your work known in Italy and in keeping you well posted in Italian (and also French) philosophical doings. As to the coming Lecture on 'Traditional Views of Human Nature' I am glad that Gustav Spiller's portentous little book is being of help. How useful, in somewhat unobtrusive ways such men are! To my knowledge he has considerably modified,

---

[65] Godfrey Rathbone Benson, first Baron Charnwood (1864–1945), liberal politician and writer, educated at Winchester and Balliol College, Oxford; Member of Parliament, 1892–1895; active in various charitable, civic, and religious works; published in 1916 his biography of Abraham Lincoln.

if not the fundamental outlook—the deep scepticism of so fine a mind as that of Sir Frederick Pollock,[66] yet his temper, the oriculation of his irritation. I *think* this was formerly a good deal occupied with us religious believers of different dyes; but now, thanks very largely to G. S., it is concentrated upon this kind of negative fanatic. I was actually pressed by Sir F. P. to join a Committee which was suffering under incubus of that ex (very much ex) Jew, and I was told that my Popery, even were it more aggressive than it is, would be a welcome relief to that childish denial. —As to hints for the Lecture, I have thought of two, and Crespi suggests a third. (1) I would rub in well the almost unescapable illusion which accompanies all insistence upon *Origins* —that these first stages of any creature or complex reveal, of themselves, this creature's or complex's nature and value. Pringle Pattison has, of course, for years been admirable on this point, so that it would come most gracefully from you in Edinburgh. But I wish you would also study and utilize Eduard Zeller's 'Ueber Ursprung und Wesen der Religion' (1877), in his 'Vorträge u. Abhandlungen,' vol. II, 1877, pp. 1–92. Admirable! esp. pp. 20– 22; 32, 33; 34, 35; 36; 40; 45; 48; 49, 50; 51, 52; above all 57–59; 89; 91, 92. —If you have not got the volume in Edinburgh, I would gladly lend it. —(2) I would insist upon the childishness of directly applying mathematico-mechanical tests and valuations to all human knowledge and worth. Do, pray, quote from Condorcet's 'Esquisse d'un tableau des progrès de l'esprit humain'—the 2nd Ed. is of 'an III'—1795. Mr. Marvin,[67] in his 'Living Past' (quite recent, Oxford Univ. Press) speaks with a

[66] Sir Frederick Pollock, third Baronet (1845–1937), British jurist with deep interest in philosophy, educated at Eton, Trinity College, Cambridge, and Lincoln's Inn; Corpus Professor of Jurisprudence at Oxford, 1883–1903; editor of *Law Quarterly Review*, 1885–1919, and editor-in-chief of the *Law Reports*, 1895–1935; became a Fellow of the British Academy in 1902, and a member of the Privy Council in 1911. Once von Hügel served with Pollock on the Executive Council of an International Moral Education Congress, and, on one occasion while riding a bus to a meeting at Pollock's chambers in Lincoln's Inn, read an article by Sir Frederick in *The Hibbert Journal* entitled "On the Relation of Mystical Experience to Philosophy." On reflection, von Hügel noted that he "thought it very thin, but less negative than I expected from him." *Diaries*, 16 October 1913.

[67] Francis Sydney Marvin (1863– 1943), British educator; staff inspector for the Board of Education, 1890–1924; in 1913 he published *The Living Past*, to be followed in later years by many books and articles on education, history, and philosophy.

good Positivist's awe of this amazing puerility perpetrated by no doubt a great mathematician and courageous character. I have studied the booklet with deepest profit—in the opposite direction!— (3) Dr Crespi would insist upon the perennial distinction between 'mankind' = the average, the majority etc. and humanity = the full, deep human beings, the trainers of the race. Government always to try to infiltrate as much as possible of 'humanity' into 'mankind'. Good, this!

As to your letter of Febr. 4. When I was in Edinburgh in June 1914 I had the advantage of meeting the Moderator of the Church of Scotland, Prof. W. P. Paterson at Dr Alexander Whyte's;[68] and I learnt promptly how fine a mind and deep character his are. I am so sorry he lost two sons in the War. I love to think of you as playing golf with him; even tho' I must admit that I hope still more, some day, from my N. K. S.!

What a strangely self-repeating pundit Ld Haldane is! I wonder whether Prof. Baillie was present at that meeting, and whether it would be tactful, if I wrote to him, in the old friendly way, asking him this or that philosophical etc. question—ignoring, of course, his non-success at last summer's election? I do so hate to drop, or otherwise to lose, old friends. And yet sometimes one makes bad worse by assuming that all is well!

I am so glad you have got the University authorities to shorten —to change—the title of your degree class; and still more that class is so inspiringly good. 'Ihr seid meine Flügel', the great Latinist Karl Lachmann used to say to his class at Bonn; may your own class continue to be your spirit's wings in Edinburgh!

I am slowly, with many rereadings, browsing thro' Bowman's Sonnets. I have now done about one third. I delight in them— with their really perfect form, their delicate, yet quite unaffected refinement, their wonderful power of expressing complex moods, their exquisite sense of the beauties of nature—Scotland especially, their generous estimate of the enemy—a desideratum not too often supplied—, his unforced utilisation of the philosophers,

<hr>

[68] Alexander Whyte (1836–1921), Scottish theologian, educated at King's College, Aberdeen, and New College, Edinburgh; minister of St. George's Free Church in Edinburgh, 1870–1916, and Moderator of the Church General Assembly, 1898.

his patriotism, so deep and so unchauvinist, and, above all, his Christian faith, impressive in its very reticence. I will report again when I have done it all. I am always a slow reader of poetry. As to H. J. Holtzmann's 'Neutestamentliche Theologie' I am deeply delighted you have got it and begun it. I am not a bit surprised that you have found but little profit in the first 100 pp. These pages really wake up to something only when you come to refer back to them in the great divisions later on. Of these divisions— Kapitel—The Second—'die Verkündigung Jesu' pp. 159–420, has taught me no end of things; the Third, pp. 420–580 is, to my mind, much poorer, far less certain; the Zweite Hälfte—vol. II— contains in its Erstes Kapitel—'der Paulinismus' the culmination of the whole work—again what have I not learnt here; the 2nd chapter, pp. 262–390 is, again, I think, much less good—it shows a good bit the Lutheran limitations; but the 3rd Chapter 'die Johanneische Theologie' pp. 398–584 is again a grand piece of work! Mind, mind, Friend, you stick to this book! You would be greatly helped in reading it by following the Synoptic differences, not in an ordinary, even if Greek, N. T. but in Hack's 'Synopse der ersten drei Evangelien', Tübingen, Mohr—put together especially for Holtzmann's works.

As to James's 'Varieties of Religious Experience', *that* is a book I have studied very carefully. I find the Lectures XIV & XV heavily scored and underlined: they are, indeed, admirable. But I also found Lecture I (Religion and Neurology) most satisfactory, it is so *vécu*, so deeply alive, sane and circumspect. And I have also learnt much from Lectures VI & VII (The Sick Soul), Lecture VIII (The Divided Soul) and Lecture X (Conversion— concluded), which St Teresa would greatly have applauded. Lecture XX (Conclusion) contains some good things; but Prof. James Ward and I, in our talks, have often agreed as to how sadly the book thins off towards the end—the importation of Spiritualism is a grievous aberration. But, indeed, there is, I am fully convinced, a grave methodological error running thro', and affecting unfavourably the choice of examples and still more the real presentation of the examples chosen. It lies in the systematic (p. 29) abstraction from institutional religion. I would indeed, very deliberately, also include cases where no institutional and historical constituents were findable, and I would sincerely describe these cases as I found them. But (and these are in J.'s collection really by far the more numerous among the cases which are characteristically religious—indeed in any careful collection they would prevail in numbers and significance) the cases possessed of institutional and historical elements, elements which can penetrate and colour what J. calls the 'personal' element thro' and thro', should, as conscientiously be *described in* ALL *their elements.* It is only J.'s Protestant, or, rather, sectarian, and American individualist prejudices which prevent his seeing how violent a 'simplifier' he is. And again it is precisely this 'simplification' which allows him, so unconsciously, to fall from cases of genuine religion to cases, really, simply of intoxication and of spasms. Holtzmann in his 'Verkündigung' chapter grandly shows how little of an 'individualist', in this hare-brained sense, our Lord really was.[69]

I am interested in Wm McDougall of Oxford succeeding Münsterberg at Harvard. Let us hope he will never again be as violently rude as he was to your friend here, the author of that big-great-book on the Emotions which you described to us at the LSSR. By the bye, unless you tell me it would not do, I should like to write to this author as to the new edition, or as to how I can get a 2nd hand copy of the 1st edition. Pray repeat his full name *and address,* and the full title (Publisher etc.) of the book.—

As to Herr Otto Schlapp, I well remember him, at Dr Alexander Whyte's house, in Edinburgh, in June 1914. I was much impressed—greatly taken—by the frank, vigourous, genial man. Do tell him please, with my kind regards, how much I want the University to honour itself by honouring him. Indeed the honour is a debt and a duty!

---

[69] These comments on William James's *Varieties of Religious Experience* should be compared with von Hügel's comments to James himself in 1909 and now published by James Luther Adams in "Letter from Friedrich von Hügel to William James," *The Downside Review,* 98, No. 332 (July 1980), 214–36.

Letter of December 7.

As to your Inaugural Lecture, I have things to say when I come to my own doings; but the questions you ask in connection therewith I will answer at once. Yes, D'Arcy's appended initials S.J. stand for Societatis Jesu. Indeed (except in France and in Germany, where *in ordinary intercourse* the designation is different), S.J. is the universal designation of a Jesuit. D'Arcy belongs to the English Province, tho' (as a good many here) an Irishman. He did remarkably well in philosophy in Oxford, and gained the Locke Essay prize there; is now competing for the T. H. Green prize. When I presented your 'Commentary' to their Oxford House of Studies—Campion Hall—he, D'Arcy at once carried it up to his room and absorbed himself in it. I shall be very grateful if you will be kind to this really fine man, if and when he consults you. (By the bye there exists a simply A 1 book about the English Jesuits under Elizabeth: 'Edmund Campion' by Richard Simpson (a worker with Acton). London, Burns and Oates. 12/6 net, alas! Every man who wishes to be just both to Elizabeth's government and to the S.J.'s, should know that book by heart. And what a grand character my darling hero, Campion is!).

Vaihinger's 'Als Ob', has not yet had its turn. The 2nd writing of my Introduction is now done; and, before I rewrite the whole in its final form, I will have to give some weeks to reading and re-reading epistemological and general psychology things: all this for section I of the body of the book.

As to W. M. Salter's 'Nietzsche, the Thinker' I *of course* at once ordered it. It was well known at Milford's, who is agent here for Henry Holt but—not in stock in England, must be got from America! Am waiting for my copy still. Could not your friend put pressure upon these tradesmen (practically all publishers are merely *that*, now-a-days) to keep a good supply of copies on sale over here? I would gladly press my friends to buy; but, as matters stand, I have to warn them that they would have to wait!

Only one of your points remains now; I take it at this point, since it leads on so naturally to my own communications—your feeling of despair and of clumsiness on starting any of your writing! Oh, indeed, I understand! You cannot have more of this feeling, you are certainly not really more clumsy, or as clumsy, as I am myself. I have never had a review, of any length, about anything I have written, but I have had to try and learn from complaints as to my clumsiness of form. I suppose this awkwardness comes, in my case, partly from my owning too many languages to be quite easy in any one, and partly from the German half of my blood. Some Germans indeed write brilliantly, but how few they are! Certainly neither Holtzmann nor Troeltsch belong to these; and indeed even Eucken,[70] who can write with much distinction, has often told me how clearly he always, when composing, feels a certain uncouthness impeding him at every turn. —I take it that this our common cross (tho' I verily believe mine to be much the bigger) can help us greatly: the danger of conceipt, so near to such brilliant creatures as Schopenhauer and Nietzsche is greatly diminished amongst the plodders; and then again the necessity for such repeated writing saves us from precipitate, immature work as certainly was e.g. some of William James's.

Well now, at last, to my own news and questions.

Some 3 weeks ago I wrote my first letters since the War—to Troeltsch in Berlin, to Prenner[71] (University Librarian) in Vienna. I received a letter of 8 closely written, very large pages from Troeltsch a week ago. It is just what I expected of him—manly, brave, humble, giving glimpses of a life of amazing activity, and the whole—hurrah, hurrah, steeped in the sense, the love and the service of God. I had sent him (as to Prenner) your Inaugural, and had told him about you, and my giving you his 2 fat vols. (Binder has not yet returned the volume which the book sellers have furnished). Let me copy out for you the following characteristic and sadly informative bits. 'Ich habe nie

[70] Rudolf Christoph Eucken (1846–1926), German philosopher; Professor of Philosophy at the University of Jena, 1874–1920; received Nobel Prize for Literature, 1908; his writings considerably influenced von Hügel in the 1890s. In 1914, after the outbreak of World War I, he signed the Manifesto of many German intellectuals in support of Germany's militarist stance—a document which outraged British intellectuals.

[71] Joseph Prenner seems to have been a Roman Catholic priest. He had been a correspondent with von Hügel since the beginning of the century.

gezweifelt, dass der Krieg unsere Beziehungen nicht zerrissen hat. Immerhin bleibt es das Vorrecht der Angehörigen der siegreichen Völker seinerseits die Initiative zu ergreifen. Für den anderen giebt es ja Gründe des Zögerns und der Zurückhaltung mehr als genug.'[72] —As to his own attitude to the war: 'Seit ich Klarheit über die Sachlage gewann, habe ich in Deutschland stets zur Besinnung und zur so notwendigen Friedenswilligkeit gemahnt. Ich habe darüber manche alte Freundschaft verloren. Mit Eucken habe ich keinen Verkehr mehr. Gierke ist feindselig gegen mich. Ich habe bei den Arbeitsgenossen sogar recht schweren Stand. Allein derartiges muss man tragen können, wenn man seiner selber sicher ist. Es sind eben tragische und schreckliche Zeiten, wo man seinem Pflichtegefühl und seiner Einsicht folgen, und die Leute machen lassen muss, was sie wollen.'[73]

As to the present German situation: 'Dass ich die moderne geistige Entwickelung, überall und auch bei uns, mit grosser Sorge verfolgte und offen besprach, dass wissen Sie ja, und das war auch schon vor dem Kriege so. Jetzt hat die Revolution grauenvolle Zustände geschaffen. Die Menschen sind wahnsinnig und zerstören den Rest. In Wahrheit herrscht Hungersnot jetzt erst recht und wird die Lage bald eine ganz Verzweifelte werden. Man lebt in altem erspartem Gut in Kleidern, Schuhen etc. Die Zukunft ist unausdenkbar. Vielleicht kommen Zeiten wo man alles verkaufen muss, was man von etwas besseren Sachen hat! Nun das Elend muss ertragen werden, und die Seele muss siegen können. Aber für die Seele bestehen erst recht die furchbarsten Gefahren, allgemeinster reiner Egoismus, giftige Verzankung aller gegen alle, Versuche alle Bildung auf das niederste Niveau

[72] These translations of passages from Troeltsch's letter have been made by Dr. David Schultenover, s.j., of Creighton University: "I have never doubted that the war had not destroyed our relationship. Still, it is the prerogative of those who belong to the conquering nations to take the initiative. For the others there is certainly more than enough reason for hesitation and reluctance."

[73] "Ever since the state of affairs has become clear in my mind, I have not ceased to exhort my countrymen to come to their senses and to that indispensable determination to seek peace. But I have lost many old friendships over this. Eucken and I have ceased to communicate. Gierke is viciously opposed to me. Even with my colleagues relations are very strained. The man who is sure of himself must be able to bear his burden alone. Indeed these are tragic and terrible times when one must be true to one's sense of duty and one's insight, and let the people do what they want."

herabzuschrauben, unerschwingliche Preise der Bücher und Unbezahlbarkeit der ausländischen Litteratur. Für den geistigen Menschen kommen schwere Tage. Vorerst verteidigen wir uns mit allen Mitteln gegen die Proletarisierung, leider sind darüber Studenten und Kollegen erst recht nationalistisch und reaktionär, wodurch die Verteidigung nicht erleichtert ist.'[74]

Then, news of his wife, a Junker's daughter! Takes up the new conditions with pluck. Their only child, the little son of 7, has, of course, had the best they could save off themselves; he is well, and clings to his parents with immense tenderness.

As to his own labours.

'Wem Staat und Vaterland nicht das höchste Gut ist, und wer von den törichten und selbstzerstörerischen Menschen nicht das letzte Heil erwartet, der bleibt ja schliesslich aufrecht und ungebrochen in Wahn und Elend, das ihn umgiebt und bedroht. Die Zeit [hat] mich in Kampf und Arbeit hineingezogen. Ich bin Abgeordneter des Parlaments, Unterstaatssekretär im Kultusministerium, muss unendlich viel reden, schreiben, lesen. Kurz ich kämpfe für Vernunft, Besonnenheit, Ordnung, Arbeit und unvermeidliche Zugeständnisse an die Massen so tapfer und eifrig als ich kann. Stunden völliger Verzweiflung sind mir nicht erspart, aber innerlich bin ich ruhig und, bis zu einem gewissen Grade, heiter geblieben. Meine wissenschaftliche Arbeit (he is Prof. of Comparative Religion, in succession to Pfleiderer and Lehmann) schreitet fort, augenblicklich auf Geschichtsphiloso-

---

[74] "You know well that I have followed with great concern the modern intellectual and spiritual development, not only among us but everywhere else as well, and have openly addressed myself to it. That was true even before the war. Now the revolution has created horrible conditions. Men are mad and set about to destroy what remains. Famine is already a widespread reality among us, and the situation will soon be desperate. People are now living off their old, stored-away possessions, such as clothing, shoes, etc. One cannot even imagine the future. The time is perhaps not far off when all the finer possessions will have to be sold! Well, the misery must be borne, and the soul must overcome. But the most dreadful dangers lie in wait for the soul—the most pervasive and purest egoism, the poisonous struggle of one man against another, the effort to force all education down to the lowest possible standard, exorbitant prices for books and absolute unavailability of foreign literature. Trying times are in store for spiritual men. First and foremost we have to defend ourselves against proletarianization, but, sad to say, on this matter students and faculty among the most nationalistic and reactionary, which does not make the defense any easier."

phie bezogen. Sie giebt mir den Halt und den Stoff für alle Arbeit.'[75]

As to his move from Heidelberg to Berlin:—

'Die Übersiedelung nach Berlin hat mich von meinem lieben Heidelberg getrennt und in die mir verhasste Grossstadt geworfen. Auch bin ich stets innerlich äusserst unpreussisch. Aber sie hat mich auch in eine grosse Wirksamkeit hineingestellt, die den Tätigkeitsdrang und das Kraftgefühl befriedigt, mir unendlich viel Kenntnisse zuführt und hoffentlich dem Ganzen ein bisschen nützt. Kurz, man kann immer noch tief dankbar sein, für das was man hat, und muss nun eben in bösen Tagen einen Glauben bewähren, den man in guten sich nicht hat rauben lassen. Gott wird weiter helfen, jedenfalls die Seele nicht aus seiner Hand fallen lassen.'[76]

About his family losses since 1914.

'Wir alle beklagen liebe Todte. Meine Mutter erlitt, beim Ausbruch des Krieges, vor Schrecken einen Schlaganfall und starb bald darauf. Mein Vater wurde dadurch gebrochen und abgestumpft und lebte noch zwei Jahre ohne den Krieg zu begreifen. Meine Schwester verlor ihren einzigen Sohn nach zwei Wochen Kriegsdienst. Mein Schwager brach darüber zusammen und starb ein Jahr darauf! So geht es in diesen Zeiten. Jeder ist glücklich

---

[75] "The one for whom State and Fatherland are not the highest good and who does not expect from foolish and self-destructive men final salvation remains in the end upright and unbroken by the delusion and misery which surround and threaten him. The times have dragged me into war and its labors. I am a member of Parliament and Under Secretary of State in the Ministry of Education, and I have to speak, write, and read endlessly. To put it briefly: I fight as courageously and zealously as I can for reason, prudence, order, employment, and inevitable compromises with the masses. I am not spared hours of total bewilderment, but interiorly I am at peace and, to a certain extent, cheerful. My scholarly work progresses [he is Professor of Comparative Religion, in succession to Pfleiderer and Lehmann]. At the moment I am occupied with the philosophy of history, which provides me with the direction and material for all my work."

[76] "The move to Berlin has separated me from my beloved Heidelberg and cast me into this despicable metropolis. Besides, interiorly I have always been extremely un-Prussian. However, it has also thrust me into a very real situation which not only satisfies my need to keep busy and feeds my sense of productivity, but also provides endless possibilities for learning, and, I hope, contributes a little to the total effort. In short, one can still be deeply grateful for what one does have, and just now in evil times one must give evidence of a faith which in good times one does not allow to be taken away. God will help along the way—at least He will not let the soul fall from His grasp."

zu preisen, den der Tod erlöst hat vom Wahnsinn dieser Welt, und wer zurückbleibt muss die Menschenliebe schon etwas stark anspannen, um es unter den Menschen aushalten zu können. Zum Glück ist die Menschenliebe eigentlich keine Menschenliebe, sondern ein Gottesliebe, die das Göttliche im Menschen, und nicht die arme, wirrköpfige Kreatur an sich, liebt.'[77]

As to his special philosophical labour just now, and his mental orientation: 'Die Religionsphilosophie hat mich, als auf den schwierigsten Punkt, zur Geschichtsphilosophie geführt. Daran bohre ich jetzt mit allen Kräften. Eine Probe davon erlaube ich mir Ihnen, als Dank für die Schrift von Herrn Kemp Smith, zu schicken. Es soll schliesslich ein neuer Band werden. Das Mittelalter wird dabei als ein Hauptproblem in den Vordergrund treten. Ich bin, im Laufe der Zeit, etwas antiklassisch und etwas mittelalterlich geworden, nicht zum Wenigsten durch eifrige Dante Lektüre, der für mich nach der Bibel kommt und mit Goethe und Shakespeare mein Heiliger ist. Ein bischen weltlich sind meine Heiligen ja immer. Aber ich suche das Heilige in ihnen, nicht das Alleinmenschliche.'[78]

About your Inaugural:

'Für den Antritts-Vortrag von Herrn Norman Kemp Smith danke ich Ihnen herzlich. Die Dinge sehen sich doch überall ein bischen anders an. Die Art, wie hier der Schotte die geistige Welt sieht, ist mir sehr interessant. Es ist doch immer wesentlich die

---

[77] "We are all grieving for our beloved dead. At the outbreak of the war my mother suffered a stroke induced by terror and died soon after. My father was broken and numbed by the loss. He lived just two years longer and died without ever comprehending the war. My sister lost her only son after two weeks of war service. My brother-in-law was shattered by this and died one year later! So it goes in these times. They are considered fortunate whom death has released from the madness of this world, and those who are left behind must earnestly stretch their love for fellow-man to be able to bear further existence among men. Fortunately love of fellow-man is in reality not love of fellow-man but a love of God which loves the divine within man and not the poor muddle-headed creature itself."

[78] "Philosophy of religion has led me, as if to the most difficult point, to philosophy of history. I am boring into this now with all my strength. Allow me to send you a test-sample in thanks for the paper of Mr. Kemp Smith. I intend it eventually to be a new book, in which I will emphasize the Middle Ages as a principal problem. Over the years I have become somewhat anti-classical and somewhat medieval, not least of all through my enthusiastic reading of Dante, whom I rank next to the Bible, and regard, along with Shakespeare and Goethe, as my patron saint. Of course my saints are always a bit worldly. But I seek the holy within them, not the human alone."

Frage der Naturwissenschaften und ihrer Interpretation, verbunden mit dem Blick auf das evolutionistische Bild der Dinge. Es bleibt alles in dieser allgemeinsten Fragestellung, und die Entscheidung ist dann mehr eine grundsätzliche Beruhigung über die Möglichkeit oder Gefordertheit einer idealistischen Deutung. Das Einzelne wird dann der Praxis oder den Spezialwissenschaften überlassen. Interessant war mir das vom Naturalismus entworfene Bild. Leider giebt er keine Namen an. Er ist in dieser Weise mir unbekannt, übrigens ein sehr inkonsequenter Naturalismus, der offenbar die Spencerische Lehre voraussetzt und sie nur in Bezug auf die Wert- und Kulturwelt etwas lebendiger macht. Mir meinerseits liegt im Moment alles an gewissen Problemen der historischen Entwickelung, und ich mustere die grossen Systematiker durch in Bezug auf das, was sie dafür geleistet haben. Das führt mich nun übrigens auch, meinerseits, zu sehr vielen Berührungen mit Bergson.'[79]

At the end, about his own position in German generally:

'Hier in Deutschland stehe ich wesentlich in Kämpferstellung, einerseits gegen das Specialistentum und seine Selbstzufriedenheit, andererseits gegen den Radikalismus und Dilettantismus, die sich erschreckend breit machen.'[80]

What a big, true, humble, Xtian soul!

Now only 3 little questions & proposals. (1) Can & will you send your 'Commentary', with a warm inscription, to Professor Dr Ernst Troeltsch, Reichs Kanzlerplatz 4[1] Charlottenburg, Ber-

[79] "Cordial thanks for the inaugural lecture of Mr. Norman Kemp Smith. Everywhere things are seen from different perspectives. It is very interesting to me the way the Scotsman here views spiritual matters. Indeed it is always essentially a question of the natural sciences and their interpretation, together with a consideration of the evolutionary picture of things. Everything is encompassed in this most universal statement of the question, and the decisive position is then rather a basic easing of mind over the possibility or the necessity of an idealistic interpretation. Particulars will then be worked out by practice or by specialists. The picture he drew of naturalism was also interesting. Unfortunately he did not mention any names. As it stands I do not recognize it, except as a very inconsistent naturalism, which plainly presupposes Spencer's doctrine and makes it a little more vital, but only in relation to the world of values and culture. However, at the moment my work is preoccupied with certain problems of historical development, and I am inspecting all the great systematicians to see how far they got with their efforts. This, by the way, has now brought me too into a great deal of contact with Bergson."

[80] "My position here in Germany is essentially contentious: on the one hand, against the specialists and their smugness; on the other, against the radicals and dilettantes, whose influence is alarmingly widespread."

lin? (2) Can you get Dr Pringle Pattison to do the same with his "Idea of God'?— (3) Can you tell me anything about J. M'Kellar Stewart,[81] Melborne, who, in 1913, published that, surely *splendid*, 'Critical Exposition of Bergson's Philosophy'. Not a soul has ever whispered a word of praise to me of the book; yet, surely, surely, it is truly great!

Your aff. old Friend
F. V. Hügel.

14 Lennox Str.

March 1. 1920   Edinburgh

My dear Baron von Hügel,

I shall not now attempt to reply properly to your most welcome, heartening and interesting letter. That I must defer until after lectures stop a couple of weeks hence. Until then I shall be kept very busy writing lectures and drawing the work of this second term to an end. Then I shall have between four & five weeks free, for quieter study & reflection.

I shall indeed be delighted to send a copy of my Commentary to Troeltsch & shall write an accompanying letter, this coming week-end, expressing my indebtedness to his 'Soziallehren' etc. Copies I must also send to Vaihinger & Adickes:[82] have been delaying unduly in doing so. To Pringle-Pattison I shall convey your message the first opportunity.

Tonight I am again writing Dr Crespi. The Secretary of the University tells me that there have been an astonishing number

---

[81] John McKellar Stewart (1878–1953), Australian philosopher, educated at the Universities of Melbourne, Edinburgh, and Marburg; appointed Hughes Professor of Philosophy in the University of Adelaide, 1923–1949, and was Vice-Chancellor, 1944–1948. *A Critical Exposition of Bergson's Philosophy* was his major work.

[82] Erich Adickes (1866–1928), German philosopher; Kantian scholar best known for his study of the "thing-in-itself," published in 1924 as *Kant und das Ding an Sich*.

of applicants for the Italian Lecturership, but that so far, to judge from the testimonials etc. submitted, Dr Crespi is the strongest candidate. There will likely be a short list made, so I am advising Dr Crespi to delay his journey north until it is made & an invitation reaches him. In that case the expenses of his journey will be paid. Quite possibly the election will not take place this month, owing to pressure of other business upon the University Court. The Secretary promises to keep me informed of the situation, & I shall see that Dr Crespi does not miss any opportunity of making good his claims.

All that you tell me of Troeltsch is absorbingly interesting. He meets the tragic situation in a manner that gives one new trust in the future—sadly needed these dark days.

In scanty half-hours I am dipping into Holtzmann's 'die Verkündigung Jesu'. Your suggestions—including Dr Crespi's fine suggestion, which I endorse cordially—towards my lecture, I am very grateful for. The Zeller I shall obtain in the Library here.

From Mr Salter another letter has just reached me, & I took the opportunity writing him your message. He sends me a copy of the 'Monist' with an article of his own in keeping with that organ's tendencies. He is floundering wildly, I fear, in a naturalistic bog. That is one of the bonds that give him sympathy—fellow-feeling —with Nietzsche.

I wish I understood better the subject—or table of contents— of your new book. You never, I think, told me exactly, or even in general, what you plan. But I must not attempt a reply to your letter. That I reserve. Meantime, my dear Baron, my most grateful thanks for your great encouragement & help. They mean a very great deal to me. I shall hope to be as little unworthy of them as may be, so far as that depends on honest endeavour to do the best that it is in me to do.

Yours ever affectionately,
NORMAN KEMP SMITH

14 Lennox Street,
March 8. 1920   Edinburgh.
My dear Baron von Hügel,

I notice that I have omitted two of your direct questions. Your suggestion as to writing Baillie is a very kindly one. I am sure that a letter from you will be a real satisfaction & help to him these days. Owing to the fact that he was an Edinburgh graduate & Pringle-Pattison's chief pupil, the passing of him over in the Election must have been painful and embarrassing to him. There is a rumour that he may soon, or in a few years, resign his Chair at Aberdeen. Whether there is any truth in the rumour I do not know. Certainly his wife, & probably he himself, would much prefer to live in London. Last year the house that they had on lease was sold: at present they are in a furnished house in Banchory up Deeside.

Alexander F. Shand's[83] address is 1 Edwardes Place, Kensington W. 8. I met him for the first time during my visit to you last summer. His personality is much less impressive than I had expected, & I fear my expectations as to his future work were somewhat diminished by this personal contact. However first impressions are not overreliable. His 'Foundations of Character' have taught me much. The 'laws' which he endeavours to formulate are, I should say, the weak part of it. But it has the immense merit, these days, of representing year-long labours, & genuinely independent thought, not the hurried & unassimilated rehash of other peoples' reflections.

I am making slow, but steady, progress through Holtzmann's 'Verkündigung Jesu', with immense profit. As I am finding, I can always rely with confidence on your recommendations of books as not only justified by their intrinsic merits but as certain to prove helpful in my own personal difficulties & needs—an immense boon for which I cannot sufficiently thank you. A friend here, a retired minister, has lent me 'Vision & Authority' by John Oman (Hodder & Stoughton). It contains much *admirable* matter, but

[83] Alexander Faulkner Shand (1858– 1936), British barrister-at-law, educated at Eton and Cambridge University; published *The Foundations of Character* in 1914.

strangely combined with a stupidly eloquent style—at the same
time frequently surprisingly good e.g. p. 36. on Christ's regarding
the child as the exemplar, not because of its supposed plasticity
but because of its *eagerness* and *earnestness*, qualities that I am
much impressed by in my gay little daughter.

Yours ever affectionately,

NORMAN KEMP SMITH

I wrote Troeltsch last night, & today am posting him a copy of
my Kant.

March 21. 1920

14 Lennox Street
Edinburgh.

My dear Baron von Hügel,

The volume of Troeltsch—so splendidly bound—has reached
me. I shall treasure it both for its inherent worth & as a gift from
you. The binder's slip is no matter. I had a copy of Kant's Critique bound once in Glasgow, in which Vernunft appeared as
Dernunst. Already I have been dipping into the volume,—reading (for the first time) with immense interest the articles on 'Die
Bedeutung des Begriffes der Kontingenz' & on 'Logos & Myths
in Theologie und Religions-philosophie'. Troeltsch I find extraordinarily congenial, & that in many different ways; & I rejoice
to know that in so doing I shall be travelling on the same road
with you.

I spoke to Pringle-Pattison; & I think he will send his Gifford
Lectures to Troeltsch, though will wait until the second edition,
now due, appears. I am giving him Troeltsch's address.

There has been an extraordinary, & very vulgar-minded, out-
burst against all things German over Schlapp's candidature, with
the most grotesque & weird letters appearing in The Scotsman[84]—
balanced by some very cogent replies. The result, I regret to say,

[84] *The Scotsman* was and is the chief   It is rather to Edinburgh as *The Times*
daily newspaper of the Scottish capital.   is to London.

is that our Principal & others have yielded. It appears certain now that Schlapp will not be appointed. Pringle-Pattison has fought nobly for him, as have many other friends; & the student-body too is strongly in his favour, & what I should describe as the better elements in the Senate. But with a weak Principal & a composite body like the Court, what can be done!

Crespi I enjoyed meeting, though unfortunately I had to be in Glasgow during the week-end. We had much good talk. Both the Principal & Prof. Grierson[85] (important because of his being Prof. of English Literature & therefore closely concerned in the appointment) were, I am glad to find, very favourably impressed. The Principal tells me that he considers Crespi will "very likely" be appointed—as definite a statement as can be expected prior to the actual election. Grierson says Crespi "will be quite an acquisition."

Last week-end I had a very pleasant visit to Glasgow, staying over the Sunday with W. B. Stevens,[86] the Professor of Hebrew, an old friend—we first became acquainted in Berlin. Over Monday night I stayed with Prof. Macneile Dixon.[87] I saw Phillimore[88] & Latta, & quite a number of others. Sir Henry Jones was not in town. Sir Henry is showing splendid courage. He has had two operations for cancer & a third is not possible, though it is again

[85] Sir Herbert John Clifford Grierson (1866–1960), British littérateur, educated at King's College, Aberdeen, and Christ Church, Oxford; held professorship at Aberdeen, 1894–1915; Professor of Rhetoric and English Literature, University of Edinburgh, 1915–1935; Rector of University of Edinburgh, 1936–1939.

[86] Kemp Smith has written Stevens for Stevenson, referring to William Barron Stevenson (1869–1954), Scottish Biblical scholar, educated at Edinburgh University and in Germany; Professor of Hebrew and Semitic Languages, Glasgow University, 1907–1937; on Admiralty staff, Intelligence Department, 1917–1919; President of Society for Old Testament Study, 1926, of Glasgow Bibliographical Society, 1932–1935, and of Glasgow Archaeological Society, 1933–1936.

[87] William Macneile Dixon (1866–

1946), born in India to an English missionary, and educated at Trinity College, Dublin; Professor of English Literature in the University of Birmingham, 1894–1904; Regius Professor of English Language and Literature in the University of Glasgow, 1904; on leave from Glasgow for service to the Department of Information, 1916–1918. Kemp Smith knew him both at Glasgow and in the Department of Information, where both worked during the war.

[88] John Swinnerton Phillimore (1873–1926), British classicist, educated at Westminster and Christ Church, Oxford; Professor of Greek at Glasgow University, 1899–1906, and was appointed Professor of Humanities, 1906–1926. In 1914–1915 he held the Sather Professorship of Classics at the University of California.

active. His great desire is that he may live to prepare & deliver his Gifford Lectures in 1921–3. The chances, I fear, are against him.

Did I tell you that Bosanquet[89] in his new book—"Implication & Linear Inference"—he sent it me ten days ago—has taken a sentence from my 'Commentary' as a motto for the volume. The book is a valuable (tho' as usual very abstract & difficult) extension of his logical position.

Do you know 'Community: A Sociological Study' (pub. by Macmillan) by Maciver,[90] Baillie's former student, now in Toronto. Have started it. It is decidedly good. His distinction betw the state & the community is fresh to me, & illuminating. Baillie, by the way, I hear, has at last received a house in Aberdeen.

On looking again into the three delightful volumes of St Beuve's 'Port Royal' (the first three, the others are very inferior in interest) I have wondered whether you find them congenial. I got a very great deal from them some years before the war, & have again been renewing these first impressions with great enjoyment —also reading Pascal's dialogue with M. Socè. The chapters in St Beuve in comment on Pascal's contrast between his favourites, Montaigne & Epictetus, are the part that I find especially suggestive. This holiday, for my W. E. A. paper, I mean to return to St Augustine's Anti-Pelagian writings. The Zeller I obtained: the article on 'Das Wissen der Religion' I had not previously read. While agreeing with it, I cannot say I have got any fresh suggestions from it; & in any case it is hardly on those lines that my paper will run. I mean to contrast & to comment on the Enlightenment & Original Sin doctrines of human nature.

[89] Bernard Bosanquet (1848–1923), British writer and philosopher, educated at Harrow and Balliol College, Oxford; lectured at University College, Oxford, 1871–1881; lived in London as writer, becoming involved in social work, 1881–1897; retired to the country to write; Professor of Moral Philosophy at St. Andrews University, 1903–1908; Gifford Lecturer at Edinburgh, 1911–1912. He was a Fellow of the British Academy, and onetime President of the Aristotelian Society.

[90] Robert Morrison MacIver (1882–1970), Scottish sociologist and political philosopher, educated at Edinburgh University and Oriel College, Oxford; Lecturer at Aberdeen University, 1907; Professor of Political Science, University of Toronto, 1917; Professor at Barnard College, 1927; President, New School for Social Research, New York City, 1963–1965, Chancellor, 1965–1966. For an account of his life, see his autobiography, *As a Tale That Is Told* (Chicago: The University of Chicago Press, 1968).

But this letter is, for the present, only to acknowledge your delightful gift. I shall treasure it always. I am, my dear Baron von Hügel,

Yours ever gratefully & affectionately,
NORMAN KEMP SMITH.

14 Lennox Street,
Edinburgh.

April 15. 1920

My dear Baron von Hügel,

My thoughts during the past fortnight have been so preoccupied in the writing of my lectures on 'The Traditional Views of Human Nature' that I have been delaying writing to you. The lecture is now more or less finished; but alas, as usual, it is twice too long; & I have the difficult task of cutting it down, without undue compression or omission of essentials. I have enjoyed the writing of it, & got some points clearer that have long been puzzling me. I wanted to finish it this Vacation, tho' it does not have to be given till June 2nd, as I shall be sufficiently busy during the coming Term, which opens on the 20th.

Over last night I have had staying with me John Anderson,[91] a Glasgow graduate who has double 1st class Honours (in Mathematics & Philosophy), & who has won both the Ferguson & Shaw Fellowships—the chief prizes in Scotland in philosophy. I have been fortunate in securing him as my Assistant for next year. He is a genuine, very able & active-minded fellow; & it will be a great satisfaction to have his cooperation & companionship. The chief philosophical influence in his development so far has been Samuel Alexander—as conveyed through his Gifford Lectures in Glasgow, & shortly to be published by Macmillan.

Yesterday I received the enclosed letter from Vaihinger. I shall

[91] John Anderson (1893–1962), Scottish philosopher, educated at Glasgow University; appointed Lecturer in Logic at Edinburgh University, 1920–1927; appointed Challis Professor of Philosophy in the University of Sydney, Australia, 1927–1958; his philosophical papers are collected and published in *Studies in Empirical Philosophy* (Sydney: Angus & Robertson, 1962). See also George E. Davie, "John Anderson in Scotland," *Quadrant*, (July 1977), 55–57.

tell him that at present you have my copy of his book; & shall be grateful if you can give me your opinion of it. I read it *most* hurriedly—& only in part—& as I told you did not then find it helpful. Shall look into the Library copy here: so don't think you must return my copy: I do not wish it at present, & shall not be wanting it this year. I can still, I think, give my name in favour of the translation, if only because of the reception accorded to it in Germany, as shown by the founding of the *Annalen*. Do not return the advertisement thereof & of Vaihinger's book; but I shall reply to Vaihinger when you send back his letter. I have also had a very pleasant note from Adickes. Troeltsch has not yet written.

A few days ago I had a walk with Pringle-Pattison. He is writing some three lectures for delivery at Oxford—on the subject of Providence.

You ask about McKellar Stewart. He is an Australian, & is now teaching in some Australian University. He came to Edinburgh to study for the D. Phil., & his "Bergson" was written in connection therewith. I have not myself read it.

The prospective appointment to the Chair of German has produced a crop of letters in the Scotsman. Those against appointing a German to the Chair have been very violent & often grotesque. Very likely the election will be at Monday's meeting of the Court. I hear that the opposition to Schlapp will probably so far succeed as to prevent his being appointed Professor. The other candidates, however, are weak, so it is probable that *no* appointment will take place, & Schlapp be continued in his present Lectureship. At the worst the authorities will at least have the good grace to allow him a pension. Dr Crespi will also probably be elected to the Italian Lectureship on Monday next. I have heard nothing further meantime regarding that.

I have had to defer my reading in Holtzmann. I shall be interested to follow your appreciations of the various main sections in his *Lehrbuch*. Many thanks too for your criticisms of James's 'Varieties'. I keep them by me for a rereading.

Richard Simpson's 'Edmund Campion' I shall hope to read in the Summer.

The extracts you so kindly send me from Troeltsch's letter I have frequently reread. They are indeed splendid in spirit. I am glad to know that a writer from whom I am learning so much has this bigness of nature. His account of the present situation in Germany is unhappy reading: I trust it may improve sooner that [sic] at present appears possible. There is very evident in this country, & as I also know in America, a steadily growing conviction that the Treaty must be modified in favour of Germany. I rejoice too to hear that Troeltsch is now working on the philosophy of history—a subject that has keenly interested me for some years.

On June 11th & 12th there is to be a Joint-Meeting in Edinburgh of the Scots Philosophical Club & of the English Philosophical Associations (which includes teachers of Philosophy in all the Universities & Colleges in England, excepting Oxford & Cambridge). Lloyd Morgan[92] is to contribute the paper for discussion: it is not likely (I mean the paper), I fear, to amount to much.

W. M. Salter—I forget whether I told you—writes me that his Nietzsche was republished by a London firm—Cecil Palmer & Hayward, Oakley House 14–18 Bloomsbury Str. W. C. He considers it strange that Melford should not know this; & is grateful for your interest in the book.

Your own work, I trust, makes satisfactory progress. The coming Spring & Summer weather should help permanently to establish your better health.

Your last letter has been a great inspiration to me. I cannot thank you sufficiently for it, & am ever, my dear Baron,
Yours gratefully & affectionately,

NORMAN KEMP SMITH.

P.S. Mrs Kemp Smith this moment has just come in to my Study with the *immensely* relieving news that a MSS. paper on Jane Austen—a *most* delightful & original one, written by the friend with whom I was staying at Melrose, & lent me by him—has been

[92] Conwy Lloyd Morgan (1852–1936), Welsh scientist, educated at the Royal College of Science; Professor of Zoology and Geology in University College, Bristol, 1884; Principal of the College, 1887– 1909, and first Vice-Chancellor of the University of Bristol. His publications include *Habit and Instinct* (1896) and *Life, Mind, and Spirit* (1926).

found. It went amissing, & we had searched high & low, & it looked as if it must have been inadvertently burned. The loss has *poisoned* the past two days for us. How queerly unmeaning are these disturbing contingencies!

P.P.S. I enclose a lecture of Bowman's which he has sent me. It *may* interest you to look through it. I have got him interested in Sᵗ Augustine & the Jansenists. The subject is very new to him, & known only in bare outline: but his paper none the less shows the fine quality of his mind. But return without reading, if, as I can understand, you cannot spare time for it.

19th April 1920
13, Vicarage Gate
Kensington, W. 8.

My very dear Friend,

I have now two more, most welcome and richly instructive, letters to thank you for. I am in one of my momentary wornout and resting days, so do not dare, even now to enter upon any except the immediately pressing, but, to my mind, far from easy point—Vaihinger and his request. I have purposely waited these 3 days, since life has taught me with painful vividness, how much any one thing leads to another thing, and how important it is to look well around and ahead before pledging oneself to what may turn out involves not this separate act alone, but this act as a link in a chain—to be willed in advance as such, or to be avoided altogether.

I should have been glad to have read by now at least part of the 'Die Philosophie des Als-Ob', particularly since your copy stands amongst my books. But, you see, I have this book of my own on my hands and in my head; and I read anything new to me, only before the composition of the Section in which that new book will have to be specially considered. My book (this is in simple confidence for yourself alone, to people generally I say 'something on fundamental religious philosophy'—I know my

will to get paralysed if it is generally known what exactly I am about)—my book is to be called (more or less):
'The Reality of God: a Study of its Self-manifestations'. The Introduction has now been written out twice—the last writing stands over till the whole book has been written twice. The body of the book is to be in 3 Sections. Section I, Human apprehension of Reality, generally considered. (God, for this Section deliberately left out.) Section II The Human Apprehension of God. (Here all the other realities taken with God, and God with them). Section III. The Chief Difficulties against the previous analyses. I have about ten: the pure Illusionism of Feuerbach and *of Vaihinger* comes here, and the latter must be most carefully studied (F. I know intimately well). —Conclusion: the positions attained in Section II, now finally restated, with such precisions and provisos, as Section III has rendered necessary. —I am now absorbed in my proximate preparations for Section I: am just finishing Kant's 'Kr. d. r. vern.', —Aesthetik—first unbroken study of what I know so well along considerable sections. The Berlin Academy text has been read in both Edˢ. up to end of Aesthetik. Your Commentary being weighed, word for word— am just finishing it to end of Aesthetic. Will sometime report about points: have gratefully learnt very much there. I intend to do at least the 'Dialektik', in the same way, before taking to starting my writing of my Section I. —You, I trust, will be my proof-reader, especially of this Section.—

Now as to Vaihinger, my points are these:

(1) I had, and have, by me the collection of reviews on the 'Als Ob' book which you send me—or rather the same for up to, and on occasion of the 2nd Ed. (1913); and it was this, very impressive chorus, from so many very different quarters, of recognition of the book as of great importance, that made me, now I had come to planning out the book so long dreamt of, ask you for the loan of the book. I find amongst these 'Urteile' and also amongst the contributors to the 'Annalen' several men I know to be sober and constructive thinkers—Benrubi[93] the Jew, and

[93] Isaak Benrubi (1876–?), German philosopher, educated at the University of Jena; published in 1904 a study of Rousseau's ethical ideas, though his chief work was a later study of contemporary French thought.

Jörgensen,[94] the devout R. C. convert. But I also note that there are declarations as to the juvenile crudity of his work, alongside of resounding praise of its range and penetration. —Certainly, I was myself much put off by the book's sub-title; it reminded me of Pico della Mirandola and Paracelsus, in its promise of all-embracingness.

(2) The book is, very clearly, as extremely *left*, as a sane and sincere mind could possibly manage, and this, not tentatively, but with complete assurance and entire self-commitment. It is a book from which you and I may, perhaps, learn much; but it is also a book which—I feel—might well rob the average, unwary, educated but untechnical reader, of his religious faith. A clear, repeated, systematised sct of assertion[s]; only the trained mind asks for proofs of them; the untrained succombs straight away. The book's introduction amongst only-English reading readers might do much harm: its resounding title and youthful assurance might secure the attention of a class of readers who, otherwise would be repelled by its subject-matter.

(3) I do not like your even recommending Macmillan to publish a translation of it—your doing so *simpliciter*; if you propose it to them at all, I should like the two *cons*—its youthfulness and considerable crudity, and its deadly negativeness (at least, for the average, even educated, reader[)]—to be put to them with the two *pros*—its great influence in Germany, and the large importance of the points it raises, as a possible stimulus to some deep reply.—

Still more am I anxious, that you should, now from the first, make clear to V. that you cannot do more than *that* for any English translation. The fact is that I feel your Commentary on Kant to have been one kind of work—and a kind admirably in keeping with your convictions and further plans; and any help (such as revising the proofs, or writing a Preface etc) to an Engl. version of V.'s 'Als Ob' to be an entirely different kind of work, and one that might easily camouflage you and your message for very many. *Of course*, you can consider the book in any new ed.

[94] Johannes Jörgensen (1866–1956), Danish poet and novelist; became a Ro- man Catholic, 1896, and resided in Italy after 1913.

of the 'Commentary'; you could even write in the 'Archiv'—I should, had I some appropriate ms, be quite ready to do so myself; you could also review 'Als Ob' in its English dress, and praise it if and where you felt it to deserve such praise. But you cannot —so the old friend feels—wisely collaborate in the direct production, or even in pressing publishers, as to the translation. —I can only fancy one situation in which this would be free from misleadingness—if you had made up your mind to write a book in analysis and refutation of this book, and if you encouraged the translation simply as material for your fully determined upon answer.—

I feel sure that, if you care, you can pretty easily not offend V. in your answer, and yet can there so plainly limit off your position and what you can do for him, as to save yourself a fine peck of very possible troubles in the future; you will have noticed, amongst the 'Urteile' how the book would in 1881 have produced a violent storm in Germany; well, even now, are we as 'far' here as they were, even at that time?—

If you feel disposed, pray tell V. that you already possess his 'Als Ob', but that *I* would be very grateful for the copy he offers you—of course, on the understanding that I study and utilise it carefully in my work on a new book now in progress, but presumably with acceptance of but little of the positions special to his work.

I thank God every day for the most solid, precious Friend He has deigned to give me in you.

Aff.

F. v. HÜGEL.

April 26. 1920

14 Lennox Str.
Edinburgh.

My dear Baron,

Very many thanks for your most kind & helpful letter. I have written in the terms you suggest to Vaihinger, & also to his translator a Mr Bergstocke who meantime has written to me. It appears that arrangements had beeen made, prior to Dr Carus' death, to have the book published by the Open Court Publishing Company, & also that Bertrand Russell has given his blessing to the book & says that he is not as far himself, as might appear, from the position it represents. I certainly don't belong in that boat. The Open Court Company, I understand, is, at present at least, without anyone to continue it, the son being more interested in active work = Chemistry.

I don't think Vaihinger will take my letter amiss.

Crespi's failure to receive the appointment here was a surprise & a disappointment to me. I fancy that the controversy over Schlapp had a decisive influence in favour of the native, whom I know & who is decidedly, I should say, inferior in every important respect to Crespi.

Your account of the scheme of your book interests me immensely. I shall be both honoured & delighted if I can assist with proofs in any way.

In writing Vaihinger I suggested that the copy of his book that he kindly offers might go to you.

By the way, you would probably see by papers, that no appointment was made here to the German Chair, Schlapp being continued in the Lectureship. So much good at least has been secured. But the principle was affirmed—surely foolishly—that no German should be appointed to the Chair.

Work is again in full swing. With kindest greetings

Yours ever affectionately
NORMAN KEMP SMITH.

May 10. 1920   14 Lennox Street,
Edinburgh.

My dear Baron von Hügel,

Just a note to say that Vaihinger has sent me a copy of his 'Philosophie des Als Ob', with a very kindly inscription. So, unless he has also sent you a copy, I shall be glad if you will accept as a gift from me my copy of the 1ˢᵗ ed. The other editions appear to contain no really important additions.

I have looked through parts, & am confirmed in my first impressions, that the position represented is crude &, as it seems to me, old-fashioned & out of date, in the way that only crudities can be. At end of Chap. XX I find the following: "Die Lüge hat dieselbe Wurzel, wie die ethische Grösse—beide beruhen auf einer Fiktion."[95] How is that for philosophical insight! Penetrating through deceptive outer appearances to the inner heart of things! And so far as I can discover he does not even attempt to explain why fictions are so serviceable as certain of them are— beyond implying that there is a struggle for survival among them & the "best" come out on top. Many of the favourable reviews must be due to knowledge of the tragic disabilities from which he has so long suffered, & against which he struggles so bravely.

With kindest greetings,

Yours ever affectionately

N. KEMP SMITH

P.S. I am rejoiced to observe that you are taking part in the philosophical meetings at Oxford in end of Sept. I expect to be there.

July 27. 1920

The Lagg,
Boat of Garten,
Inverness-shire

My dear Baron von Hügel,

The pleasing leisure of the vacation brings with it, I find, a great unwillingness to put pen to paper; but none the less I have

---

[95] This is from a passage in Hans Vaihinger's *Die Philosophie des Als Ob*, 8th ed. (Leipzig: Meiner, 1922), p. 143, which reads: "Wie Irrtum, Fiktion und Wahrheit theoretisch nahe verwandt sind und oft ineinander übergehen, so auch praktisch: die Lüge hat dieselbe Wurzel, wie die ethische Grösse—beide beruhen auf einer Fiktion." Dr. David Schultenover, S.J., has rendered the line quoted by Kemp Smith as: "The lie has the same root as ethical nobility—both are based on a fiction."

been thinking of writing you ever since I got North, which I did on July 12th. My little daughter & I are staying with my wife's sisters, while Mrs Kemp Smith is visiting in England. In August my little family settles in a cottage close by, where we remain until I come South for the meeting at Oxford. I am glad to know that you will be there.

The concluding weeks of Term were very busy ones, especially as I had considerable extra work in connection with the Workers' Educational Association. I think I told you that I had become President of the Edinburgh branch.

My friend, A. A. Bowman, spent a few days with us. He is over from Princeton for the Summer, & has taken a house in St Andrews, with his wife & two children. My wife & I stayed with them when I went to St Andrews to receive the LL.D. I liked to think that my name was being inscribed on the same roll of honour as your own.[96] Also, I was presented for the degree by my old-time teacher, John Burnet.[97] The Baroness, as I remember, said to me that the St Andrews LL.D. gown is too impossible to wear. I thought then there must be some mistake. As St Andrews goes on the principle of having the distinctive colour (white) only in the hood, the gown is uniform scarlet, trimmed with silk of the same shade. This makes it, I think, quite the most distinguished gown of all the Scotch LL.Ds. Owing to Herkless's[98] recent death, the proceedings were subdued; but there was a very pleasant luncheon at which we were all required to make five minute speeches.

[96] On 9 July 1914 von Hügel had received the honorary doctor's degree from St. Andrews University. This was his first academic honor, and his deeply felt gratitude to St. Andrews was reflected two weeks later when he wrote in his will that all the books in his personal library, with the exception of his own writings and manuscripts, were to go to St. Andrews University Library. *Diaries*, 9 and 27 July 1914.

[97] John Burnet (1863–1928), Scottish classical scholar, educated at Balliol Col-

lege, Oxford; Professor of Greek at St. Andrews University, 1892–1926; Sather Professor of Classical Literature at the University of California, 1925.

[98] Sir John Herkless (1855–1920), Scottish minister and educator, educated at Universities of Glasgow and Jena; Regius Professor of Ecclesiastical History at St. Andrews University, 1894–1915; Provost of St. Andrews, 1911–1915; Vice-Chancellor and Principal of St. Andrews, and Principal of the United College of St. Salvator and St. Leonard, 1915–1920.

Lord Robert Cecil[99] did not appear for the Edinburgh Graduation. Kipling[100] however was there. Barnes,[101] the Labour M. P., was also receiving a degree; & I liked his modest & dignified utterances.

The chief satisfaction of the past winter to me has been the hold I got over my University classes. From the Degree class a number of the best men—& two of them *very* good—are continuing next year into my Intermediate course. Next after that comes the W. E. A. work which I have found thus far very congenial, & which has very considerably enlarged & diversified my circle of acquaintances in Edinburgh. People are extraordinarily willing to work for it. Next year we are having several new courses (each with a weekly meeting of about 2 hours for 20 weeks)—one to be given by Morley Fletcher,[102] the Director of the College of Art, & one by our Astronomer Royal.[103] In all there will be some 12 courses. Next year too we cooperate with the British Association, which visits Edinburgh in September, in arranging 3 public lectures to working-men—probably on the general theme of Science & Education.

Now that leisure has come—amidst walking & cycling over the

[99] Edgar Algernon Robert Gascoyne-Cecil, Viscount Cecil of Chelwood (1864–1958), third son of the third Marquess of Salisbury, and one of the creators of the League of Nations; held various government posts; Chancellor of the University of Birmingham, 1918–1944; among the many honorary degrees he received was one from Edinburgh University to which, apparently, Kemp Smith was referring.

[100] Joseph Rudyard Kipling (1865–1936), British writer; defender of imperialism and authoritarian government; *The Light That Failed* (1891) and *Captains Courageous* (1897) among his best-known books; "Recessional" probably his best-known poem; received Nobel Prize for Literature, 1907; refused Poet Laureateship, 1895.

[101] George Nicoll Barnes (1858–1940), Scottish labor leader; Assistant Secretary of Amalgamated Society of Engineers, 1892; General Secretary, 1896–1908; Member of Parliament from Glasgow, 1906–1922; member of War Cabinet, 1917; gave special attention to old-age

pensions, taxation of land values, care of discharged soldiers, League of Nations, the Irish Question, and all industrial problems caused by the war.

[102] Frank Morley Fletcher (1866–1949), English artist who became a naturalized citizen of the United States in 1926, educated at University College, Liverpool; exhibited his paintings internationally; head of art department at University College, Reading, 1898–1906; H.M. Inspector of Schools of Art, 1906–1908; Director of Edinburgh College of Art, 1908–1923; Director of School of Art of Community Arts Association, Santa Barbara, California, 1923–1930.

[103] Ralph Allen Sampson (1866–1939), British astronomer, educated at St. John's College, Cambridge; Lecturer at King's College, London, 1889–1891; Professor of Mathematics at Durham College of Science in Newcastle, 1893–1895; Professor of Mathematics at Durham University, 1896–1910, and of Astronomy, 1908–1910; Astronomer-Royal of Scotland, 1910–1937.

moors, & some golf, I am getting arrears of reading done—
Fustel de Coulange's 'Cité Antique' (a first reading), Bosanquet's
Gifford Lectures, & the two very tough volumes of Alexander's
Giffords. I am inclined to think Alexander may be right in his
view that space & time are inseparable; in that part of his work
I am greatly interested; but his philosophy as a whole is a most
God-forsaken one. The conjurer producing rabbits from a hat is
not in it [sic] compared with Alexander's generating everything
out of space–time, alias motion. For Alexander himself, as a man,
I have the deepest respect; & certainly his work is always thorough
& utterly sincere. By & bye I hope to be able to get some new
class-lectures written, or at least partially thought out, for the
coming winter.

Boutroux,[104] it appears, is unable to come to the Oxford Congress. A. J. Balfour is presiding at the Symposium in which you
take part. Wildon Carr[105] writes asking me to speak in a profound
Symposium on Neo-Realism in U.S.A. I excuse myself: it is the
last subject on which I desire to speak.

Your health, I hope, has been good these summer months; &
allows you a satisfactory morning's work. Or are you taking a
complete holiday?

Stout in Sᵗ Andrews told me that in resigning his editorship of
'Mind' he proposed Wildon Carr as his successor, but that there
was opposition to this suggestion. The opposition, I should say,
is justified: Carr's philosophy seems mainly to consist of the last
new cry. He continues to combine most new things in a general
Bergsonian blend.

Have you ever looked into Moffatt's[106] translation of the New
Testament? I met him this afternoon for the first time. A colleague

[104] Etienne Emile Marie Boutroux
(1845–1921), French philosopher and
educator.
[105] Herbert Wildon Carr (1857–1931),
British philosopher, educated privately and
at London University; President of the
Aristotelian Society, 1916–1918; held professorships in philosophy at London University, 1918, and the University of Southern California, 1925.
[106] James Moffatt (1870–1944), Scot-

tish theologian, educated at Glasgow University and the Free Church of Scotland
College; Professor of Greek and New Testament Exegesis at Mansfield College, Oxford, 1911–1915; Professor of Church
History at Glasgow Free Church College,
1915–1927, and at Union Theological
Seminary, New York City, 1927–1939;
published translation of New Testament
in 1913, and of Old Testament in 1924.

of his at the Free Church College in Glasgow, A. B. Macaulay,[107] a very charming fellow, is here for the summer, & we meet from time to time.

I send you these very dull & disjointed pages as token only of my grateful appreciation of your kindly & generous interest. I am, dear Baron,

Yours ever affectionately,

NORMAN KEMP SMITH.

30th July 1920

31st   "   "

Clonboy,

Englefield Green,

Surrey.

My very dear Friend,

Really with you—I mean, with the fact of our friendship—I feel every day the deep truth of Browning's 'What a thing friendship is, world without end!' For here are you, amongst other things, heaping one most interesting and most helpful letter upon me—I have quite five of them at my elbow as I write this—not withstanding my shameful mumness all these many months! But you will have guessed that the silence meant no slackening of the friendship, of the deep and steady affection, and bracing feeling of support which have been cheering me on, more than ever since I last scribbled to you. Indeed such an increase of in-touchness could not fail to come since, up to July 12 when I found I *must* slip away for some weeks from my work-table, to leisure and much open air, I have ever since Christmas been immersed in the to me closest possible study of your 'Commentary'. I am happy to say that I finished the mostly treble study of all the chief parts of that great book by the end of June, so that I could, at

---

[107] Alexander Beith Macaulay (1871–1950), Scottish theologian; onetime Professor of Apologetics and Systematic Theology at Trinity College (Church of Scotland), Glasgow; external examiner to the Universities of St. Andrews, Aberdeen, Glasgow, and Edinburgh.

last, again start composition—this time, the first, pencil, draft
of Part I of the body of the book. I have now decided (a little
change) to make Part I study and (I trust) establish the presence, the inclusion of the Unconditioned in every at all full and
sane human experience; and to devote Part II to the elucidation of
the transition of the evidence and the conviction from those concerning the Unconditioned to those involving a Personalist God.
(I deliberately write Personal*ist*). The other two Parts of the book
remain, so far, unchanged in my scheme. —Now I am already
quite clear in my mind that Part I will owe, and will gratefully
avow, *hugely* to yourself; and next to you, to Stout: to you two
more than to any other English thinkers (this, although I am
starting there with James Ward, whom I continue to find very
tine in parts, but unsatisfactory in places—less uniformly sound
than yourself and Stout). —I had hoped to learn much from
Bosanquet's *Giffords*: I have very carefully studied both vols.:
but I did not. Certainly, his form is admirable, and he possesses
much of the sense of dependence so characteristic of religion.
But he is, I think, just simply fanatical about the category of
wholeness: it brings us, I am confident no further than to the
fringes of religion. The Pantheistic trend becomes thus marked
and operative on many a crucial point: it would be easy to quote
astonishing examples of this.

I intend to read Webb's[108] *Giffords* when I get to my Part II.
Here again, tho' I expect less systematically than in Bosanquet,
I am prepared to find certain Pantheistic elements: W's partly
Indian blood. As to Alexander's *Giffords*, I feel that I must not
now delay my work over the study of so difficult, and religiously
so arid a book. Certainly the *précis* of their main contention on
the wrappers, doubtless from A's own pen, reads most oddly with
regard to *Gifford Lectures*—Lectures which are all supposed to
be expositions or defences etc. of Theism. But pray tell me more
about the volumes, as you get through them!

[108] Clement Charles Julian Webb
(1865–1954), British philosopher, educated at Westminster and Christ Church,
Oxford; Wilde Lecturer on Natural and
Comparative Religion, Oxford, 1911–
1914; Gifford Lecturer, Aberdeen, 1918–
1919; first Oriel Professor of the Philosophy of the Christian Religion, Oxford,
1920–1930; long-time friend of von Hügel's.

How I envy you the *toughness* of your brain, your ability to study such works whilst resting! I never was like that; and, naturally enough, I am now less like that than ever. I find that if I am to get a real rest, I have to get away for these 6 weeks, from philosophical, and still more from all new or systematic *religious* reading. I am reading, instead, *The Browning Love Letters*, which a most discr[im]inating lady friend, pressed me to read, in spite of my strong feeling that I would be committing an indecency, a prying into the innermost secrets of two souls, never intended by them for any other human mind. I am now very glad to have followed her advice. They are hard reading often; indeed some of *his* letters are largely unintelligible. But what a *splendid* couple! and how God, the sense of God, the presence of God, the need of, the dependence on God runs through it all majestically! I read and re-read, I side-mark and I underline the finest thoughts and reasonings as carefully as I have done with my N. K. S.'s 'Commentary'.

And then, with these letters, I have gone back to his poetry, in parts to things I had never properly mastered there—especially to 'La Saisias', assuredly a most beautiful and touching work, even though some of its arguments appear to me part too simply individualist, part curiously over-subtle.—

But, as to your own reading, pray do not drop the study of H. J. Holtzmann's 'N. T. Theologie', till you have ruminated through every word of 'Die verkündigung Jesu', 'der Paulinismus' and 'die Johanneische Theologie'. You will never regret the time and trouble; it will bring much additional precision, penetration and richness, to your ethical and religious teaching and influence.

How delighted I am to learn that you are so happy with, so pleased concerning, your classes; and again that your labours for those working men are turning out so congenial, so fruitful. I think I can fully enter into all your feelings concerning both ranges of labour and of learning through the teaching. *That* is one of the joys of friendship, —by sympathy born from such friendship, one quadruples, or more, one's own interests, indeed even influence!

I am very, very glad too about your Hon. LLD at St Andrews,

and very proud we should thus be fellow Doctors of Scotland's oldest university! Forgive me that I did not discover this most pleasant event, and did not congratulate you on it. I do so now, most delightedly! What my wife must have *meant*, or at least what must have, for the moment, confused her, was the certainly strange-looking, canary-coloured Doctor of Philosophy robes of A. E. Taylor, which were very *voyants* throughout that day in June 1914, and which, at the time, she declared to be impossible things to wear. But, equally at that time, she was so little hostile to the LLD gown and hood and cap, that she warmly approved my getting measured for a set to take away with me as my own. This set I wore, for the first, this June at Oxford at the Christ-Church *Gaudy* Dinner. It was admired, and I had to explain to Webb what it exactly was.

I think that you, on your part, have, conversely, missed *my* recent honour. I daresay you read some months ago how the limitation to Anglican clerics of the Oxford DD Degree (a limitation extant since the Protestant Reformation) had been removed. Well, the first batch of such non-Anglican cleric-Doctors of Divinity, *honoris causa*, received their title and gowns on June 24, and of these six, I was one. I pointed out to my fellow Doctors that, once again, Scotsmen had secured the lion's share. For of the six Doctors, 3½ were Scotch: Sir George Adam Smith,[109] Aberdeen, Old Testament; John Skinner,[110] Cambridge, Old Testament; Very Rev. Dr Cooper,[111] Glasgow, Ancient Church History: these three, whole Scotsmen, Presbyterians and clerics; and myself, Biblical Criticism and Philosophy of Religion, Roman

<hr />

[109] Sir George Adam Smith (1856–1942), Scottish Biblical scholar, educated at Universities of Edinburgh, Tübingen, and Leipzig; Free Church minister in Aberdeen; held visiting lectureships in America at The Johns Hopkins University, 1896, Yale University, 1899, The University of Chicago and University of California, 1909; Principal and Vice-Chancellor of the University of Aberdeen, 1909–1935.

[110] John Skinner (1851–1925), Scottish Biblical scholar, educated at the University of Aberdeen and the Free Church

College, Aberdeen; Professor of Old Testament Language and Literature at Westminster College, Cambridge, 1890–1922, and Principal of the College, 1908–1922; with von Hügel one of the original members of the LSSR.

[111] James Cooper (1846–1922), Scottish theologian, educated at Aberdeen University; Regius Professor of Ecclesiastical History, Glasgow, 1898; leader in Scottish ecumenism and first Secretary of Scottish Church Society; Moderator of General Assembly of the Church of Scotland, 1917.

Catholic and layman, half Scotch. The remaining two Doctors were also laymen—Arthur Peake,[112] Primitive Methodist, Biblical Commentator, and St. John Thackeray,[113] Anglican: Septuagint and other Hellenistic Greek religious literature. —The whole thing went off in the most friendly way; and I was personally very glad to find two good, well-tried friends—Skinner and Peake—amongst my fellow Doctors. —The previous evening, at the Gaudy at Christ-Church, I was able to watch, and in part to speak with, the Hon. D. C. L. Doctors promoted in the morning of that June 23rd; and opposite to me sate the very Barnes, that fine, sane labour leader, whom you met and admired so at St. Andrews. I could also watch closely Venizelos,[114] the Greek Prime Minister, of whom Canon Headlam,[115] who sat beside him, told me next day, that polished and *distingué* as V. looked and indeed very largely was, he, nevertheless, had *for years*, been a highway robber in Crete, and that he still had numerous relatives and intimate friends upon the highroads of Crete!

—You generously kind Friend have offered me—alas, already long ago!—your first copy of Vaihinger's 'Als Ob' book, V. having now sent you another copy from, and inscribed by, himself. I gratefully accept, and must get you, sometime, to write your appropriation of it to me into this copy. This, tho' I have come to feel that it would really not be worth my while to study thro' the whole of this crude effusion. I feel sure you are right, and that

[112] Arthur Samuel Peake (1865–1929), British Biblical scholar, educated at St. John's College, Oxford; held lectureships at Oxford and Manchester, and in various Methodist colleges; edited *Holborn Review*, 1919–1929; edited well-known *Commentary on the Bible* (1919).

[113] Francis St. John Thackeray (1832–1919), British classicist, educated at Eton and Merton College, Oxford; Fellow and Tutor of Lincoln College, Oxford, 1857; Assistant Master of Eton, 1858–1883; Vicar of Mapledurham, 1883–1919.

[114] Eleutherios Venizelos (1864–1936), Greek statesman; first appointed Premier of Greece, 1910; championed allies in World War I, and forced to resign by pro-German king; took Greece into war on side of allies after abdication of king; resigned premiership, 1920; again Premier, 1924, 1928–1932, 1933; exiled, but later granted amnesty, 1935.

[115] Arthur Cayley Headlam (1862–1947), English theologian, educated at Winchester and New College, Oxford; Fellow of All Souls College, Oxford, 1885–1897 and 1924–1947; held various lectureships at Oxford and Cambridge; member of Senate of London University, 1903–1913; Principal of King's College, London, 1903–1912; and Professor of Dogmatic Theology, 1903–1916; Regius Professor of Divinity, Oxford, and Canon of Christ Church, 1918–1923; Bishop of Gloucester, 1923–1945.

much of the, even so disconcertingly resounding praise, his crudity has received, is really the result of compassion for his blindness and of respect for his plucky fight against it: these, mixed doubtless with great, and entirely merited esteem for his truly monumental 'Kommentar'. (I have carefully studied large sections of it, by now, and have some right to a definite opinion). I feel we can even go further, and can assume, with great probability of truth, that it was his pathetic crippledness and inability to produce any new work of any dimension which drove him to look and see whether he had nothing ready to his hand that he could give the world: the 'Als Ob' affair would thus readily offer itself to him for publication. And, once decided upon publication, V. himself would be as pathetically ready to believe he was thus giving an epoch-making volume to the world, as all his old pupils and friends would (as far as ever they conscientiously could and indeed a good deal further) encourage this his, in a way touching, overestimate. —Even so, it still remains passing strange to find the truly *exquisite* balance and circumspection of the 'Kommentar' preceded and—much more strange—succeeded by such crude and rude violence and *sans-culottism!*—I got my wife carefully to copy out his long letter to you; and I have now closely studied the 'Kant-Studien' *précis* by himself, referred to in his letter. I hope to make effective use of one I think quite unconsciously, hence all the more instructively, deeply irreligious affirmation contained in the *précis*. Has the poor thing been always thus blind spiritually as well as corporally? The entire affair is strange indeed!

I am so glad we shall meet in Oxford, even tho' I am so far feeling no enthusiasm as to my own participation. Eduard Le-Roy,[116] who was to have opened that *Symposium*, and this by an examination of *Loisy's* religious philosophy booklets, cannot come; and thus I, who had accepted really to please L., or rather to avoid displeasing him, have now to follow upon Jacques

116 Edouard LeRoy (1870–1954), French philosopher and mathematician; student of Henri Bergson's, and collaborator with Pierre Teilhard de Chardin in several publications; his *Dogme et critique* condemned by the Vatican during Roman Catholic modernist crisis; collaborated with von Hügel in effort to save Loisy from total condemnation by the Vatican.

Chevalier[117] (Lyons), a good friend of mine, but whose (very sound) Paper contains certainly no direct, or at least explicite, reference to L. I have still to write my own Paper, and am inclined to read up L., but to leave out any direct reference to himself. But J. A. Smith is second, I am third, and Jacks,[118] that clear and clever but (I think) never very deep thinker, is fourth and last. —May you yourself be given a large and a thoroughly appropriate share in the Congress!—

Please, when the Congress is over to *come and stay three nights with us at Vicarage Gate*. I can then show you my annotations (with the very few criticisms and corrections of misprints and the great series of warmest admirations and gratitudes). I found I should ruin my holiday rest if I tried to write out these notes and what and where I chiefly learnt from you. There are especially three great facts and insights which I thus owe, most gratefully, to my fine N. K. S. Friend!—

Your letters contain other, still unanswered queries. But I dare not miss the belated sunshine out of doors; so must stop, after two concluding remarks.

The first is: Oh, *how* humble, how unworldly, how un–self-occupied, how pure of heart—pure, not only from all sensuality but from all hate, all jealousy, all rationalist forcing one's poor thinking machine, how passive (in the right sense) one has, I have, to be, to gain any steady, useable light in these deepest facts and burrowings! *That* is one, perhaps the chief, encouragement to such toil: it makes one better, smaller in one's own poor eyes!

And the second is this prayer of Leopold von Ranke, composed when in his late seventies (?) and found after his death amongst his Papers. But I had better copy it out on to a separate card for me—oh how right it is & none of your Pantheisms, no Hegelisms,

---

[117] Jacques Chevalier (1882–?), French philosopher and educator; Professor of Philosophy in the University of Grenoble; his lectures, *Henri Bergson*, were translated into English and published by Macmillan in 1928.

[118] Lawrence Pearsall Jacks (1860–1955), British philosopher and writer; entered ministry as assistant to Stopford Brooks in Bedford Chapel, 1887; Professor of Philosophy at Manchester College, Oxford, 1903–1931; editor of *The Hibbert Journal* from its foundation in 1902 until his retirement in 1947; helped to make Loisy's work known in England.

but an awed sense of otherness, of the distinct Reality of God!
Your devoted old Friend
F. V. HÜGEL.

Prayer of Leopold von Ranke.[119]
Wer ist die Kraft,
die Leben in mir schafft?
Wer gibt Erkenntniss
und Verständniss?
Wer bewahrt die Seele
dass sie nicht fehle?
Allgewaltiger,
Einiger und Dreifaltiger:
Du hast mich aus dem
Nichts gerufen,
Hier liege ich vor Deines
Thrones Stufen.

To N. K. S. from F. v. H.
July 31 1920.

Sept. 4. 1920

The Lagg,
Boat of Garten,
Inverness-shire.

My dear Baron,
Many thanks for your letter. Need I say how great a satisfaction, & how encouraging a support, it is to me to hear that my Commentary has really proved helpful. To my mind—at least

[119] The following English translation of von Ranke's prayer was made by Dr. David Schultenover, S.J.:

Who is the power,
    who gives me life?
Who gives knowledge
    and understanding?
Who guards the soul
    that it does not fail?
Almighty,
One and Trinity:
You have called me
    out of nothing,
Behold me
    at your throne's step lying.

that is my hope as well as my feeling—the book is very much of a *transition*-book. Had I been able to defer the writing of it for some years I could have made much more of both the negative & the positive side of my criticism of Kant. However I suppose that had I waited I should have lost the benefit, so very considerable, of writing under the *compulsion* of early publication—it makes one work so much harder. Already I begin to move away from some of the positions indirectly & directly suggested in it, though, I should think, in so doing I am moving on lines that in the main would probably meet with your approval. In particular I now recognise more clearly the untenableness of Kant's phenomenalism—his alternative to subjectivism. A *much* more objectivist or realist view can, I think, be taken as regards the object of perception & of knowledge generally. Here I find that I can profit considerably by parts of S. Alexander's argument. Stout will be lecturing on these problems in his second Gifford course (I'll send you his syllabus as soon as it appears) at the opening of session in October. Thus far, tho' he has been steadily developing away from Ward's very unsatisfactory pan-psychism (to my mind a kind of philosophical measles), he does not yet seem to have successfully broken with subjectivism.

You ask me to write further my impressions of Alexander's 'Giffords'. Perhaps I had best enclose the rough draft of my letter to him & his reply.[120] The doctrine of 'emergences' is that they are unpredictable, & are evidenced solely by brute empirical experience. Space–time (ultimately, it would seem, = motion) is the matrix out of which all things arise by 'emergence'. First emerges matter, 2^{ndly} the secondary qualities (related to their space–time patterns on the analogy of relation of mind to body), 3^{rdly} life, 4th consciousness—the highest emergent that has yet occurred. Deity is our name for the next higher quality—beyond Consciousness. When it emerges, however, it will necessarily realise itself (as must all existences in Space–time) in *finite* centres, & the name Deity is shifted to the next higher still: i.e. Deity, qua Deity is

---

[120] See Appendix III for Kemp Smith's rough draft. Although Kemp Smith's draft is with his manuscript letter to von Hügel at St. Andrews, the manuscript reply from Alexander seems to have been lost.

incapable of existence. All this sounds most preposterous: but there is an immense deal of very sincere & genuine solid work in the book, especially on the asserted inseparability of space & time, & on the realistic interpretation of sense experience & knowledge. Also his conotional psychology has considerable interest. But I should not, I think, advise your turning aside at present to read Alexander. In reply to his point upon miracles, I am replying that miracle may arise through breach of continuity as well as of law.

I fully intend to follow up my study of Holtzmann, already so illuminating. Indeed I had set his two volumes aside to bring with me, but on second thought, reserved them for the winter. They form an excellent occasional alternative to my University work.

No, I had not observed in the papers your receiving the Oxford D.D. That is splendid! Many thanks for your own kindly congratulations to me.

In the past month I have reread carefully Bosanquet's larger "Logic" & his Giffords, with much profit as well as disagreement. The former I had not read since I was a student, & the latter only glanced through previously. One thing that strikes me very forcibly is the strange & even weird inappropriateness of much of his terminology, e.g. his equating universality with system or wholeness, & both with individuality, also his *constant* use of purely *logical* terms to describe dynamical & conative processes. Both, I fancy, are in considerable part his legacy from Hegel & Caird, & in lesser degree from Green & Nettleship. His field of reading seems to be extremely narrow—though with occasional signs, I should say, of fairly recent enlargement.

I have not, also, been able to do the writing of lectures, I had hoped, not even, thus far, the preparing of an address I have promised to one of the Students' Societies at opening of Term— on, I propose, 'Mediums & Mediumship'—or perhaps on the general history of Modern Spiritualism with comments. Have been reading 'Raymond'—a *very* unpleasant handling of that gallant youth: his letters from the Front are the best of the book. Also am rereading F. Podmore's 'History of Modern Spiritualism'. Is there any book on the general subject you would especially recommend? As an unhappy consequence of these arrears of writing, I am beginning to fear I may be prevented from getting South for the Oxford Congress: but shall try in the next fortnight to earn the holiday. How very good of you to ask me for three nights thereafter in London! There is nothing I should enjoy or value more. May I delay a definite decision until later, or may that be inconvenient? It is a very great added inducement to my coming South.

I have left to the last the thanking you for your inspiring & illuminating address on 'Christianity & the Supernatural'.[121] That in the ethical & religious field, the distinction between sin & virtue is less significant than that between the good & the good only makes explicit for me a truth which I have more & more been coming to recognise; and you do so with many touches & suggestions—"social-solitary" & the like—that help me greatly. I have ordered a number of copies to send to friends. Some day I hope that you will write directly upon ethics: the usual academic treatises are sadly barren, & go far to account for—tho' not, I should say, to justify—S. Alexander's exclusion of them from his reading.

Many thanks also for Ranke's fine prayer: I shall keep your transcription of it as one of my many momentoes of your goodness to me.

Yours ever affectionately,
NORMAN KEMP SMITH.

20th Sept. 1920
13, Vicarage Gate,
Kensington,
W. 8.

My ever dear Friend,

I had intended not to write again, till I had well digested the abstract of your letter to S. Alexander, and his answer to you. But I have still not done with these two very interesting enclo-

---

[121] In *Essays and Addresses on the Philosophy of Religion*, First Series (London: Dent, 1921), pp. 278–98. This address was originally delivered at Oxford in May 1920, and printed in the June issue of *The Modern Churchman*.

sures, and yet find that I have several happenings and thoughts
I want to put to you, together with my warm thanks for those two
letters and especially also your most cheering and stimulating
letter to me, in which they came.

First then (leaving out S. A. altogether, till I return—soon I
hope—those two letters) a word as to the Philosophy Congress
—as far as that *Symposium* on the Relation between Morals and
Religion goes. I dare say you know that the whole idea of holding such a S. originated with *Edouard LeRoy* (Mathematician
and Catholic Bergsonite), or rather (I think *in petto*—all this in
strict confidence) with Loisy, who, poor thing (brilliant but I am
confident more and more oversubtle and too radical historical
critic, and feeling his isolation keenly) has been trying his hand
(I myself think with indifferent success) at the philosophy of religion, in 'La Religion' and 'De la Discipline Intellectuelle'.
Whereas in his critico-historical work there lies an erudition believed equal or surpassing that of Wellhausen or of H. J. Holtzmann, and a practice of all his wonderful mind of forty years: in
this psychological 'philosophical' writing, his reading and training are ever so slighter: indeed his mind is (I think constitution-
ally) so sceptical at least in these fields, that it would be almost
like asking Hume to give renewed and most careful attention to
the various *believing* analyses and outlooks of his day, as to get
my much loved L. to study carefully, say, your 'Commentary'.
Certainly as to Troeltsch, as big as L. at L.'s best, and what? ten-
times L.'s size in religious philosophy, I have been unable to get
L. beyond the irritated exclamation: 'mais ne voyez vous pas,
que cela est encore orthodoxe!' How subtle is that kind of inverted dependence—that shutting out of all further light and
growth, from allowing negation to take the place in the mind and
will, which only affirmation ever can fruitfully occupy!

Well: L. wrote to me about LeRoy's getting the first (opening) place for this discussion at Oxford; would I accept the second? Similarly Wildon Carr wrote to me, with J. A. Smith as 3rd
and Jacks as 4th. I had to tell both L. and Jacks that I could not
in conscience simply back L.'s delicately but thoroughly anti-
transcendent, entirely immanental re-explaining (really: explain-

ing away) of religion. But that, since L. himself desired it, and as I certainly was now the oldest and closest friend he possesses, perhaps anywhere, certainly in England, I would accept and would do my best. —The long vacation arrives, and what does J. A. Smith do, but go off to a still quite inaccessible part of the Tyrol—with not a wire or letter even capable of reaching him— till now 4 days ago. Meanwhile—but *weeks*, at least a month, ago, LeRoy had fallen out of the running—brain-fag and imperative need of entire rest. But Wildon Carr (having then already many adhesions from France to the Congress especially because of this Morals–Religion Symposium) wrote pressing me to remain in, and sending me a Paper by *Chevalier* (Prof. of Philosophy at Grenoble) which he intended to make the first in the proposed new arrangement. I again accepted but this time with the condition that I should not be expected to speak about L. That I could follow, as a discreet Critic, a more or less endorser of L.; but that I could not be the first, and probably the only one, to speak of L., and this in disparagement. W. C. wrote back very grateful, entirely understanding; and that now the S. (entirely dissociated from LeRoy and L.) would consist of Papers by Chevalier, myself, Smith, and Jacks. Good. —Yes: but what was far from 'good', was that tho' J. A. S. was bombarded by W. C. and others at every probable address abroad, he returns only last Thursday (16th) from abroad, and promptly discovers that he could not possibly see his way to discuss Ch.'s Paper; and on Saturday first sees my own Paper in print, and tells me that *that* proves he has no sense either of Ethics or of Religion, and that deeply sorry tho' he is to upset our plans (Jacks too was now in print), he could not possibly remain in. —I thereupon wired and wrote to W. C. that unless a substitute (why not himself) were even yet found for J. A. S.—an Immanentist etc.—I really could not come to the Discussion. W. C. has, I think, very good-naturedly accepted, and promises to come fully out of his shell. In this way we shall really have, already in the 4 Papers, the two fundamentally divergent positions; instead of (with J. A. S. out, and no one to replace him) three shades of the same metaphysical, transcendental position only. (*Quite* between ourselves,

J. A. S.'s to me strange refusal *may* spring, at least in part, from an experience at Woodbroke Summer School in 1917—'Progress and History'. Marvin, the Positivist, was our boss; he gave me 'Progress in Religion' and to J. A. S. the 'Progress in Philosophy' and the Conclusion to all—the outlook into the Future. Marvin pressed me to read the whole volume of our Addresses when in proof and candidly to give him my precise impressions. I only accepted for Miss Stawell (Greek History) A. J. Carlyle (Mediaeval History) and J. A. Smith (besides correcting my own proofs). Miss St. and C. I greatly admired, but as to J. A. S. I wrote that his position was one of such practically sheer Becoming—it was such a Heracleitean πάντα ῥεῖ affair—that I felt really ashamed to appear within the same covers with something so destructively one sided. And Marvin, as he later on told me with glee, went and told J. A. S.! Do you not feel it wrong of people to act thus! Now I am sure of the real fineness of J. A. S.'s character: it [is] large and sweet—no meanness will ever lodge there. Yet, without any *rancoeur*, he might well feel, after *that*, uncomfortable in discussing deep matters in public with me. —And yet the man is an odd, curiously changeable, pure Celt (from Dingwall 'not a drop of Saxon blood in me' he has told me proudly). Thus, he must just have seen Chevalier's Paper before he left for—the clouds, for Carr wrote that 'J. A. S. finds it *excellent*. *Now* this same Paper he cannot possibly discuss etc.[122]

What a long, too selfish account of *one* incident. But it is told in part that you may understand how dearly your support will be welcomed I am sure by us all, but very certainly by myself, at Oxford, if you *do* turn up there for the Symposium next Sunday, 27th.

Your ever devoted Friend
F. v. HÜGEL.

Time still only for 2 points: (1) How strange that Jacks, Principal of a Unitarian College, shd delibreately put forward McTag-

[122] At the last moment Smith actually took part in the symposium. For an after-the-event account of the symposium, see Friedrich von Hügel, *Selected Letters,* *1896–1924*, edited with a Memoir by Bernard Holland (London: Dent, 1928), p. 310.

gart's[123] and Royce's[124] immortal finite spirits (their substitutes for God) as giving a real, full equivalent for Theism, as regards the effect of such views upon Ethics. I am sorry now I did not take the sense of awe, adoration as one of my virtues: *that*, at all events, has no real place in those views and their effects. But, even apart from this, I am shocked by the mental levity of J. in the matter: as if God, not Immortality, were not the entire of the religious experiences and thirst etc. etc.—

(2) I am delighted to find you always so refreshingly anti-Hegel, so clear from all that dreary identification—, that circle-business. Hurrah, hurrah!

F. v. H.

Thanks for the 'New Statesman': have promised the author of the book there reviewed, to read at least the chief parts of it, and give him an opinion on it—he was very severely handled by the 'Times Lit. Suppl.'

Next time I will tell you something of the financial anxieties that—1st time in my life—have closed in around me. Some relief has come; but next year we *must* do up this big house, with the money from where? This has, for the moment driven me from my dear God-book, to promptly lucrative work.

Devoted. F. v. H.

The Lagg,

Sept. 20. 1920 Boat of Garten.

My dear Baron,

I have so far got my work in hand as to feel I can come South. So it will be a very great pleasure for me to look forward to if I can avail myself of your kind invitation, & stay with you in London after the Oxford meetings. I should come to London on the

---

[123] John M'Taggart Ellis M'Taggart (1866–1925), British philosopher, educated at Trinity College, Cambridge; Fellow of Trinity College, 1891, and Lecturer, 1897–1923; Fellow of the British Academy; student of Hegel's thought.

[124] Josiah Royce (1855–1916), American philosopher of religion, educated at the University of California and The Johns Hopkins University; taught philosophy at the University of California for most of his adult life, and wrote numerous books and essays.

Tuesday, & stay that night & the following, travelling back to Edinburgh by the night train on the Thursday.

If this is still convenient for the Baroness & yourself, please do not trouble writing.

Your paper on 'Morals & Religion' has only just reached me by this morning's post, so I have not yet been able to read it.[125]

With kindest greetings & many happy anticipations of our meeting,

Yours ever sincerely,
NORMAN KEMP SMITH.

P.S. I leave here for Edinburgh tomorrow, & shall reach Oxford on the Friday afternoon. Am to be at New College.

14 Lennox Street,
Edinburgh.

Oct. 4. 1920

My dear Baron,

I had a quite comfortably sleeping journey North on Thursday; & my wife has insisted upon my spending the week-end in bed, to get rid of the remains of my cold. While in bed I have been thinking over the winter's work, & going through my lecture-notes material. Classes start in a few days, & meantime there is much to be done. So I shall not attempt to write more than this note of thanks to Lady Mary and to yourself for your splendid hospitality. My visit to you made my journey South so very worth while; & you have given me much to think over in your many helpful talks.[126] I shall endeavour, to the best of my powers, to

---

[125] In *Essays and Addresses on the Philosophy of Religion*, Second Series (London: Dent, 1926), pp. 157–64. This paper was first delivered at the Oxford symposium in late-September 1920.

[126] On 28 September 1920 von Hügel and Kemp Smith traveled down to London together by train from Oxford, following the philosophical symposium. On the 29th and 30th they had a number of long and serious talks about philosophical topics; Kemp Smith made suggestions and criticisms of the various essays to be in-cluded in von Hügel's soon-to-be-published collection of occasional writings, and von Hügel gave Kemp Smith his various criticisms of the latter's *Commentary*. During one walk in Hyde Park they discussed the "period in life of greatest spiritual mortality; Christianity & Rigorism; the sufferings of parents etc." *Diaries*, 28–30 September 1920. A more detailed account of the conversation about the "period in life of greatest spiritual mortality" can be found in von Hügel's *Selected Letters*, p. 311.

prove worthy of your generous interest in me & in my work. May you have great strength and inspiration this coming winter for your thinking & writing! My kindest greetings to Lady Mary for giving me so happy a visit. My wife too requests me to convey her kind regards. I am,

Yours ever affectionately
NORMAN KEMP SMITH

P.S. I hope Pucky[127] is well, & that the picture-puzzle has worked out.

17th Dec. 1920.
13, Vicarage Gate,
Kensington,
W. 8.

My dear Friend,

This is to commend to your kindness Mr Paul Brodersen, a student of the University of Copenhagen—of course, a Dane and a Lutheran Christian—who has been residing for a term or two in Oxford, and who is now about to go to Edinburgh for a term. Mr Brodersen is preparing an Essay on *Revelation*—his is indeed a philosophical and theological head and interest. He reads, speaks and writes English remarkably well. I am giving him also a note to Professor Paterson. And if there is anyone in Edinburgh, besides yourself and Dr Paterson, likely to be of use to Mr Brodersen: will you be so good as to bring such an one into contact with this pleasant Dane?

Perhaps I had better explain that I have been urging Mr Brodersen to master certain (specified) portions of your great Commentary, and that generally I am recommending him to begin

---

[127] Puck was von Hügel's Pekingese dog.

with a sound and clear position as regards knowledge generally and its, in a very true sense, revelational character.

Your devoted old Friend
F. V. HÜGEL.

Jan. 8, 1921.
" 10, "
13 Vicarage Gate,
Kensington,
London, W. 8.

My very dear Friend,

I am a bit late with my New Year's wishes and yet, even so, this is only the 3rd real letter I write so far in 1921. First to Troeltsch, then to Loisy, now to you. And indeed, as far as union of convictions and bracing influence go, you come immediately after Troeltsch, my poor friend L. remaining sadly negative and purely immanental.

Let me first say that the last I heard from you (indeed about you) was in your note of October 4th: your wife had, most wisely, put you to bed so as promptly to kill off that cold in you. But I do not even know whether you ever got up and out again. Surely, yes! And indeed with such a world of things to do, as not to be able to get back, during these 3 months to that habit of yours, so bracing and profitable to me of pregnant notes to myself. Pucky and I on our rambles in the Parks think over the matter and *that* is our explanation of the change!

(By the bye: I am fully aware that I have your valuable approximate reproduction of your letter to Alexander, and Alexander's answer—both, about his Giffords. I have still not properly studied these Papers; and wanting to find them just now, had to give up the hunt for the moment—they are not with your many other letters. I promise to return the 2 Papers carefully, when found out and properly digested).—

Let me tell you, first, how grateful I was for your kind and useful impressions and suggestions as to my *interim* volume. The affair has dragged on with somewhat depressing slowness— Dent[128] seemed unable either to refuse the book or to conform to the minimum concessions which Thring,[129] of the Society of Authors, considered I must insist on. But the day before yesterday, on Twelfth Night we signed and exchanged the copies of an Agreement which embodied Thring's main point—that, tho' Dent does not begin paying me anything till the 1000th copy has been sold, yet that he, D., pledges himself to print, in the first Edition, not less than 2,000 copies. —I have, ever since you left, with very few and short breaks, devoted all my weekday mornings to sorting out and correcting—improving, I hope, the form of—the papers to be printed. I have dropped all the biographical sketches; have let fall, not only the Eucken article (thanks to you, Friend!) but also the one on Campbell's 'New Theology'. (C. declares he has changed his view since then, so I thought it hardly chivalrous to attack, however courteously, his old positions in his person). I have also omitted the 'Idea of God' paper, partly because I doubted whether the bit of it (the introductory, critical bit of it) which you read, had much impressed you; but still more, because the second, directly constructive part still required writing out— only its skeleton existing so far. I am reserving these materials for my God book. —And finally, I am omitting a Letter upon Moral Evil and Theism which I wrote to Fogazzaro's[130] granddaughter, because my R. C. friend and critic Edmund Gardner,[131]

[128] This is the London publishing firm which produced von Hügel's books.

[129] George Herbert Thring (1859–1941), British solicitor, educated at Hertford College, Oxford, and, after two years in an office on the Stock Exchange where he gained considerable business experience, was articled to a London solicitor and from there practiced on his own; Secretary of the Authors' Club, 1891–1906 and 1935–1937; Secretary of the Incorporated Society of Authors, Playwrights, and Composers, 1892–1930.

[130] Antonio Fogazzaro (1842–1911), Italian novelist and senator; involved in the liberal Catholic movement for Church reform and reconciliation with the Italian

government during the modernist crisis of the first decade of the twentieth century; condemned by the Vatican.

[131] Edmund Garratt Gardner (1869–1935), British scholar of Italian literature, educated at Beaumont and Gonville and Caius College, Cambridge; abandoned medical studies for the study of Italian literature and history; Barlow Lecturer on Dante, University College, London, 1910–1926; Professor of Italian Studies, Manchester University, 1919–1923; Professor of Italian, London University, 1925–1934; trusted friend of von Hügel's and his literary executor. See *Diaries*, 20 and 22 June 1910.

thought at least some of our R. C. fellow believers might be shocked (I *think* he was a little himself) at my insistence that so much is the sex instinct, in whatever may be its healthy, ideal degree and kind essential to the human being, at least for this life, that we must, if we would not be Doketists as to the humanity of our Lord, assume its presence (of course also its perfect control and profoundest spiritualisation) in Jesus Himself; hence even more so, or at least as much so, in His Mother. I still feel this so strongly, and the argument looked so little driven home, after I had (tentatively) omitted all reference to the case of Jesus and Mary, that I (somewhat reluctantly) decided to drop this Paper altogether.—Could you some day get out of Professor William Paterson how he feels about this point?

I had not expected E. G. to be shocked at this point at all, and yet he *was*. I had expected him to be alarmed at quite another point, but he was *not*—not a bit. He accepted, thanked me for, and urged the publication of, my Paper on the *Parousia* in the actual teaching of Jesus, a paper based throughout upon H. Holtzmann's masterly sections in the *N. T. Th.* I trust he is right, and that this my Paper will not seriously perturb, or at least will only perturb on to eventual benefit, any or many of my readers. But I have now done my best as to the prudential matters, and will peacefully abide by these two, negative and positive, decisions.—

I have loved to retain, and still more greatly to improve, I think, the two, especially the 2nd Paper upon Troeltsch's analysis of Christianity. I was glad to find how greatly you, Friend, had helped me in epistemology towards much firmer grasp of what is wanted in those matters in T. —You will, I hope, read these two Papers when they are out, although, in very truth, you can get more out of T. alone, if and when you read him on a large scale and with close scrutiny. (By the bye, I have remembered with interest that T. also, for long, in his letters to me, and indeed in his printed articles, deferred to Eucken and was glad to be classed with him, declared himself E.'s disciple etc. True, he has not done so for the last 7 or 8 years, yet not, I think, with any clear sense of the inferiority of E. —My impression persists that as an exponent of the systems and tempers of mind of others, i.e.

especially in his 'Lebensanschauungen' E. is really good. Certainly James Ward distinguishes clearly between E. when thinking out a scheme of his own, and E. when drawing out and appraising the mind of others. I have heard him say to me as to the latter: there E. is better, very much better, another man. *That is different!*)[132]

Well, I now can hope to have done with the *Essays* by the end of this month till their printing I believe in June. Dent is pledged to have them out before Oct. 20; and he now writes he will publish them in September. —As soon as I have done them all up, inclusive of the Preface (which however we will print last, with, I hope, some good final touch's introduced into it after I have seen the whole body of the book in print) I will turn, oh how gratefully and happily, to my book, getting on a good bit, I hope, before the long vacation.—

I have had especially two big experiences in my life since you were here.

For one thing, a Mrs F. R. Lillie, wife of the Professor of Biology of that name at Chicago University, came to Europe and to London, and, a woman of 53, alarmed but at last reassured me by her determination to go over to Rome. She is the daughter of a self-made American millionaire (now dead)—her brother is American Minister at Tokio. Her husband and his brother (also a scientist and Professor) are Canadians, British subjects, by birth, and were originally Presbyterians, but are now just clean lived spiritual minded men who, I take it, are at heart still Theists and who I am not sure would admit straight away the designation. She herself has all along had a strongly agnostic bent, with a strain of mysticism of an increasingly R. C. type checking, or alternating with the agnosticism. A somewhat crotchetty woman: would not be married in the Episcopalian Church, since she could not promise to 'obey' her husband—they were married by a Congregationalist Minister; was and is so much 'for and with the people' that she insisted upon being a picket in the strikes (in, I

[132] Kemp Smith had persuaded von Hügel to omit from his forthcoming book an essay on Eucken because Kemp Smith considered Eucken a second-rate thinker and felt that von Hügel treated him as first-rate in the essay. *Diaries*, 30 September 1920.

think, her Father's works); and, tho' she had 5 children of her own (four remain), carried thro' her determination to adopt three more. As she said with pretty smiles, her poor man has had to suffer not a little at her hands. And then she has gone and crowned her excentricities with this Popery. I first heard anything about her directly from herself, telling me of her going up to a log-cabin in the mountains for her Lents with my 'Mystical Element' for her sole reading. I was of course glad if this book helped her, but I did not expect, nor indeed did I actively wish, that she would go the very long, yet apparently irresistible, for her own best self irresistible, road she has actually travelled. Her fine old mother-in-law, still a definite Presbyterian, called upon me here and wanted to make sure that I understood, or even merely *could* understand, how greatly she and her sons disliked all Romanism. I think I was able to convince her that [there] was one considerable side of average Popery which I disliked as much as even she could do. Then, too, she wanted to know why the daughter-in-law should not be satisfied with all the elaborate ritual of the High Episcopalian Church she had been frequenting these last few years: was it not petty to attach so much importance to this or that further ceremony? To this I answered that I could promise to pour as much cold water as I could find upon any inclination to move for any such reason. But that my impression was that there was here no ritualist interest or *attrait* at all. That the daughter-in-law simply seemed possessed by an instinct that somehow, within the R. C. Church (an institution which, as such attracted her but little and, in part, repelled her much) there did exist, somehow, a more massive and a more penetrating sense of the supernatural than in any other body. Might this not be true? or, at least, might not the daughter-in-law strongly feel this to be true? And if she did, might not a moment come, when we really would have to let her go her way? The fine old lady agreed that such a point might be reached, but warned me that I should find Mrs F. R. Lillie distinctly unlike other people—not normal, altho' in her own way, very good.

Then came Mrs F. R. Lillie herself, after 3 weeks of Paris to London for a fortnight—an M.D., a humourous, shrewd, self-knowing woman, drawn by just one thing to Rome—the crowd, the praying poor in our Churches. Had spent her days in Paris in such crowds. Had seen in Paris also Père Léonce de Grand-maison[133]—a fine scholarly cleric, who told her, when she informed him she intended to come over to Rome: 'Well be slow, deliberate, circumspect; and if you find you *must* come and you do come—*don't expect too much!*'. Good!—she came on to London, and here she was actually received; and, on the evening of her reception she told me: 'I think it will stick: I do not remember ever feeling so Protestant as I felt today!' I believe I well understood *that*.

Since getting back to Chicago we have seen letters of hers saying how completely her husband is reconciled to her act—that they never were more united than they are now. But indeed it is interesting, and to me very attractive, to note how little *priestly* her religion is. A Francis—to be a Franciscan Tertiary, *that* is her *attrait*. So I was able to ask her mother-in-law, as she mourned the coming disgrace of the Lillie family, whether it might not, after all, be an honour for that family if one of its members were buried in a habit like unto that in which Dante was entombed? —As Mrs F. R. Lillie left for the station I gave her Mother Julian's 'Revelations of the Divine Love', A.D. 1360—such glorious things; and she said smilingly: 'Yes, beautiful; you remember the interior voice which warned her: "beware of priests!".'—

The second big recent experience came after this American episode, and once more tested the reasons and the extent of my Church appurtenance severely. My good friend F. T. Scotti[134] published the Life of his close friend Antonio Fogazzaro in June last. It is most carefully, beautifully written, but so entirely leaves

---

[133] Léonce de Grandmaison (1868–1927), French Jesuit theologian; taught theology to young Jesuit seminarians at Fourvière, France, and later at Hastings, England; became editor of *Etudes*, 1908, and founded *Recherches de science religieuse*, 1910.

[134] Francesco Tomassino Gallarati-Scotti (1878–1966), Duke of S. Pietro in Galatina, Prince of Molfetta, Marquis of Cerano; educated at University of Genoa from which he graduated in law; helped to found Popular University of Milan; co-editor of *Rinnovamento*, 1906–1907, a liberal, scholarly journal advocating ecclesiastical and political reform which was condemned by the Vatican; befriended and advised by von Hügel; fought in World War I; published anti-fascist newspaper until exiled from Italy; Italian ambassador to Court of St. James's, 1947–1951.

the *Liberal* in F., as something dead and gone, unstressed, that I wondered a little, whether it had been worth while to publish such a book thus severely restricted to a study of F. as a man of letters —to his writings, and to F. as a moral and religious character— to his interior life. But here comes—to his surprise (as he now answers me as much as to my own) a condemnation not even by the *Index*, but by the Holy Office, giving no reasons nor specifications. Our surprise is largely grounded upon the still undoubted fact that Benedict XV is so little Pius X, that Pius X's Secretary of State, Cardinal Merry del Val,[135] did all he could to prevent Cardinal della Chiesa becoming Pope. But behold Cardinal Merry has now become Chief executant at the Holy Office— doubtless a sign that, at least for the moment, the militant black party are again in the ascendant, tho' very certainly this time, not led by, but drawing with them, the Pope. I wrote to Scotti hoping he would show great dignity and moderation as to any question of acceptance, and to Fogazzaro's favourite daughter that Providence seemed determined upon a course different from that aimed at by her Father—that It appeared bent upon allowing these Roman Congregations, by their very excesses, to discredit their own acts. Scotti has answered that he has answered the summons to formal submission by declaring that even tho' not understanding the reasons that have decided this official act, he will respect the authority of the Church by a complete silence and abstention from every defence or attack; but that he cannot go further, and formally accept a Decree which gives no reasons no details no limits, and which he could not thus accept without an insincerity which would dishonour not only himself but the Church. —So far, so good. May this be the end of *that*. Maria Fogazzaro has not answered yet. —Meanwhile there was a fine, sober, strong article in the 'Corriera della Sera', comparing what Dante had said about worldly Popes and worldly Curia, putting even contemporary office holders into his *Inferno*, and what

[135] Rafael Merry del Val (1865– 1930), cardinal of the Roman Catholic Church, of aristocratic Spanish ancestry; educated at Ushaw Seminary, England, and the Gregorian University, Rome; Vatican Secretary of State under Pope Pius X, 1903–1914; fierce and intransigent persecutor of liberal Catholic thinkers and social reformers, among whom were von Hügel and his Catholic friends.

Fogazzaro had written, even in his most daring moods—how mildly, in comparison! And then it described the official solemn participation of the Church authorities in the sixth centenary celebrations for Dante, and the condemnation of Fogazzaro. Why this difference asks the writer? 'Because', he answers, 'Dante is dead 6 centuries and Fogazzaro is dead a decade'.

Two more simply bibliographical points to end with. —Do you know Professor James B. Pratt,[136] of Williamstown University, and his recent work 'The Religious Consciousness'? He has just written me a most cheering note, saying he thinks I will like his book at least as much as its notice in the Times Lit. Suppl., since so much of it was learnt by him from my 'Mystical Element'. He is soon to visit England.

Then you once asked me for a good book on the non-Jansenist, the non-Rigorist school in French ethics and spirituality. Exactly what you want does not exist—not good, says Henri Brémond,[137] an excellent authority. But he himself has just published, as the 4th volume of his really great 'Histoire Littéraire du Sentiment Religieux en France', Paris: Bloud, a history of Jansenist Piety, a criticism and supplementation of Sainte Beuve which you *certainly* ought to read. But the whole work—4 vols out and 3 more to come—is valuable. I hope the Edinburgh University or the Advocates Library takes in the work.

Now good bye at last. Forgive this deluge in return for your few drops, and give me soon something between the two. My wife and Daughter send their kind regards, and Pucky does the same.

Your aff. Friend

F. V. HÜGEL.

[136] James Bissett Pratt (1875–1944), American college professor of philosophy; educated at Williams College and Harvard, Columbia, and Berlin Universities; taught philosophy at Williams College from 1900; studied Oriental religions in India, 1913–1914, in Japan, China, and Siam, 1923–1924, and in Java, Indo-China, and India again, 1931–1932.

[137] Henri Brémond (1865–1933), French priest and literary writer; became a Jesuit, but eventually left the Society, 1904; friend of von Hügel's and various French and English modernists; his major work is the multi-volume *L'Histoire littéraire du sentiment religieux en France, depuis la fin des guerres de religion jusqu'à nos jours* (1916–1933); in 1923 he was elected a member of the French Academy.

Jan. 10. 1921   14 Lennox Str.
                                         Edinburgh.
My dear Baron von Hügel,

My Christmas vacation has been rather interrupted by an attack of influenza, mild in itself but weakening in its effects; & my
time-table has therefore been considerably upset. Otherwise I
would have written you sooner, to send you greetings for the new
year. Please do not regard my letters as demanding an answer,
tho', I need not say, a letter from you will always be more than
welcome. I know well how you have to husband your energy, &
how many calls there are upon it.

The other day I received a letter from my friend Bowman, &
enclose that part of it which refers to your "Christianity & the
Supernatural".[138] With what he says I myself fundamentally agree,
though he sets the natural & supernatural in greater antagonism
than I should feel justified in doing. I am hoping that when Sir
Henry Jones resigns his Chair of Moral Philosophy in Glasgow,
as he must soon do—he has not been able to take his classes this
winter—that Bowman will be an applicant; & if the Glasgow University authorities be wise, they will appoint him, even tho' he
has yet to give proof of his quality by published writing. Fortunately, he is known personally to some of those with influence
in Glasgow. He was my successor in the Lectureship there in
1906 until I got him over as a colleague in Princeton in 1912.

In rereading your 'Christianity & the Supernatural' I feel again
that the two instances you cite of humility—of Darwin & of Tiele
—are hardly in the same class with the others. You mentioned
yourself the Darwin instance: do you not feel the same regarding
the other? Are the arrangements for your volume of collected
papers now definitely made. Also, I hope your writing has been
making good progress.

My old & honoured teacher, Sir Henry Jones, is now entirely
disabled, but is bearing his malignant & depressing ailment with
heroic courage. He is indeed so ill that the 'Scotsman' has asked
me to write an obituary notice in appreciation of his academic

---

[138] See Appendix IV for that part of Bowman's letter which Kemp Smith sent to
von Hügel.

work. I have been making some notes, & find the task very difficult—not the less so, that I am in very partial agreement with his teaching; & doubtful of its entire beneficence as an influence. However there is much that I can very sincerely say.

Classes restart tomorrow, & I have much work to catch up with. So I shall content myself meantime with sending to Lady Mary & to yourself my kindest greetings. May the new year & the coming years make me worthier of the friendship you have so generously extended to me! Your photograph on my mantelpiece is a perpetual, (delightful as well inspiring) challenge.

Yours ever gratefully & affectionately
NORMAN KEMP SMITH.

P.S. I enclose a cutting from the Scotsman on Dʳ Whyte.

13 Vicarage Gate, W. 8. 13 Jan. 1921

Our letters have crossed. This is to make sure, by my earnest entreaty, that *you do not write again—not for a long, long time.* I have been slow in learning one thing about you; that you are indeed a healthy yet not an overstrong man. You require rest almost as much as I do. —I will return Prof. *Bowman's letter*, when I next write you in an envelope. —I am, of course, deeply grateful to you and to him about this his warm appreciation. One ¼ th of it would still make the writing of that Paper of mine abundantly worth while. As to the Church and a philosophical duty, I think his position is most plausible, indeed true if one does not take the Ch. very wisely and widely; but I do not doubt that some confusion of thought or the like lurks here. My new book will discuss this in its Introdⁿ As to *Sir H. J.*, I shd. be glad if you cd find space and inclination to praise his *Browning* book, and then, in his *Lotze* book (1895), the pp. 102–118 (surely, excellent!). But indeed I understand yr feeling abt his philos. generally. Thus I found his

'Idealism as a Practical Creed', 1909, so thin that I ceased thereafter to study him. —Darwin & Tiele are both *certain* mistakes, used as they are in '*Chr. & Sup.*' Am putting a note to say so. —I loved your letter.

> Gratefully,
> F. V. HÜGEL.

Jan. 16. 1921   14 Lennox Str.
                                                 Edinburgh

My dear Baron,

Your most interesting letter & card have been indeed welcome. Last night too I had a very pleasant visit from Mr Brodersen; & feel that our lines of communication have been very happily reestablished. Apposamy[139] also I enjoyed seeing twice: I was out of town most of his time in Edinburgh.

M[rs] Lillie I had heard of in U. S. A. & rather think I told you, or at least Lady Mary, about her adoption doings. Did she tell you how, after adopting the children, she had felt that the one thing still awanting to complete her household was a grandparent, & that she accordingly approached an apparently lonely old man serving in a draper's shop in Chicago, & had asked him if he would like to be a grandfather! He was duly installed in an ample armchair by the Lillie fire-side, & *his* duty—all members of the Lillie household having duties—was to drive the pony-cart that took the children to & from school. Otherwise grandfatherhood was his sole profession for the remainder of his days! There is a pleasing suggestion—somewhat American, it is true—of St Francis about this, is there not?

---

[139] Apposamy was a young Indian Christian from the south of Madras who was studying at Queen's College, Oxford. He called on von Hügel early in 1920, and the latter gave him a copy of Kemp Smith's Inaugural Address. *Diaries*, 14 January 1920.

I rejoice to hear that arrangements have been completed for the publication of your volume of essays and addresses. May I make a plea for modifying your reference to Socrates in 'Christianity & the Supernatural'? How, after reading the 'Apology', you can speak of his outlook as 'dry & shallow', I cannot understand. And on Burnet's view of Socrates the Pythagorean, & therefore mystical, elements of his teaching have—if we accept it, as I am myself inclined to do—to be more fully recognised.

I have been meaning to try how W. P. Paterson will react to your 'Christianity & the Supernatural', but have not yet done so. I shall soon, on first opportunity. He has very considerable influence here, especially in appointments to the Gifford Lectureship. He is *very friendly*, as it is, to the suggestion of your appointment here; but I hope to enlist his *more active* participation, tho' owing to Pringle-Pattison's appointment (made just before I came) to be *followed* in 1923–4 by Bergson's second course, next nomination is a considerable way of [*sic*]. Glasgow, after Sir Henry Jones, has one series (the second) still to come from A. J. Balfour. Latta (Logic Chair in Glasgow) I was glad to hear saying some ten days ago that you ought to have been appointed before this to a Gifford Lectureship. When it comes to an actual appointment all sorts of influences are at work: but I hope for the best—& that, for me, would be to have you in Edinburgh. But if Glasgow had the wisdom to step in ahead of Edinburgh, I should congratulate Glasgow very heartily. These things, like all else, are on the knees of the gods!

Stout has restarted his Gifford Lectures, & I enclose his syllabus. A cursory reading of it leaves me *very* disappointed. He has not been moving in the direction I had hoped, to a genuinely realist view of knowledge. His universal mind seems to me to come in much too easily, & chiefly to *buttress*—indeed to afford *justification* for—his subjectivism: not much of a compliment surely to the U. M. Stout is another example of how it is well-nigh impossible for the professional psychologist ever to become a philosopher—don't you think? The tares that he sows as psychologist spring up & choke his intimations of deeper things. Stout has indeed been struggling valiantly to break away: that, however, is over. Evidently he has at last long [*sic*] heart, & capitulated unconditionally to the enemy. Objects, he declares, can exist only so long as they are being experienced: they 'belong to the mind-complex'. Don't you agree with me that the dependence of objects on mind is a question for theology & is *not* established by any valid theory of knowledge?

Bowman (he is about 35 years of age, & has lost (for philosophy) 5 years in the army) has been greatly influenced by Tolstoi (as I once was also) & (an enthusiasm I could never share) by Dostoievsky. His present excessive insistence upon dualism is, I should conjecture, a phase that will demand & receive from him many qualifications. It is a very healthy starting-point. Bowman has great things in him, & especially a quite unusual strength & fineness of character which impress even those who know him less intimately. In a Chair of Ethics he could do much for philosophy. Heaven knows that moral philosophy stands in need of more competent handling in our philosophical Chairs!

I have always heard J. B. Pratt very well spoken of. Owing to a trivial contretemps on our first meeting—my not knowing who he was—& my forgetting his name & face on again meeting him —we started off unfortunately, & though I met him again several times never came, as I should have liked, to be better acquainted with him. Williams College is one of the best of the New England Colleges, & one of my Princeton students, now back in Princeton as an Assistant Professor, was assisting Pratt at Williams last year & liked him greatly.

Many thanks for your reference to Henri Bremond: & also for all your other news, which is immensely interesting.

Yes, I have a miserably small stock of *reserve* strength, & am driven to economise it in every way possible. But my health is growing steadily, however slowly, better with the years, I think. With kindest greetings to all your household, not excepting Pucky.

Yours ever affectionately,
NORMAN KEMP SMITH.

Jan. 19. 1921

J. W. Scott,[140] formerly Lecturer in Moral Philosophy in Glasgow, was appointed last Spring Prof. of Philosophy at Cardiff. As you will gather from his letter he is *still* befogged by Hegelianism, & still not quite sure that the moral ideal is *not* self-realisation. But he is moving towards better things.[141]

N. K. S.

March 27. 1921

14 Lennox Street
Edinburgh

My dear Baron von Hügel,

The Second of our Terms closed on the 18th, whereupon I spent the week-end with a friend at Melrose, & on getting back to town on Monday at once fell victim to influenza. My wife (she is needing a holiday much more than I am) & I had planned going this past week to Provence & possibly also North Italy. But now that we have been thus delayed & I have to be back by April 18th, we go direct on Wednesday to Antibes in the Riviera, staying at the Grand Hotel du Cap D'Antibes for at least the first week. We shall only have some 18 days altogether, but that is better than nothing.

I have so much to write you about, & so little time, in the hurry of detaching ourselves from entanglements, & indeed still considerable listlessness owing to the influenza, that I must write more briefly than I had wished.

Your review of Heiler's 'Das Gebet' is splendid.[142] I can so heartily agree with your 'et-et' method, & with what you say about remaining in the crowd for our own sakes, & about the needs of

---

[140] John Waugh Scott (1878–?), Scottish philosopher, educated at Glasgow University where he was assistant to Sir Henry Jones, 1905; Mills Professor of Philosophy at the University of California, 1921–1922; associated with Sir Arthur Rose in working to alleviate unemployment in Scotland.

[141] With this brief covering note Kemp Smith sent von Hügel a letter which he had recently received from Scott. The letter is found in Appendix V.

[142] "A Great Book on Prayer," *International Review of the Missions*, 10, No. 38 (April 1921), 266–70.

sense & of society for us all. All that you say in these connections, & also regarding the need of hard-headedness represents so much that I have been learning from your writings. But it is a long, long way from this to the orthodox Catholic doctrine of sacraments; & in the latter the hard-headedness seems to me personally to be entirely lost sight of. However, very happily for me, I can deeply profit by what you say, this reservation notwithstanding.

Stout gave his last lecture on the 18th, & I had to move the vote of thanks to him. I took some trouble in preparing myself for it, & was glad I did. His wife & son from Oxford were present; & Stout was evidently touched—saying so himself—by what I said. As a *lecturer*, he is most unsatisfactory; but I have obtained his complete MSS from him, & find that I have to form a much higher estimate of their value when thus read in detail. He is steadily moving more & more consistently in the direction of idealism, though his subjectivism in certain fundamental respects has accentuated rather than weakened. At the same time his increasing divergence from his Master, James Ward, is very pronounced. Altogether I feel that his Giffords will be a very considerable contribution to the literature of pure philosophy.

He and Mrs Stout stayed with us lately. There is a simplicity & genuineness about him that I admire & appreciate the more I know him. He feels somewhat isolated in St Andrews; his colleague, Taylor, is very difficult; & Burnet, apart from College business, lives in almost complete seclusion.

The past term has been a very busy—*over*-busy—one. My teaching has gone really well in all my classes, & that is cheering. For the past two years I have given my best energies to making a really good start in this respect, & feel that I have succeeded. And in a University, where traditions among the students regarding classes & teachers counts for much, this is a great gain. I shall hereafter feel more at freedom to think of my own work.

Very regretfully, I shall probably drop my W. E. A. class. It has been a great pleasure to me to teach it, & the extraordinary gratefulness of these adults—I started with an enrolment of 66, & finished with an enrolment of 99—makes one feel that much should be sacrificed for its continuance; but on top of the other work, & lasting 2 hours at a stretch, & necessitating the expenditure of more energy than goes to teaching an ordinary class of juniors, it takes too much out of me, I fear. However I shall keep on the Presidency of the Bench, & find ways & means of doing what I can.

In the coming Term I have only 3 hours per week to the large Degree class, & rejoice in the leisure I shall have till October. There are a few matters, especially regarding the theory of knowledge, that I mean to write out, & shall send you some notes upon them. They will serve to make clearer points in my *Commentary.* I shall welcome your criticisms, if you can spare the leisure.

Recently I have been reading Father Tyrrell's[143] letters, & have copied out in full your glorious letter on mysticism.[144] How brilliant a creature Tyrrell was, & considering his powers of insight and of feeling, how unstable! His enthusiastic appreciation of Sir Henry Jones's 'Browning'—(a book I have never been able to read, perhaps because I benefited so greatly by his class-teaching & had got there what he has to say)—I was glad to find, for on finishing this letter, I must write him again. He is passing through the Dark Valley, under the most distressing circumstances of great pain, sleeplessness etc. His son—an Indian Army Doctor, D.S.C. & a splendid fellow—is in attendance upon him in Wales, & keeps me informed of his condition.

I delayed giving W. P. Paterson your article until an auspicious occasion offered, & in the absence of that gave it to him at a recent Senate meeting. The influenza has prevented me seeing him again, except at Stout's last lecture, where there was no op-

---

[143] George Tyrrell (1861–1909), Irish convert to Roman Catholicism who became a Jesuit and priest; expelled from the Society of Jesus because of his liberal thought, 1905, and excommunicated for his outspokenness against clerical abuse, 1907; brilliant reform-minded apologist and liberal theologian; considered by the Vatican to be the chief English modernist, and condemned as such; close friend of von Hügel's for the final ten years of his life. For a thorough and scholarly exposition of Tyrrell's thought, see David G. Schultenover's *George Tyrrell: In Search of Catholicism* (Shepherdstown, W. Va.: Patmos, 1981). For an account of Tyrrell's interaction with some individuals mentioned in the von Hügel – Kemp Smith correspondence, see John David Root's "George Tyrrell and the Synthetic Society," *The Downside Review,* 98, No. 330 (January 1980), 42–59.

[144] The letter from von Hügel to Tyrrell to which Kemp Smith refers is found in *George Tyrrell's Letters,* ed. M. D. Petre (London: Unwin, 1920), pp. 40–44.

portunity of talk. But I shall be calling upon him when I get back. I was hoping that I might be able to see you while *ên route* for Antibes, & to introduce my wife to Lady Mary & yourself, but the delay makes this impossible, even if you *are* in London. We reach London late on Wednesday evening, & leave by very early train on Thursday, to catch express from Paris the same evening.

Now you *must* not regard this as requiring an answer. Your energies are too precious to be squandered in any such way. Meantime with kindest greetings, & the best of good wishes for your health & work, Yours ever affectionately

NORMAN KEMP SMITH.

Next term I mean to get back to Holtzmann, reading a little each day.

2nd April 1921
13, Vicarage Gate,
Kensington,
W. 8.

My very dear Friend,

I really must not wait longer for the full leisure I would require to write to you properly, but will just do so *tant bien que mal*, which, after all, is pretty well our enforced way with almost everything we manage to do at all. I want all the more not to delay because only thus would I catch you in the sunshine at Antibes more at leisure than in Edinburgh for your friend's odds and ends of news and impressions. Especially too—and I must begin with this—because my wife and I want you both to understand how gladly we will sleep you both here, if, on your way back, you can and will stop a night in London—or better still, two. My wife begs me say, with her kind regards, that there is only one limiting condition attached—that it should not be for a Saturday night, when we could only take in one of you. But all the other nights we cd. easily manage you both; and we much want to see Mrs Kemp Smith. To know a married man and not to know his wife is, indeed, a very lopsided affair!—

Meanwhile I am delighted that you should both have the sunshine and the wonderful blue sea for a bit—a very short bit, alas! —so short that it feels a bit of selfishness to try and tempt you to curtail this rare change. So do not worry, please, about the above proposal, unless it somehow fits in with your plans and needs. But if you do not stop with us now, I trust we may meet somewhere and for a bit before we both get back to work—during the long vacation.

Now, first for your very interesting letter, which, as always, I loved to get; and then for my own news.

I was *most* interested, cheered and reassured by what you tell me about Stout. I have so much loved his series of epistemological papers in the Procs. Arist. Soc., I so cordially like the utterly modest, humble man, that it pained me to think he had gone back —had become more, and not less, subjectivist. But now I can believe, on your most competent opinion working upon much material, that the change, such as there exists, is really upon the whole, in the right direction. I *am* glad. And tho' I care for James Ward also—indeed tho' I know him personally much better than Stout, I expect to find that Stout's moving away from W. is on points where I have long felt W. profoundly unsatisfactory—as to his Panpsychism and the like.—

As to your own working out of certain epistemological positions, I am sure to learn LOTS from your mss, so please get them tidy as soon as you conveniently can and let me gratefully profit by them.—But you are not, I hope, losing your book 'The Conception of Man in the XVIIIth Century' out of mind: *that* will be your first (nobly, rightly) 'popular' book—it will do a huge amount of good, I am very sure.

I am sorry you have to drop your lectures to those highly intelligent *workers*; I so well understand how it must be a wrench to do so. Yet I do not doubt it is a wise step—you have not sufficient strength, physico-psychic force for those lectures given on top of your University work. And it delights me to think that you will now only have those three Lectures to your Honours Class a week—leaving you fine time for study and incubation and writing. And then you do keep in some real touch with the workers by continuing the Presidency and thus, I suppose, addressing them more or less informally every now and then.

As to Prof. Bowman's Lecture, I will venture to keep it till you are home again, in hopes of being able to read it before then— the subject greatly attracts me. I am as full worked just now, as my brain- and nerve power will hold, and it is strange how easily those poor instruments become feverish and restless the minute I bring them even slight additional work when this does not fit in with the main work I am busy with at the time.—

As to Tyrrell—yes, his strength and his weakness were what you say. Henry Jones's 'Browning' I had first read and greatly admired, and then I won an easy convert to it in Tyrrell who revelled in it.—

I am deeply grateful for your caring about my 'Mysticism' letter to him, and for what you say about my Heiler review. Such words from yourself make me feel my labours well worth while even if they led to nothing else. Of course I am grateful for the criticism also. I will only say now as to Sacraments that I have been practising and testing them in and for the spiritual life for over half a century, and that I have found them for myself of the greatest use, and in very truth extensions and applications of the principles which you yourself so clearly see and so firmly accept.—

This leads me, quite naturally, over to your past, very wise and helpful 2 criticisms of my 'Xtianity and the Supernatural'. I have carefully studied John Burnet on Socrates—his indebtedness to the Pythagoreans and Orphics etc. You and he are quite right, I am sure. So Socrates has disappeared from that passage of mine, and Confucius has gone in—he and Bentham really do there, I think. —Also I have dropped those Darwin and Tiele anecdotes —you and other friendly critics are quite right—they are charming but not of the heroic and supernatural type. A much less immediately attractive example has taken their place, but one which is *essentially* heroic and supernatural. I have also, I believe, strengthened the Paper in its wording here and there. It is to stand as the last in my 'Essays and Addresses'—the volume to be out in September—I hope Sept. 14th, Dante's six hundredth death day. I have dedicated the volume to his great memory—that grand white[145] Catholic that I have loved ever since, his fellow townsman, I began to observe and to think, in his and my beautiful Florence.[146]—

You may be interested to hear that the Swedish Lutheran Archbishop Soderblom[147] writes to me somehow more argumentatively, and less pleased, about this article than about my review of Heiler. Dr S. appears annoyed that God should have brought me to Him as He did: that the manner is very foreign to their ways in Sweden etc. But is *that* my fault and can I go and tell lies—making out my conversion to have been a satisfactory Lutheran affair when it was *not*? —Also he says that, after all, my supernatural good never excedes the Good! Well, of course not: God Himself does not exceed goodness—at least, outside of Swedish, Lutheran, circles! —He is going to address our LSSR on April 12 on 'Luther's Humour and Pathos'. I *think* he had thought of something more controversial about Luther, but that he has thought it wiser to select this theme which sounds to me more fit for some Literary Debating Society.[148]

I enclose you my letter on Cardinal Manning, which you may well have missed in the *T. L. S.* I am glad to have done it. I never much cared for M., but the legend about his feeling concerning his wife was a monstrous error, and here I have been able to kill

145 This is not a racial comment, but a cultural one. In the course of the Roman Catholic modernist crisis and his involvement in it, von Hügel referred to Catholics who sympathized with his own large aims and goals as "white," and those Catholics of a heresy-hunting and professionally orthodox mentality as "black." It is in this sense that he here uses "white" in speaking of Dante, since Dante too had his trouble with popes and Roman officialdom as any reader of *The Divine Comedy* will recall. See *Diaries*, 22 June 1910.

146 While his father was Austrian Minister at the Grand Ducal Court of Tuscany, von Hügel was born in Florence, Dante's native city.

147 Nathan Soderblom (1866–1931),

Swedish theologian and Lutheran archbishop, educated at the University of Uppsala; minister of the Swedish church in Paris, and then Professor of Theology at Uppsala, 1901–1914; became Archbishop of Uppsala and Primate of the Swedish Lutheran church in 1914.

148 Although von Hügel did not attend the LSSR meeting on April 12, he noted in his *Diary* that Soderblom spoke on "The Psychology of Luther as the Root of His Doctrine." On the following day the Swedish Archbishop and his wife had lunch with the Baron and Lady Mary at 13 Vicarage Gate, after which Mme Soderblom, in walking to a taxi, fell to the pavement and twisted her ankle. *Diaries*, 12–13 April 1921.

it beyond all chance of resuscitation.[149] I have to speak before our LSSR on 'Suffering and God' on May 2nd; to speak at Swanwick on July 3rd, and to get on with my book, which, D. G., is steadily progressing. Am learning a lot.

Yr v. aff. Friend
F. v. HÜGEL.

Hotel Crillon
Avignon   13th April 1921
My dear Baron,
    Very many thanks for your most welcome letter, & for your very kind invitation. My wife & I would have been only too delighted to take advantage of the hospitality of Lady Mary & yourself; but, as it happens, I have to be in Edinburgh for an early Tuesday morning lecture & we arrive late on Sunday evening, taking the 2 p.m. train from Paris, to allow me to catch the 10 a.m. train North on the Monday morning. If we came over Sunday night, we should simply be disturbing your household, & have no real opportunity of seeing you. My wife, however, expects to stay on in London & in Haslemere for a few days—her plans will depend upon a sister who lives in Haslemere—and she looks forward to calling upon Lady Mary some afternoon next week. She will take her chance of finding Lary Mary at home. I should greatly like that she should have the pleasure of meeting you both.

[149] *The Times Literary Supplement* (No. 999, 10 March 1921, pp. 149–50) carried a front-page leading review article on Shane Leslie's newly published *Henry Edward Manning: His Life and Labours* (London: Burns, Oates, and Washbourne). In a lengthy letter to the editor of *TLS* (No. 1001, 24 March 1921, p. 195), Baron von Hügel commented on the review and on Manning whom he had known, and communicated a fact which Purcell, Strachey, and Leslie had not recorded in their biographies (and apparently had not known). Common opinion held that Manning, as a Roman Catholic cleric, had never ever mentioned his wife, who had died before he had left the Anglican Church. But Herbert Vaughan (who succeeded Manning as Cardinal Archbishop of Westminster) was with Manning at his death in 1892, and shortly before Manning lapsed into unconsciousness he had given Vaughan an old notebook filled with prayers and meditations in Mrs. Manning's handwriting and from which, according to the dying cardinal, he had prayed every day of his Roman Catholic life. Vaughan himself related the fact to von Hügel on the very day of Manning's death, and, because no biographer had told the story, von Hügel now felt compelled to do so.

To your letter I shall make no attempt at answer—defering that until my return to Edinburgh. We have been enjoying our holiday immensely, especially Provence. Avignon entirely surpasses all my expectations; & we are seeing it in glorious weather. Today we were over the Palace of the Popes, & in the evening crossed to Villeneuve.

Your letter on Monday has interested me greatly. Strachey's 'Eminent Victorians' seemed to me a very vulgar-minded book, & though praised for its French 'lightness of touch' (! forsooth) is surely crude & coarse in a surprising degree. I was not therefore unprepared to find that on this particular matter he was as unreliable as in so many others. I return the cutting in case you have need of it.

My wife joins me in kindest greetings & thanks to Lady Mary & to yourself.

Yours ever affectionately,

NORMAN KEMP SMITH.

We expect to stay over Sunday night next at the Hotel Russell. P.S. I have tried to plan some way of seeing you, in my passing through London, but alas none seems practicable; & I am greatly disappointed.

14 Lennox Street,
Edinburgh.

June 6, 1921

My dear Baron,

Even though with the briefest of notes, I must break this long silence. Since I returned I have been very lethargic, & beyond reading through Tom Paine's works (with enjoyment & an ulterior motive), Macintosh's *Vindiciae Gallicae*, Fitzjames Stephen's 3 vols of *Horae Sabbaticae* (good), I have done little beyond my University teaching. Well yes, there is one other item to my credit. I have more or less completed the editing of some translations of Kant's Inaugural Dissertation (quite horrible Latin) & a couple of his other pre-Critical writings that were left in an unfinished form by John Handyside, a former graduate of Edinburgh & Lecturer in Philosophy at Liverpool, who was killed in the war. Probably the Liverpool University Press will publish them. Pringle-Pattison is arranging that.

Then there was the worry of owning *two* houses. This house is *full* of stairs & difficult to work, so my wife decided we must move; & we purchased another house at Term. No sooner had we done this than my wife, exercising the prerogative of her sex, decided we had better, for several reasons, *not* remove. So we have had two houses for the past fortnight, & the task of selling one or other, with the alternative of a very restricted income. It now looks very like the other going, so I rejoice there will be no removal for the present.

Lastly, there has been a cat & mouse game proceeding between Professor Seth[150] & myself. He is resigning the Chairmanship of the Executive Committee of the School of Social Study, after having held it for 5 years, & has had his eye severely upon me as his successor. He has a variety of reasons why it is my duty to take the Chairmanship: I have strong objection to this additional distraction. So it see-sawed. Finally, in a fit of extreme tiredness last week—it has had at least this good result to its credit—I wrote definitely refusing on any account to consider the suggestion. So that at least is settled.

My last lectures are tomorrow & next day to my big Degree class; & as usual I part from it very reluctantly on pleasant terms, but feeling how inadequate an account I have given them of my stewardship.

I am stupidly used up, but have hopes of work in the summer months, which we expect to spend almost entirely in Edinburgh.

Some weeks ago I demanded of W. P. Paterson what he had to say of your 'Christianity & the Supernatural'—to find he had, on my giving it to him, very characteristically at once, before read-

[150] James Seth (1860–1924), Scottish philosopher, educated at the Universities of Edinburgh, Leipzig, Jena, and Berlin; assisted Professor Campbell Fraser at Edinburgh University, 1883–1885; held professorships in philosophy at Dalhousie College in Halifax, Nova Scotia, 1886–1892, Brown University, 1892–1896, Cornell University, 1896–1898; and was Professor of Moral Philosophy, Edinburgh University, 1898–1924.

ing, mislaid, & it had not turned up again. I shall leave it now till your volume of essays & addresses appears. However I had the satisfaction of hearing him say that he felt very favourably to the suggestion of your appointment as Gifford Lecturer in Edinburgh. I don't base many hopes on that, but it is satisfactory so far as it goes. Though his vote probably counts for more than that of any one of the rest of us on the Committee, the Committee has some 14 members. One of them, our Prof. of Mathematics has two great interests in life, mathematics & mysticism—so I have good hopes of *him*.

Mrs Kemp Smith was sorry to miss Lady Mary: she rang up before calling but no answer could be obtained; & she went on, as it was her last afternoon in town.

But this note is only to send greetings & the best of good wishes for your work. By & bye I shall be able, when the degree examinations are over, to write out of an ampler leisure.

Yours ever gratefully & affectionately,
NORMAN KEMP SMITH

P.S. Lord Haldane sends me his new book: 'The Reign of Relativity'. I fear it is a sad & unreadable hodge-podge. But I respect him the more personally from meeting him twice in the past year: he has a kindly, & quite unembittered spirit. Evidently he is at his worst when [he] writes on philosophy, & I have taken the wiser line of acknowledging the gift before sampling it!

Aug. 8. 1921   14 Lennox Str.
Edinburgh.

My dear Baron,

I trust you are having a very real rest, with some good work thrown in, during these wonderful summer months. For me they have, since end of Term, worked more by laziness than by the fruitful labours I had been optimistically looking forward to: the fatigue of the rather foolishly strenuous winter is unfortunately still with me, & after some baulked attempts at strenuous writing,

I have been filling in the working-hours merely by translating Kant. I find the translating soothing & restful, like playing patience or doing picture-puzzles; & it has all the satisfactoriness of manual labour, with something always to show for the time expended. In the past month I have translated the sections on the Antinomies.

Adickes' large volume on Kant's *Opus Postumum* is very interesting. He proves conclusively—& much to Kuno Fischer's discredit in his violent controversy with Pastor Krause of Hamburg—that it is by no means a work of Kant's senility (though he was in 1796–1800 very much the invalid). Its main aim is to bring the empirical element in nature within the scope of a transcendental philosophy, thus curiously in some ways anticipating Schelling. Also Kant entertains, & seeks to develop a doctrine of Selbstsetzung, in the manner of Fichte. On these lines, however, as Adickes seems very justly to conclude, really getting nowhere. What is most valuable is (1) his doctrine of double affection, upon which he is very definite & eager—of noumenal self by noumenal object, & of sense-organs by empirical object, confirming (if it needed confirmation) the realist interpretation of his Refutation of Idealism in the second ed. of the Critique; & (2) his anxiety to demonstrate (at *great* length) that the thing in itself is not at all to be conceived as a second *object* behind the empirical, & that when so conceived it is a mere figment of the mind. Adickes shows (as one would expect) that there is, however, no justification for Vaihinger's view that Kant is here applying his 'als ob' doctrine to the notion of the thing in itself, & reducing it to the level of fiction.

What is also very interesting is that Kant throws overboard as unsatisfactory his proof of God's existence as necessary to combine virtue with happiness, & substitutes for it *Glaube* of a more genuinely ethical inspiration.

I was rather perturbed to find a heading in Adickes' table of contents: —'Das Ding an sich as "transcendentaler Gegenstand = x" '; for if, as this implies, Kant in the Op. Post. uses the phrase 'transcendental object', my contentions in the Commentary would be rather upset. However in *none* of the many quotations from the Op. Post given by Adickes does the phrase occur, & I fancy it is Adickes & *not* Kant who is using it. I shall write Adickes & enquire probably.

Adickes urges the publication of the Op. Post, though it would be a *very* expensive understudy; involving, to be satisfactory, typographical reproduction of all the erasures etc. of the original.

Troeltsch has sent me a copy of his Dante address, & I shall write acknowledging it. I have read it with admiration.

Did I ask you whether (as you must be) you are acquainted with de Maistre's 'Essai sur le Principe Generateur des Constitutions Politiques'. I only came upon it at the end of Term. It is extraordinarily interesting, & quite the most philosophical of his works—historically significant as an early anticipation of Bergson & other recent anti-rationalism. I fancy de Maistre must have been to some extent influenced by Burke, while going further on similar lines.

Another book from which I have got much is J. S. Haldane's Yale lectures—a small & readable book—on 'Organism & Environment as Illustrated by the Physiology of Breathing', quite the best & most helpful work I have come across on the general subject of vitalism.[151] Haldane was north, at end of Term, getting an LL.D., & I had some talk with him: he is very delightful. Also made the acquaintance of Ernest Barker,[152] now of King's College: an attractive soul.

[151] John Scott Haldane (1860–1936), Scottish scientist and philosopher, educated at the Universities of Edinburgh and Jena; from 1885 engaged in scientific research, lecturing and writing; held lectureships at Oxford, Yale, Glasgow, and Dublin Universities. Of interest, in the light of Kemp Smith's letter, are the comments of J. S. Haldane's older brother, Richard Burdon Haldane, in his autobiography: "My next brother, John, had already [1877] begun to develop the passion for biological investigation which has engrossed him through his career at Oxford and elsewhere. He was working at Physiology, with ideas of his own. He was interested also in Philosophy, and he and I wrote together the essay on the Relation of Philosophy to Science which appeared in 1883 in the volume to which I have already referred, *Essays in Philosophical Criticism*. In that essay we sought to demonstrate, from our respective points of view, that the phenomena of life were unintelligible unless there entered into the constitution of biological experience relations of a wholly different order from those of mechanism. He has pursued this theme undeviatingly since then from the standpoint of experimental science, while I have been occupied with it from that of the theory of knowledge" (*Richard Burdon Haldane: An Autobiography* [London: Hodder and Stoughton, 1929], p. 28).

[152] Sir Ernest Barker (1874–1960), British political theorist and educator, educated at Manchester Grammar School and Balliol College, Oxford; held positions at

Bertrand Russell's 'Analysis of Mind' is on behaviourist lines: he goes [*sic*] not go the whole way, but very nearly, & adopts Wm James' theory of the emotions!—which I fancy the latter-day W. J. had really given up: so do men's evil deeds live after them! Behaviourism, so far as I can make out, is simply a restatement in biological terms of the epi-phenomenalist view of consciousness. Naturalism could hardly go further, & in going so far is surely very much a *reductio ad absurdum* of itself.

On the 15th of this month I have to be in London for a meeting of the Nominating Committee for the Challis Chair of Philosophy in Sydney, recently advertised: I am member of it. Probably my wife will join me for a ten days holiday on the Yorkshire moors, as I return on the 16th—meeting at York or Darlington. We have to be in Edinburgh for the Brit. Assoc. meetings Sept. 7th to 14th, & thereafter join my wife's sister at Biggar for a fortnight.

We are both very ignorant of the geography of Yorkshire, but am trying to work it up from Murry's Handbook.

Please tell Lady Mary that a quite readable writer of detective stories is Isabel Ostrander, an American: 'At 1-30' & 'The Clue in the Air'. But she may already know of them. I have also by me, recommended by a friend, 'The Cask' by Crofts, likewise a detective story: but have not yet read it. "Lighting Up Time" by Ivor Brown, who I notice has recently two books published on 'Democracy' is very entertaining, likewise 'Simple Souls' by Hunter. You may judge of the relaxed & unstrenuous nature of my present existence!

With kindest greetings & best wishes,
Yours ever affectionately,
NORMAN KEMP SMITH.

Merton, Wadham, St. John's, and New Colleges, Oxford, before becoming Principal of King's College, London, 1920–1927; Professor of Political Science and Fellow of Peterhouse, Cambridge, 1928– 1939; his numerous publications brought many honorary degrees and other honors from universities and governments around the world; he was knighted in 1944.

The Red Lion Inn
Thursley nr. Godalming,
Please read red* at once.   Surrey.
Sept. 3–5, 1921

My dear Friend,

It was, as always, a deep pleasure and help to get your two letters of June 6 and August 8, as usual so full of homely details and suggestive reflexions. I trust you will continue, when you can do so without effort, thus to talk aloud to me—I find it a very real support for my inner life—one, in many a respect, like unto your own. I have not answered for so long simply from physical and psychical weariness—up to August 8 from my work, and since then—as now always in my summer vacation—from nature somehow crying aloud for drifting and do-nothing or its equivalent.

In your June letter I was glad indeed to find evidences of your not neglecting your 'Human Nature' book, upon the achievement of which within measurable time I have set my heart: Tom Paine, Mackintosh and Fitzjames Stephen will have furnished you with much further valuable material. And then the editing of those translations from Kant by John Handyside and—in August—the working on at your own translation of K's big Critique—this too is a fine continuation of your noble Kant labours. I feel pleased by your refusal of that Chairmanship of the Executive Committee of the School of Social Study, because tho' you would fill the post admirably, I have got to see, more and more clearly, that your health forces are sufficient indeed to your pledged work and duties, but to *not much more*. Wise living, then, demands pretty frequent refusals—refusals bound to be frequent in the case of so sought-after a man. But, of course, I am delighted you *should* be thus sought after.

As to your two houses, I hope that now, for quite a good while, they have become one again. My Bollandist friends tell me there exists no well-authenticated case of bilocation amongst the saints; but, in any case, bilocation is not desirable amongst philosophers!

* The line drawn under this sentence, as well as the marginal rule directing Kemp Smith's attention to the final four paragraphs, are written in red.

My wife and I much regretted not seeing Mrs Kemp Smith when she kindly called on us—we even, unjustly, grumbled that she had not warned us to be in by telephone. But this point, I now remember, I made clear by a P. C. to you. I much appreciated your kindly discrimination about Lord Haldane, your putting general character above specialis[t] competence. Fénelon would have approved of you, he who could not rest till he had got that over-fastidious ex-huguenot Carmelite, Soeur Charlotte de S. Cyprien away from her non-appreciation of all folk not of the very highest intellectual or spiritual gifts and achievements. Oh, Oh! what would some of Ld H's admirers say to this our confab. upon their hero!

And your kind thoughts and attempts as to my own work and prospects: I can but simply thank you for them and try a little to deserve them!

Your letter of Aug. 8, tho' written—as you declare—when very weary—is even more rich in food for my mind than the June one. All you write about Adicke's volume on Kant's *Opus Postumum* I find most deeply helpful towards my own new book. I must get that volume, and, with this your summary of its main points before me, utilize it as wisely as I can.

As to Troeltsch, I will take him in another connexion presently. But as to de Maistre's Essai sur le Principe Générateur . . .' I must confess at once, to my shame, that I do not really know it—firsthand and as a whole. I say emphatically 'to my shame', because my uncle, Clemens Hügel, was a devoted student of de Maistre —I possess his comple[te] copy of all de M's works. In this I have studied carefully one of the 'Soirees de S. Petersbourg' and a little of 'Du Pape', but none of that 'Essai': I promise now to read this 'Essai' very carefully.

Dr Haldane's Yale Lectures ought, doubtless, also to be considered by me; and Bertrand Russell's 'Analysis of Mind' may turn out very useful for one or other of my purposes.

As to my wife, she is getting a separate little holiday in Worcestershire; she will be most glad of your Detective Stories list, when she gets it after we meet and settle down again on Sept. 9.

You yourselves will now be having your last days in Yorkshire

before the British Association meeting in Edinburgh. Of Yorkshire I know only York itself, Scarborough and Richmond (the
last two very well). It seems clear that, even had I been in London on Aug. 15th, you could not have found the time for a meeting between us.

And now a few words about the chief doings and experiences
on my own part, during these last 3 months.

At the beginning of June John Nicolas Farquhar,[153] that Non-
conformist Scotchman and Indian Missionary specialist you are
sure to know something about, gave us, at our LSSR, a very careful and stimulating address on *Karma*. Since then, I got his 2nd
or 3rd call, and have now studied rather more than half his remarkably interesting 'Modern Religious Movements in India',
which will help me, on some points, with my book. I much like
and greatly respect the man—so clear sighted and so courageous,
so discriminating and so wise. I feel I have now made a real friend
there, and one of very genuine value. The book just mentioned is
hardly a great book—*that*, to my mind, his 'Crown of Hindooism'
really is; but it is a far more faultless book than is the 'Crown'—
which latter suffers from the author's Bible Christian bringing up
and his ignorance (contrasting so curiously with his mastery in
the facts and the criticism of Hindoo religion) of New Testament
criticism and Church history. He would be almost twice the
man he is, intellectually, had he studied and assimilated H. J.
Holtzmann's 'N. T. Theologie'. What about my closer friend's,
N. K. S.'s, progress towards the complete study of those 3 out of
the 6 parts of this great work? I am so very anxious that anything
N. K. S. may write, even indirectly, as to the Christian religion,
shall show clearly his assimilation of the large discriminations
worked out in that great book.

Then, beginning of July I was in Swanwick (Derbyshire), for
an 'Interdenominational Summer School of Social Service' where,
carefully eschewing the week-day subject-matters of a technically

[153] John Nicol Farquhar (1861–1929), Scottish missionary and professor of comparative religion, educated at the University of Aberdeen and Christ Church, Ox-ford; missionary in India, 1891–1923; Professor of Comparative Religion in the University of Manchester from 1924.

Economic or Political kind (worked out, in part, by fine specialists of a markedly non-denominational kind) I spoke, on the Sunday, as the second of 3 speakers (Mrs Creighton[154] being the first;
and Dr Selbie,[155] of Mansfield College, Oxford, being the third)
on the General World Outlook and the Help Afforded by Xtianity.
I tried to develop what I found to be the four chief weaknesses
and dangers of all Nationalisms, and the corresponding helps and
antidotes inherent in Christianity. My fourth and last danger and
help were the fierce materialism which largely possesses every
present-day Nationalism owing to the Industrialisation of modern life—the vehement competitive lust for coal, petrol etc.; and
the unchangeable otherworldliness, the theocentrism, of Christianity, in its central motive, evidence, and end. That groups and
outlooks of Christians had a real title to the great name of Church,
insofar as the[y] were thus primarily orientated to God, and His
Adoration, and not, in the first instance to man and his social
service.

How modest, Friend, we ought to be, not only as to the intrinsic
worth of our performances, but as to how far our hearers even
understand what we are at! An educated, intelligent-looking lady
stopped me as I hurried along a passage 24 hours after that immortal harangue of mine. She told me she felt it might cheer me
to learn first hand, from even one instance, how deeply I was
understood and appreciated. That she had been profoundly moved
by the passage in which I had insisted that Churches existed for
the worship of God. That her dear old Rector, in the village where
she lived, unfortunately kept his church locked on week-days. She
was now at once going to have this out with him, and, supported
by my impressive words, believed [s]he would succeed in getting
him to let his Church remain open on week-days. —I told her,

154 Louise von Glehn Creighton (1850–
1936), wife of Mandell Creighton, Anglican Bishop of London (d. 1901), and
writer; her publications are mainly historical, autobiographical, and editions of
her husband's writings. She published a
Life and Letters of Dr. Creighton.
155 William Boothby Selbie (1862–

1944), British Congregationalist minister
and educator, educated at Manchester
Grammar School and Brasenose and
Mansfield Colleges, Oxford; Principal of
Mansfield College, 1909–1932; Wilde Lecturer in Natural and Comparative Religion, Oxford, 1921–1924.

very sincerely, that this would be a good change and that I was glad of my long double journey if *that* was to be its result. And surely, we ought so to feel!

Then, shortly afterwards Professor J. B. Pratt of 'The Religious Consciousness' came to Vicarage Gate, with his very winning Italian, Roman, R. C. wife—a cultivated, spiritual-minded woman, evidently deeply happy with her man. They spend most of their holidays in some haunt of one of the great saints—Subiaco and Monte Cassino, Siena, Assisi, Avila. I am very sure that this contributes greatly to the balance and richness of this remarkable last book of his. We found, on comparing our experiences, that we both had, to our initial surprise, discovered the least balanced, the most easily captured by the last craze, to be the actual or future clerics of our respective countries (with I think the sole, and even there more seeming than real exception of the R. C.'s); and our explanations of this fact turned out to be identical. I was delighted to find that he lectures much to candidates for various Christian ministries; also how clear and firm he is as to the metaphysical, evidential character of all deep religion, and as to the persistent worth of moderate mysticism. I was only a bit surprised to find his book so largely occupied with questionnaires and their results—surely, a childish method, the unsatisfactoriness of which P. is, however, himself in process of seeing thro'.

Then, beginning of August and of my holiday, at Farnham Castle, the Bp of Winchester[156] had a meeting of Clerics to discuss Faith-healing, and asked me to speak a few words to these 12 men. I could not help feeling strongly the unreality, amidst all the amiability, of these men, when I felt myself driven to point out that, surely, the first question was not whether, in St Paul's time, such powers existed, or again whether there was now a demand for such powers, but simply, whether such powers—such, not official but charismatic powers—were now, in fact, working

---

[156] Edward Stuart Talbot (1844–1934), Anglican Bishop of Rochester, 1895–1905, of Southwark, 1905–1911, and of Winchester, 1911–1923, educated at Charterhouse and Christ Church, Oxford; he contributed an essay to *Lux Mundi*, and his open and tolerant views in religion eventually brought him and von Hügel into contact, with a resulting warm friendship.

among them. After all, St Paul had merely regulated, moderated those powers, unruly in their exuberance at that time. Did they find themselves thus pressed and tossed about by similar forces? That I was sure my own clerics were not: were *they*? And I then noticed a wistful, humourous look as it lit up the countenances of the more alive of my listeners.

Here, in this village, surrounded by lovely moors and endless walks I have done only two 'learned' things at all.

I have, for one thing, now finished a little over half of the text of Salter's 'Nietzsche The Thinker'—a *very* fine book; I thank you, Friend, most gratefully for urging it upon me. I am learning lots from it, for my work.

And, for another thing, I have ended by inducing Troeltsch to come and speak at the late July 3rd Christian Student Movement Summer School of next year (1922) at Swanwick. I will translate his ms. for him, and this will get typed in 100 copies for the 700 hearers he will have.—

Now here you come in; and *please, please*, don't say 'No' but 'Yes' and *as promptly as possible*. I want you too to come and to speak; that, in itself would be grand. But I want you also badly there, to help with Troeltsch. You know what a cripple I am with my deafness. I so much want a man at the meeting who knows German well, who hears all right, who appreciates T., and who could and would—especially with the questions and in the larger conversations—look out for T., explain to him when he did not entirely understand etc. I believe this visit of his to England (a week or 10 days with us after 3 days at Swanwick) may really do great good. Come and help to make it a success.

I can (apart from your huge activities already booked) think of but one objection—that the meeting might somehow commit you to some ecclesiasticism etc. If you suspect this, pray be reassured—the audience will be as many coloured, as non-committed as a whole as any one could wish. And yet your fine constructive fundamental side could have full play. Don't, don't say 'No'; say promptly yes to

Your aff. old Friend
F. v. HÜGEL

| The Committee which settles the programme for next year meets within not many days; hence my hurry for an answer.

14 Lennox Street,
Sept. 9. 1921   Edinburgh.
My dear Baron,

Many thanks for your most welcome & interesting letter. I did not reply by return as I have had three guests with me for the British Assoc. meetings. One of them, a former colleague at Princeton, a mathematician, has just left for Liverpool, whence he sails to U. S. A. tomorrow. Another, a son of the late Prof. Adamson, who is a Botanist is off for a week-end expedition to Ben Lawers. So I have a breathing space, before dinner, after which I am due to meet Lloyd Morgan at James Seth's.

I have been attending the Anthropology & Physics Sections, especially the latter, which had a very helpful discussion this morning on the newer views regarding the electron theory. Next week I hope to learn something regarding the *quantum* theory, which has only just risen upon my horizon, tho' I hear it has been prominent in physics for quite a number of years. There is also a 'relativity' discussion in which Eddington[157] takes part.

In order to profit by my Princeton Colleague's visit—Veblen[158] is his name—I have been reading Einstein's[159] own little book.

[157] Sir Arthur Stanley Eddington (1882–1944), British astronomer, educated at Owens College, Manchester, and Trinity College, Cambridge; Chief Assistant at the Royal Observatory, Greenwich, 1906–1913; Plumian Professor of Astronomy at Cambridge University from 1913, and Director of the Observatory there from 1914; knighted in 1930.

[158] Oswald Veblen (1880–1960), American mathematician, educated at the University of Iowa, Harvard University, and the University of Chicago; taught mathematics at Princeton University, 1905–1932; Professor at the Institute for Advanced Study, Princeton, 1932–1950; member of numerous learned societies

both in America and abroad, and collaborator in various international mathematical projects; President of the International Congress of Mathematicians held at Harvard in 1950.

[159] Albert Einstein (1879–1955), German theoretical physicist, educated at Luitpold-Gymnasium, Munich, and Technical University, Zurich; after teaching in Zurich, Prague, and Berlin, he came to the United States in 1933, and became a citizen in 1940; he discovered and was the chief exponent of the theory of relativity; awarded the Nobel Prize in 1922; appointed a life member of the Institute for Advanced Study, Princeton, 1933.

Though difficult, it is quite the most satisfactory piece of reading I have done on the subject. It is *always* best to go to original sources, when one can. I only get very *dim* notions of what Einstein is working to; but Veblen has helped me, as he used to help me in Princeton, quite a good deal. He had many conversations with Einstein when the latter spent 3 days in Princeton, & was immensely impressed by him. Einstein, he says, regards his theory as quite *empirically* based, & is ready to cast it overboard if the appearances conflict—regarding mathematics as merely an instrument of interpretation, & the simplicity or elegance of a theory as rendering it an object of doubt & suspicion rather than otherwise. Veblen was also much impressed by the simplicity & otherworldliness of Einstein himself, who rather regards his fame as obscuring the worth of those physicists & mathematicians from whom he has himself learned.

My wife & I never got to the Yorkshire moors. Just after I wrote you, a telegram came from her sister who has been taking a cure for neuritis in Aix-les-Bains saying that she was worse & asking her to come to her aid. So I went South alone, & had my former Princeton pupil with me for a week.

As to the Australian Chair it turned out, happily, that the two best applicants were Australians—one being McKellar Stewart, with whose book on Bergson you are acquainted.

On my way back to Edinburgh I spent a couple of days in Lichfield, partly for Samuel Johnson's sake, & partly to see the Cathedral, which surpassed all my expectations. My wife returns on Monday, & when the Brit. Assoc. closes on Wednesday, we join the little daughter for a fortnight in Biggar in Lanarkshire.

How splendid that you are inducing Troeltsch to come to England next year. I should be immensely interested to meet him, though I fear your estimate of my powers of talking German is very far from correct. I could never do more than *jabber* it, & even that dexterity I have well-nigh entirely lost. However, if I could be of any service at all, I should not like to decline your very kind suggestion, & should certainly do my best to come to the Swanwick Summer School. The difficulty of any ecclesiastical entanglement does not alarm me: if it does not *you*, it need not me. And by the way I am giving two lectures on—& against—Spiritualism in the beginning of October to a sort of Summer School for Scottish Episcopal Clergy to be held in Edinburgh. W. P. Paterson & my colleague Grierson (Eng. Literature) are also to be addressing them. Wildon Carr is here, & says there is to be a small Congress of Philosophy in Manchester about July 9ᵗʰ next year: he wants me to join in a Symposium on 'The Philosophy of History'—with A. E. Taylor & Collingwood.[160] The subject appeals to me, but not the symposium method.

But I must close, & that without referring to the many other interesting items in your letter. I sincerely hope you are rested & refreshed by your holiday.

With kindest greetings,
Yours ever affectionately,
NORMAN KEMP SMITH.

I enclose a syllabus of our next winter's W. E. A. courses. We have increased them from 17 to 24. Arrhenius[161] & Kapteyn[162] from Groningen are in Edinburgh.

[160] Robin George Collingwood (1889–1943), British philosopher and archaeologist, educated at Rugby and University College, Oxford; Waynflete Professor of Metaphysical Philosophy, Oxford, 1935–1941; formerly Fellow, Tutor, and Librarian at Pembroke College, Oxford, and University Lecturer in Philosophy and Roman History; published many original works and a translation of Croce's autobiography.

[161] Svante August Arrhenius (1859–1927), Swedish physicist, educated at the University of Uppsala; one of the founders of modern physical chemistry, and developer of the theory of electrolytic dissociation; offered a post at University of Giessen, 1891, but refused it to become a lecturer at the Technical University in Stockholm where he became Professor of Physics, 1895, and Rector, 1896–1905; refused offer from University of Berlin, and became Director of Physical Chemistry Department at Nobel Institute, Stockholm; received Davy Medal from Royal Society of London, 1902; won Nobel Prize for chemistry "in recognition of the extraordinary services he has rendered to the advancement of chemistry by his theory of electrolytic dissociation," 1903; received Faraday Medal, 1914.

[162] Jacobus Cornelius Kapteyn (1851–1922), Dutch astronomer, and Professor at the University of Groningen from 1878; plotted the stars of the southern hemisphere and discovered that all stars whose motion can be detected are part of one of two streams moving in different directions at different speeds.

13 Vicarage Gate, London W. 8.
   Oct. 11, 1921.

I was able—at last!—to send you your copy of my 'Essays' yesterday. I much hope that a good deal in what is there new to
you, may comend itself to your judgment—that of a half-dozen
such, at most, which I had in my mind all the time I was editing
these things. —I now write to beg you kindly to put on a P.C.
to me titles, publishers etc. of the wisest and most penetrating
books or articles read by you on *Spiritualism*. A country vicar
finds his parish much infected by sp.— He is a very honest, solid
man, but with only little discrimination—this latter would have
to be already done for him in the prints now sought for. If your
own Address is in print—*that* would be best of all.

Aff. Friend F. v. HÜGEL.

Oct. 13. 1921   14 Lennox Str.
                                            Edinburgh.

My dear Baron,

Very many thanks for your most welcome gift, made all the
more valuable & precious by the inscription, & by your kindly
reference to me in the preface. I am very proud to be even so distantly associated with your magnificent work. The preface is thus
far the only part of the volume that I have been able to read: it
is close packed with interest & suggestion, & makes me very eager
to get at what follows.

I find especially congenial your method of treating such problems as evil & the Parousia. Just these days, for my advanced
class, I am working at what is,—may I say?—a parallel view of
the categories—that we have to *think* substance & causality in
formal terms, & can *locate* them—saying they are here & here,
but are never in position to *specify*, that is, to profess *understanding* of them.

I like too—& it gives light that I was seeking—your distinction between the Patristic view of Augustine, that man is pri-

marily wicked, & the Scholastic view of Aquinas that he is primarily weak. Hitherto I have mainly read in Augustine, the Port Royalists & Calvin. That is why I asked you for the reference you so kindly obtained for me to a statement of the counter-position. Unfortunately I have not yet found leisure to study it.

But I must not attempt to write at length. Classes have just started, & I am rather swamped by work & a number of other engagements. Last week Sir Henry sent me his first three Giffords to make suggestions upon. I think his Gifford Series is likely to be the best of his published work. He is printing forthwith, as not likely to be able to deliver any more of them, & wishes me to help in seeing them through the press. I fear he may not survive to hold the work in his hands. Also I am addressing a few Trade Union Branches, to obtain their affiliation with the W. E. A. It is amusing; & generally involves a tustle with adherents of the 'Labour College' just started in Edinburgh this winter, in rivalry to our 'capitalist' W. E. A. And lastly, just these days two very elderly Aunts, who were very good to me as a boy, are seeking a house, that they may settle in Edinburgh, & I wish to help them all I can.

I fear I know of no *brief* author of the Spiritualist propaganda. Frank Podmore's 'History of Modern Spiritualism' (Methuen 1902) I recommend heartily, but it is in 2 vols. 'Spiritualism & Psychical Research' by J. A. Hill in People's Books Series (Jack & Nelson, London & Edinburgh) is the best quite brief account, I know of, but it is too favourable & non-commital. Still your friend, by reading it will be in some degree able to draw his own conclusions. The trouble is that those who dislike Spiritualism dislike it so heartily that they don't wish to write about it. I am urged to publish my 2 lecs. but hesitate as all my knowledge of it is at second-hand. Enclosed are summaries of them & a leader support[ing] my argument from the Scotsman wh. you can send on to your friend. I do not wish them back.

The past week-end I spent with Pringle-Pattison at the Haining in Selkirk. He starts his Giffords here in February—chiefly on immortality.

I also enclose (don't return, just destroy when read) a note expressing my view on a point—perhaps the main point—you criticised in my Inaugural. It will have nothing fresh for you, but I should like you to know the position I am taking & have any criticism of it.

With kindest greetings,
Yours ever affectionately,
N. KEMP SMITH.

14 Lennox Street
Oct. 30, 1921   Edinburgh,
My dear Baron,
I must again write to thank you for your magnificent volume of essays & addresses. For to the neglect of my duties, but to the great good of my mind and spirit, & consequently to the ultimate benefiting even of my University work, I have read through the volume, & am restarting on a rereading of it. Not in a very long while have I found any book so congenial, so inspiring, & so helpful in so many different ways. Your style has that personal quality which makes it, to me at least, more & more attractive, & lends to your argument an added charm & persuasiveness, from the sense it affords of being the outcome of a life's rich experience, backed by very much more than obtains expression in the logical steps of your massive argument.

On Thursday night last I was so unfortunate as to have to listen to an address by Prof. Herford[163] of Manchester on 'Approaches to Religion in the Literature of the Past 60 Years'. His 'Age of Wordsworth' I once read and liked, so I was interested to see and hear him. But alas, a drearier & more commonplace or less discriminating treatment of the subject it would be difficult to conceive. By his account no one—Wells, & Doistoievsky &

---

[163] Charles Harold Herford (1853–1931), British writer and academic, educated at Owens College, Manchester, Trinity College, Cambridge, and the University of Berlin; lectured at The Johns Hopkins University and University College of Wales, Aberystwyth; Honorary Professor of English Literature at Manchester University; in 1916 he delivered the Warton Lecture to the British Academy on "Is There a Poetic View of the World?"

Lowes Dickinson etc. etc.—each introduced with appropriate laudatory adjectives, had his contribution to the *ever*-deepening modern consciousness, & what the conclusion could be except the inerrancy of the human mind (!) in this field, I failed to see. Fortunately I had refused beforehand to serve the vote of thanks, and was not called upon to express my mind. Had I had to do so, I should have been tempted to refer to Malebranche's theory of swooning—that it is *not* due to the mind's losing consciousness but to its thinking of too much *all at once*. I wish Herford could be induced to read your opening address on 'Responsibility in Religious Belief'. I am sure he has sufficient intelligence to profit by it. But how many other people (including myself) are in the same position. I am glad you criticise Tennant.[164] I was annoyed some years ago, in Princeton, to find *such* a view in such a quarter. But I shall not attempt to refer to the many *positive* suggestions in this paper that delight me. There could not be a better introduction to the volume as a whole.

'Religion and Illusion' has very happily recalled the evening— I shall ever be grateful to Mʳ Mead's Society!—in seeing and hearing you for the first time.[165]

'Progress in Religion', especially in its view of the Christian development, & in its criticism (especially illuminating to me) of the violence & rigour of Sᵗ Paul & Sᵗ Augustine, & its references to

---

[164] Frederick Robert Tennant (1866–1957), British philosopher of religion, educated at Gonville and Caius College, Cambridge; held various ministerial positions in the Church of England, including curate of Great St. Mary's, Cambridge; University Lecturer in Philosophy of Religion, Cambridge, 1907–1913; Lecturer in Theology, 1913–1931.

[165] The essay on "Religion and Illusion" was originally presented in English (as opposed to its first publication in Italian in 1909) as an address by that name which von Hügel gave before The Quest Society at Kensington Town Hall on 29 November 1917. He was invited to speak to the group by George Robert Stow Mead (1863–1933), British writer on re-

ligious topics and editor of the *Quest Quarterly Review*, and fellow-member with von Hügel of the LSSR. About 150 people attended the address, including a number of friends, relatives, and acquaintances of the Baron's. These included, among others, his wife, second daughter, and brother; Herbert Weld-Blundell, Evelyn Countess de Vesci, Lady Encombe, Adeline Duchess of Bedford, Mrs. Stuart Moore (Evelyn Underhill), Rev. Albert Way, and Adeline Chapman (who did the proofreading for his first volume of *Essays and Addresses* in 1921). At the time of this meeting in 1917 von Hügel was unaware of Kemp Smith, although the latter apparently was in the audience of his hearers. *Diaries*, 29 November 1917.

the position of Aquinas, setting Nature & Supernature in place of Sin and Redemption. This is a distinction in many respects quite new to me, & it is what I have long—vainly—been looking around for. Your remark, in the Preface, on original sin as standing for human weakness & foolishness rather than for human wickedness I had myself been feeling my way to in the past ten years—but with no sufficient definiteness.

I note that on page 97 you refer to Ernest Scott[166]—now in the Union Theol. Seminary in New York City—a very interesting man, with a touch of genius. I knew him when I was a Lecturer in Glasgow & he was at Prestwick in Ayrshire.

In 'Preliminaries to Religious Belief' you supplement very helpfully certain considerations in your opening address. Your treatment of evil throughout this whole volume will, I am sure, be counted by a multitude of grateful readers, now and in years to come, as one of its greatest excellences—tho' I have difficulties regarding parts of No. 7 that I must reserve for further reflection on rereading. The parallel you draw between the parousia problem & the problem of evil, & your whole method of meeting the former is full of suggestion. You certainly do not in any way shirk the problem. Also that part of your teaching which reinforces what—among so many other things—first so attracted me in your 'Mystical Element in Religion'—regarding the necessity of the other activities of the spirit to the religious & vice-versa— form so *integral* a part of your argument, & give confidence when you stress the other truth.

Your summaries of Troeltsch, & your criticisms that follow, I have read throughout with very complete sympathy & agreement.

Nov. 3. I have been twice interrupted, by visitors etc., since I started this letter last Sunday. Sir Henry's proofs have been coming in at the rate of at least one lecture per day, & that, with my

[166] Ernest Findlay Scott (1868–1954), Scottish Biblical scholar, educated at Glasgow University and Balliol College, Oxford; Professor of New Testament Literature at Queen's University, Kingston, Ontario, 1908–1918, and at Union Theo-logical Seminary, New York City, from 1919. His numerous books include *The Apologetic of the New Testament* (1907) and *The Validity of the Gospel Record* (1937).

other work, has more than fully occupied my time. So far I have managed to keep up with the coming of the proofs, & am now starting in on his 11th lecture. The disabilities, very crippling, of his illness have not, I am greatly relieved to find, seriously affected the quality of his lectures, though they must have made the writing of them terribly hard. Indeed I think these Giffords will be his most important, & best, published work. I am so glad to be able so sincerely to write him cheerily about them. His last note makes the ominous statement that the disease is affecting his eyes.

In *many* main points I am in hearty agreement with Sir Henry's positions—and of yore learn't much from them—but the relative emphasis, the *atmosphere* of much of his thinking,—the very mention of contingencies is a red rag to him—& his way of speaking of reason as if it were, which it really is not even for him, a blessed divinity, & the source of all blessings, take much away from the real merits & beneficence of his work. I could wish— had he been younger it would be different—he might read and profit by your 'Essays and Addresses', but I know well the counter-influences are too strong to allow of his even beginning to appreciate what you can add to his own teaching. So I abstain from even recommending them to him—I mentioned your kindly references to him & the quotation from his Lotze.

This morning I had a letter from my friend Macneile Dixon —Sir Walter Raleigh's[167] successor in Glasgow. The religious consciousness—at least in some of its forms—has been more or less omitted from his make-up, distinguished & delightful, full of charm indeed, as that make-up his [*sic*]. So I have abstained, in his case too, from *summoning* him imperatively to read your book; & advisedly, as it appears. For he writes that he has come upon it & been looking through it. He knows well how I feel about your writings, & he deplores that he 'can make nothing' of the book. "They're subtle, but, alas, I can make nothing of him. I suppose it is that he's building on quite different foundations.

---

[167] Sir Walter Raleigh (1861–1922), British literary writer, educated at University College, London, and King's College, Cambridge; onetime Professor of English Literature at the University of Glasgow, and from 1904 Professor of English Literature at Oxford; knighted in 1911.

And when it comes to Heaven—and Hell [this essay by its title would especially draw Dixon's attention for he is writing a book on the nature of tragedy]—well, he's a dear, good man, but a vision crossed my mind of the mothers of men, the pious souls, 'oftener upon their knees than on their feet', praying for their sons.... Will they not care a damn & be happy among the blessed? I know, if my poor mother is not changed past all recognition, she will leave the angelic choir, & be down with me in the shades before eternity has got fairly started. But I suppose it argues an inferior & unspiritual mind in me to aire these problems. But we must just work with the instruments God has given us."

I am not sure I could myself whole-heartedly give adherence to your teaching on this matter: as I have said No. 7 is the one paper that I have most difficulty over.

But here am I wandering on, & disgracefully consuming your time, with this already too lengthy epistle. And yet instead of *really* closing, I shall threaten you with still another, with a few of my reflections on the later parts of the book, sometime soon, when leisure allows. For me they are by no means the least interesting portions of it.

Yours ever gratefully & affectionately,

NORMAN KEMP SMITH.

14 Lennox Street
Dec. 19, 1921   Edinburgh,
My dear Baron,

The Term closed on Friday. It has been a very busy one for me, as quite a number of unexpected outside engagements & extra work—all of it more or less unavoidable—kept cropping up. But it has also been unusually fruitful in various ways. I have got a series of lectures written for my Honours Class, developing further than I had previously succeeded in doing a theory of knowledge. Have also written a paper on Whitehead's[168] "Concept of Nature" for the University Physical Society, & a paper "In defense of Reason" for a Dining Discussion Club. One of the main extras has been the helping with Sir Henry Jones's proofs of his Gifford Lectures. I am more than glad to be of this little help to my old Teacher; but it has taken up half of every week for two months; & that has been one of the reasons why I have not written you sooner. Happily the terrible disabilities of Sir Henry's illness have not affected the essentials of his work: these lectures will, I think, be the best work he has yet published: they give the quintessence of what he has been teaching his classes for the past 30 years. All the paged proofs are now completed; & the book will no doubt appear before very long. You will have noted that Sir Henry's "Life of Edward Caird", as finally edited by J. H. Muirhead, was published a fortnight ago.

Two weeks ago I spent a Sunday with Sir Henry, & was at his second last Gifford Lecture. He bears up heroically: but it is to be hoped that now he has completed the Lectures, he will allow himself to be placed under anodynes. His doctor told me, however, that *conceivably* he may live for another 18 months or even two years. But the strain is so excessive both for himself and those about him, that a more speedy end may be hoped for. Even before this illness, they had a series of family tragedies. First their eldest daughter—the flower of the flock—died; then their third son; & during the war their youngest son was killed in France. The remaining daughter is a nervous invalid. Happily their other two sons are pillars of strength to them. The eldest, in the Civil Service in Brussels wrote the "Road to End-Or"—a book you must have heard of, describing his Spiritualist hocussing of the Turkish Prison-Camp, after his capture at Kirte.[169] The second

---

[168] Alfred North Whitehead (1861–1947), British mathematician and philosopher of science and religion, educated at Sherborne School and Trinity College, Cambridge; most of his adult life centered in Cambridge and Harvard Universities; in 1922 he was the first recipient of the James Scott Prize of the Royal Society of Edinburgh, and in 1927–1928 he delivered the Gifford Lectures at Edinburgh University; his ideas have greatly influenced the contemporary process theology movement.

[169] E. H. Jones, *The Road to En-Dor: Being an Account of How Two Prisoners of War at Yozgad in Turkey Won Their Way to Freedom*, with illustrations by C. W. Hill, 7th ed. (London: Lane, 1921).

son is an Army doctor, & after attending his father for 18 months had to return to India in November. Lady Jones, a very gentle & rather fragile creature of strong character, has come amazingly through it all. She and Sir Henry are living in a few rooms—they prefer that—in the top story of their house in Glasgow, with a niece in attendance upon them.

In November I got entangled in controversy with Dr Norman Maclean[170] of St. Cuthberts—the chief Established Church in Edinburgh—he is the junior colleague of Dr Fisher. He wrote a very violent article—as it seems to me, also a very vulgar one—against America, following upon his return from being a representative at the Pan-Presbyterian Conference at Washington. This he followed by a still more violent diatribe in a Sunday evening sermon, when he aroused applause (!) in his Church from an audience of about 2,000 by saying that U. S. A. is "bleeding us white" in payment of interest for munitions of war—the fact, of course, being that we have not yet paid a cent of interest. As no one else intervened, I felt that I must do so—especially as I had, as President of the Univ. America Club, to act as Chairman at its Thanksgiving Day Dinner (we have 27 American students here this winter) & could not face them until some reply had been made. So I indited a letter to the 'Scotsman', & then a second in reply to Dr Maclean's reply. After which, I am glad to say, "the rest was silence". St Cuthbert's is the church that Dr Pringle-Pattison is a member of; but I have been relieved to hear that he counts Dr Fisher alone his Minister & has so disliked Dr Maclean that he never attends when the latter takes the service. How Dr Maclean ever attained his present position I cannot understand: I do not like to think that it indicates (what it *might* be taken to show) a terrible decline in the personnel of the Scottish Established Church. I enclose cuttings of the letters & you may care to

---

[170] Norman Maclean (1869–1952), Scottish ecclesiastic, educated at St. Andrews and Edinburgh Universities; ordained in the Church of Scotland, 1892, and was a minister at St. Cuthbert's Parish, Edinburgh, 1915–1937; served as a chaplain in the First World War, and visited the United States and Canada in 1921; preached the inaugural sermon for the 11th Assembly of the League of Nations in the cathedral at Geneva, 1930; published many works of fiction, studies on social and religious questions, and an autobiography.

glance at them. (I find I have no copy of D^r M's.) But these are my only copies; & I shall be glad to have them back. I have a very real affection and admiration for America & Americans; & have felt very strongly in this matter.

But to turn to happier themes. I took advantage of my renewed leisure since Friday to reread part III of your "Essays and Addresses". Your article on "The Catholic Contribution to Religion" has been most welcome—further comment thereon. This is certainly not the least interesting & valuable part of your book —which, indeed, is surprisingly unitary in argument & impression, notwithstanding the occasional character of so many of the papers.

On p. 233 (8 lines from foot of p.) you express, very emphatically, as "truly Catholic" what so many of us outsiders feel to be a great defect of the Catholic Church: it seems to be *committed* to treat as final what is not final. Do you think it is capable —well, I need hardly ask: I know that you do—of making again the great effort it made so successfully in the Middle Ages—of assimilating to itself, & of adjusting itself to a newer and different world? Certainly when you expound your *Ideal* of the Catholic position, I find it difficult not to give you my hearty adherence on many perhaps most points, tho' not, I fear, on doctrinal points that to you are the most vital of all. Your view of Nature & Supernature, as the really fundamental distinction, I find most illuminating & am obtaining from it much real help in my own difficulties. It is what I have been myself obscurely trying to work to —very unsuccessfully—& many things fall at once into place, when you propound & illustrate it—as you do from start to finish in this volume. Your contrast of Catholicism with Protestantism is most masterly,—if I may presume to praise it—& gives me much food for reflection—more than I am yet in a position to digest. Even should you, in the main, achieve only the bringing about of a better understanding each of the other, I can think of few things more worth doing at the present time. In my 'Defense of Reason' I worked in some most helpful points from your reference to the Protestant sympathy with the Occamist position.

I like your phrase (p. 255)—"the half-educated man: the Individual".

p. 268–9. Your distinction between "necessary" realities of religion & "deductions or details" seems to me, from a "Catholic" position, one that needs much elucidation. Your sentence on p. 269 that the historical nucleus has its "unshakable foundation" "*not* in the God of Revelation & Supernature, but in the God of Reason & of Right Nature" etc intrigues me greatly: & the "and both" at end of sentence appears to me to indicate that you are yourself doubtful as to whether you can really commit yourself to this assertion. Or am I misinterpreting the 'and both'? Christ in the Trinitarian sense, which to you is *the* great strength, is to me *the* great stumbling-block. Is this, by your contention here, an ultimate part of the "sufficient nucleus"? Troeltsch, as I remember, has indicated that he is not willing to equate the Religion of the Future with any such position.

On p. 272 is 'Dominion' a misprint for "Dominican"? Again reading your concluding Address on "Christianity and the Supernatural", I find it even more inspiring than on previous readings: it takes time for me to *grow* into the positions you outline. But coming as it does after all the previous papers, its teaching at once illustrates & enforces all that goes before, while the presuppositions you are all along making have become so much clearer.

I shall not attempt, my dear Baron, to express all that I have owed to this volume. It will be my constant companion. If I may judge by my last rereading, it still has not by any means yielded up to me all that it has to give.

Lord Salisbury's 'Life' by his daughter I have just taken out of the Univ. Library & look forward to it. Am started on vol. I of Disraeli's 'Life'. On Monday next I go to St Andrews till the 31st—with a party for rest and golf. Mrs Kemp Smith has been sadly overworked of late, owing to lack of domestic help. (But we have now a cook & a housemaid comes tomorrow.) She has had many outside engagements—among them the organising of a 'Jumble Sale' for the University Settlement & training of girls in Christmas Carols. In connection with former occurred an amusing incident. A copy of bill of Sale was sent to St Cuthbert's Church Hall; & it was returned with word that as the name Kemp Smith was on it (my wife's name as Convener of Committee) it could not be exhibited there!

W. P. Paterson asked me ten days ago to join him with other members of the Established Church Committee on Spiritualism at a Seance. I did: it is my first, but I have promised to attend also the next. As W. P. P. remarked—I heartily agree with him —he "does not like the smell of them". The woman-medium was, I think, genuine enough—a simple uneducated woman, a trance-medium. W. P. P., I was glad to find, on the whole approved my Maclean letters.

Your health has, I hope, been good of late, & that your great work makes satisfactory progress. My ambition for Edinburgh University is that its substance may yet, someday, be given here as lectures.

My colleague, Whittaker,[171] Prof. of Mathematics, whose two great interests are Mathematics and Mysticism, knew, I find, your Mother in Cambridge; & he has lent me the copy of your Father's biography which she gave him. Needless to say, I have read it with the greatest interest.

Yours ever affectionately,

NORMAN KEMP SMITH.

13 Vicarage Gate, London W. 8.

Dec. 31, 1921 – Jan 3, 1922.

My very dear Professor,

What a lot I do owe you—I mean, even since I last wrote to you! I wonder whether you at all realise how much, how rarely

[171] Sir Edmund Taylor Whittaker (1873–1956), British mathematician, educated at Manchester Grammar School and Trinity College, Cambridge; Professor of Mathematics at Edinburgh University, 1912–1946; lectured at various times at Oxford and Cambridge Universities, and at the Universities of Durham, Dublin, and California; his Riddell Lectures at Durham were on *The Beginning and End of the World* (1941), and his Donnellan Lectures in Dublin on *Space and Spirit* (1946); he was knighted in 1945.

much, your kind support and sympathy are to me! I am deeply touched by your pretty care of your two old aunts; yet *they* did so much for you, when you were young! Whereat *I*, whom you treat as if I were two uncles rolled into one, have only had some 5 years or so in which to be grateful to you, and in which I could do so little for you! —My not writing for so long, with those two fine last letters of yours all unanswered, means just nothing other than my little health, which, even more than yours, is just equal to its work, and hardly anything more.

But now I want to make this letter the last written in 1921 and the first written in 1922. Taken thus in two bits, of an hour each, I can hope to say the chief of what I have in my mind about your own doings apart from myself; about your points concerning my 'Essays'; and finally about my own further, other doings.

As to yourself, let me first thank you for the two 'Scotsman' letters against Dr Maclean—which I herewith return. I like them very much, throughout, and am very glad you spoke out against that unmannerly Philistine. Of course, they take America at its best—rightly so, against a man who sees nothing but a caricature, a universalising of its worst. I mention this only because your *complete* impression of America is, to my mind, these letters *plus* the things you have told me of your *William-Salter-like* depressions when there.

I strongly feel with you the sadness that such a man as that— vulgar, sensational, semi-educated—should be the second minister of the first Established Church in Edinburgh. I do hope he has not the right of succession to his chief. Professor James Ward told me, some 8 years ago, how sadly the quality of the average student for *Anglican* orders had sunk during the last 30 years or so. And in Ireland, for our *R. C.* clergy there, what a come down the Maynooth-trained clerics represent, compared with such ripe scholars as Bishop Moria[r]ty of Kerry, Cardinal Newman's friend; Abbé Hogan, of Saint Sulpice, whom I used to love to learn from; and some of the older priests who appear in Thomas Creevey's Papers, under date of 1828, I think, of one of whom the Protestant Lord Duncannon, out there in Ireland, said: 'Now I will take you to the man whom I trust as *my own brother*'. In all three cases—Presbyterian, Anglican, R. Catholic—, the causes of this decline do not lie in any change in the religions concerned, nor in their being really played out, but in a concurrence of various circumstances which have prevented the careful selection and the large cultivation of the subjects for the clerical call. A thousand pities. But for Ireland I hope now that a revival may come, in this, immensely important, respect also.

Then I have cared much for what you say about—for your direct impressions of—spiritualism. Fancy you and Dr Paterson assisting at scéances! It makes me think sadly (tho' with no fears for you two!) of an able man, the son of a very zealous R. C., himself still claiming to be an R. C., of one of the oldest noble families in England, who, obsessed with the miserable mysteries of spiritualism, has gone and married a little (I believe, Spanish) medium—utterly uneducated and highly hysterical. I can quite believe that the medium you watched is sincere; so was, and is, the little woman I refer to—yet what shoddy stuff they moves amongst! One interesting fact (as I believe) is how greatly an exclusively mathematical or physical science mentality and education exposes men to the crassest credulity in such matters— e.g. Sir William Crookes[172] and Sir Oliver Lodge.[173] Altho', no doubt, humanists can manage pretty well also—as Frederick W. H. Myers[174] and Edmund Gurney.[175]

[172] Sir William Crookes (1832–1919), British scientist, educated at the Royal College of Chemistry; made many chemical and physical discoveries, and was honored by several countries for his discoveries and publications; knighted in 1897.

[173] Sir Oliver Lodge (1851–1940), British physicist, educated at Newport Grammar School and University College, London; Professor of Physics, University College, Liverpool, 1881–1900; Principal of the University of Birmingham, 1900–1919; Fellow of the Royal Society; interested in psychical research and spiritualism; knighted in 1902. For an important study of Lodge's thought, based on hitherto unused materials, see John David Root's "Science, Religion, and Psychical Research: The Monistic Thought of Sir

Oliver Lodge," *Harvard Theological Review*, 71, Nos. 3–4 (July–October 1978), 245–63.

[174] Frederic W. H. Myers (1843–1901), British writer and sometime President of the Society for Psychical Research, educated at Cheltenham and Trinity College, Cambridge; his own intellectual odyssey and that of several of his contemporaries are discussed in Frank Miller Turner's *Between Science and Religion: The Reaction to Scientific Naturalism in Late Victorian England* (New Haven: Yale University Press, 1974).

[175] Edmund Gurney (1847–1888), British writer and one of the founders of Society for Psychical Research, educated at Trinity College, Cambridge.

You will, I hope, get 'In Defence of Reason' printed somewhere. I feel sure that I shall greatly like it.

As to Sir Henry Jones's Gifford Lectures, I am so glad that they are so good—so really, in your mind, the best thing he has done. For thus you can and do bring deep gratification to that fine man, your teacher, just when he wants it most. Poor thing! And (one more instance out of a thousand) there are people who can, who do, *explain* Evil! What next?

But, Friend, there is only one thing which, about all this and other activities of yours, a bit distresses and alarms me: *I want 'The Conception of Man in the XVIIIth Century' to get on*; and how, on earth, under such circumstances, *can* it get on? Pray, do not lose this out of sight! I so much want that book, and how many others want it too!

Yet it is a shame to scold you for those activities and not to feel guilty at your reading, and re-reading, my 'Essays' during your strenuous term time and proofs correcting etc. I can say however, in all simplicity, that you have thus cheered me on to try and do better, much better, in my new book—that you have done so more than has any other notice, printed or ms, which the book has so far called forth. I daresay you saw the 'Times Literary Supplement' review and my rejoinder. I do not doubt that the review is by Canon Barnes,[176] of Westminster Abbey, late Master of the Temple, a great Mathematician, who, some 2 or 3 years ago, wrote incidentally about my writings in the highest terms. So I have thanked Mr Richmond for his evidently most friendly intentions in giving the 'Essays' to B. for reviewing. —Of course, I began by thinking it better *not* to rejoin; the presumptions are, of course, *greatly* against rejoining. But it increasingly pressed in upon me that a good many readers of that much read

---

[176] Ernest William Barnes (1874–1953), Church of England ecclesiastic and mathematician, educated at King Edward's School, Birmingham, and Trinity College, Cambridge; became Fellow of Trinity College, 1898, and also ordained, 1902; Master of the Temple, 1915–1919; Canon of Westminster, 1918–1924; Bishop of Birmingham, 1924–1953; Fellow of the Royal Society. Von Hügel's views of Barnes are, ironically and unintentionally, borne out by the latter's son in a recent study of his father: John Barnes, *Ahead of His Age: Bishop Barnes of Birmingham* (London: Collins, 1979).

T. L. S., if I said nothing, would assume that I not only was, but recognized myself to be—that I aimed at being, an Apologist, and that I was only too pleased to be accepted as 'the first of R. C. Apologists'.[177] What a strange affair is the human mind! There is Barnes, a great *mathematician*, yes! But this very man has a quite unreasonable opinion as to the place and demonstrative, values-deciding power of *history*! When I lunched with him, 3 years ago at the Middle Temple, he talked of Lord Acton, as tho' he were one of the world's deepest thinkers and deciders. And in his review of me, he declared that there existed only two real religious problems now, both historical! And what about God? about what you and I sweat and toil at as utterly central, as quite fundamental! The man flies—or tries to fly—by mathematics and history, whilst, between, metaphysics are strangely ignored!

I *deeply* appreciate your precise indications as to what you like best and as to slips of writing or printing. But most useful of all are your objections or difficulties. Let me say a few words about each of the three great points you bring up.

1. As to *Abiding Consequences*. When I first discovered, to my deep delight, that you insisted upon the irreplaceableness of Fear in Religion, I felt (I still feel) that, at bottom, you ought

[177] Under the heading "A Great Apologist" von Hügel's first series of *Essays and Addresses* had been reviewed in *The Times Literary Supplement* (No. 1039, 15 December 1921, p. 839). The reviewer opened with the sentence: "Baron von Hügel is, we think, the most powerful apologist for the Roman Church now living." And while praising von Hügel's book the reviewer proceeded to "prove" that he was in fact an apologist. In the following issue of the *TLS* (No. 1040, 22 December 1921, p. 860), von Hügel's protest appeared, under the heading "Apologists of Religion." He began his letter with this moving statement: "Your review of my 'Essays and Addresses on the Philosophy of Religion' is so excessively handsome and so resonantly sympathetic that I may well appear ungrateful if I beg you to allow me a short protest concerning the main point of this same review. A dog who is quietly conscious of being but a dog, and of having long striven just to be a dog and nothing more or other, may be allowed, perhaps, to feel some perplexity amidst his gratitude upon finding himself first prize among cats. Much though I love religion, I have long been greatly tried by the apologist's mentality; my private life history would spell nonsense if this costly combination were not, in simple fact, its outstanding feature." After meeting the reviewer's point directly, von Hügel concluded: ". . . I should feel myself fatally hampered and oppressed by such a *role* as that of apologist, even though it be the first of all living Roman Catholic apologists, and though it be for the Church, or for Christ, or for just God Himself. More and more to live the spiritual life, increasingly to penetrate into the living Realities it reveals, and to express my discoveries, indefinitely deepened, extended, tested, and steadied by those of others, as faithfully and fearlessly as I can: this alone I can strive to do."

to be, that in some way and degree you are, however little clear about it yourself, with me there. For, pray, what *has* Religion, at its deepest and in its most characteristic instincts, to do with intermediate, methodical etc. things and conditions? Is not one of its chief differences from the other levels and ranges of human apprehension, experience etc., just that instinct flying to, that persistent pressing on to, the Last, the Abiding. Yet you teach us (I am so grateful you do) that Fear is an abiding part of man's Religion. The Fear, tho' a religious Fear, is, here, then, busy with only temporary alternatives? This, to me, will not do; but either there should always be fear in Religion, and then this is because Religion intimates Abiding Consequences; or, if there are no Abiding Consequences, there may still be good reasons for Fear, but not in Religion proper, not in Religion at its deepest. —You quote the touching objection of your friend—that his mother must indeed be changed, in her deepest, best nature, if she could possibly be happy for ever, with him suffering such Abiding Consequences. In such deep matters I do not see how we can ever hope to get beyond difficulties and obscurities; we can only opt between contrary difficulties. There is, however, a mitigation of the difficulty, your friend advances, which I believe entirely compatible with the position I have striven to maintain. *Aquinas* first taught me that the great presumption for the Theist is that God creates nothing (and especially no human soul) whose existence is not better than would be its non-existence. And he again made clear to me that there exists only one grave obstacle to holding that presumption to be the fact—i.e. Our Lord's words at the Last Supper about Judas—that it would have been better for that man not to have been born. Now *Wellhausen* shows, I think clearly, how difficult of belief is the Last Supper scene, in this respect, as the Synoptic Gospels give it us. For Our Lord speaks these tremendous words, He has emphatically asserted the presence of this traitor in their midst etc: yet the disciples remain sitting on, to the end. There is no leaping up in horror, no driving out of the traitor etc. Wellhausen concludes that Jesus may well have had premonitions of *something* traitorous, He may also have made some vague allusion to them; but that the immense emphasis and denunciation are expansions of this scene, due to the brooding of the first generation of Christians upon that aweful treason. And then *Dr Abrahams*,[178] the Rabbinical scholar, has found that very saying 'It were better for such and such a man not to have been born' to have been a tag which knocked about in the Rabbinical schools of those times. Hence nothing would be easier than for these words to become incorporated in those expansions.

But with the going of those words, as actually spoken by Our Lord Himself, would go the one serious objection which even so orthodox a Theologian as Aquinas sees against holding that the fate of *all* souls will be better than if they had not been; that *all* souls possess a real good in their existence indefeasibly. This outlook I believe to be quite compatible with the teaching that souls can, and do, harden into abiding evil consequences—that they can, and do, end in a condition of various degrees of *abiding* disharmony, regret etc. If even this cannot and does not take place, I cease to find any satisfaction given to the immense, all-pervading earnestness of Jesus's preaching of the two ways, nor indeed to your fine Fear outlook and requirement.—

2. As to *the Christology.* I was and am keenly aware that my second section contains a larger number of problems, perplexities etc., than do either of the other sections. But I felt and still feel that this does not spring from my being somehow much weaker at this middle subject than at the two other, but because we are now fronted by difficulties and obscurities far greater (at least for us, for our times) than those which confront us in the other two regions. And I felt that it would not be nothing if, in the 'Apocalyptic Element' I succeded in deciding if only a few students, not to *tidy up things for God,* but just quietly to admit certain great facts as the result from a strictly sincere study of the documents, and to remember themselves, and to remind our Unitarian friends, that *all cannot be cleared up in Pure Theism either.*

[178] Israel Abrahams (1858–1925), British writer and lecturer in Talmudic and Rabbinic Literature at Cambridge University; educated at the Universities of London and Cambridge; President of the Jewish Historical Society of England, 1905; co-editor of *The Jewish Quarterly Review*, 1889–1908; author of numerous books and articles; one of the original members with von Hügel in the LSSR.

I will not now enter into a careful consideration of the pages you feel require re-thinking; but I promise to do so, if and when I am brought again to these points. I am only quite clear about one thing as to Troeltsch—that that splendid mind and best of friends is—in spite of his grand historical sense etc.,—too intellectualist, too purely thought, in these matters. I have just again been reading a passage where he reduces all religion, as now possible to the cultivated man, to a thought about God—to a thought of Him as Good. No, no: we, even we, cultured, have bodies, have senses still! I cannot away with such reductions. A wide, wise Incarnationalism of some kind: the future is with *that*, and not with just a Thought of a Thought of God.

3. Your third point—as to whether the Church can be conceived as capable of assimilating the best in the modern world, as she assimilated, in the Golden Middle Age, the best in the Graeco-Roman world—is one that certainly, after suffering under Pius X, I ought fully to understand. My answer is threefold. (1) Single Roman Catholics—not only laymen, but priests, but religious—have, to my deepest mind and conscience, already achieved this assimilation: I am, of course, specially thinking of Huvelin. They have achieved an interpenetration, oh—how far more substantial and spiritually sane and solid than I can find even in Holtzmann and Troeltsch, in de Lagarde or Pringle Pattison! —I know, of course, that single men are one thing; an entire huge Institution is another thing. Still, in this poor world of trouble and inevitable, difficult choosings, it is not nothing to find such an assimilation a *fact*, and no mere hope. (2) Next, I do not feel that I can do more, with regard to the Church authorities, than to include such assimilative action of theirs, amongst the objects of my *faith*. I find I can believe such action possible, and even such belief I find to work well and ennoblingly in my life. After all, it is not as though my nine long stays in Rome had confirmed me in the fear, with which I first went to Rome, that the men in authority there were unanimously opposed to such assimilation; for very certainly it did *not*. At this very moment I know of several high authorities at the Vatican itself who are, as before Pius X, definitely friendly to, and believers in, such

assimilation. —True, this enlightened party has not so far succeded against the ultra-conservatives; and it is very certainly easier
to think that this will continue on and on. Yet I do not, myself,
find it impossible, even now, to believe in such a future triumph.
(3) But, above all, and without any emphasis upon future possibilities, the essential, the most indispensable of the dimensions
of religion is, *not breadth, but depth*, and above all, *the insight
into sanctity and the power to produce saints*. Rome continues—
of this I am very sure—to possess this supernatural depth—possesses it in far greater degree than Protestantism, and still more
than the quite unattached moderns.

As to my own doings since last I wrote—the little doings and
the little experiences—they have chiefly been the following. I
went and spoke at that *Conference on Prayer at Beaconsfield*, in
an old house 'The Yews' not 300 yards from Edmund Burke's
grave and modest monument in the Parish Church there. I went
and carefully gazed at it three times. I have loved Burke ever
since I was eighteen: a great soul! We were only seven in all, two
laymen (the fine Governor of Greenwich Hospital and myself)
and five clerics (all, with the Governor, High, Ritualist, Anglicans). One of the clerics struck me at first as a strange combination—an Anglican Benedictine. But this Father Denys turned
out a very genuine and thoughtful man and a reader of philosophical books on the vertiginous scale of Crespi's reading. One
thing about him delighted me: he has your Commentary upon
his worktable continuously; has carefully studied every word;
and is constantly consulting it. —They were all most kind and
eager to listen; indeed I had to rebate some of their enthusiasm.[179]

Then I got it into my head that perhaps a remarkably able
Doctor I had watched improve the working power of a man of
50, might be able to help me also. But he succeded only in the
most careful diagnosis of my condition of very high arterial pressure, which affects my nights as often as, or more often than, not,
leaving me next morning too weary for composition. But I now

---

[179] These lectures on prayer were published posthumously twice: once as chapter 8 in *Essays and Addresses on the Philosophy of Religion*, Second Series (London: Dent, 1926), and again as a small
booklet entitled *The Life of Prayer* (London: Dent, 1927).

recognize that I was asking for a miracle; and that, at 70, you can only somewhat moderate this condition by careful diet etc., but cannot cure it. So I have dropped my new Dr, with thanks for his care and hints.

I have been having a good deal of bother and distress about *Troeltsch*—about his speaking at Swanwick next July. Mr Tatlow[180] had spoken of the acceptance by the Executive Committee of the C. S. M. as very likely, and I had thereupon told T. of my plan for him, and secured his undertaking to come to England (his first visit) next July. But, alas, the majority of the Exec. Committee in Sept. were hotly against having T.; that the Movement's Constitution requires the speakers at this meeting to be accepters of the historic Creeds, and that if they accepted T., they would have no standing ground against accepting Quakers, Unitarians and Theosophists. —Certain friends of the Movement have been consulted and now, at Christmas, I have been definitely told that they cannot have T. at Swanwick, and propose his coming instead in September to the London meeting of their paid secretaries, and to speak to them. I wrote a long explanatory letter to Tatlow in November; but, tho' I still feel it somehow unanswerable, it, as you see, failed in its object. —I have now written to Clement Webb at Oxford, whether he could not undertake to get a meeting together there for T. at end of July. I have done this, in hopes, when I presently write about all this woe to Troeltsch, of having two substitutes for Swanwick to offer him. But I have a sort of an impression that I may not know the *real* reason of this commotion, and that it has to do, in part at least, with T.'s Germanness. They say that they want me, that *I* am all right for them. But I want to postpone any decision till I know whether T. will still come this year. If he does, I shall reserve myself for accompanying him. He is absolutely engaged to the London University for 1923, and may, very possibly, now prefer to drop coming in 1922, which anyhow I had difficulty in getting him to promise. (Webb has just told me that an *Austrian* Pro-

[180] Tissington Tatlow (1876–1957), Church of England cleric, educated at Trinity College, Dublin; General Secretary of the Student Christian Movement, 1898–1900, 1903–1929; Chairman of SCM, 1929–1933; chairman of various church-related organizations, and Select Preacher at both Oxford and Cambridge.

fessor, a fine savant and a charming personality has quite a short time back been at Oxford, by special invitation; but that there were painful incidents—men refusing to shake hands etc.—oh, what poor little bits of things we poor humans are![)].

Just now I am plunged in preparations for an address 'Priest and Prophet' at Liddon House (before Bishop Gore[181]) on Jan. 19. I am finding very interesting points, I think; but I shall delight to get back to my book which is beginning, after much toil on my part, to support me.

Most cordial good wishes for the New Year, Friend, in all your Professorial work, your incidental Lectures, your home life, and indeed in everything.

My wife joins in kind regards to Mrs Kemp Smith, whom really we must get to know. My wife has had endless botherations as to servants, so can well understand the trials of Mrs Kemp Smith.

Yours most sincerely
F. v. HÜGEL.

Thank you for reading the *Mémoire* of my Father. My Brother put it together with meticulous care, and I made the translation of von Reumont. But I have a certain feeling of shyness as to men who never knew our Father, reading the thing. For 'stars and garters', titles etc. somehow seem to predominate there as they did not do with the living man. The fact is that neither my Brother nor I ever directly knew him well except as a worn man of 70–75; and it is the absence of a vivid experience of him, at his fullest which, I think, gives that somewhat worldly, almost snobby, touch to the little volume. I possess quantities of charming family letters of my Father's parents, his brother, and his 3 sisters, as well as of himself. But what tragic things are there!—

---

181 Charles Gore (1853–1932), British theologian and Church of England ecclesiastic, educated at Harrow and Balliol College, Oxford; editor of *Lux Mundi*; Librarian of Pusey House, Oxford, 1884– 1893; Vicar of Radly, 1893–1894; Canon of Westminster, 1894–1902; Bishop of Worcester, 1902–1904; Bishop of Birmingham, 1905–1911; Bishop of Oxford, 1911–1919.

14 Lennox Str.

March 7, 1922   Edinburgh

My dear Baron,

I have—I need hardly say—long been intending to thank you for your most cheering & wonderfully interesting letter of Dec. 31st, which I have tonight been again rereading & pondering over. But even this is not to be a proper reply thereto. That I shall reserve, also my promised comments on the concluding sections of your 'Essays & Addresses'—tho' they are much in my mind as I write my concluding lectures, for my advanced class—concluding a course semi-historical in which the nature & function of reason has been the main connecting theme. If you saw the lecture I gave today on what I call the historical or *institutional* view of reason (as ags the 18th Cent. "natural reason") you would recognise many points as showing the influence of your book.

Two things stir me up to write: first, that the Term is nearing its close & that my wife & I plan a six weeks holiday to Greece—allowing 4 weeks in Greece itself. It has long been my ambition to see Greece. Also on way back we hope to visit Ravenna, Mantua, Remini & Bologna—all towns new to us. Something may at the last intervene to prevent our going. But I trust, & expect, not. We propose starting about March 19th or 20th. We both need a good holiday, & I especially desire to be in good form, that I may get much writing done in the leisure of Summer Term & the long vacation. Next Term I have only 3 hrs. per week of teaching; & in August & September we are to occupy a cottage in Iona. For I am by no means forgetting my hoped-for book on "Human Nature", though probably some other book—systematic on theory of knowledge with indications of a corresponding theory (objectivist & ontological) in ethics. But how far my views are ripe & really will bear writing out clearly I can only test by trial & failure or success—& that is what I want to do this coming summer, if all goes well. I have been preparing the way in my lecture courses; but lecturing to students, however satisfactory as a method of learning, is somewhat deceptive, I think, as a test of what is fit for publication.

Lately, P. H. Wicksteed's[182] book on Aquinas—'His Reaction between Dogma & Philosophy'—has *greatly* delighted me—especially in the light of the broad outlines you yourself dwell upon in your 'Essays'.

Then 2[ndly] I have been aroused to write by a letter that has just reached me from my friend Bowman. I had sent him at Christmas your 'Essays & Addresses' as I knew he would appreciate them, & (the mutual understanding between him & myself means so much to me that he [*sic*] I wish him to be profiting where I have been so immensely) that his reading of it will help to keep us in step. My anticipations have been more than fulfilled; & you must therefore pardon my quoting exactly what he says: "I wish to thank you very warmly for the splendid present you sent me. It only arrived lately (evidently delayed in transit), & I have not yet got through it, but have read enough to be profoundly impressed. I share to the full your feelings with regard to von Hügel. His spiritual insight, his power of synthesis, his sense of historical reality—all these mark him as a master-mind of his generation. Incidentally he has done me a service for which I cannot adequately thank him—viz., he has enabled me to precipitate into clear consciousness the theme of my book. Did I tell you it is to be entitled: "Naturalism & the Supernatural"? A title in itself doesn't mean much, but in this case it has furnished a rallying point & a point of view which has given unity & coherence to a great mass of heterogeneous material which had long been pressing together in my mind. Very many thanks for your gift."

Since last I wrote Sir Henry Jones has passed to his rest. It was really an immense relief for *all* his friends when the end came: the strain was too excessive, tho' he bore it heroically to the very last, both for him & for those about him. I attended the funeral in Tighnabruaich—in a simple old-world Churchyard high in the hills. I meant to send you the notice that I wrote of him in the Scotsman, & shall if I can still find it.

[182] Philip Henry Wicksteed (1844–1927), British Unitarian minister and scholarly writer and lecturer, educated at University College, and Manchester New College, London; held ministerial positions at Taunton, 1867–1870, Dukinfield, 1870–1874, and Little Portland Street Chapel, London, 1874–1897; University Extension Lecturer, 1887–1918; an authority on Dante.

Principal McAlester[183] of Glasgow has written asking me to submit to him my impressions of possible occupants for the Chair. It is possible that the Chair may be offered to someone, or failing that, that two or three may be invited to apply. In the latter case it is just possible that Bowman might be one of them. Unhappily he has not yet published, & is known only to a few in Scotland. Latta, whom he assisted in Glasgow, & Macneile Dixon both heartily agree with me that he is *the* man for the Chair; but we see no way of bringing his claims home to the Electors (the members of the University Court) though we could probably be certain of receiving, say 3 votes. So in writing the Principal I shall dwell on the other possibilities—A. E. Taylor, John Laird[184] (whom I met at Christmas & was impressed by), W. D. Ross[185] of Oriel, & A. D. Lindsay[186] of Balliol—I should place them in that order, as regards their claims, with Wm MacDougall (now of Harvard) somewhere in the list as a possible addition. Then I shall finish up by saying that there is one other man whom I have not so far mentioned because his claims are not sufficiently known in philosophical & wider circles, A. A. B., but that if I were a despot & had the power of appointment I should elect him without hesitation—& refer the Principal to Latta & Dixon for conformation of my judgment. This may just possibly bear fruit

[183] Sir Donald MacAlister (1854–1934), Scottish scientist and physician, educated at St. John's College, Cambridge, St. Bartholomew's Hospital, London, and the University of Leipzig; chairman, consultant, and lecturer for various medical and scientific groups; Principal and Vice-Chancellor of Glasgow University, 1907–1929; recipient of numerous honorary degrees and awards; created baronet in 1924.

[184] John Laird (1887–1946), Scottish philosopher, educated at Aberdeen Grammar School, and the Universities of Edinburgh and Heidelberg, and Trinity College, Cambridge; Professor of Logic and Metaphysics at Queen's University, Belfast, 1913–1924; Regis Professor of Moral Philosophy, Aberdeen, 1924; Mills Lecturer at the University of California, 1923–1924; Gifford Lecturer at Glasgow, 1939–1940.

[185] Sir William David Ross (1877–?), British philosopher; sometime Provost of Oriel College, Oxford, Honorary Fellow of Merton College, Oxford, and Fellow of the British Academy; Gifford Lecturer at the University of Aberdeen, 1935–1936; his Memorial Lectures (1948) honoring Sir Samuel Dill were published in 1951 by the Clarendon Press as *Plato's Theory of Ideas.*

[186] Alexander Dunlop Lindsay (1879–1952), Scottish philosopher, educated at Glasgow University and University College, Oxford; Shaw Fellow of the University of Edinburgh; Professor of Moral Philosophy in Glasgow University, 1922–1924; Master of Balliol College, Oxford, 1924–1949; Vice-Chancellor of Oxford University, 1935–1938; created 1st Baron Lindsay of Birker, 1945.

in his inclusion among the invited candidates. Bowman's book won't be ready for a year or more.

Pringle-Pattison's Gifford Lectures—on Immortality—have been, to me at least, very disappointing. They are little more than compilations, rather padded out, tho' of course very pleasingly written. The reason is, I think, that of late years, & for many years, he has not really been working hard, & has said all he has to say in the first series. Also 'Immortality' is so *derivative* a belief, that it hardly serves for these lectures, especially as he has nothing *really* of his own to say regarding it.

W. P. Patterson, the Convener of our Gifford Committee, is always speaking of summoning it, but has not yet done so. However he cannot but do so some time next Term—in May or June. Have been at two more of his Spiritualist Committee seances— one with previous medium & one with a Mr Vant Peters. I look forward with some curiosity to the Report they have promised to submit to the Established Church Assembly in May. Lord Sands[187]—a Judge in our Court of Session—a member of the Committee is quite evidently impressed, & since last seance has written me two letters dwelling upon the valuable & surprising results obtained. They were very far from at all impressing me, quite the reverse. At least one other member of the Committee appears to take the Spiritualism very seriously. But do not mention this to anyone. I am only an invited guest, & not (I am glad to say) in any way called upon to express views in or about the Report.

But I must not run on—especially as there are so many much more interesting matters to talk about in your last letter, & these I am deferring. I trust your address on 'Priest & Prophet' worked out to your satisfaction, & that your book makes reasonably good progress.

Perhaps I ought to have mentioned—as *part* excuse for my delay in writing—that I have twice had influenza since the New

---

[187] Christopher Nicholson Johnston, Lord Sands (judicial title), (1857–1934), Scottish jurist, educated at the Universities of St. Andrews, Edinburgh, and Heidelberg; held numerous official appointments; Senator, College of Justice, Scotland, from 1917; Chairman of Edinburgh Employment Committee (Ministry of Labour), from 1922; knighted in 1917.

Year, or something like it, with resulting lethargy. But latterly have again been getting good work done. These are the ups & downs that have to be met with equanimity.

Meantime, my dear Baron, I send you my kindest greetings & all good wishes. I trust that Lady Mary is well. Mrs Kemp Smith also wishes to be remembered to you both.

Yours ever affectionately,
NORMAN KEMP SMITH.

March 9.

I have delayed posting until I knew the date of our leaving Edinburgh. In order to catch steamer at Brindisi we have to leave London on Friday the 17th, & that means my staying in Edinburgh till the last moment for University work. So I must defer seeing you till our return at end of April, when I trust I may have the privilege.[188] We come South on Thursday, & leave early on the Friday morning. Yesterday the Editor of 'Mind' wrote asking me for an obituary notice of Sir Henry. As I have no time to write one specially, have sent him my remaining copy of the Scotsman notice. He can use it if he thinks it suitable.

3rd June 1922.
13, Vicarage Gate,
Kensington,
W. 8.

My dear Professor,

What a Kind Friend! Of course I owe this entirely to you, in the sense that unless someone had cared and watched and pressed, as occasion offered, and had worked with both wisdom and devotion for it—someone, too, in a position to render his action strongly effectual: I should never have attained to this biggest

---

[188] Kemp Smith did call on von Hügel, and the Baron's *Diary* notes: "*Kemp Smith*, just back from Greece, Ravenna, Rimini, Bologna, Parma, *came at 11.10.* With him and Puck into K[ensington] G[ardens]. Sat and talked about Time & Space—whether Finite (I) or Infinite (he); and as to simultaneity of God. Puck & I saw him off to Euston [Station], at Ken-s[ington] High Str[eet] Station at 12.40." *Diaries,* 29 April 1922.

chance for doing something somewhat abiding.[189] And so, I thank you most gratefully, and [am] deeply touched by your simple, sincere devotedness and service. I should love to think of an opportunity arising when I could serve you even distantly as largely.

I will certainly accept. The two years still for preparation are, of course, an excellent feature, although I must not and do not forget that I may not be in this world when the time for the first lecture arrives. Still, I am in very fair health (for me), and I can trust that I may be allowed to get through this big affair. I certainly incline to the one-lecture-a-week plan; but it may be wise to ask for this to be left open till nearer the time.

I have some other pressing notes to write to-night; but the official invitation, received this morning, shall be duly answered on Monday.—

I am very glad you are taking up the Troeltsch affair now. I have found out from the Registrar to the London University that, as Troeltsch's Lectures there have been put off to next year, Troeltsch has chosen, and they have accepted, *March* (1923) for the delivery of these 4 Lectures. I have been trying to get the Cambridge people to arrange something for T. then; but a hitch has occurred—this time, not as to his theological, but as to his political, correctness. That letter to the 'Times' of Professor *Sherrington*,[190] reproducing a bit of his, S.'s diary, giving his interview with T. in 1912 (?), in which T. appeared a good bit of a man for State Omnipotence, a non-moral state etc., is being brought up against T. and any plan to honour him. One of the Cambridge Professors (a personal friend of mine) who began by offering his Lecture-Room for T. to address his students, now first requires

[189] This is in reference to von Hügel's official invitation from the University of Edinburgh to be Gifford Lecturer there. A letter from Kemp Smith to von Hügel with the *un*official announcement seems to be lost. In his *Diary* von Hügel notes on June 2: "Letter from Kemp Smith; the *Senatus Academicus of Edinb. University has elected me Gifford Lecturer for 1924, 1925 and 1925, 1926*; ten lectures each year, salary abt £1300 per annum." And on the following day his *Diary* records: "*The Official Announcement as to*

the Gifford Lectureship came. Letter of grateful thanks to Kemp Smith for all he has done & achieved." *Diaries*, 2–3 June 1922.

[190] Sir Charles Scott Sherrington (1857–1952), British physician and lecturer on physiology, educated at Gonville and Caius College, Cambridge; member of numerous international medical associations, and recipient of various honorary degrees and awards; Gifford Lecturer at Edinburgh, 1936–1938; knighted in 1922.

evidence from me that T. is not what that interview seemed to show he was. I am getting 3 sets of documents, in typed form, to send to this friend.[191] (1) The section in my 'German Soul', which analyses, and quotes everything at all criticisable from, T's two War-Addresses of Jan–Febr. 1916; (2) the 3 long letters from T. to myself of 1921; and (3) a statement drawn up now by T. himself, as concerns these points. (This I wrote off to him to send me, yesterday; I think he will do as I propose he should). I am, for myself quite sure of two things: that T. *now* is thoroughly moderate and Christian in his *state*-views; and that I never knew nor suspected that he felt otherwise before the war. It is a fact that he refused to sign any of the Professorial Manifestos, and equally a fact that in the 2 big vols. of his collected works I have found anti-Junker bits but no chauvinism. —I write all this in order that, if any hitch occurs in Edinburgh, you may ask me for a copy of these 3 sets of documents. (I believe, but this as utterly confidential, that it is Prof. Sorley who, in Cambridge, keeps up this fierce Inquisition against all things and persons German).

I was in Cambridge, just over a week ago, for my Brother's getting the Hon Dr Sc., after his 38 [years] work at and for the Museum of Ethnology there. I saw James Ward, now 82, busy finishing up a book on Kant as a man. We had a long talk, and I thought him strangely influenced by his 32 years old only son out in Rangoon (Burmah) who has there taken up violently with Theosophy and the like. J. W. declared he now felt just God alone too far off; the Incarnation was necessary; but indeed also further mediations were wanted. Strange, strange; this poor Papist was alarmed at the pace at which his austerely Puritan friend was unlearning his Puritanism!

My wife and I hope indeed to be alive and well for two long stays in Edinburgh, thus seeing you much and getting to know Mrs Kemp Smith thoroughly. By the bye, will you please tell her with my compliments that I felt cross with myself when I had

[191] From von Hügel's *Diary* one can conclude that this "friend" was Francis Crawford Burkitt (1864–1935), Norrisan Professor of Divinity at Cambridge University from 1905, brilliant Biblical scholar, and friend of von Hügel's from their early days in the LSSR. See *Diaries*, 20, 29, 30, 31 May, and 1, 19, 22 June 1922.

let you go off this last time in London, and I had not woken up to the fact that of course I could get to know Mrs Kemp Smith, if only I came with you to Euston! —I am horribly stupid about all such things.

As to my Lectures, I will, of course, simply work on at my book, gradually getting it, I hope, fit for these two courses of Lectures. It is anyhow planned as two large Parts.

Your very grateful and aff. Friend
F. v. Hügel.

P.S. I dare not write on, but want just to say that *of course* I at once sent off, most gratefully, your two important corrections for the new Preface of my 'M. E.' to Dent, urging their immediate putting right. Young Dent wrote back they had just finally finished, up to the 'jackets' on the casings of the volumes, and could not touch these. But that only a small number of copies had been printed off for this 1st issue. Yet I have just caught them napping over some 20 further off prints they have sent me. They have however now solemnly undertaken to send me the two pages printed, showing their execution of the corrections now at once. You shall have the Troeltsch volume now in not many days.

H.

June 29. 1922   14 Lennox Street,
                                               Edinburgh.

My dear Baron,

You do not need in any way to thank *me* for assisting, in however minor a way, in your election to the Gifford Lectureship. The Lectureship is even more closely bound up with the Chair I hold—at least so I should maintain—than with that of Theology, & it was my bounden *duty* to consider nothing but the securing of the best possible incumbent. What very much calls for explanation, especially in view of the people who have been chosen in the past, is why you should not have been elected in one or

other of the Scottish Universities long ere this. But at least Edinburgh is the gainer thereby. When I mentioned your appointment to Latta in Glasgow, he replied: "What, you have snapped
him up! He was my candidate to succeed Balfour in Glasgow."
'Snapped up' forsooth!

Speaking of Glasgow, you will have heard that A. D. Lindsay
of Balliol has been appointed to succeed Sir Henry Jones in
the Moral Philosophy Chair. He has some influence in Glasgow
through the friends of his Father who was Principal of the U. F.
College there, though what chiefly counted probably was his Oxford backing. He has been very popular as a Tutor, & has a very
pleasing personality. But he is, I should say, much better fitted
to teach young Englishmen who have no real belief in philosophy, & who take to the very mild & easily digested diet of Aristotle–Kant–Hegel pap (à la Oxford) & of Liberal–Labour ethics
in which he deals. The Principal & the City Members of the Court
who look to him for a lead voted for Lindsay. The runner-up was
Bowman, who had nearly all the support of the University rep-
resentatives. Taylor did not apply, & probably wisely: his health
is not good, & he has much more leisure for writing in St Andrews
than he could have in Glasgow. Bowman will not be disappointed,
I think. He is proving a quite extraordinary success in Princeton,
& obtaining great influence there: his decision to apply in Glasgow was largely determined by a sense of duty, on the part of
his wife & himself, to their parents who are aging & live in
Glasgow.

I have got W. P. Paterson & Curtis[192] interested in the
Troeltsch visit, & they will in due course get into direct touch with
Troeltsch. They would like to give him an Honorary Degree, but
fear the time is not ripe for that just yet. Paterson also stated in
our Gifford Committee some time ago that he would hope that
public feeling would allow of his being nominated sometime to

[192] William Alexander Curtis (1876–
1961), Scottish theologian and Biblical
critic, educated at the Universities of
Edinburgh, Heidelberg, Leipzig, and Oxford; Professor of Biblical Criticism at
the University of Edinburgh, 1915–1946;
Dean of the Faculty of Divinity, 1928–
1946; Principal, New College, Edinburgh,
1935–1946.

the Gifford Lectures. MacKintosh & Principal Martin[193] of the U. F. College (they are *both* admirers of your own works) are likewise much interested in Troeltsch, & would help towards having him visit Edinburgh next year under friendly auspices.

I have been very busy finishing off the Term's work, & am now very nearly disentangled, with three clear months ahead for writing.

Probably I shall be able to secure the leave of absence— January to June—required for accepting the invitation to the University of California, as Professor J. H. Muirhead,[194] Professor-Emeritus in the University of Birmingham agrees very kindly to take over my duties while I am away. At least our Dean, Sir Richard Lodge,[195] now says that tho' there is no precedent for anyone being granted from Edinburgh so long leave of absence, he will do his best to carry the matter through the Court. The visit to California should not interrupt my work, but rather help it. For besides being something of a holiday, & very much of a mental change, these are the best months for that part of the world & the worst months for Edinburgh—much worse in Committee meeting & other time-wasting engagements as well as in weather. Also I shall be compelled to adjust myself to new conditions, & write special lectures, which I always find a great help in the fight against sloth & dilatoriness. My wife, I should hope, would join me there & return with me. She is at present at Haslemere, until July 24th, with the daughter, to see the end of her old school which is being closed for good or rather bad. She was to be in London this week, & hoped to call upon Lady Mary.

The Labour Party Conference has been meeting in Edinburgh

[193] Alexander Martin (1857–1946), Scottish philosopher and theologian, educated at Edinburgh University and New College, Edinburgh; Professor of Apologetics and Practical Theology in New College, 1897–1927; Principal, 1918–1935; Moderator of General Assembly of the United Free Church of Scotland, 1920 and 1929.

[194] John Henry Muirhead (1855–1940), Scottish philosopher, educated at Glasgow University and Balliol College, Oxford; Professor of Philosophy and Political Economy at the University of Birmingham; author of numerous articles and books.

[195] Sir Richard Lodge (1855–1936), British historian, educated at Christ's Hospital and Balliol College, Oxford; first Professor of History at Glasgow University, 1894–1899; Professor of History, Edinburgh University, 1899–1925; Dean of the Faculty of Arts, Edinburgh, 1911–1925; President of the Royal Historical Society, 1929–1933; knighted in 1917.

this week, & Robert Adamson's[196] eldest daughter, who has been caught into that movement & was here to report the Conference for the Westminster Gazette, has been staying for a week with me. Through her I have been meeting Ramsay Macdonald[197] & M[rs] Snowden,[198]—good types both & likeable, though somewhat ordinary surely, to be leading an influential party, as at least the former does. Looking in at the Conference debates yesterday, the assembly was well worth a visit: it is extraordinarily alive & alert. The delegates look more or less middle-class, with the revolutionary element hardly at all in evidence. The leaders speak well, but with no great distinction. It is surely surprising, & rather depressing, that out of some four million trades-unionists so little really first-class personalities seem to emerge. Probably Smillie,[199] the miners' leader, is somewhat of an exception. The Webbs[200] strike me as extraordinarily well-informed, but otherwise quite unimpressive.

Your account of Ward is not very reassuring. Surely the strang-

[196] Robert Adamson (1852–1902), Scottish philosopher; Professor of Logic and Mental Philosophy at Owens College, Manchester, and from 1895, Professor of Logic and Rhetoric at Glasgow University.

[197] James Ramsay MacDonald (1866–1937), British labor leader; Secretary of Labour Party (L. R. C.), 1900–1912; Treasurer, 1912–1924; Leader of the Labour Party, 1911–1914; Chairman of Parliamentary Labour Party, and Leader of H.M. Opposition, 1922; Prime Minister, First Lord of the Treasury, and Secretary for Foreign Affairs, January–November 1924; Prime Minister and First Lord of the Treasury, 1929–1935; Lord President of the Council, 1935–1937.

[198] Viscountess Ethel Annakin Snowden (1881–1951), British leader in Women's Suffrage Movement and Labour Movement, educated at Edge Hill College, Liverpool; member of the Labour Commission of Enquiry to Russia in 1920 from which she reported unfavorably on Bolshevism; member of the first Board of Governors of the B.B.C., 1927–1933.

[199] Robert Smillie (1857–1940), British labor leader; President of the Scottish Miners' Federation, 1894–1918, and 1921–

1940; President of the Miners' Federation of Great Britain, 1912–1921.

[200] Sidney James Webb, Baron Passfield (1859–1947), and Martha Beatrice Potter Webb (1858–1943), English social reformers, and social historians and economists. Sidney was introduced in 1885 by George Bernard Shaw to the Fabian Society of which he became one of the most influential members through his writings. Beatrice was influenced by Herbert Spencer, and assisted Charles Booth in research for his *Life and Labour of the People in London*. After their marriage in 1892 both worked as a team for socialism and trade unionism in England, and published in 1894 their influential *History of Trade Unionism*. They founded the *New Statesman* in 1913, and helped to establish the London School of Economics in 1895. Sidney was made President of the Board of Trade, 1924, and against his desire raised to the peerage, 1929; he became Dominions and Colonial Secretary, 1929–1930, and Colonial Secretary, 1930–1931. A valuable selection of the letters of the two Webbs has been edited by Norman Mackenzie: *The Letters of Sidney and Beatrice Webb*, 3 vols. (Cambridge: Cambridge University Press, 1978).

est of moods in him. But his philosophy is so barren—to me at least—that *any* rebellion therefrom may be counted for grace.

You continue, I trust, in good health, & make progress with your work.

Yours ever affectionately,
NORMAN KEMP SMITH.

P.S. I *must* send you the Kant volume!

Oct. 1. 1922   14 Lennox Street,
Edinburgh.

My dear Baron,

The volume of Troeltsch was a very cheering welcome home yesterday, on our return from our two months' sojourn in Iona. My most grateful thanks, also for the honoured inscription. I shall, as opportunity offers, make a fuller study of the book. In my previous reading I was only able to sample it here & there, & to appreciate how much I could hope to learn from closer perusal. As a rest in the midst of unpacking, I have already reread the admirable 'Schluss' section.

I have been meaning to allow myself the pleasure of again writing you. For you must not feel—I refer to the note on outside of the packet that you are to be writing soon—that each of my letters at all needs an answer—else I should feel constrained to hold my hand. I have better health, more leisure, & less important work in hand—not to speak of the numerous correspondents that I fear make sad incursions on your invaluable time & energy. I mean this remark as to your writing sincerely—my sincerity in this respect is only equalled by my delight in a letter when it does come.

Iona has far surpassed all our highest expectations. My wife & daughter fully share my enthusiasm; & I have found it as good for work as for holiday. Indeed this past summer I have got more writing done than in any summer since before the war. What surprised us is the extraordinarily bright & varied colouring of land & sea, & the variety the little island affords in its tiny compass of moor & hill & bays etc. A number of artists were busy at work—it has been quite a haunt of the professional artist for some years —one of them a friend & near neighbor here, John Duncan.[201] The natives are very superior and intelligent types. Add to all this the historical associations & the absolute quiet—not even broken by the daily incursion for a couple of hours of sight-seers from the Oban steamer: we were almost a mile from the village —Scotland cannot offer a more delightful retreat.

My book on the theory of perception—and problems connected therewith—is well underway. But I shall not hurry it on: time will help to mature it; & in California—between January & May I should have leisure to put in work on it—the more so as I am to use it in the post-graduate course that I give there. I am endeavouring to work out a thoroughly realistic view of perception & of the categories, & am, I think, making some headway. At least if my views break down, I shall at least have come definitely to terms with them at last, & they have been in my mind, vaguely, for years.

My coming visit to California has led me to read 'Idealism & the Modern Age' by G. Plimpton Adams[202] (Yale Univ. Press), a member of the philosophical staff at Berkeley. It is a very interesting book, & able. He is acquainted with Troeltsch's work, but not, I observe, with your own. Adams' standpoint I find, in the main, congenial, & look forward to much helpful discussion with him. The other book that I read—apart from the Odyssey & the Iliad—in Iona, & with still greater profit—it seems to me a very outstanding work—is one that you must know: *Das Heilige* by

[201] John Duncan (?–1945), Scottish artist, educated in Dundee, London, and Düsseldorf; Associate Professor of the Teaching of Art at The University of Chicago, 1901–1904; executed many paintings and art works in Scotland and northern England.

[202] George Plimpton Adams (1882–?), American philosopher, educated at Harvard University; the greater part of his life was spent at the University of California teaching philosophy; from 1932 he held the Mills Chair in Philosophy there. His *Idealism and the Modern Age* (New Haven: Yale University Press, 1919), has several sympathetic references to Kemp Smith's thought.

Prof. R. Otto[203] of Marburg. Not for long have I read any German book that has so impressed me. It is a really important contribution to the philosophy of religion, do you not think? My copy is I notice from the 8th ed.: & original, first published in 1917.

This week work begins. Tomorrow & Tuesday I speak at Nelson's, the Printers, & at an Engineering Works, at lunch-hour on behalf of the Workers Educational Association, & also for same to Leith Women's Liberal Club on Wednesday evening. Then there are the usual Senate & Committee meetings of the opening of Session. Classes start on the 10th.

Last year I was asked to edit some translations by John Handyside of Kant's *Inaugural Dissertation & Early Writings on Space.* Handyside, who was a pupil of Pringle-Pattison and Lecturer in Philosophy at University of Liverpool, & killed in the war, left these translations in a somewhat rough first version. I have gone over them carefully, & now have them completed & ready for the printer—the Open Court Publishing Co., i.e. Heath on this side. The volume should prove useful to English students of Kant. The Latin of the Dissertation is very difficult & frequently obscure. Shall send you a copy when the book appears.

It seems very strange to be back in the crowded modern world —and not over-pleasing—after these two months' retirement. We are fortunate above our fellows, & am glad too that the little daughter should have so happy early associations with its old-world life.

With kindest greetings to Lady Mary,

Yours ever affectionately & gratefully,

NORMAN KEMP SMITH.

[203] Rudolf Otto (1869–1937), German theologian and philosopher of religion, educated at the Universities of Erlangen and Göttingen; Professor of Theology at Göttingen, 1907–1914, at Breslau, 1914– 1917, and at Marburg, 1917–1937; his major work was *Das Heilige* (1917), translated into English as *The Idea of the Holy* (1923).

13, Vicarage Gate, W. 8.
24th October, 1922.

My very dear Friend,

It is high time to write to you and thank you for your two charming letters, especially the last one about Iona and the rest. I am dictating this to my secretary for letters, who saves me much in this way; and she will sign the whole for me.

Let me first tell you how delighted I was to think of all your happiness in Iona, and that the little Margery[204] should so early in life get those grand simple impressions of ocean and land and the great monastic traditions of the past. I should think that in two or three years' time you might be able to read her some of the brief stories in Bede's Ecclesiastical History, where there is so much about Iona.

Then I was so pleased to think that your Perception Lectures for California have got on so well. And, finally, that you finished that English translation of Kant's Latin Treatises: thank you for promising to give me a copy. I have studied the 1770 one very carefully in parts.

Now as to myself. I was full eight weeks at Thursley, and did simply nothing there but walk and sit out and sleep, with simple little German books read out to our dear old Eva.[205] Puck and a lady friend were out with me every day, generally twice. I came back four weeks ago, distinctly better, with more margin for work, but seeing very plainly how carefully and wisely I have to manage such strength as I have got. I have now taken to dictating my book from the beginning, which I hope will give a greater lucidity and freshness; but I am as yet some distance from where I shall have to dictate parts never yet written.

As I look ahead a little, I see three enterprises, of which two appear to me still quite capable of execution, but the third of which, alas, appears to me now more or less problematical. I really believe that I shall achieve that book and have it ready

[204] One of von Hügel's many idiosyncrasies was constantly to confuse first names, even of people he knew rather well. Kemp Smith's daughter's name was, not Margery, but Janet.

[205] Eva, a German lady, had for decades been a servant in von Hügel's household, helping to raise his three daughters, and always accompanying the family, or its individual female members, on their trips abroad.

for the printer, say, by Easter, 1925. Also I do not see why I should despair of coming to Edinburgh, and telling such people as may care what I think I have got clear for myself. I feel as though three Addresses at a distance of a fortnight between each would remain possible to me, even then. But what seems to be now too much to hope for is that then I should be fit for ten successive Lectures at a distance of but a week between each, and then to have to begin again such a long close series only one year later. I want then for you kindly to consider how long you think it would be considerate for me not to decide. I thought of a year from the appointment,—i.e., June 1st, 1923,—but then you would not be in Edinburgh at that time, and I would sooner, if I must give up, do so with you in Edinburgh capable of kindly explaining for me.

After all, in any case I have had a most kind encouragement and support, and if I came to Edinburgh for those three times I could get into touch with a good many hearers who would, I think, have me at my best—as a speaker and not a writer. You see I have never in my life spoken at greater proximity between Address and Address than three weeks or so; and the cumulation of the effort is, of course, where they are ten,—a very different thing from what I ever have experienced.

I quite understand how, with the Gifford appointment, the only alternative is to take all or leave all; but I daresay you would be able when the time comes, if I live till then, to get me an invitation from some group or Society in Edinburgh.

Perhaps I better add that both my wife and my home daughter are somewhat irritated with me at already thinking of resignation; but I feel myself not by any means alone in the world, and that at least I must put the matter into your hands and decision.

Thank you about the books you have been reading. I always make a note about them. I myself am slowly assimilating Oswald Külpe's "Die Realisierung," which surely, had he lived, would have been a very considerable book, and even so the first volume is refreshing and supporting me greatly; and for light reading the "Experiences of a New Guinea Resident Magistrate" interests me much, even though certainly not literature but slang. Professor

Rudolf Otto himself sent me his "Das Heilige." I entirely agree with your judgment of it, although I still have not read it as carefully as it deserves.

I have had a genuine consolation in the success of attempts to get Troeltsch invited to Oxford. Clement Webb is going to invite him to give an Address in his Lecture Room. But this is still a secret, please.

But, on the other hand, I have had a great grief. Dear Puck suffered so much from cardiac asthma that last Wednesday he had to be put an end to in my chair in my study, in which I am now sitting.[206] The little fellow was full of trust and affection towards me up to the moment when unconsciousness came on; and once again I had my doubts as to whether all we fine reasoners are right, and whether such a little mind, heart, and character, which so obviously is more than just material or the product of simple materiality,—whether all this really ends at such a moment after nine short years of life. Perhaps you will remember the splendid parallel which St Catherine of Genoa loved so much, between the trust and love of a dog who knows his master, but without analysis or reasoning, and the human soul's attitude to God where this attitude is a right one. There, too, the knowledge far transcends the discernment, and there especially the reality far transcends the knowledge. The shock was all the greater to me because two days before the end the vet who knew him best had told me that he might quite well get over the asthma, and that in any case he would certainly not think of having him destroyed; and, indeed, I find that Pekinese live to 14 or even 15 and 16 years of age, so that as his race goes he was certainly not old.

Your very affectionate and grateful old friend,

F. VON HÜGEL.

p.p. Es[telle].B[lyth].

[206] A detailed account of Puck's last illness, death, and burial is to be found in von Hügel's Diary. The Baron himself accompanied the dog's "little corpse" to the pet cemetery at Molesworth in Huntingdonshire where it was buried in the same grave with von Hügel's earlier Pekingese, Teufel. Diaries, 14, 18, 19, 21 October 1922.

Nov. 6. 1922.   14 Lennox Street,
                                               Edinburgh.

My dear Baron,

I must ask you to pardon my delay in replying to your letter
of Oct. 24ᵗʰ. Your suggestion that your health may unhappily constrain you to resign the Gifford Lectureship, & the questions you
ask in connection therewith, called, as I felt, for much careful
consideration; & as it happened there supervened thereupon a
quite hectic week of engagements & other preoccupations. I had
to prepare & deliver an address on 'The Nature of Democracy' to
a W. E. A. audience. Then I had to inform myself regarding the
business of the 'City of Edinburgh Council of Social Service' (the
Organisation that takes the place of the older Charity Organisation Society), as I have had to take on the Chairmanship of its
Executive Committee & it had its first meeting last Thursday.
Twice, too, I had to take the Chair at public, students' meetings.
(One on Sunday night in the Operetta House, when Dʳ Sclater[207]
addressed the students; & *as it happened he quoted a saying of
yours, from one of your books*). To crown all, Mʳˢ Kemp Smith
& I have had some difficult decisions to make, in regard to a new
house—happily with the almost incredible good fortune that we
have secured one of the most delightful houses in all Edinburgh,
& that at a very low figure, in the Grange district, with a quite
charming garden, & open outlook on to the Blackford Hill. We
shall hope to welcome there Lady Mary & yourself—might we
also dare to hope Baroness Hildegarde—as our most honoured
guests. But I must come to business. As I have said, these multi-
farious preoccupations have hitherto kept me from obtaining as
clear a mind as I should like upon the important issue you raise.

Let me first of all say, that the possibility of your having to
resign from reasons of health only makes me rejoice the more
heartily that Edinburgh has made itself right with posterity, by
placing on record its desire to have you add distinction to its list

---

[207] John Robert Paterson Sclater (1876–
1949), British Presbyterian minister, educated at Emmanuel College, Cambridge,
and Westminster Theological College;
minister of New North Church, Edinburgh, 1907–1923, and from 1924 minister of Old St. Andrew's Church, Toronto,
Canada; held various lectureships in Scotland and at Harvard and Yale Universities.

of Gifford Lecturers. That will always remain as a great satisfaction, whatever be the decision to which you ultimately come.

On one other point I am also, I fear, likewise clear, & that is that I must agree with you that in fairness to your successor, whoever he may be, your resignation ought to be intimated immediately you are certain as to its inevitableness. But I sincerely trust that you may still see your way to holding the Lectureship at least for one year. Should you, upon good trial, find the burden too heavy, resignation as for the second year, could then be made. There is no uncertainty as to your being able to complete the lectures as for publication, & that, after all is really the main requirement of the Lectureship. *Many* Gifford Lecturers have been so ineffective as speakers that their audiences have dwindled to a mere handful; & yet no one has thought of questioning, when their published work has proved worthy, the *essential* worthiness & worthwhileness of the appointments. Could you consider residing in or about Edinburgh during *both* Spring & Summer Terms of one year (each Term is of 9 to 10 weeks), & delivering the 10 lectures at fortnightly intervals?

We have, however, to face the possibility that this may not be possible to you. In that case, I am afraid, I must, as I have said, concur in your deliberate judgment, & admit that there is no alternative to early resignation. As to how the Senatus would then act, I cannot say. Doubtless it would regretfully accept your resignation. I can only speak for myself, but I should certainly make every effort as a member of the Gifford Committee to prevail upon it to allow, on grounds of health, for one year at least, still better for both years, your giving four or five instead of ten lectures, with, of course, the explicit condition, which, as I understand, you fully expect (your health not further failing) to be able to fulfil, that you publish, in book form, the full, required 20 lectures. However this is merely my own personal feeling as to how I should act; I have no grounds for thinking it would be of any avail, & I take the liberty of mentioning it at all, only in order to define my own feelings in the matter.

I should like, if you have to decide on resignation, to have the opportunity, if I may, of consulting Prof. W. P. Patterson before you do so. He is much better able than I am to advise as to times & procedures, & also to judge as to how the Gifford Committee & Senatus would regard the proposal I have outlined. I note in the University Calendar that Professor Flint[208]—Patterson's predecessor in the Chair of Divinity—is entered as Gifford Lecturer for 1907–9 with the following after his name "(no lectures delivered)". That may be an important precedent: but what the circumstances were I do not know.

If the worst comes to the worst, I shall at least hope that your health may allow of your coming to Edinburgh; & it is more than generous of you to consent to a few lectures to our philosophical & theological group. That is a promise I shall hold you to, if Lady Mary can give her approval to your undertaking the journey in some early year.

I fear that the prospect of Edinburgh inviting Troeltsch next Spring, while he is in England, will not after all mature. Prof. Patterson is to have leave of absence during the Summer Term & Prof. Curtis who took the matter in hand says he cannot now himself undertake the arrangements. But I shall speak again to Principal Martin & Prof. Mackintosh of the New College next time I see them.

My most sincere sympathy in what I know is indeed a great great grief to you, little Puck's death. My daughter, wife & I are looking forward to having a dog friend, now that we are to have a garden. But it is late, & I must close.

Yours ever affectionately,

NORMAN KEMP SMITH.

P.S. I sail on Dec. 27th, but shall be back in Edinburgh by middle of June, & University does not close till end of July. Mrs Kemp Smith will, I fear, be prevented from going to California with me by the necessities of the new house etc.

[208] Robert Flint (1838–1910), Scottish churchman and theologian, educated at Glasgow University; Professor of Moral Philosophy and Political Economy at St. Andrews University, 1864–1876; Professor of Divinity at Edinburgh University, 1876–1903; Stone Lecturer at Princeton University, 1880.

14 Lennox Street

Nov. 13. 1922

My dear Baron,

Professor Paterson was out of town over the week-end, but I have seen him this evening. We went over the Gifford Deed, & were glad to find that it does not quite definitely require that *ten* lectures be given each year, but on the contrary leaves this to the discretion of the Lecturer. Paterson, who is Convener of the Gifford Committee, in his present mind favours endeavouring to obtain sanction from the Committee & the Senatus to which it reports, that you be asked to hold the Gifford at least for one year, giving such lectures as you see your way to, while publishing in full. Meantime he agrees that it will be best to do as you desire, that is to submit your resignation, explaining that you do so regretfully, because though you expect to be in a position to fulfil the requirement to publish a volume representing at least 20 lectures, you feel doubtful as to your having the strength to deliver more than a smaller number thereof. Your letter is to the Senatus, but should be addressed to the Secretary of the University, Wm Wilson, who in August last was elected to the Chair of Civil Law. So address the letter: —Professor William Wilson, The Secretary's Office, The University, Edinburgh—asking him to submit your resignation to the Senatus. There should be time for a meeting of the Gifford Committee before next meeting of Senatus on December 7th.

In haste, & with kindest greetings,

Yours ever affectionately,

NORMAN KEMP SMITH.

19th Nov. 1922
13, Vicarage Gate,
Kensington,
London, W. 8.

My very dear and most helpful Friend,

Thank you much for your interesting and important letter. I cannot, just now, write fully about either its other contents or about various further things which have occurred here. But I must and will now without further delay, put the following clear perceptions and definite decisions of my own *re* the Gifford Lectureship upon paper to you.

1. *I definitely resign the Gifford Lectureship*, into the hands, I suppose, of the University Registrar. But I will await your instructions as finally culled from Prof. Patterson, concerning how I am to put it and to whom to address it. I can promise to send off this resignation at latest on day after receipt of these instructions.

2. I suppose I shall have to say *why* I do so, with or without discriminations. But it can do no harm if, at least to yourself thus privately (or also for Prof. Patterson), I once more declare that I continue thoroughly hopeful of achieving the book, in 20 chapters (at least). I find I can dictate to my very able and most sympathetic short-hand secretary, twice a week, even after extra bad nights, and this with freshness in the composition thrown out. —This, of course, would have been a large part of my obligation as Gifford Lecturer.

It is, then, entirely only with regard to the oral delivery of the above in two courses of ten lectures each, at distances of time no more than a week between each lecture, and of no more than a year between the two courses, that I resign my trust. I am already quite sure that I could not so lecture.—

3. I feel already strongly that I should *at most* say the above. But I can thank yourself for so devotedly looking around as to some arrangement possible to the Committee and *Senatus* and feasible by myself.

Yet I am clear, on this point, that it is only because of my wife and home daughter that I do not already beg you to abstain from any step or question which would aim at any exception for myself. I have always shrunk from exceptions in all matters. But *they* might feel differently (they know nothing about all this), so I will simply leave action or no action in your hands, with perfect readiness to follow your further hints, sure you will, above all, consider the rights of others, the dignity of the Trust, and my own little self-respect.

4. This, again, does not prevent my still and already looking forward, with (I feel) reasonable confidence to coming to Edinburgh—if and when I am ready and you can arrange for me, for up to 3 addresses (at a fortnight between each) based on the then ready book. But all I allow myself thus to forecast is entirely outside the Gifford Trust. I would come simply in my private capacity, at, I should hope, the invitation of the Edinburgh Philosophical and Theological Society.

I am so delighted to think of your lovely new house, with the fine garden, and thank you much for your handsome invitation to us three. My wife and Hildegard will also be most touched and grateful, when they hear. But I am waiting to tell them all, until all is fixed up.

I am myself feeling deeply grateful for my present working capacity and for all the encouragement I already and permanently have from Edinburgh: I should be greedy indeed to want anything more. And thus, too, I can suit my own time and pace.

Your grateful old Friend
F. v. HÜGEL.

Nov. 24. 1922   14 Lennox Street,
                                                        Edinburgh

Private

My dear Baron,

This afternoon there was a meeting of the Gifford Committee, to consider your letter of resignation. Professor Paterson moved that you be requested to continue in the Lectureship, giving such number of lectures as you felt able to give. Unhappily—at least so I see the situation—the Committee considered that this would be contrary to the intention of the Gifford Deed which lays great emphasis upon the giving of the lectures, and does not even exact publication. I suggested as a compromise that you be asked to hold the Lectureship for one year, giving such lectures as you can, & publishing in due course. But this motion also failed to obtain sufficient support. The decision of the Committee was that the Senatus be recommended to accept your resignation regretfully.

I wish it could have been otherwise. You will be hearing from the Secretary in due course, doubtless after the meeting of Senatus on the 7th Dec. Meantime, & with immense regrets,

Yours ever affectionately,

NORMAN KEMP SMITH.

Your thoughtfulness to the University in so anticipating what you have considered to be inevitable has been warmly appreciated by the Committee, & the cause of your resignation deeply regretted.

25th Nov. 1922
13, Vicarage Gate,
Kensington,
W. 8.

My dear Professor,

You and Professor Paterson have been most kind and generous in your endeavors; and please let me thank you, and beg you to thank him, as warmly as if you had succeded. But indeed the Deed of Foundation standing thus and the Committee taking (I doubt not, correctly) that view of it, I could not have failed myself to find this out before long, had it—*per impossibile*—been achievable for me to secure such a limited appointment. And *that* would have been much worse for me than anything I may now lose. But indeed even this is not the right view to take. For I have had nothing but gain, and great gain, as the sum total effect of your kind efforts. I remain one who was appointed to that post and who has given it up for purely health reasons. This will cheer me on greatly. And now, too, there is nothing to strain me or to make me anxious, but only work which is, thank God, going well, tho', of course, I have to pass thro' times of deep disgust at it.—

I have had *Adickes* handsomely bound, with care not to cut

off any of your annotations. He looks really very handsome now! I shall have finished with him before you leave for California, and will return him in sufficient time unless you say you do not want him till you are back.

Your devoted Friend
F. v. H.

Dec. 17. 1922   14 Lennox Street,
Edinburgh.

My dear Baron,

I have only just been contriving to keep my head above the waters of work & engagements, else I had written sooner. It is very good of you to have bound the Adickes, & I shall value you [*sic*] it the more as thus ever reminding me of you. Just yesterday I had a postcard from Adickes in reply to my query whether Kant ever uses the term 'transcendental object' in the *Op. Post.* He cannot say offhand, & is unable to verify in detail, but does not think that it does. So, thus far, my assertion that he definitely gave up using the phrase seems to hold. I have to have a new edition of my *Commentary* ready for the Macmillans by May, & shall do this in California. As the *Commentary* is stereotyped I am not permitted to throw out the paging, but short of that can make changes. Also I mean to add an Appendix on Adickes' account of the *Op. Post.*, & shall therefore be glad to have the Adickes' volume *not later* than Christmas morning, as I leave the next day. My steamer sails from Southampton on the 27th. I go to London by day on the 26th, & leave Waterloo at 8.45—boat train—on the Wednesday morning. So unhappily I shall not be able to look in upon you: had it not been for Christmas Day I should have come a day sooner. For the same reason I shall unfortunately miss seeing J. H. Muirhead. I'll take an Hotel near my Stations.

I rejoice that Prof. Mackintosh is now arranging for Troeltsch's visit to Edinburgh, & am only sorry that I shall myself be away. At last meeting of Senate W. P. Paterson moved & I seconded that Troeltsch be invited by the University to lecture. There was, however, some opposition, & though the motion might very possibly have received a majority, it seemed best not to rouse antagonisms that are rapidly dying down—so the motion was withdrawn. This does not in any way stand in way of arrangements proposed by Mackintosh—quite the reverse. With feeling towards France changing so rapidly, many of us believe that in a very few years it will be feasible to propose Troeltsch for the Gifford Lectureship.

The question of your successor as Gifford Lecturer is still under discussion. Patterson proposes Archbishop Soderblom (is that the right spelling?) of Upsala. The nomination that I should, on the whole, myself prefer, is A. E. Taylor. The Science & Medical people want a scientist, but seem unable to propose a satisfactory name. Balfour in his Giffords in Glasgow is ambling along very amiably, but does not seem to be saying anything at all.

The Stouts were with us over last week-end. I have got some very helpful criticism of my new book from Stout, & he promises more in mss. In haste, but kindest greetings,

Yours ever affectionately,

NORMAN KEMP SMITH.

Last week we sold this house, at the figure we asked for it; which removes one anxiety, & lets me sail with a freer mind.

20th Dec. 1922.
13, Vicarage Gate,
Kensington,
W. 8.

My dear Professor,

Thank you much for your letter, as always so full of news and of kindest advice—indeed you never fail to be able to tell me of at least one generous piece of help towards ends I love so much.—

I greatly regret, but quite understand, that we cannot meet in London, now on your passage through to—California! Your objective does sound such an immense distance off! —But I trust you will be able to stop anew at least, on your way back through,—preferably at our house. A day's notice wd. be quite sufficient.—

To make quite sure that you get back your *Adickes: Kant's Opus Postumum* I am sending it you, very carefully packed, this afternoon; this note shall go separately, to reassure you, supposing the parcel is a little late in coming. But in the parcel will be a little Christmas card for dear little Marjorie, whom I indeed think of, often. How pleased she will be to have you back! I wanted a more certainly suitable card, but from those I foraged at the Medici Society's delightful shop, this is the one I feel sure will, at least, not be directly unsuitable.—

I have got my philosophy secretary to type out for me all the chief passages you have marked in the Op. Post., and a few noted by myself about space and time. So I shall not ask for the volume again. But if later on I am better off, I intend to rejoin the Kant Gesellschaft, and to buy the volume—I hope at sub-scription-price.

I have now got my first eight chapters all in type—which makes me very happy. But, of course, the whole will have to be gone over again twice: when I have done it all, D. V., thrice, you are to see Part I—specially your domain.—

I have read, as you suggested Einstein's own accounts of his Theory. I understood all pretty well—except where he *would* be 'clear' and give me fearsome algebraic formulae. That man is no quack, and he may turn out right ere we are, say, 5 years older. Do, please, put some note or other—something—into your 'Commentary' about this. I simply cannot I find treat Space and Time as certainly infinite. I never, somehow, could believe in that infinitude, and now E. comes along apparently on the point of demonstrating that they are not infinite. —I delight in E.'s *Real-*

ism—it shows everywhere; and I feel that somehow the finitude point will not really weaken Realism—if we somehow manage well.—

How kind and useful of Prof. Paterson and yourself in proposing that Troeltsch shd be now invited to lecture before the University! And how wise, not to press the point! T. will certainly now come to Edinburgh—to the New College very kind people —and will, I feel sure, go down beautifully. The future is in God's hands!

Goodbye then, one of my two closest living Friends.

May you do excellently well with the Lectures, the new book, the 'Commentary' and all else!

Gott befohlen! We both believe in, adore, love God! What a gift of His *that* is!

Very aff. Friend

F. v. H.

Best season's greetings to Mrs Kemp Smith, from us both.

Thanks, too, about that point as to Kant's dropping of the 'transcendental object' term. I shall enter what you say into my copy of your 'Commentary'.

Dec 25. 1922   14 Lennox Street,
                                                              Edinburgh.

My dear Baron,

Your letter & the Adickes have reached me. The latter does indeed look magnificent in its gorgeous attire. The little daughter has also been delighted with your card, & will be writing you herself.

We have a Christmas Tree today with some students & friends of the daughter. The latter (mostly aged about 10) are to act 'Little Red Riding-Hood'. A strange choice, but settled on for mysterious reasons, which I do not attempt to fathom.

I shall only just manage to be ready for 10 a.m. train tomorrow morning, bag & baggage.

M[rs] Kemp Smith joins me in kindest greetings to Lady Mary, the Baronness Hildegarde and yourself.

Yours ever gratefully & affectionately,

NORMAN KEMP SMITH.

May 28. 1923   Princeton, N.J.

My dear Baron,

The intention to write you has been constantly with me, & now that I am hoping to see you so soon a letter seems of little service. I sail on June 5th on the S.S. Berengaria for Southampton, & should gladly avail myself of your hospitality for a couple of nights if this is entirely convenient for Lady Mary & yourself. The Berengaria is a six-day boat (I always choose the largest & fastest I can find), so should reach Southampton about the 11th. A letter addressed to me as: *Passenger* 2ND *Cabin, S.S. Berengaria, due June 11th, Cunard Line, Southampton*, will find me on arrival.

I was deeply grieved to hear of Troeltsch's death; & greatly enjoyed your notice of him in the *Times*.[209] Very many thanks for so kindly sending it to me.

But I shall not attempt to write of the many things about which I should like to talk to you. The months in Berkeley have been most interesting & stimulating. Your friend D[r] Clark I enjoyed meeting. He is a fine, gentle spirit.

Here I am in a social whirlpool. Last week I spent with my friends, the Bowmans, & this week I am with the McLean Harpers.[210] It is delightful seeing old friends in this beautiful little town.

My wife is busy this month removing into our new house; the daughter is a regular correspondent.

---

[209] For von Hügel's letter to *The Times* on Troeltsch, see Appendix VI.

[210] George McLean Harper (1863–1947), American writer and university professor, educated at Princeton University; worked on *New York Tribune* and *Scribner's Magazine* before taking up teaching at Princeton, 1889–1932; an authority on Wordsworth.

With kindest greetings to Lady Mary & to your daughter, & with happy anticipations of seeing you,

I am, Yours ever affectionately,

NORMAN KEMP SMITH.

P.S. I enclose a printer's proof of the Appendix for the new edition of my Kant. I hear that J. G. Fraser[211] has been appointed your successor in the Gifford Lectureship: Seth & I hoped for Taylor, but the science people intervened.

June 28. 1923   67 Great King Street
                                            Edinburgh.
My dear Baron,

Since I reached Edinburgh I have been plunged into a multiplicity of engagements & duties, that still ought not to have prevented me writing you sooner.

In the first place, J. H. Muirhead, who has been taking my work in my absence, was staying with us & left only on Tuesday of this week. Then secondly, there were quite a number of University matters to be attended to, including the Pass & Honours Examinations. Thirdly, the Secretary of the Workers' Educational Association has to relinquish part of her work, & there is the task of finding a substitute to take it over, to carry on meantime. And lastly, not least, there is our new house. Unhappily the drains have to be relaid, & that together with the usual delays of painters etc. means that we cannot get in until the end of next month. We are staying in a sister-in-law's flat until the house can be occupied. To top all, the work on the roof has not been properly done, & I am carrying on a somewhat heated correspondence with the contractor.

All this has come somewhat heavily on my wife, who, however, is well, as also is the little daughter. I was greatly flattered to hear

---

[211] Sir James George Frazer (1854–1941), Scottish classical scholar with an anthropological and literary approach to religion, educated at Glasgow University and Trinity College, Cambridge; his best-known work is *The Golden Bough* (1890).

that when someone during the winter said to her that she would be forgetting her Father in his absence, she replied "Oh, no: I know Daddy off by heart"! As further compensation our new garden, which has been kept in perfect condition, is looking most attractive & beautiful. Edinburgh too—besides being home—is the best of cities to return to.

Tomorrow I have to go over to St Andrews, to propose a friend at the Graduate Council for membership of the University Court. Shall be dining tomorrow night with the Stouts & meeting John Laird of Belfast who is going to Berkeley for the whole of the coming Academic Year as Mills Lecturer. John Burnet has also been asked to go as Sather Lecturer in Greek, & asks me to advise him in the matter on Saturday. I fancy his health is hardly such as to justify his attempting it. He is still showing the effects of his recent nervous breakdown.

Harold Joachim[212] was to have been in Edinburgh today, *en route* to St Andrews to receive the LL.D.; but has been delayed by the illness of his son. Tho' not much older than myself, he was a Lecturer & one of my teachers, when I was an undergraduate in St Andrews.

I am sorry that Troeltsch's lectures have set you so difficult a problem; but they will gain so much by the setting in which you will place them, that I cannot regret—for the general reader's sake—that friendship & loyalty to his memory constrain you to the task.[213]

Muirhead, who delights in editing, is preparing a volume of 'Selbstdarstellungen'—modelled on a German volume—representative of British philosophers—or rather, as is likely, two volumes—the second being composed more of younger men & those who send in their contributions later. Unfortunately Muirhead's standards of selection are not, I think, very strict or happy. He is

[212] Harold Henry Joachim (1868–1938), British philosopher, educated at Harrow and Balliol College, Oxford; Assistant to Professor of Moral Philosophy, St. Andrews University, 1892–1894; Lecturer in Philosophy at Balliol, 1894–1897; Fellow and Tutor in Philosophy, Merton College, Oxford, 1897–1919; Wykeham Professor of Logic, Oxford, 1919.

[213] The lectures which Troeltsch would have delivered in England in March 1923, had he lived, were carefully edited in translation, with a lengthy Introduction, by von Hügel as *Christian Thought: Its History and Application* (London: University of London Press, 1923).

including Wildon Carr & May Sinclair[214]—unworthy pair to couple together, but!!— He has an interesting contribution from Bosanquet, largely biographical, & written just before his death. I had the honour of an invitation to contribute, but feel neither old enough nor mature enough for doing so. The coming Summer will, however, I am still hoping, allow of my completing my first book in statement of a point of view of my own.

It was a great delight to have the privilege of seeing you again. I mean, by hard work, to try in some small degree to justify, so far as in me lies, the immense boon of the friendship you generously extend to me. The older generation, when it has profited by the years as you have done, carries so great a store of wisdom in so vivid & contagious a form that I, as a younger man, can never be sufficiently grateful to you for allowing me access to it in this full measure. Please convey to Lady Mary my greetings & warm thanks for her kindly hospitality.

Yours ever affectionately,
NORMAN KEMP SMITH.

4th July 1923
13, Vicarage Gate,
Kensington,
London, W. 8.

My dear Professor,

It was most kind of you to write me so full and variously interesting a letter. I always enjoy your letters very specially, especially in their fullness of detail as to all you are doing and planning.

I wish I could, just now, write at length, but I dare not. The fact is that I want to get everything passed and finished with the

---

[214] May Sinclair (?–1946), British writer, educated at the Ladies College, Cheltenham; first novel published in 1896; first really successful novel, *The Divine* *Fire*, published in England and America in 1904; her writings more appreciated in America than in England.

Troeltsch volume before I leave this for my holiday on Tuesday July 31st. I have still to revise (on top of Principal Barker) the last London University Lecture in galley proof—it has not yet reached me; I have to get my Introduction improved chief in galley proof but also still a little in page revise; and I have to compile the Index—I think even for so small a volume, an Index of Persons and an Index of Things.—

But this morning I at last sent off the (typed) Introduction for an early return in galleys-proof. Mr Murrell (Manager of London University Press) is, apparently, going to allow me appreciably more than 3,000 words—I have just over 4,000 in the ms so far.—

Now I chiefly write to find out whether, I should think by Monday or Tuesday next, you will be a little less rushed, and could do me the great kindness of reading the thing thus when it still can be greatly altered. It has cost me much (also interior, emotional) trouble, and I feel that the points are all important and substantially right. There may, however, be inconsistencies or slips in taste etc which I have overlooked, and those points themselves may be over-iterated or otherwise ineffective.

If you read it you will find a bit about the English Hegelians, which Webb wanted put in and similarly Barker. But *perhaps* (?) there ought to be a word to show that I am with Troeltsch in my conviction that Hegelism has strangely little to give to religion and takes from it its very roots. (Am saying something of this sort in my new Preface to 'M. E.' 2nd ed.).

Frau Troeltsch is annoyed at the translation into German (in the 'Christliche Welt') of my *T. L. S.* letter on her late husband —dislikes the intimate bits appearing thus for Germans to read. I have written her that no one asked for permission to translate, and, had they done so, I should have required them to cut out those parts which I still feel not excessive for over here, where I hoped to soften readers out of their militant anti-Germanisms.

I mention this as a further reason why I want to be circumspect (but not timid—*that* will ruin any piece of writing!) in this Introduction as regards its human bits.

I shall expect a P. C. (but nothing else!) before this week is out with 'yes' or 'no'—meaning 'able to read the thing' or 'unable'.

We are full of sympathy with you too about the new house—we ourselves had drains to be re-laid in one Hampstead house and the roof to be properly doubled in the other.

My love to Janet please; I do not forget the letter I owe her.

Yrs aff'tely

F. V. HÜGEL.

P.S. Only Principal Barker wd., besides yourself, see that proof.

H.

July 5. 1923   67 Great King Street,
                                                        Edinburgh.

My dear Baron,

I was delighted to have your letter this evening, as we were having tea & feeling somewhat distracted & upset over the discovery just made at our new house of *very* extensive dry-rot—how extensive we don't yet know. There are evidences that it was *partially* dealt with some 12 or 18 months ago; & this may enable us to have a legal claim on the sellers of the house. Altogether we are having a run of bad luck in this matter! So your letter, with messages of better things, was a godsend, to turn our minds to happier thoughts.

Yes, I shall be honoured & delighted to read the Introduction very carefully, & to make any suggestions that may occur to me. The earlier it arrives next week the better. I am to be in St Andrews on Monday night taking the Chair at a reunion of old St Andrews class-mates—the first since I graduated. I return on Tuesday, & on Friday go to Durham for the Philosophical Conference. On Tuesday, Wednesday & Thursday I can reserve time for the Introduction.

Please note that my number in Great King Street is *67* (*not* 7 as on your letter of yesterday).

Enclosed is Meinecke's article; which I at once seized upon, further to help clear my mind of house worries. It is *most interesting*, if a little diffuse & indefinite.

I was in St Andrews over Friday night, to propose a friend for membership of the Court as representative of the General Council of the University. At night, at the Stouts', I met Professor & Mrs Laird: my wife & I also had lunch with them in Edinburgh today. Stout says that the *first* volume of his Giffords won't be out till next year: I doubt there may be even longer delay. Also a letter has come to the Secretary of the University from Bergson saying that the state of his health will not permit his giving his 2nd Series here next Spring. I have not yet heard further details.

My wife & little Janet join me in kindest greetings

Yours ever affectionately

N. KEMP SMITH.

Up to the 26th July
67 Great King Str.
After the 26th
14 Blackford Road,

July 21. 1923   Edinburgh.

My dear Baron,

I have been immensely interested to read through the proofs of your most admirable Introduction. You have indeed solved your difficult problem in a wonderfully satisfactory manner. All my numerous suggestions—I jot down *all* points, that you may select as you find good—concern only questions of expression. There is just one exception, & that concerns the passage at ft of p. 2862 (also numbered p. 5). I should criticise the passage 1) because it seems to make out the earlier Troeltsch to have been an unqualified eulogist ("without reserve") of the Medieval Roman Church; & 2) because you may seem to Protestant readers to be narrowing your argument from the general (& alone strictly relevant) thesis, that institutional religion is necessary, to the special case of the Roman Church. You may or may not be right, but is it necessary in dealing with Troeltsch, who recognises institutional values also in other Churches, to direct your argument in this manner? Also, as the passage stands, there is a difficulty in the phrase "during the Golden Middle Ages in the *Soziallehren*".

Please take my numerous suggestions on the galley-proofs only for what they are meant to be—the suggestions that occur to me as I read. I have gone over the proofs carefully twice, & should have liked to do so a third time; but fear I may be keeping them too long. If I can be of any aid in reading the next proof of the Introduction, please don't hesitate to call upon me. There is no privilege I value more, or feel to be a greater honour, than that of being of aid to you, in however minor a way. Very many thanks for your generous reference to me in the Preface: I read it with immense pride.

The limits of the dry-rot have been reached, & we are being very philosophical about it.

Last week-end I was at the Philosophical Congress at Durham. There was an *excellent* session on 'Relativity'—Whitehead & Sampson (Astronomer, Edinburgh) & Percy Nunn,—with Wildon Carr sticking in with great nonsense. Stout's new theory of universals was discussed but G. E. Moore so indulged in dialectics as rather to ruin it. In the session on the Sunday night, on 'The New Idealism (meaning, it would seem, Croce & Gentile!) & Mysticism', Miss Underhill[215]—Mrs Moore—was quite good; & Dean Inge was amusing & quite irresponsible—so much so as to call down a reprimand (!) from the Chairman, Prof. J. A. Smith of Magdalen, who spoke extraordinarily dully for 20 minutes without saying anything at all. Our friend, Meade, got an inning—about half an hour of it, I think—to such effect as you can conjecture. Samuel Alexander was easily the most delightful & effective participant at the meetings. I saw a little of Mrs Moore

---

[215] Evelyn Underhill (Mrs. Stuart Moore) (1875–1941), British writer on religious topics, educated at King's College for Women, London; Upton Lecturer on Religion, Manchester College, Oxford, 1921–1922; considerably influenced by von Hügel both personally and through his writings; among her many books probably the two most significant are *Mysticism* and *Worship*.

who is very attractive, & we spoke of you. There were a number of younger men whom I was also glad to see.

A Physiological Congress is in session in Edinburgh all this week. On Wednesday next the University confers 8 Honorary LL.Ds.—one on Albrecht Kossel, Professor of Physiology at Heidelberg, & one on Hans Horst Meyer, Professor of Pharmacology at Vienna. This is a good step forward. The others are to Italian, Dutch, American, Swedish, Russian & French physiologists.

I remove to the house of another sister-in-law, on the 26th at 14 Blackford Road, near our new house, into which we expect to get in September.

May you have the best of holidays, & return with renewed zest to your own great book! I grudge this Troeltsch interruption, tho' only for that reason—as you must yourself.

With kindest greetings,

Yours ever affectionately,

NORMAN KEMP SMITH.

And please let me help further with the Introduction, if I can at all.

Aug. 25. 1923.   14 Blackford Road,
                                                  Edinburgh.

My dear Baron,

I herewith return the proof of your Introduction.

V 'Titles' have no fronts & backs, so it will have to be title-pages (as on p. XI).

V 'between us' is colloquial. I should suggest 'in collaboration'.

VI Twice on this page you give Webb's initials in the wrong order, as J. C. instead of C. J. I have verified this in the list of members of Aristotelian Society.

VII   Again Webb's initials wrong—this time as J. E., instead of Cl. C. J.

XII   comma after complete.

XIV   "large mistakes" is unfamiliar in English: I suggest *"grave* mistakes".

XVII 8 lines from top—"to each formulation"—Something is wrong here. I make *two* suggestions on margins.

XVII lower middle of page—type not properly aligned.

XX   Two lines of confusion, requiring omission.

XXI   Two *m* s in Mohammedanism.

XXII Sentence towards top of page does not run well. I should suggest comma after "conclusions" & substitution of 'philosophical' for 'considerable'.

XXII For *sublimierten* I should suggest, as better than penetrative *'speculative'*. This, I think, is really what Meinecke means.

XXVI 'this' a misprint for 'thus'

XXVII "all-growth" is probably a printer's error for "all growth". At first I read it otherwise & so suggested cutting out the "all-". All that is required is cutting out the dash.

XXVII 'with' has to be omitted.

XXIX Can requirement be used thus in the sense of 'need'? I suggest substituting 'need' as more correct English.

XXX   'Difference' will have to be changed to 'distinction'. A difference cannot be "drawn"; nor can we speak of a "difference" "coming from a politician".

XXXI Stimulus is certainly better than stimulation. But I should suggest 'inspiration': by a *free* use of language a person can be said to be an inspiration.

You will rejoice to have this piece of work finished. I look forward greatly to reading the Addresses.

I continue busily at work on my book, & am making reasonably good headway, & find myself strengthening in conviction as to the fruitfulness of the lines upon which I have been working —a good sign so far. Have also rejoiced to find—quite an unanticipated windfall for me—some valuable empirical evidence in support of a main thesis in Dr Head's[216] extraordinarily interesting physiological work on the senses & brain. It strengthens greatly one of my weaker links where I had seemed driven to seeming paradox on *speculative* grounds.

A Princeton colleague—Harper, author of the 'Life of Wordsworth'—is with me these days & we are going for week-end to Ayrshire to visit a mutual friend. The house makes progress. We shall get in it beginning of October. Mrs Kemp Smith & the daughter are both well. We may go to Windermere to my sister-in-law's cottage for a few weeks in September.

I have hesitated to send to you while on holiday in Surrey the volume of Külpe. If you wish it sent on, I am now finished with it, & can post at once if you send me a card. Otherwise I shall keep it in reserve for your return to London. With kind greetings to Lady Mary,

Yours ever affectionately,

N. KEMP SMITH.

P.S. Only today have I sent on to Pringle-Pattison the copy of your Preface to new edition of 'The Mystical Element of Religion'. I told him a fortnight ago that I had it, & have been waiting until I was writing him on another matter.

Oct. 20. 1923.   Ellerton,

Grange Loan,

Edinburgh.

My dear Baron,

Yesterday I posted to you the volume of Külpe which I ought to have returned earlier. I trust that you have not meantime been needing it. We are now at last happily, & very comfortably, set-

[216] Sir Henry Head (1861–1940), British medical doctor, educated at Charterhouse, and the Universities of Halle, Prague, and Cambridge; made many contributions to neurological studies, and received numerous honorary degrees and awards; Goulstonian Lecturer, Royal College of Physicians of London, 1901, and Croonian Lecturer, Royal Society, 1921.

tled at the above address; & I write in my new study, with the sun pouring in from its South window & the open garden in front. Mrs Kemp Smith rejoices in the garden which has been a long-cherished ambition of hers: it bears in plenty both flowers & vegetables—& a few fruits. A row of pine-trees seperate off the lower kitchen-garden from the lawn & flower-beds. The house too we increasingly like.

You have, I trust, had a restful summer, & are in good health for work. The Troeltsch volume is, I suppose, due to appear any day now. August & September I spent fairly busily writing, & by the end of September had finished my 'Prolegomena to an Idealist Theory of Knowledge'. The Macmillans have accepted it for publication. Do you know who their reader is?—since Sir Henry Jones's death? The Macmillans sent me on—without giving his name—his suggestion that I add to my introductory chapter an outline of my later argument: he seems to have made no other criticism, at least that they have thought good to communicate to me. I shall make a final revision, & place in printer's hands, I expect by end of next month. The views I propound are, at least, sufficiently *realist*, I think, to appeal to your sympathies on that score. It is a great satisfaction to have the book completed. I shall gladly be done for the present with theory of knowledge, that I may turn to other problems.

Classes started last week. I have twenty more than last year in my Degree class—191 in all; & 11 in my Honours class. The present week has been a busy one, as I had to give three addresses —the result of my last year's refusals accumulating—to three students' Societies, one being the University Theological Society & one the New College Society. Now I am quite free till December, save for my classes.

Lloyd Morgan is to be in Edinburgh in a few days. I have not yet got his Giffords (St Andrews) read, but do not expect to get much profit from them. Pringle-Pattison called yesterday with a copy of his 'Immortality' volume, & tells me that he has been corresponding with you. Am interested in a volume 'Essays of a Biologist' by Huxley's grandson, Julian Huxley. It is interesting to observe—the volume also is charmingly written—how he di-

verges toward a religious standpoint, & away from T. H.'s agnosticism, but is still at a very *half-way*, & I should say impossible, position.

  With kindest greetings to Lady Mary & to yourself.
                      Yours ever affectionately & gratefully,
                      NORMAN KEMP SMITH.

13 Vicarage Gate, London, W. 8.
    All Saints 1923.
My dear Professor,
  Your letter of 10 days ago cheered me greatly. To think of
you working at your own table, in that big house of yours, looking out on to the great garden, so loved by your wife; and then to
learn that your 'Prolegomena' is finished in the ms: all this rejoices, braces and points me on, in my own life. —You do me a
great, much valued kindness in thus keeping me abreast of all
your vicissitudes and labours; it helps me to grow and to expand
so happily.

  I am rejoiced too at being able to tell you that since last Monday Oct. 29, I am again at, indeed engrossed in my big book;
and this morning (really Nov. 2, but I could not resist putting
that Feast of yesterday, so dearly loved by me, at the head of
this scribble!) I dictated with much happiness 1,600 new words,
introductory to Part II. to my Secretary. I hope to get this middle
Part done (thus, for the 1st typing) before the winter is out.
Then will remain Part III which, I believe, I shall find the easiest
of the three. How one grows, how sustained and yet humbled one
feels and *is* when thus plunged in work of a modestly creative
kind! I always find it to become a sort of prayer. And my health
has, at once, benefitted by my return to my own pastures. And
as I work I think spontaneously of the possibility of pleasing you,
my Friend.

                      Aff. and grateful. F. v. HÜGEL.

Ellerton,

Grange Loan,

Dec. 8. 1923.   Edinburgh.

My dear Baron,

Just a line to acknowledge receipt of the Troeltsch volume. I am eagerly looking forward to its perusal. Indeed I have already reread your Introduction, with great appreciation. I am proud too of your generous reference to myself in the Preface. When I have studied the volume at leisure, I shall again write you.

The past eight weeks have been very busy. I had to write two addresses—one on American Life and Conditions (already given twice & to be given three (!) times more), & one for the annual Scottish Conference of the Workers' Educational Association, on 'Education & Propaganda'—which have gone reasonably well. I have been teaching too with more than the usual success in both my classes, (208 in one, 10 in the other). This encouragement has been balanced by much searching of heart & sense of failure in many matters, by which I trust to profit much more than by the successes. So, on the whole, all goes well with me; as I know it *must* with yourself & your work, so immensely much more richly & fruitfully.

My household is busy preparing for Christmas. We have a Christmas tree for the daughter & her friends, & next day for 12 children of parents connected with the University Settlement. Janet is the happy possessor, just this week of a kitten & an Irish terrier pup.

With kindest greetings to Lady Mary. Yours ever gratefully & affectionately,

NORMAN KEMP SMITH.

13 Vicarage Gate, London, W. 8.

Dec. 22, 1923.

My dear Professor,

I want to write you just a short note, partly to thank you warmly for your last *lettrina* or *letterina*—I am now wobbly about a word I used, in Rome, to hear and to use so often! It was most kind and dear of you to continue there your simple, but much loved chronicles, of your doings, joys and pains—especially this time, my mentioning those humiliations. Don't I just know the kind of things you mean, and don't they just evoke little tumbles or thumps that came to me, some of them over 50 years ago and that make me ache still whenever the memory comes across them. How lonely and yet how close to our fellows we all are in such things; lovely, because not only was it *you*, and not the nearest of your loved ones who felt those rubs, but because even if they ever are, materially, ideotical, our individual reactions to them are so different. But how much more you know than this poor psychological stuff; you see that these humiliations furnish unique occasions of interior purification and growth—happy man! Still, a friend can also hope and pray for the other that direct encouragements may also not fail, since we do indeed require these also, and since, in the relations between you and me I receive so many, many of such.—

I am beginning to-day (Christmas Eve) a little week's holiday, and can look back to what I have been able to do, since resuming at the beginning of September. I have had *some* weeks when health left me a fair margin of strength for work; but the last fortnight and over has pulled me up short, with much, and repeatedly most, of the night in my arm chair, where I indeed escape the strangling feeling of the high arterial pressure and the plague of that perpetual little requirement, but where I cannot so far, succeed in getting beyond very light dozing. Still of the book planned as: Introd., 2 cc.; Section One of Body, 8 cc.; Section Two, 8 cc.; and Section Three, eight cc., with a Concl. of 2 cc.: I have now got all the Introduction, all Section One, and the first four cc. of Section Two behind me—all written or dictated three times. It will, doubtless, all still require at least one very careful re-writing or equivalent before first printing. I am finding this Section Two much my hardest piece; I believe Section Three will be much easier.—

I have just had to lose my 2nd Secretary—a young curate's wife, 1st baby coming—but have secured my 3rd, trained Secretary—London Univ. (Philosophy) Degree, and expert short hand and typing. She comes for the first dictation on Jan. 1st.—

Our excellent cousin, Evelyn Lady de Vesci, has given my wife and me, each, £25 for our Golden Wedding on Nov. 27 last; and I have been buying books as I never can as a rule—things wanted, tho' for many a year, e.g. Adam's Plato's 'Republic', Höffding's 'Modern Philosophy' etc.; also one very noble book of travel—Doughty's 'Arabia Deserta', which I love to browse in of afternoons in hopes of catching some of its greatness—a something that does not pass away.

So glad you have got on so well with your classes and with the secondary, but very interesting and useful work. I have now no engagements outside the book, except one, throughout 1924—two little addresses to the Christian Students at Swanwick June 23–26.

How constantly you are before me in those wakefull nights! God bless you for all you are and all you do for me.

Very aff. and grateful

Old Friend

F. v. H.—

So proud, amongst Macmillan's announcements to find my name amongst the helpers towards your *Commentary*, ed. 2. But I wish they would not print my 'von' with a big V.: it ought always to be small—not part of the name. So Ranke, Bismark, Harnack, etc. always did and does.

Dec. 31. 1923   Ellerton,

Grange Loan,

Edinburgh.

My dear Baron,

Very many thanks for your most welcome letter. The daughter has also been delighted with the letter all to herself and with the charming old-world book with its beautiful woodcuts, which we have all enjoyed. Janet is herself writing you. I am so sorry, however, to hear that of late you have had to work under such difficult conditions of ill-health & sleeplessness. May the week's holiday have brought, or be bringing, much relief! Your new book is now just precisely half written, is it not? And that, for you, the more troublesome & difficult half? Don't you find it generally the best method, to press on to the finishing of the whole in rough, before setting yourself to polish & give more or less final form to the earlier sections? I always find that after 'finishing' the concluding parts, there is much to alter, as well as so much that can be improved, in the earlier sections, & that these necessary improvements can then be made so much more easily, as well as so much more effectually.

The change of Secretary is a great pity. But may the new comer prove to be a treasure! I note that you speak of purchasing a Höffding. I shall be interested to know how you find him. I gave up reading him some years ago, after some considerable trial, as profitless—perhaps wrongly. Doughty's 'Arabia Deserta' I happened to have put in a request for at the University Library just a few days before your letter came, & I look forward to wandering through it in the coming months—with the more interest that you are doing likewise. One of my chief friends here is an enthusiast for it.

The Macmillans promise to have my 'Prolegomena' out in March, or in 'April at latest'. The first proofs are due this week. It will be a volume of some 250 pp.

Troeltsch's 'Christian Thought' I have now read very carefully twice, & with the greatest profit. The lectures are very worthy of him, & make a very massive impression. Your own Introduction seems to me, if I may say so, of the happiest, both as appreciation & as criticism. The root of what is unsatisfactory in Troeltsch's ways of thinking, so far as I can see, ultimately lies in the very strange dualisms that run through all his discussions. I remember your saying the word 'merely' ought *never* to be used. Troeltsch is constantly talking of the merely natural, the merely individual, the merely formal, the merely rational even. Yet when he closes with his problems, all sorts of qualifications that really render his dualisms & his 'merelys' quite meaningless, are brought in by a back door. He carries his dualisms so far as to speak e.g. on p. 164, as if rationalism & idealism (surely as 'isms' quite incompatible & incapable of being *both* true) met on a parity & had to 'compromise' with one another. And on p. 165 it is, it would seem, the idealism that is 'Utopian'.

How loosely he uses 'Nature'. The term acquires a wider or a narrower meaning, in his hands, just as required by the exigencies of his argument. Thus on p. 63 'Nature' is equated with 'the demands of subsistence' "merely" (in the legitimate sense). "The conflict between Nature & Morality, between the demands of subsistence & the shaping of moral personality, can never be completely solved." So, on p. 60, he speaks of "Reason *disengaging* itself from its natural basis".—rather, is it not? emerging *with the aid* of its natural basis—that surely is at least an equally true point of view. Indeed Troeltsch himself recognises this, but still continues to speak in the sheerly dualistic manner.

Then how perverse a view he takes of individuality—cf. p. 106 as the source of inevitable & essential imperfectibility! This no doubt connects, as you suggest in your Introduction, with his refusal to recognise how meaningless & impossible individuality becomes when he denies the saving presence & efficacy of universals. I should suspect that a Neo-Platonic type of metaphor— his constant use of the term 'Tension' suggests this—has had evil as well as good effects on his thinking. The Supernatural & Supraindividual he seems to picture as standing over against the *merely* natural & *merely* individual, & the latter (quite inagreeably & unintelligibly owing to the 'merelys' necessitated by his dualisms) as being set in a state of ferment & 'self'(?)-conflict, & tension by the former. Not only all initiative, but all worthwhileness are ascribed to the former; to the latter remains only the power of thwarting, imposing temporary compromises etc. In consequence, like Dean Inge, he is in position to run with the hare & to hunt with the hounds. Constantly he awakens interest by saying things which seem to promise so greatly, only to dash our hopes on the very next page. In *pure philosophy*, is he not, like the Dean, essentially an *essayist*—using certain philosophical, & favourite, doctrines, with very little reflection on the other philosophical problems—equally important, & *often much more fundamental*—that are inseparably bound up with them? And are not Schopenhauer & Bergson thinkers of this type—very *luminous*, but at the same time by no means lucid. We can always appreciate their *immediate* conclusions, but must not allow ourselves to look too closely into their grounds, connections, consequences. But I am, I see, in danger of saying considerably more than I mean—in *my* attempt to get my own immediate conclusion. The little volume has benefited me greatly & left me with an increased respect that was already great—for Troeltsch & his work.

For the past month I have been studying with *immense* interest Schweitzer's 'Decay & Regeneration of Civilisation' & 'Civilisation & Ethics'. Have now read both twice. But I shall defer comment, beyond saying that Schweitzer's view of 'Nature' as essentially *enigmatic*—the more so that it is *akin* to, & also manifests itself through what is best as well as what is less good or even evil in ourselves—seems to me immensely more true, & more in keeping with a religious standpoint, that [*sic*] the so-contrary attitude of Troeltsch emptying all that is best in Nature into a Super-Nature conceived as opposite to it. Meantime I shall continue my study of Schweitzer. Another book that of late has interested me for somewhat similar reasons is 'The Heart of Nature' by Sir Francis Younghusband. I owe you an immense debt in drawing my attention both to Troeltsch & to Schweitzer.

Yours ever gratefully & affectionately,
NORMAN KEMP SMITH.

The 'von' with a capital must have been an error of the particular journal; I have been careful to have it correctly printed in the Pref. to Comment.

P.S. This week-end I have read, for the first time, Pringle-Pattison's Gifford's on 'The Idea of Immortality'. Most of it is more compilation—very pleasantly done—than a contribution,

& a little commonplace, for lack of having something really his own to give, at times. But also at times his fineness of character & wise discretion have given me much that I have found very helpful.

                                        Ellerton,
                                        Grange Loan,
                                        Edinburgh.

Jan. 14, 1924

My dear Baron,

Enclosed is an offprint of a paper on 'Whitehead's Philosophy of Nature', the only part that is my own is the concluding part in criticism of Whitehead & Bergson, & in defence of universals.

We were alarmed a few days ago by Janet falling ill. The doctor diagnosed the trouble as probably diphtheria, & administered the anti-toxin. However, happily, it has turned out to be tonsilitis, & a mild case at that. She is well on the way to complete recovery already.

I am very busy with the proofs of my book, & with University work.

                    Yours ever affectionately,
                    NORMAN KEMP SMITH.

                              13 Febr. 1924.
                              13, Vicarage Gate,
                              Kensington,
                              W. 8.

My very dear Kemp Smith,

I have cared so much for the little one's bad time—for your anxiety during those days of uncertainty and acute fear. But how good that it turned out to be something so much less and that she was well on the mend when you wrote! And then I was so glad of your criticism with the fine defence of the reality of universals—*mir aus der Seele gesprochen.* And then your recommendations of books have been followed carefully—Schweitzer's first two *Civilisation* volumes lie before me, and shall be carefully studied. Only, with Sch. I always fear excessive dualisms, chasms dug too deep and wide for him (or any one following him) ever to be able to bridge again. That is certainly the case with his purely eschatological Jesus: we *all* felt this (I *think*, all of us) when the fine man spoke to us, before our LSSR. But he is genuine and earnest, and no mistake.

The gloomy Dean has just given me (on my application) his most touching new booklet ending up with a sketch of his little Paula (+ 10½ last Holy Week).[217] He there gives also her photograph and a set of most touching Latin Elegiacs in her memory. But in his covering note he rises fiercely in favour of birthcontrol, a point I had ventured to express my deep regret about as to his now *full* absorption in that slippery pathway.

But what has forced me my pen into my hand *hic et nunc* is a note from the Publisher of the Troeltsch Lectures 'Christian Thought' this morning to say the volume is selling very badly— only 200 copies sold outside of America (where 500 are taking their chance). He warns me that, unless the sale gets promptly better he will have to take distressing measures (I suppose he means 'remainder' it). He asks me whether I know of no Society or group of men who could help. I have just written to Clement Webb at Oxford, and now, thus write to yourself in Edinburgh, before finishing up with Ernest Barker, London University. I have again over-drawn my credit at my Bank, so dare not now buy more copies than I have bought already; nor indeed do I think of, or wish, any one else to do so. Yet it ought certainly to be possible to find some booksellers willing to hold out for a while with copies to sell and to secure 2 or 3 well wishers to the

---

[217] This refers to Dean W. R. Inge of St. Paul's and to the death of his daughter. The "booklet" to which von Hügel refers is W. R. Inge, *Personal Religion and the Life of Devotion* (London: Longmans, Green, 1924).

book, men with opportunities for directing others to its study and possession. —I was vexed at Augustine Birrell's[218] *Athenaeum-Nation* review—as flippant as he could make it. And now I have before me another which contrasts, all in Jack's favour, as so lucid and persuasive etc., some lectures of J. with these of Troeltsch. But the *Guardian* pleased me much; and 2 or 3 other notices were right in their tone.—

I am expecting the German originals, as just published, by any post now, with a Preface by myself, somewhat different from the Introduction to the English translations.

Your ever aff. grateful Friend
F. v. Hügel.

Have got another Pekinese, *Wu*, since Jan. 1st.

24th Febr. 1924
13, Vicarage Gate,
Kensington,
W. 8.

My dear Professor,

This is but to tell you that I have had from Principal Ernest Barker so zealous and vigourous a letter, and one so showing his grasp—far beyond where I saw to—of the real situation of the Troeltsch Lectures affair I wrote to you about, that I now regret having troubled either yourself or Clement Webb, at least for the present, in this affair. It was E. B. who recommended Mr Stanley Murrell, London University Press, as publisher for the Lectures; and, as Head of King's College, which constitutes so important a part of the University of London, Dr Barker must have a large voice in the keeping of Murrell in that post or in the dismissing of him from it. Dr Barker writes indignant with Mur-

---

[218] Augustine Birrell (1850–1933), British lawyer, politician, and writer, educated at Trinity Hall, Cambridge; Quain Professor of Law, University College, London, 1896–1899; Member of Parliament for Fifeshire, 1889–1900, for North Bristol, 1906–1918; President of Board of Education, 1905–1907; Chief Secretary to the Lord Lieutenant of Ireland, 1907–1916; author of numerous literary studies.

rell and telling me he has just written Murrell a piece of this his indignant mind—that the book has appeared far too recently for any sane judgement as to its eventual sale; that if the reviews have not, so far achieved much, *advertisements* are now the right means, and means which it is Murrell's duty to employ; that the sale of 200 copies so far (outside of America) is nothing to despair about—this kind of book very rarely selling markedly better than that, from the first; that he E. B. published a little book with the Clarendon Press years ago, which sold at first even worse, but is still selling reasonably—and that great house never dreamt of treating himself as he, S. M. had now treated me etc. Bravo! —I am writing Murrell to-morrow (since I promised him an answer beyond the P. C. which but told him I had received his letter and was consulting 3 friends (the Principal included), that I do not doubt he, M., will see with myself that the Principal's opinion is decisive as to the course to adopt; and that I now look to his acting upon it. Pray forgive any trouble you may have kindly taken—it may still come in usefully later on.

Aff. & grateful old Friend,
F. v. HÜGEL.

March 2, 1924.   Ellerton,
                                        Grange Loan,
                                        Edinburgh.

My dear Baron,
    I have been wondering how it is that not till today have I answered your two letters! And I find *no* answer to this question. Barker is surely right. I should have expected a larger initial sale; but the vagaries of the purchasing public are uncalculable. What is certain is that the book will make its way in the end. The publisher must be fussy, & very commercial-minded, surely! The Scots Philosophical Club met in Edinburgh the week-end after your letter came, & I mentioned the Troeltsch volume to some of the members, as I got opportunity to do so.

Prof. Latta has resigned the Secretaryship of the Club & I have had to take it over. Fortunately there is not much work, as we only meet twice a year, once in Edinburgh or Glasgow alternately in the winter months, & once in St Andrews or Aberdeen in the Spring. We have a dinner one evening, & a discussion in the forenoon of the following day. At the past meeting A. D. Lindsay from Glasgow read a paper on 'Sovereignty.'

We are in the throes of an economy campaign in the University. The University Court has appointed a Committee to enquire into possible economies to meet the £5000 deficit of the present year; & the Senate has appointed a similar committee to make a parallel enquiry. I am on the latter committee. Arts, happily, is not so greatly concerned as the Medicine & Science Faculties. The number of students in the latter has, as might have been anticipated, gone greatly down.

My book is out of my hands, & should be published this month: the greater leisure is very welcome. The Term closes in a fortnight, & we have a six weeks vacation. Whether I shall go off anywhere, I have not yet decided. My wife will not be able to get away, as painters are to be finishing off the two rooms that had dry-rot.

Yesterday some of us initiated a Committee to raise funds among Pringle-Pattison's pupils for a portrait to present to the University. There should be no difficulty in doing so.

I am very glad to hear that you have another Pekinese, but I cannot decipher his or her *name*. May it develop some of the finer qualities of character of the departed Puckie! We still are without a canine member of the household, but hope to secure one in May or June.

Morton Prince[219] (from Boston) is lecturing at the University on the 'Subconscious'. He has the psychiatrist's very usual loose reasoning: he deduces a vast amount from very circumscribed

[219] Morton Prince (1854–1929), American medical doctor, educated at Harvard and Tufts Universities; practiced medicine in Boston for most of his life, specializing in nervous disorders, lecturing at both Harvard and Tufts, and also the University of California; outspokenly anti-German during World War I, and in Paris during 1918–1919 in an official position; his publications include *Nature of Mind and Human Automatism* (1885), *Dissociation of a Personality* (1906), and *The Unconscious* (1913).

evidence: His 'Sally Beauchamp' was, I am convinced, mainly the creation of his own suggestions to a very clever & suggestible patient. But I have only shaken hands with him so far & heard *one* of his lectures. He is coming to dine with us on Wednesday night. I shall look forward to reading Dean Inge's little book on his daughter Paula. Meantime with kindest greetings,

Yours ever affectionately & gratefully

NORMAN KEMP SMITH.

Ellerton,

Grange Loan,

Edinburgh.

March 11. 1924

My dear Baron,

I have been [intending] to write you again ever since I heard from W. P. Paterson that our D.D. Committee of Senate had recommended you for an Honorary D.D. from the University. I was the more delighted to hear this that I had myself had no hand in it. Indeed I only heard *after* you had declined the honour, on the ground that you would not be in sufficient health to make the journey North. Had I known earlier I should certainly have added my persuasions to Paterson's, in the hope that we could have had you as our guest at Ellerton. However I can very well understand that you are reserving all your energies for the writing of your great book: & if that is necessary thereto, must even, however regretfully, applaud your decision.

We have had Morton Prince lecturing on the Subconscious— a pleasant man of *no* mental distinction. Our Principal—he is an engineer—spoke of Prince as a 'man of genius' & his lectures as 'fascinating'. I attended only two, & they sent me away feeling very angry-minded. I doubt if he has any sense of what is & is not evidence, & I distrust his highly coloured stories of his cases. I should conjecture that Miss Beecham absorbed his theories— through his indirect over-subtle suggestions—& gave them back to him in dramatic form. Pringle-Pattison agrees with me *heartily* about Prince, & has just given me his own Hertz lecture on 'The Philosophy of History'. It is very pleasant reading but *very* slight. I am, my dear Baron,

> Yours ever affectionately,
> NORMAN KEMP SMITH.

P.S. My book should be out by end of month, & I shall have a copy sent you. I *may* in a fortnight go to Paris for a fortnight. Our Term closes this week.

	Ellerton,
	Grange Loan,
March 26, 1924	Edinburgh.

My dear Baron,

I am deeply grieved to hear from Baroness Hildegard of your illness, though rejoiced to have such good news of your speedy recovery.[220] This time of the year is usually the period of lowest vitality, after the long strain of the winter, & I trust that your body has in this illness worked off its excess of accumulated fatigues & strains, & will respond now, after some seasonable rest, only the more generously to your need of its services. Happily— is it not so?—the parts of your book with which you are now working deal with those matters with which you have always been most deeply concerned, & which you can therefore write directly out of your own experience & thought, & so with less of the strain involved in writing upon other people's views or upon secondary questions of a more academic character.

I shall not now write at any length, but shall hope to be seeing

---

[220] On March 18 von Hügel's doctor thought the Baron was dying. He had an unconscious spell, and the last sacraments of the Church were administered. Although he rallied from the attack, he gradually became weaker and died ten months later (see *Diaries,* 18 March 1924). His own account of this illness is found in personal letters to Mrs. F. R. Lillie of Chicago, Bishop Edward Stuart Talbot of Winchester, and Professor Clement C. J. Webb of Oxford, in *Selected Letters,* pp. 369–71.

you someday soon. My present purpose is to spend next week-end with Professor J. H. Muirhead near Birmingham. Thereafter I come on to London on the Tuesday.

My book is out tomorrow, & I am sending you a copy, not that you may read it, but that you may glance at my Preface in which I am glad to be able to make acknowledgement of my debt to you.

Our daughter continues to make splendid progress, as I trust you yourself are also doing.

Yours ever gratefully & affectionately

NORMAN KEMP SMITH

13, Vicarage Gate,
Kensington,
W. 8.
1st April 1924

My very dear friend,

I should love to write at least this little note in my own old hand but dictation is so much less tiring and I want if I can to regain my freshness as soon as possible. How delightful if you could come in from your friends to see me here. I fear not for much profitable discussion but just to let me look upon a man whom I so dearly care for and who has now again so solidly cheered me up. I mean of course in your Prolegomena of which I have so far only been able to read the short Preface which, however, encourages me so greatly, the passage on page 233n. and then the Index with all its suggestiveness. Need I say that if and as soon as I get fit I shall read and re-read, ruminate and weigh every word of what you say. I do not doubt but that I shall be greatly supported and on not a few points shall be further enlightened by your strenuous utterly sincere thinkings.

What a pleasure it is to have friends whom one can admire, nothing surely makes one grow like that.

I love to dwell too upon the little one getting on again so nicely and upon all the good and happy things and events that surround you, staunch supporting friend.

This of course means also to thank you for the letter of the day before the book with its fine new stamped address. This must go thither but will doubtless follow you promptly to Birmingham I take it. I know Professor Moberly[221] there and much esteem him. Please if you know him and meet him give him my kind regards. Professor Muirhead I also know though less. I have been so pleased at his attitude during the War.

Yours ever affectionately and gratefully,
F. VON HÜGEL.

13 Vicarage Gate, W. 8.

April 2, 1924.

How delightful to have you within reach for 'about 3 weeks'. Before they are over I may be quite fit for your staying here! I find it would be difficult to put off the one person a day I am now seeing, either to-morrow (Thursday) or Friday. But will you, very kindly, come on *Saturday*, 5th, at 4.30: my wife would give you tea; and I would be ready for you at 5—an hour of homely talk? Silence to mean 'yes'.[222]

Wrote you a letter (dictated) yesterday, about the book, so far only walked round and round, but with deep delight.

Aff. old Friend   F. v. HÜGEL.

---

[221] Sir Walter Hamilton Moberly (1882–?), British philosopher; son of Robert Campbell Moberly, a contributor to *Lux Mundi*, and whose chief work, *Atonement and Personality* (1901), influenced his son's final work, *The Ethics of Punishment* (1968). In this work of his extreme old age the younger Moberly discussed at some length von Hügel's ideas on eternal punishment.

[222] "At 5, *Kemp Smith came to see me,* after tea w[ith] M[ary] at 4.30. —Invited me, for Prof. Muirhead, to contribute a 20 pp. long acc[oun]t of my life & philos[ophical] convictions to the 2nd vol., now being edited by him, of self descriptions by Engl[ish] living philosophers. Talked much of Felix Adler, the N. Y. Jewish Ethical writer and his dissatisfaction with every pure ethicism." *Diaries,* 5 April 1924.

Thackeray Hotel
(Opposite the British Museum)
Great Russell Street
London
April 6. 1924.   W. C. 1
My dear Baron,

The two books of Felix Adler are entitled: 'The Reconstruction of the Spiritual Ideal' (lectures delivered at Manchester College, Oxford) & a larger work entitled 'An Ethical Philosophy of Life'. Both are published in U. S. A. by Appleton. Professor Muirhead has them, & would, I am sure, be delighted to lend you them any time you might care to look into them. I wrote him last night & he will be communicating with you.

I cannot properly tell you how great a pleasure it has been to me to have seen you again. I always feel, however, that I do not manage to convey to you how great I feel my debt to you both for the inspiration of your writings & for what I value so greatly the high privilege of the friendship you so richly extend to me in my unworthiness—unworthy save perhaps in my knowledge of its value & of my own undesert.

I pray that your health may be so restored as to enable you to carry your book to a happy completion.

Unless I hear that you are unable to see me on Friday, I shall call about 4-30.

Yours ever gratefully & affectionately,
NORMAN KEMP SMITH.

Ellerton,
Grange Loan,
April 28, 1924   Edinburgh.
My dear Baron,

I trust that you have been making good progress. The weather that came to us yesterday, if also with you—it was here the most perfect of days—seems to promise that the long cold winter of our discontent is over & past, & the summer with its sunshine really returned again. The day before yesterday I had a letter from C. C. J. Webb, just returned from Italy where he had met Moberly & so heard of your illness, & begging me to send him news of you.

Our garden is a great delight these days with its spring flowers: & we look forward greatly to a quiet summer in it, before we go to a cottage we have taken for September on the slopes of Skiddaw, at some distance from Keswick.

My journey North was most enjoyable. I spent one night at Ely: the cathedral I had not seen before & had not expected to find it one of the finest in England. Then another night at Peterborough, one at Lincoln & one at York: four days on the Yorkshire moors. Then a bee-line to the little daughter who is quite herself again, at Windermere with an Aunt. She is deep in nature study, with insects & fish in jars & boxes. She returns to her parents tomorrow, & starts in at day-school again on Thursday.

My own school starts tomorrow & I find it a little difficult getting back into harness. Have spent the week-end reading students' essays on Berkeley: *not* an inspiring task, but very necessary, & to them, I trust, beneficial. Have not had time yet to see my colleagues. But I shall write very soon more at length, when work is underway. Meantime Mrs Kemp Smith joins me in kindest greetings to you & sympathy in your illness & to Lady Mary. Yours ever affectionately,

NORMAN KEMP SMITH.

Ellerton,
Grange Loan,
Edinburgh.

May 16, 1924

My dear Baron,

I am very sorry to hear that you have had another, though milder attack, of your malady. Its immediate effects have, I trust, passed off by now, & your strength returned to you again. But I had been hoping to hear of very real progress, with no steps back; & sympathise with you in your disappointment.

The year is behaving with the same perversity as your health: here we are in midsummer—as you are, say, in the middle of your book—& only in the past week has Spring descended upon us. The trees have been folding out their leaves with incredible industry—making up, as they can, for the lost time. The Term's work, too, is in full swing. Last week I was reading the essays of my 3 best advanced students—in competition for a £20 prize that has the dignified title of "Bruce of Grangehill & Falkland's Prize", in memory of an 18th Century holder of my Chair—& *two* out of the three quote from your "Essays & Addresses". So my teaching must carry *some* measure of genuine guidance to the springs of truth—would you not agree?

My colleague, James Seth, has fallen very suddenly ill—heart-collapse. He is in charge of two nurses since yesterday. His constitution is excellent; & the doctor considers he will soon get back to his ordinary health, but orders no work for some months. Pringle-Pattison has been spending the Easter in Rome with M^{rs} P-P., but is returning this week. Before leaving Edinburgh he asked me for your address: returning sooner than he had anticipated, on account of his brother's illness, he may not, however, have been able to call.

I am now Secretary of our Scots Philosophical Club which is to meet in Aberdeen on 30th & 31st of this month. Seth was to have opened the discussion on the 31st. Now I must find a substitute. I have much correspondence with Baillie; he is not over-easy to cooperate with.

My book has fallen into the hands of Wildon Carr for review in the *Times Literary Supplement*. He deals kindly with me: but I could have wished a reviewer of more understanding. He cannot understand which [sic] I don't refer to, & have no debts to, Croce & Gentile! So far my chief encouragement, regarding the book, has been a letter from A. D. Lindsay from Glasgow (Sir Henry Jones's successor) saying that mine is the gospel that he has long been looking for! Lindsay is spoken of for the vacant Mastership of Balliol: but I fancy they are libel to look for an older & more distinguished man. For that they may have to go outside the ranks of Balliol Fellows. I understand that the election is on the 26th.

I have procurred to myself the two volumes just published, in the new Benedictine translation (which is *excellent*), of Aquinas 'Summa contra Gentiles'. Am enjoying them greatly. Have also on hand two books by Emil Brunner (Prof. in Zurich, & one of the leaders of a new School of Philosophy in Germany & Switzerland)—'Die Mystik u. das Wort' & 'Erlebnis, Erkenntnis u. Glaube'. From preliminary dipping into them I find promise of considerable illumination & help. They were given me by a postgraduate student. I had not heard of Brunner before. It appears that an older man of the same School was a Pastor in Switzerland, Dr. Hermann Kutler.

The week-end after this, my wife, daughter & I are going off for the quiet of 3 days to Gifford, a small village in the Lammermuir Hills. Next week we have old friends from Glasgow visiting us, during the days of the Church Assembly—a Mother & daughter. The Mother is well over eighty, but very active, somewhat of a poet, & the Head of a large family of grandchildren. Four years ago she climbed, on her own feet!, to the top of Snowden. Here is an example to emulate! But you do it, on the spiritual heights instead.

Edinburgh is busy preparing to welcome the Browns[223] to Holyrood Palace! It is a most popular appointment. The Church too is glad to have this demonstration that it is not the Church only of the rich. By all accounts the Browns are a very decent, choice couple. The many feel that they are being honoured by proxy.

I shall write very soon again, & am, my dear Baron, yours ever affectionately & devotedly,

NORMAN KEMP SMITH.

[223] Rt. Hon. James Brown (1862–1939), Scottish labor leader and politician who was appointed Lord High Commissioner to the Church of Scotland in 1924, 1930, and 1931. He was a Member of Parliament for South Ayrshire from 1918 to 1931, and again from 1935 until his death. In 1931 the University of Glasgow awarded him an Honorary Doctor of Laws degree.

Ellerton,
Grange Loan,
June 1. 1924.   Edinburgh.

My dear Baron,

I trust you have been making progress of late, & shall be grateful if Baroness Hildegarde can send me a card as to how you are. These days I am rather anxious regarding my wife who had to have an operation on Thursday last. We had known for some time that it would have to be faced—(it is nothing malignant), & Amy wisely decided to get it over. Happily the doctors are very well pleased, & she is getting along very well, though still in considerable pain & discomfort. I was able to see her this morning for the first time. But as the reports of her were good, & all visitors interdicted till today, I went to Aberdeen over Friday night, for the Scots Philosophical Club meetings of which I am Secretary —a dinner on the Friday night & a discussion on the Saturday forenoon (on Plato's theory of Art). I was staying with Professor W. L. Davidson,[224] a most delightful man—over 70—who lives with his sister. Principal George Adam Smith came to the dinner & discussion.

Dr. Deissmann[225] from Berlin lectured here 10 days ago. A very attractive man, but gave a very dry lecture on recent epigraphical discoveries (*very* minute ones) bearing on the New Testament. At the lunch afterwards Professor W. P. Paterson, by whom I was sitting, suddenly opened upon Deissmann as follows: "I don't see why you should despair of finding, in the Palestine excavations, something really big—connected say with the apostles. There is John: he took Mary to stay with him after the death of Christ. Now we know that John wasn't the sort of man to have Mary die in his house, & not give her a really fine monument. It might turn up." Deissmann looked rather stunned

[224] William Leslie Davidson (1848–1929), Scottish philosopher, educated at the University of Aberdeen; Examiner, Mental Philosophy and English, Aberdeen, 1881–1884, 1887–1890, Edinburgh, 1889–1892; Burnet Lecturer, Aberdeen, 1891–1894; Croall Lecturer, Edinburgh, 1918–1919; published numerous articles and books, and edited Alexander Bain's *Autobiography* (1904).

[225] Adolf Deissmann (1866–1937), German Biblical philologist and evangelical theologian; held Professor's Chairs in the Universities of Heidelberg (1897) and Berlin (1908); an early and scholarly leader in ecumenism.

at this! He does not know our Paterson. Deissmann was talking very warmly of yourself.

I have had a very pleasant review of my book by Wildon Carr in The Times Literary Supplement of the week before last. I could, however, have wished to fall into other hands. McTaggart also reviews it briefly, but in a very friendly manner, in The Cambridge Review.

A. D. Lindsay was appointed, after all, Master of Balliol. He should make a good Head, tho' hardly a brilliant one, & will be well liked personally. He is a member of the Independent Labour Party, & so will continue on many of the lines of his predecessor, who tho' a Liberal, leant that way.

Dr Whyte's son, Sir Frederick Whyte, the Speaker of the Indian Legislature, is home on leave; & I have met him twice at dinner. He says the Indian situation is better than two years ago, but still very dangerous. Gandhi, he reports, has lost much of his influence owing to his imprisonment. The less educated natives had thought him divine, & this to their minds is disproved by his being imprisoned!—a strange mentality.

Professor Seth has been very ill—heart-failure—but is making good & steady progress. I expect to see him, for the first time, since he fell ill about a fortnight ago, on Tuesday. Meantime, my dear Baron, I am,

Yours ever affectionately & gratefully,
NORMAN KEMP SMITH.

P.S. If you are able, & in the mood, to have a *very* light novel read to you, I can recommend 'The Bishop out of Residence' by Victor L. Whitechurch.[226]

[226] Victor Lorenzo Whitechurch (1868–1933), Church of England cleric and novelist, educated at Chichester Grammar School and Chichester Theological College; held various ecclesiastical appointments from 1891; Vicar of Aylesbury and Chaplain, Royal Buckinghamshire Hospital, 1914–1922; Rector of Hartwell-with-Stone, 1923–1931; authored numerous novels.

June 8. 1924.   Ellerton,
                                   Grange Loan,
                                     Edinburgh.
My dear Baron,
    I am delighted to hear that you have so far recovered as to be
able to work at your book, from time to time. This is splendid
news. It is also good that you are able to be out in the open air
in the afternoons—from now on, I trust, more in summerlike
sunshine.
    My wife, I am glad to say, continues to make excellent prog-
ress. She is not good at standing monotony: that is the danger,
that she will see too many visitors etc. If only she will cultivate
an idle mind, all should go well.
    My classes close the week after the coming one; & what with
essays to read, examination papers to set, concluding lectures to
prepare etc., *and* committee meetings, there is little philosophic
calm. Also I am Examiner for Degrees at Durham, & go there—
always a pleasing city to visit—for a night on the 19th.
    Last week I had a son of Boyce Gibson[227] (who I think has
corresponded with you) visiting me. He is acting as an Assistant
in Moral Philosophy in Glasgow. Wildon Carr writes suggesting
a joint-meeting of the Aristotelian Society & the Scots Philosophical Club in Edinburgh in the summer of 1925. But with Seth so
very ill—he is recovering from his last week's relapse—& for
other reasons, I am suggesting it be in 1926 instead. Next Spring
too Seth intends to resign. Whom we shall get in his stead, I don't
yet know. Possibly we might be best to get A. E. Taylor; & probably could, if we did not advertise the vacancy but *offered* the
Chair to him. The Moral Philosophy Chair in Glasgow will have
to be filled this summer.
    Macmillan has sent me a very friendly review of my book by

[227] William Ralph Boyce Gibson (1869–
1935), educated in mathematics at Oxford, and in philosophy at the Universities
of Jena, Paris, and Glasgow; he lectured
in philosophy at the Universities of London and Liverpool, 1898–1911, and held
the Professorship of Philosophy at Melbourne University, Australia, 1912–1934.
He and von Hügel had corresponded before the former went to Australia, both
having an interest in Eucken's thought.

McTaggart in the Cambridge Review. Like the reviewer in the Guardian, he objects to me, with my realism, calling myself an Idealist, instead of entitling my position Spiritualism. I should certainly refuse to adopt any such title, as I believe you would too. Plato believed in dead matter: so did Locke. None the less neither was a spiritualist. And if Plato does not have the right to call himself idealist, who has? Surely the proper counter-opposite to realism is not idealism but subjectivism. And the true alternative to naturalism, idealism. I have just come from a University service in St Giles at which the preacher, Dr Fisher of St Cuthberts,[228] said that for him the chief proof & evidence of immortality was in the existence of great men, & he cited Plato & Shakespeare!! Well *that*, I should say, *may* be called spiritualism. But surely it is queer doctrine from the pulpit of St Giles. I should greatly like to put Dr Fisher on a diet of your books—preceded by a sufficiency of personal tribulations & self-questionings. And a question I should greatly have liked to have asked him is where Plato & Shakespeare, the unhappy creatures, were to look for evidence of immortality. I doubt if Dr Fisher's evidence would have satisfied *them*! And what is evidence that does not satisfy the people who knew it best!

I am, my dear Baron, yours ever affectionately,

NORMAN KEMP SMITH.

13 Vicarage Gate, London, W. 8. 9th June 1924

I want to try just a P. C. to you, since letter-writing still tires me so much, and yet I want just to say 'Thank you' for these delightfully full and enlivening letters of yrs. —Have minded w. you so much Mrs K. S. having to have that operation; but, by now, she will be her normal self again: how good! Yet I do wish and pray

---

[228] Robert Howie Fisher (1861–1934), Scottish churchman, educated at Edinburgh University; University Lecturer on Pastoral Theology, Edinburgh, 1911–1914, Lecturer on Apologetics, 1913–1916, Baird Lecturer, 1922; Minister of St. Cuthbert's Parish, Edinburgh, 1914–1925.

you may now have a good long spell of no anxiety either as to yr house, or the little one, or your wife: you have had such a series of crises w. all 3! —Glad you cd get off to preside at Aberdeen: You have said nothing about B. when the affair actually came off: have always felt him a very sensitive, hence diff., man, poor thing, but I feel so truly sorry for him. —As to the rev.[s] of your 'Prol.' it certainly was a sheer mistake of the *T. L. S.* to have *their* notice done by W. C. It is indeed polite and well-meaning, but a rev. was evidently wanted of weight bec. of its very author. Mr Bruce Richmond wrote me some time ago that he was off for a complete, much-needed holiday of a month; so he may have had nothing to [do] w. this selection. Am hoping for fine rev.[s] in 'Mind', 'Kant Studien', 'Rev. de Metaph. et de Morale'. Have spoken strongly for the book to Prof. Liebert, for the 'Kant Stn.' But do rev.[s] really matter much? I doubt it. —Refreshed my mind w. reading Felix Adler on 'Marriage' in his Hibbert Lect[s] 1923—have now bought them: warm thanks f. telling me of so alpine a mind. I want too to master in Hocking's 'Meaning of God' Pt IV, and, still more, all yr 'Prol.' But the 'book' is now distinctly getting on, this is by dodging abt to catch a fair morning after a good night, and the latter comes only about 2 or 3 times a week, and any little thing can give me a bad night: get out daily in bath-chair & sleep with wide open windows.

Aff. gratef. Friend F. v. HÜGEL.

Ellerton,
Grange Loan,
June 15, 1924   Edinburgh.
My dear Baron,

I was delighted & honoured to have your postcard, but I also feel that if I am to entrench on your all too small reserve of energies, by making you feel that my letters must be acknowledged, I must cease writing forthwith. It is splendid that you are again able to keep your book progressing, even if only at intervals.

All goes well with us. Amy is making the best possible progress & will get back to Ellerton next Saturday or else tomorrow week. The other day I received from Paul Elmer More,[229] from Princeton, a copy of his 'Christ of the New Testament'. Shall let you know how I find it, when leisure for reading it comes. The past week has been the busiest in my year: correcting students' exams, reading their essays, & preparing the concluding lectures of the Term which closes next Wednesday. Have also had to read Durham papers, & go to Durham for two nights on Thursday.

John Laird of Belfast has just got back from his year in California, & called on Thursday night.

Seth, I am sorry to say, has been forced by his illness to resign his Chair—this is *strictly private* until the announcement appears in the papers. The Chair, I trust, will not be advertised, & instead be offered either to John Laird or to A. E. Taylor. Whether Bowman will apply for the Glasgow Chair, I have not yet heard. Laird saw him before sailing back, & reports that his (Bowman's) book —'Prolegomen–to the Philosophy of Religion' is finished. I should have liked to have Bowman here as my colleague: but that is not possible, as he has not yet published, & no one knows him here except myself. Laird should prove a congenial & stimulating colleague, however; & our views are sufficiently different to give the student free & open choice.

Have you seen the kindly & appreciative reference to yourself in the current issue of the 'New Statesman': I send you my copy (which you need not return), in case you have not—on p. 292 (marked). What the reviewer's last sentence, in his last paragraph, means, I cannot conjecture. Do you know who the writer is? (But I *must* not ask questions, after *forbidding* you to write!)

A letter came yesterday from my Princeton friend Harper, who is in Italy with his wife. He writes from Florence & is now in Ravenna. He gives no very assuring account of Fascist activities.

[229] Paul Elmer More (1864–1937), American philosopher, educated at Washington University (St. Louis), and Harvard University; lectured at Smith Academy (St. Louis), Harvard, and Bryn Mawr, 1887–1897; Literary Editor of the *New York Independent*, 1901–1903; Editor of *The Nation*, 1909–1914; sometime Lecturer in Greek Philosophy, Princeton University.

Now I must return to my examination papers! I am, my dear
Baron,
        Yours ever affectionately,
                NORMAN KEMP SMITH
Yes, I saw Baillie in Aberdeen, & we were quite friendly together.
But he is a *very* difficult man, but I should not say that *sensitive-
ness* is a prominent feature in him.

June 22. 1924.   Ellerton,
                                          Grange Loan,
                                            Edinburgh.
My dear Baron,
My busy-ness is happily over—it *destroys* all true work—&
from now on I look forward to a leisurely summer of hard work.
The visit to Durham & Newcastle was quite pleasant. I met a colleague of Glasgow days whom I had not seen for some 16 years
—Nicol Smith of Oxford (English Literature Reader), & some
others whom I see only at long intervals. The Authorities at Durham arrange what they call an 'Examiners' Dinner' annually in
the old baronial hall of the Castle, pleasantly informal, with ad-
journment to the Common Room. Then the following night I
spent with Ferguson,[230] Hoernle's[231] successor in Newcastle—a

---

[230] Alexander Stewart Ferguson (1883–
1958), British philosopher, educated at St.
Andrews University and University College, Oxford; Assistant Professor of Philosophy, 1909–1911, and Professor of
Mental Philosophy, 1911–1923, Queen's
University, Kingston, Canada; Professor
of Philosophy, Armstrong College, New-
castle-upon-Tyne, 1924–1926; Visiting
Professor, Columbia University, 1931–
1932; Terry Lecturer, Yale University,
1947. His culminating position was that of
Professor of Logic at Aberdeen.

[231] R. F. Alfred Hoernlé (?–1943),
British philosopher of German extraction
and secondary education, educated at Balliol College, Oxford; Professor of Philosophy at the South African College,
Cape Town, 1908–1911; Professor of Philosophy, Armstrong College, Newcastle-
upon-Tyne, 1912–1914 and 1920–1923;
Assistant Professor of Philosophy, Harvard University, 1914–1920; Professor of
Philosophy, University of the Witwaters-
rand, Johannesburg, South Africa.

pleasant man, whose wife is a daughter of Bradley,[232] the philologist. In the train going & coming I perused Paul Gaugin's
letters. Gaugin was not so definitely insane as van Gogh, but ab-
normal & degenerate, & yet with an extraordinarily disinterested
devotion to his art.

You will have read in the papers—or heard—of James Seth's
resignation—hastened by his illness by one year. It came quite
suddenly upon us all here. Seth himself is making good progress
towards recovery. His successor will have to be appointed forthwith. And that brings up the J. B. Baillie issue forthwith! This
time James Seth agrees with Pringle-Pattison in supporting Baillie. In the competition for my Chair, he stated emphatically that
he did not desire Baillie for a colleague. Now he declares that he
only preferred me to Baillie. Evidently Pringle-Pattison has persuaded him in the matter, & I can quite sympathise with the personal relations that make out & out opposition to Baillie difficult
for them both. Yesterday I had a long talk with the Principal,
& I have good hopes that he will support me in opposing Baillie's
election. The more I think over the suggestion of Baillie, the
more severely I find myself hoping that the suggestion may not
prevail. For myself I favour either A. E. Taylor or Laird (Bowman not having published & not being known here save by myself, I am not bringing up his name). The Principle rules out
Taylor in the ground of age & health, so I am concentrating on
support of John Laird; & have just been inditing a carefully
worded epistle to the Principal, confirming what I said by word
of mouth to him yesterday—especially as regards my opposition
to Baillie, & my reasons therefor. A preliminary meeting of the
Curators (3 for the University including the Principal & 3 from
the Town Council of the City—the same electing body as for my

[232] Henry Bradley (1845–1923), British philologist, educated at Chesterfield
Grammar School, and awarded honorary
degrees by Oxford, Heidelberg, Durham,
and Sheffield; engaged in private teaching
and clerical work until 1884; editor of
Academy, 1884–1885; President, Philological Society, 1891–1893, 1900–1903, 1909–
1910; President, Oxford Philological Society, 1921; Fellow of the British Academy, 1907; joint-editor, from 1889, and
eventually senior editor, from 1915, of
The Oxford English Dictionary.

own Chair) is to be held tomorrow. In view of the vacancy in the corresponding Glasgow Chair, I trust they will act promptly, not advertising the Chair, but instead making their own choice & offering the Chair. A congenial colleague in what is virtually a single Department is greatly to be desired: Baillie would most certainly not be that. He shows at his best with those considerably senior to himself; by his contemporaries & juniors he is very generally disliked—for he is more than difficult, I think. *And* his philosophical work is wooly & half-baked.

I have Dʳ Whyte's 'Life' by me to read: I see there are references to yourself contained in it. The book makes progress, however slowly, I trust. I am, my dear Baron,

Yours ever gratefully & affectionately,
NORMAN KEMP SMITH.

P.S. My wife has continued her splendid recovery, & returns home tomorrow.

Ellerton,
Grange Loan,
June 29. 1924.   Edinburgh.
My dear Baron,

No gift from you could have given me greater pleasure than this copy of Abbé Huvelin's little book.[233] Since you lent me your own copy, I have wished to have one of my very own, that I might reread & study at leisure. My most grateful thanks. The inscription too makes it one of my treasured possessions.

This past week I have been enjoying comparative leisure, lazying much in the sunshine of our garden—with only occasional committee meetings. My wife is immensely profiting by the openness & sunshine; & continues to make good progress.

[233] See note 40.

VON HÜGEL – KEMP SMITH

The situation here, as regards the election to the Moral Philosophy Chair, is so far clearer that Laird is ruled out, for reasons into which I need not enter. This has helped to increase Taylor's chances, though also, I fear, Baillie's. However I have good hopes that the Principal may be finally brought round to support Taylor. The only objections made to him are his health—which I counter by laying at the door of his *excessive* devotion to study; a *consuming* desire for truth is no bad quality in members of an academic community, & not *over*-usual there—& his 'difficulty' as a colleague. The latter report I ascribe to the notorious effect of St Andrews' East Wind on the liver; or if that explanation be challenged as unworthy a Christian & a Philosopher, on the smallness of St Andrews that throws its residents too much together. Certainly they dwell not together in charity, in that little town.

How far Pringle-Pattison is *actively* working for Baillie, I do not know; so far I observe no signs thereof; & would gladly believe that he is contenting himself with formal support. He knows quite well Baillie's personal unpopularity & the relative disesteem in which his books are held.

Probably the Principal will have made up his mind by the end of this week. I have done my best, in begging him to seek first distinction for our School of Philosophy & the University: certainly Taylor will bring us immensely more prestige than any one else in the field: & I should myself count it a high honour to be his colleague. Our Principal is a very decent sort of man; but as Head of University mediocre and uninspired.

The only alternative suggested, apart from Baillie, to whom the Chair can appropriately be *offered*, is now W. D. Ross of Oriel, Deputy-Professor of Moral Philosophy in Oxford—a very scholarly, quite competent, Aristotelian & a successful tutor. Otherwise he is, of course, not in the same boat with Taylor.

Taylor sent me last week his very delightful lecture on 'St Thomas Aquinas as a Philosopher'. I am asking my bookseller to send you a copy: if, as is very likely Taylor has himself sent you one, please hand on the extra copy to someone likely to appreciate it.

Of Huvelin's book I shall write later, when I have meditated

upon it. Meantime again, my dear Baron, my most grateful
thanks.

Yours ever affectionately,
NORMAN KEMP SMITH.

Ellerton,
Grange Loan,
July 6. 1924.   Edinburgh.
My dear Baron,

The situation, as regards the Moral Philosophy Chair, has ma-
tured very satisfactorily since I wrote you last Sunday. On Tuesday the Principal so far came to a decision as to ask me to write
Taylor enquiring, confidentially, whether he would be likely to
accept the Chair if offered. Taylor answered that he would require information as to duties, assistance etc. & some days to
think the matter over. After writing him again, he gives a definite
favourable reply. The Principal now tells me that he has himself
decided to recommend to the 'Curators of Patronage', at a meeting tomorrow, that the Chair be formally offered to Taylor. I
trust he will carry them with him. *All this*, of course, *is strictly
private*, until a public announcement is made. The letters from
Sᵗ Andrews are very reassuring as to Taylor's health etc.

On Friday I called on Pringle-Pattison & had a very friendly
talk with him. He still presses Baillie's claims, but will accept
Taylor's appointment without further protest.

Should all go well, without further hitch, I shall greatly rejoice.
Taylor will be a stimulating colleague, & a great inspiration to
the students. His coming too will confer no little prestige on our
Department & on the University. S. Alexander put C. D. Broad[234]
first in his recommendations, & Taylor second. James Ward put

---

[234] Charlie Dunbar Broad (1887–
1971), British philosopher, educated at
Trinity College, Cambridge; Fellow of
Trinity College; Professor of Moral Phi-
losophy, Cambridge; Fellow of the British
Academy; President of the Society for
Psychical Research, 1935. Among his in-
fluential publications were *Examination of
McTaggart's Philosophy* (1933), *Scien-
tific Thought* (1959), and *Lectures on
Psychical Research* (1962).

Moore first, & then Broad. But I had little difficulty in convincing the Principal of the unfitness of Broad & Moore for a *Moral* Philosophy Chair, at least for a Scottish one. The other letters, even when they questioned Taylor's fitness owing to health or age, placed him first in distinction & work done.

Have just finished André Maurois' 'Ariel'—a *life* of Shelley, written from the documents, as if the author had been present on all occasions, in the English translation that does not read like a translation. It is flippant & at times cynical—tho' not as regards Shelley himself—in the Lytton Strachey style: but vastly entertaining & well worth reading.

Had Oliver de Selincourt, son of Prof de Selincourt of Birmingham,[235] staying with us for a couple of nights: he is Lecturer at Aberdeen in Political Philosophy—a very attractive & able young fellow. On Tuesday next Alan Dorward[236] comes for a night—another young philosopher & our External Examiner, Lecturer in Queen's University, Belfast.

I had a pleasing encouragement this past week in election as a Fellow of the British Academy, which rather impresses me as bringing me into the august company of those who have been my teachers from student days on.

All goes well with yourself, I trust; & strength not too unequal to the continuing of your book. I told you I was reading the Life of Dr Whyte: well, just today I have read, for the first time, his reply to your letter of Jan. 1916—also the account of your address in Edinburgh on 7th July, 1914.

I am, my dear Baron, Yours ever gratefully & affectionately,

NORMAN KEMP SMITH.

[235] Ernest de Selincourt (1870–1943), British scholar and littérateur, educated at Dulwich and University College, Oxford; Lecturer in English Language and Literature, University College, Oxford, 1896–1909; Professor of English Language and Literature at the University of Birmingham, 1908–1935; Dean of Faculty of Fine Arts, Birmingham, 1919–1930; Professor of Poetry, Oxford, 1928–1933; President of the English Association, 1935–1936.

[236] Alan Dorward (1889–1956), British philosopher, educated at Edinburgh University and Trinity College, Cambridge, where he was influenced by the thought of Moore, Russell, and Whitehead; Professor of Philosophy, Liverpool University, from 1928; published papers and notices in various philosophical journals.

Ellerton,
Grange Loan,
July 10. 1924.   Edinburgh.
My dear Baron,

Just a line to say that Taylor has accepted the Moral Philosophy Chair here. I am immensely relieved & delighted that it has worked out thus.

With all greetings,

Yours ever affectionately,

NORMAN KEMP SMITH

Ellerton,
Grange Loan,
July, 20. 1924.   Edinburgh.
My dear Baron,

The past week has been a very busy one. On Tuesday I went to Dundee for a night to see my people, including two quite old Aunts who live at Coupar Angus & whom I used constantly to visit when a boy. On Thursday came the Graduation. And in addition we have had visitors staying with us. On Thursday next Professor J. H. Muirhead comes for a week. However, the winter's hurly-burly is now practically over, & quiet will descend upon us, I trust, for the summer.

I do not quite understand from your last letter whether or not you *leave London* for a 6 weeks' holiday on August 1st, as you speak also of staying on till Sept. 15th. But I am delighted to hear that your book makes such good progress. To have so much of your book completed will enable you to give yourself up to a holiday spent the more thoroughly.

You will have noticed that Baillie has realised the ambition of his wife & himself to obtain an administrative post. It is no easy task that has come to him, in the Vice-Chancellorship of Leeds: but it is perhaps just for that reason the greater an opportunity.

Hetherington[237] who has been appointed to the Moral Philosophy Chair in Glasgow is a former pupil of Sir Henry Jones: he won't make any contribution to Philosophy & I should have thought that his gifts lay more in administrative work (he has been for some years Principal of University College, Exeter), but he is a very sensible, capable fellow, & will do his best by his students.

Taylor is finding it difficult to find a house at this season in Edinburgh, & may go into rooms for the winter.

I have been doing so [sic] reading in anthropology in Elliot Smith & Wissler, with considerable profit: & today have been looking into Romain Rolland's 'Mahatma Gandhi'. A very delightful Indian student of mine, of Brahman caste from Madras, has carried off my copy of your 'Mystical Element in Religion' to read during his vacation. But I fear he has too much of the Gandhi – Tagore (of whom he is a pupil) – Rolland simplicity & sentimentality of mind to profit fully: however Providence through me is giving him his chance. My wife continues to make good progress.

I am, my dear Baron, Yours ever affectionately,

NORMAN KEMP SMITH.

Ellerton,
Grange Loan,
Aug. 3. 1924.   Edinburgh.

My dear Baron,

You are now, I trust, most happily started on your well-earned holiday, under favourable auspices. I feel myself much in the same

[237] Sir Hector James Wright Hetherington (1888–1965), Scottish philosopher and national labor arbitrator, educated at Glasgow University and Merton College, Oxford; Lecturer in Moral Philosophy, Glasgow, 1910–1914; Lecturer in Philosophy, Sheffield, 1914–1915; Professor of Logic and Philosophy, University College, Cardiff, 1915–1920; Principal and Professor of Philosophy, University College, Exeter, 1920–1924; Professor of Moral Philosophy, Glasgow, 1924–1927; Vice-Chancellor, Liverpool University, 1927–1936; Member and Chairman of various Trade Boards, 1930–1940; Member, National Arbitration Tribunal, 1940–1948; knighted in 1936. His chief and ultimate academic position was that of Principal of the University of Glasgow.

position. For up till the present week there have been alarms & distractions of all kinds. Seth's funeral was on Monday, & Taylor came over for it. I took him to see one or two possible houses. Then on Tuesday J. H. Muirhead & I proceeded to Tighnabruaich —a five hours journey—on the Kyles of Bute. Lady Jones stays on there in a small house looking out South down the Western Kyles to the mountains of Arran. In the evening we motored out with her to Sir Henry's grave, upon which, with Muirhead's help and advice, a very suitable stone has been erected giving simply his name & dates & the inscription '*Amor Omnipotens*'. Lady Jones is a very gentle little lady, of great natural dignity & abounding humour. She has recovered from the strain of Sir Henry's long illness, & though frail is looking well. With her she has a daughter, somewhat of a nervous invalid, & a very competent niece.

Next day we travelled to Tarbet on Loch Lomond, & stayed overnight with the MacCunns.[238] He is very alert & active, full of interest in all things; & Mrs MacCunn (a daughter of Sellars sometime Prof. of Latin here, & herself born in St Andrews) is also a very able woman: she writes books on history. Their son, who was a Lecturer on History at Glasgow University, was killed in the War. Muirhead is most energetic: he bathed, before breakfast, *in the rain* at Tighnabruaich, & again next morning in Loch Lomond! I did not emulate him!

On Thursday night, to the great delight of the daughter, the airedale pup arrived—a splendid little fellow: we are already all very fond of him, & have named him "Roy". I forget your own new dog's name, Puckie's successor. The daughter has John Duncan (the artist's) two little girls staying with her now, for a week. They keep us lively.

Lady Jones was speaking of Sir Henry's 'Early Memories', which read so delightfully. She says he dictated them without effort. I have wished that you could prepare some form of auto-

[238] John MacCunn (1846–1929), Scottish philosopher, educated at Glasgow University and Balliol College, Oxford; taught for five years at Oxford upon graduation; elected Professor of Philosophy, University College, Liverpool, and held same post when that institution became Liverpool University; Emeritus, 1910; Justice of Peace, Dumbartonshire; wrote *The Ethics of Citizenship, The Making of Character, Six Radical Thinkers, Ethics of Social Work,* and *Political Philosophy of Burke.*

biography: it would be invaluable, & an inspiration to us all. Have you ever thought of doing so? Sir Henry's 'official life' (I do not expect much from it) has been prepared by Hetherington who has been appointed to the Moral Philosophy Chair in Glasgow, & is due to appear in September or October.

I am struggling with W. E. Johnson's Logic: it is very stiff, but full of interest. It is hardly a 'book': rather a series of somewhat disconnected notes on logical topics. The assumptions upon which he proceeds but does not discuss are numerous. Otherwise I am lazy, & am looking forward to abiding in that state for some time. My wife continues in her happy recovery; & we revel in the garden.

The Leseur[239] volume I have for the coming week.

I am, my dear Baron, with the best of good wishes,

Yours ever devotedly,

NORMAN KEMP SMITH.

August 11. 1924.

My dear Baron,

You have, I trust, been having in London the bright sunny weather that is visiting us here in the North. We are having most of our meals out of doors, in the garden.

The chief event of the week has been the arrival in Edinburgh of Paul Elmer More & his brother who is a Professor of Physics with their families.[240] More was a neighbour of mine in Prince-

[239] Elisabeth Leseur (1866–1911), French spiritual writer, educated in a small private school; married Felix Leseur, a medical doctor with atheistic convictions, 1889; read Renan's *Vie de Jesus* with unusual result of deepened Catholic convictions; began leading unostentatious but ascetic spiritual life and began writing her *Spiritual Journal*; died of cancer at 48; her husband converted six years later, and died a Dominican priest in 1950.

[240] An account of this trip by the More families is found in Arthur Hazard Dakin, *Paul Elmer More* (Princeton: Princeton University Press, 1960), pp. 223–24. Although Dakin mentions that the Mores moved "up the east coast to Edinburgh," he does not mention the visit with Kemp Smith in 1924. However, in June 1931 More was again in Scotland to receive an honorary LL.D. from Glasgow University (on the recommendation of A. A. Bowman, by that time on the Glasgow faculty);

ton. More after teaching first Sanscrit, & later Greek, at Harvard, became editor of the New York 'Nation'—then a conservative organ. Since his retiral to Princeton he has been devoting himself to a series of books upon the Platonic Tradition, beginning with 'Platonism' & 'The Religion of Plato', the latter of which was very warmly eulogized by Taylor in 'Mind'. His last book is 'The Christ of the New Testament', done in order to equip him for treating of the Platonic influence upon Christian doctrine. More has a profoundly sceptical mind, rather of the A. J. Balfour type. I find it difficult, while frequently agreeing with his conclusions, to connect them with his premises. His last book is a defence of the all-divine, all-human (supernatural) nature of Christ. Most of his middle life he has been a sceptic in religion, now, like A. E. Taylor, he moves steadily towards more positive views.

He has also published some eleven volumes of 'Shelburne Essays'—very varied in quality so far as I have looked into them. I remember liking his essay on Newman—at least parts of it—greatly.

Tonight I am having a small batchelor dinner for More & his brother here, & on Tuesday am taking them over to see St Andrews. More, by the way, has a philosophy in common with Irving Babbitt,[241] whose 'New Laocoon' you may perhaps know. They have an historical significance as standing for nearly everything that is least popular in U. S. A.

H. W. Garrod's[242]—the newly appointed Professor of Poetry

and in discussing that trip Dakin does mention that More also stayed with Kemp Smith in Edinburgh, and he quotes More as saying of A. E. Taylor, whom he met there, that he was "the most volubly continuous talker I ever tried to interrupt, but interesting and enormously learned" (ibid., pp. 300–301).

[241] Irving Babbitt (1865–1933), American literary scholar and critic, educated at Harvard College and in Paris; taught romance languages at Williams College and Harvard University, at which latter school he became Professor of French Literature in 1912. He believed that the Romantic writers, who had been nurtured on Rousseau's thought, had so exaggerated the ideas of *liberté* and *sentiment* as to have caused an egotistical revolution which was subversive of the very foundations of law, artistic standard, and sound social theory.

[242] Heathcote William Garrod (1878–1960), English poet and writer, self-educated; Tutor at Corpus Christi, Oxford, 1902–1904, and at Merton College, 1904–1925; held various positions in the Ministry of Munitions, 1915–1918; Professor of Poetry, Oxford, 1923–1928; Norton Professor of Poetry, Harvard, 1929.

at Oxford—Inaugural is pleasant but slight. His sole thesis is the *difficulty* of all art, as of all theory! The Clarendon Press has published an open letter by J. A. Smith, addressed to Garrod on 'The Nature of Art'—very footling, it seems to me, in advocacy of Croce's—surely—very unenlightening views on that subject. Garrod's appointment led me to look into his 'Religion of all Good Men' (issued in 1906): it is crude in the extreme & *not* even well-written. His recent volume, on the other hand, on 'Wordsworth' is on a different level.

Last, & best of all, I have this week read through the Elisabeth Leseur volume in the sequence you recommend, & shall complete the rest of the book in a few days. You have placed me under a great debt in sending the little book. What perhaps has impressed me most of all are the virility & balance & delicacy of her judgment & insights, & her insistence upon serenity & gaiety of spirit. While intensely emotional, there is not a trace of sentimentality —rather a horror of it. She gives me added faith in France & in France's future—as in the possibilities of life. And I trust to benefit yet more in rereading.

Our dog 'Roy' is growing in stature & in all the virtues: so is the daughter. My wife continues to make also the best possible progress.

With kindest greetings, I am, my dear Baron,

Yours ever gratefully & affectionately,

NORMAN KEMP SMITH.

Ellerton,
Grange Loan,
Aug. 18. 1924   Edinburgh.
My dear Baron,

The weather has hardly been holiday-weather, but perhaps is warmer in the South. I can picture you out in Kensington Gardens between the showers. On Tuesday I went with Paul Elmer More & his brother to St Andrews, that they might see the ancient city. Otherwise the week has passed very quietly, with none of us out of the garden hardly, save to give our dog Roy exercise on the Blackford Hill. Such little work as I have attempted has mainly been on W. E. Johnson's Logic, which is tough reading, but on the whole thoroughly profitable.

I have looked into Schweitzer's 'J. S. Bach', but find it much too technical for my very elementary knowledge of music. My wife is reading Lady Gwendolen Cecil's 'Life of Salisbury', & that has led me to look into it again. The chapter on Salisbury's 'Religion', in the first volume, is quite packed with good things.

The Elizabeth Leseur volume I have now finished. The concluding section—Pensées de chaque jour—is almost the best in the whole volume. Many thanks again for it: I feel that I have gained much that is really new & valuable from it. In ways difficult to define, it is quite individual, differing from other books of a similar kind, & worthy to rank with the best of them.

A junior member of the Department of Philosophy at Harvard, who is working on Greek & Mediaeval Philosophy—a sometime pupil of Hocking's—& settling in Edinburgh for the winter to get aid from A. E. Taylor, is living closeby—not, I think, particularly able, but eager & hard-working. Am taking him this afternoon out to Eskbank to visit my Assistant, John Anderson, who lives there.

On Wednesday I have promised the daughter to go picnicing with her to the seaside, on the Portobello-Joppa sands!—thermoses in a knapsack, with ice-cream at a tea-shop on the way, & Roy to be taught to swim! Such are the gay delights of our Edinburgh life! Then on Monday next we go South to Lake Derwentwater.

The news of the signing of the Treaty in this morning's papers is cheering.[243] May it be the beginning of better times!

[243] This refers to the conclusion and agreements of the London Conference held from July 16 through August 16, in which Britain (under Ramsay MacDonald's leadership) deflected the French determination to ruin Germany and dominate the Continent. The Conference settled details of how the Dawes Plan for German reparations should be made operative, and arranged a time schedule for the evacuation of the Ruhr. Reports of these conclusions reached by the Allies and Germany were in the British papers on the day before Kemp Smith wrote this letter.

You are, I trust, my dear Baron, profiting by your well-earned rest from all writing, & not feeling like a dog held on leash.

Yours ever devotedly,

NORMAN KEMP SMITH.

13, Vicarage Gate
Kensington,
London W. 8.
Aug. 23 [1924]

My very dear Friend

How you *do* deserve that time. Here you are writing to me the most interesting letters once a week in the midst of Heaven knows what mass of important work & calls, with me dumb as a fish at the other end & still unfit even to read this Friend's new book.

You are now off to the English lakes, how fine & so I want at least to dictate this little letter in view of the full letters I should so love to write.

First of all then a few words about the chief things you have told me or sent me, indeed 4 letters.

What a charming little snapshot that is of Janet & you—her father. I am delighted to have it & to note the rare quantity of intelligence & heart already visible in that little countenance & not less so in that pair of black stockings so expressive of a sturdy quite sweet & wholesome determination. Tell her please with my love, that I do not write her a separate little note only because I still knock up easily over my poor scriblings. But this is the answer to the question that evidently really comes from her: the new little Pekinese I had to lend away to a very kind young lady friend of ours, since tied to my chair indoors or out, as I always am now, I could not myself give him proper exercise, nor could I expect our maid or my nurse to add such exercising to their already considerable work on my own behalf. I do not think it at all likely that I shall ever again be able to keep a dog. The little thing's name on his Pedigree chart is Wu-Pei-Fu. The name of one of the 4 Chinese Generals now warring against each other out there in the huge home of the little thing's ancestors. So I called him Wu for short.

I am so very glad you now have that promising young dog Rover & have to take all that exercise with & for him. By "you" I of course mean Janet as well as yourself.

I was so glad to learn of Baillie's final securing of a post & it is one in which I feel sure that at least his wife will speedily feel at home & happy. —How interesting about those 2 brothers More. I hope to get "The Religion of Plato" from among the works of the Philosophy brother. Altogether I want you please to realize how no recommendation of yours is ever passed by me without effect. I have now quite a little library of such recommendations among my books—Hocking's "Meaning of God in Human Experience", Schweitzer's 2 vols. on "The Philosophy of History" & others, I have also carefully read the chapter on his religion in Ld Salisbury's biography, but must admit frankly to being puzzled at your enthusiasm for it. I must read it again & shall perhaps then not find it somehow so dry, agnostic & arid. Something to my mind, so far, so strangely unlike the Living Waters we both search after.

How good that you have been able to have Prof. Muirhead with you like that; & altogether what a joy as well as the most useful activity is what you have now such ample room for in your large house & lovely garden.

To go over to the chief points on my side, I am happy to say that on Saturday August 2nd I finished up as before my holiday beginning on Monday the 4th with the complete first dictated & type written draft of my entire book. I feel as though Section I practically all of it written 3 times, is fairly decent & interesting already as it stands, although even it badly requires careful insertions, or at least verifications & quotations & minor references. Section 3 which I only began some 8 weeks before the holiday break came upon me is almost all of it merely 1st draft but somehow I was going up in mental & nerve force during those weeks of quiet concentration upon this work with much open air & gentle peace of soul. And so this section has a dash & a go & a bite about it which I had much doubted whether I should ever feel within myself again. But of course this section still requires 2 more re-writings as well as the fillings in necessary in section I. Section 2 I took up these last weeks last of all at a point where I broke down before the crisis on March 18. I did not go back upon the extant part about one half & am prepared to find it terribly arid & inoperative; but the remaining part of that section has come out, I believe, as fresh & to the point as I could expect to make it this my 1st dictation concerning a path of my road which I knew, from the first, I should find exceptionally difficult. I do not yet know whether I shall resume my work after the expiring of next week on Sep[t]. 1. I think I may find it wiser to make the break one of 6 weeks in which case I shall begin on Sep[t]. 15. with prayer to God that He may furnish me with at least as much health as I had during those last weeks before my rest began. And beyond this, Friend, please we shall not speculate nor lay down dates for ourselves. I have always found that such things weaken or delay my working powers.

This last week I have had quite a bit of literary work, in spite of my supposed entire holiday. I had let myself in for it many months ago. You shall have a copy of the thing when I have any myself—a German translation of a paper of mine, made by others, but developed & improved in this German by this old friend.

I have taken due note of your proposal that I should later on dictate an autobiography & how Sir Henry Jones had found this kind of work strangely easy & the most attractive he had ever done, although he did it on his death bed. I must not occupy my mind with such a plan whilst I have still my big book to think of & cannot hope for more just now than strength to finish it. But if I am spared to achieve such a finish & find myself then still with some strength & freshness, I think with you that that would be a good last thing to do with abounding materials all around me & with lessons from a long life which are not necessarily less valuable because they have come home to oneself.

And now Friend, among a thousand, may you & your wife & the little daughter have a most happy further holiday. Continue in your kindness to write to me & not to expect any frequent answers. And remember, of course that if I could see you here, before Sep[t]. 15 especially, for a night or two, I should be deeply happy, even though, as you know, I cannot yet read much in your grand new book.

Your very affectionate & grateful Friend

F. VON HÜGEL.

I am so delighted that you care for Elizabeth Leseur. You could hardly give me a greater pleasure.

The Ghyll,
Underskiddaw,
Keswick

Aug. 25. 1924

My dear Baron,

We are this morning setting off South for Lake Derwentwater. My packing is finished, & I use the interval, before we start, to write you. My sister-in-law motors us down. We start at 10 a.m., have lunch & tea by the roadside, & should arrive about 6 p.m.

The past week has been a very quiet one. We had friends from England staying with [us] for two nights, on their way to the Island of Tiree, a few last social engagements, & now we are free. I mean to take as complete a rest as the weather permits, without ambitions in the way of work or reading. But I take a bag of books as a safeguard against the rainy days, of which the Lake District is not usually sparing.

Owing to the cottage we are going to being the property of maiden-ladies who treasure it as the joy of their hearts, we may not take our dog, Roy, with us, greatly to the sorrow of Janet. But one reason why the dog may not go has compensations for her, namely, that it might catch the squirrels that have to be fed each morning.

I have heard nothing about the Moral Philosophical Chair that Baillie vacates in Aberdeen—It is the Secretary for Scotland who appoints—save for J. W. Scott & a couple of younger men asking me for testimonials. A. E. Taylor is coming over this week to settle about rooms for the winter—to allow him time to look around for a house, at leisure. There is good prospect of comfortable rooms nearby here.

The settlement with France & Germany seems likely to be a big step forward to more settled conditions.

But I must write you next from the South. The daughter summons me. I wish our itinerary could have included London, that I might have seen you this month while you are at greater leisure. That, however, is not feasible.

With the best of good wishes,

Yours ever affectionately,

NORMAN KEMP SMITH.

The Ghyll,
Underskiddaw,
Keswick.

Sept. 1. 1924

My dear Baron,

Needless to say I was *more* than delighted to have your letter, but you are breaking all the rules. For it was understood that you were not to reply—or at the *very* most & even that only at long intervals, by a postcard. I am sure you ought not to be writing or dictating letters. But how good is your news regarding your book, that the third Section came to be written, in the end, so comparatively easily & with such congeniality of spirit, that section 2 has also worked out with freshness & vigour (at least the latter part that you have now written), & that when you expected to be meeting with difficulties of a more insuperable kind. That the whole book is thus completed in first draft, with Section 1 almost in final form, is wonderful news. For if I may judge from my own books, the happiest & most satisfactory stages in the writing of a book are the earliest & the last. The middle stages when the book as a whole is being brought into being are, have you not found, the hardest? Then often the mind is freed from its biggest effort & can be allowed to relax & to dwell on this & that part at will, polishing & interpolating & eliminating, with so much less strain. And rereading one part enables one to see how some other part can be improved & strengthened. I rejoice too that your holiday has come on top of such good work, to give it relish & to give you the better heart for the last stages of the journey, after, as I trust, Sept *15*TH (*not* 1st).

We motored here in rather wet weather on Monday of last week. The cottage is sequestered in a woody dell, with a stream flowing through the garden—the home of two maiden ladies who have it in almost too spik & span a condition, to make our holiday camping in it altogether free from responsibilities. We continue the owners' happy custom of placing food out for the squirrels which are very tame, & come feed quite close to us, greatly to the daughter's delight, & our own. They even come, now & then, & feed on the window sill while we have meals at a table drawn up to it. But the weather all week has been miserably wet, & we have not been out as much as we should like.

Last night my wife & I went to evening service at St Kentigern's, the Parish Church of Crossthwaite, a mile from here. In the Church is a monument to Robert Southey—his figure recumbent in white marble. He is buried in the Churchyard. This is the Church of which Canon Rawnsley,[244] who died two years ago, was Vicar.

I had not meant that I agreed with Salisbury's views, as given in the chapter on his 'Religion'—save, with you, in his attitude to the problem of evil & his belief in Providence—but I liked the incidents regarding the young man who wished to choose the profession in which he would do most good, & also Salisbury's reply regarding the weight of responsibility in making decisions. But I thought the chapter extraordinarily interesting as an account of a typically English attitude, with all its many limitations, & especially as the candid avowal of his bewilderment— honest, & surely only what was inevitable to a candid mind that

[244] Hardwicke Drummond Rawnsley (1851–1920), Church of England cleric, educated at Uppingham and Balliol College, Oxford; ordained 1875; Vicar of Wray, Windermere, 1878–1883; Vicar of Crosthwaite, Keswick, and Rural Dean, 1883–1917; author of many volumes of both prose and verse.

has so typical English a contempt for "the subtleties of philosophy"—as to how Christian ethics are to be reconciled with the
tasks of the statesman. The solution—as outlined in your 'The
German Soul'—is so entirely beyond his ken. Denouncing metaphysics, Salisbury was condemned to rest his beliefs on a pre-
cariously sceptical, & as you say dry & arid, foundation—just as
does A. J. Balfour, & also P. E. More in his 'Religion of Plato'
& other books. But I admire the courage, the stout heart, & the
otherwise sound insight which Salisbury shows—allowing for the
limitations of his outlook & interests—with so much honesty &
levelheadnesses, in holding to so much as he does. P. E. More's
book you need not, at present at least, I should say, trouble with.
And that reminds me that I spoke of a novel called 'The Bishop
out of Residence' which had given us much innocent amusement
by Victor Whitechurch. Well we brought with us here to read,
two others of his books, & my wife started reading one of them
aloud of evenings after dinner—'The Canon in Rendener'. But it
is so deplorably bad in comparison with the other, that we have
had to stop it; & it leaves me wondering whether 'The Bishop out
of Residence' can have been so good as we then thought it. The
third book is also disappointing. Now we are reading aloud, alternately, a Scott & a Trollope. My wife is also reading with
great appreciation Elizabeth Leseur's Journal.

For work, when it rains, I am wrestling with W. E. Johnson's
3 vols. on 'Logic'. They are really important but very hard reading, for he has little gift of exposition & he does not sufficiently
disclose the philosophical position which underlies & determines
many of his logical doctrines. I think of reading the book with
my Honours students during the coming Term. Then I am also
using my leisure to read through my volumes of notes & excerpts,
& have been especially glad to reread my notes of your letters
as given in F^r Tyrrell's Letters p. 41 ff, & with which I so heartily
agree, having so greatly profited, summarising, as they do, your
teaching in the 'Mystical Element in Religion'.

Little Janet says she can sympathise with you in being separated from Wu. We miss Roy, having had to leave him behind
because of the miserable spic & spanness of this cottage.

Tonight I have to go up to Edinburgh; on unexpected business; but am hoping to be able to return tomorrow.

I am, my dear Baron,

> Yours ever affectionately,
> NORMAN KEMP SMITH.

The Ghyll,
Underskiddaw,
Keswick.

Sept. 7. 1924

My dear Baron,

You have, I trust, been sunning yourself in Kensington Gardens now that the sun has again visited us; & I also trust that you are still on holiday with yet a week of complete rest ahead of you.

We have taken advantage of the sunny days to go a picnicing —one day up Barrowdale, surely one of the most beautiful places in all England, another day at Lake Buttermere, & yesterday on the slopes of Skiddaw.

The daughter has so made friends with the squirrels that one of them now feeds out of her hand. Another of her many sources of happiness is the making of a doll's bed out of a cardboard boot-box, covering it with cloth, with lid devised to form a canopy, & with bed-clothes made from "*half a quarter* of a yard" of various fabrics purchased from a patient & benevolent draper in Keswick. We are reading 'Rob Roy' to her, not that we consider it anywise suitable (even with large omissions) but because it is required as her school reading during her holidays.

My wife can now walk excellently. So we make pedestrian expeditions further afield than we had expected. And I am glad to say, she is as delighted & impressed as I have been with Elizabeth Leseur's Journals.

This afternoon we had a visit from Prof de Selincourt of Birmingham & his son Oliver who is going in for Philosophy-teaching as his profession & is a Lecturer at Aberdeen. The Father is bringing out, through the Clarendon Press, the original MSS. of Wordsworth's Prelude, in the form in which it was submitted by Wordsworth to Coleridge. It differs from the published Prelude considerably in length, & varies in all three respects of omissions, alterations, & additions. The Wordsworth family have allowed him access to papers for purposes of this publication.

This cottage, as it happens, belongs to Gordon Wordsworth who has leased it to the present occupiers. Over the mantelpiece printed in brass is Wordsworth's sonnet—not much as a sonnet —beginning: "Beaumont. It was thy wish that I should rear A seemly cottage in this sunny Dell . . ." I understand Beaumont gave Wordsworth the ground here, but the latter never himself built on it. He & Dorothy, during their first stay together in the Lakes, lived however in a farm-house, quite close to us—almost across the road—; with the Calverts, one of whom left him the money that gave him independence.

Skiddaw is a glorious mountain. I have found an old packtrail that leads right round behind it, high up on the mountain-side, & gives open views onto the side glens.

With all good wishes, I am, my dear Baron,

Yours ever affectionately,
Norman Kemp Smith.

The Ghyll,
Underskiddaw,
Sept. 15. 1924   Keswick.
My dear Baron,

We are still living amidst rain & mist, hoping that the sun may yet appear in all his summer strength ere the winter is upon us. We had sharp frost one morning, & since then the trees have been showing more & more of their autumn tints.

I have little to report this week beyond the daily round of our quiet life. The daughter has a girl-friend staying with her for a week—daughter of a physician in Windermere. They keep the house very cheerful.

This morning I had a letter from a former Princeton pupil, now Professor of Philosophy in the University of Iowa. He tells me that he is almost the only teacher of philosophy proper in Iowa, tho' it has 2½ million of a population. For the rest, usually only psychology is taught, not philosophy, & very strange psychology at that, as you can well conceive. He is an energetic young fellow; & America, whatever else it may or may not do for its sons, at least sets them tasks that are inspiring in their magnitude. For the minds of its millions are often soil almost as virgin & unworked as the unploughed prairie lands.

I have been reading, with great appreciation Dean Inge's last little book, with the Latin poem & concluding chapter on his daughter.

Have you, I wonder, restarted work this morning? (*NB* My queries are 'rhetorical'—*not* meant as suggesting a reply. I can very well picture in imagination what needs no external confirmation). I generally find it *very* hard after a holiday to make the first start-in. But I trust that all inevitable obstacles & difficulties such as always recur, allowed for, you have entered auspiciously upon a winter of congenial work on your great book. With every good wishes, I am, my dear Baron

Yours ever devotedly,

NORMAN KEMP SMITH.

Have a request from Professor Liebert of Kant-Gesellschaft asking me to allow my name to be added to their editorial staff. I very gladly agree.

The Ghyll,

Underskiddaw,

Sept. 22, 1924   Keswick.

My dear Baron,

You have, I trust, been able to make a satisfactory start to work again, after your time of rest. The weather is no better with us, rather worse, sunless & cold; but we still hope for a week of sunshine before we return home on Monday the 29th. The daughter was delighted to have your card. She has had a girl friend with her all week; & they have been very full of plans & 'plays'. And 'Rob Roy' has had to wait upon her greater leisure.

You may have noticed in the papers that my colleague, Professor Darroch[245] (of Chair of Education) has been missing in Jura, his native island, for almost a fortnight. He had a mental breakdown some two years ago, from which he recovered, to have another relapse last Spring. There can be no hope now of his being still alive. A pupil of Simon Laurie's[246] (Laurie of 'Metaphysica Nova et Vetusta' which he wrote under *nom de plume* of 'Scotus Novanticus'), he had sufficient philosophy to recognise the weakness of the popular psychologies & theories of education, but hardly sufficient strength of character to stem the tide. He did his best work as a man of business & administration, on Committees etc. Did you ever look into Simon Laurie's books—quite able, & with much insight. But Laurie was so unwise as to invent a special terminology, & I have never found study of his writings really repaying,—again my queries are only rhetorical! you understand.

Had a request from Clarendon Press through W. R. Ross of Oriel asking me to contribute to a philosophical Series. They project a volume covering Descartes, Spinoza & Leibnitz. I decline. I have no present desire to write further on them. You spoke of my returning to my work on traditional views of human nature. I always have it in mind; but first I must write a book developing the logical doctrines that underlie my general position: Unless I do that now, I shall never get back to it. Thereafter

---

[245] Alexander Darroch (1862–1924), Scottish education theorist, educated at the University of Edinburgh; Assistant Lecturer in Education, University College of North Wales, Bangor, 1900–1901; Lecturer in Psychology and Education, E. C. Training College, Edinburgh, 1901–1903; Professor of Education, Edinburgh University from 1903; appointed first Chairman of the National Committee for the Training of Teachers in Scotland.

[246] Simon Somerville Laurie (1829–1909), Scottish educator and philosopher, educated at Edinburgh University; Secretary to the Endowed Schools (Scotland) Commission, 1872; one time President of Teachers' Guild of Great Britain and Ireland; Gifford Lecturer at Edinburgh, 1905–1906; among his many published works is *Metaphysica Nova et Vetusta by Scotus Novanticus.*

I shall feel free to devote myself entirely to problems more directly bearing upon human & spiritual life—capable, I hope, of treatment in a more generally readable form. At present I am striving to get myself really clear on the fundamental problem of universals. I cannot away with Bosanquet's view, & have difficulty about a substitute. Am finding W. E. Johnson's disjointed & difficult discussions of some little help.

F. H. Bradley's[247] 'Appearance & Reality' I profited by in my student days; but for the past 20 years I have not been able, on returning to his books, to make much of them, & have not been able quite to concur on what appears to be the prevailing judgment as to the value & influence of his teaching.

This past week I have again been looking through Schweitzer's second volume of Dale Lectures 'Civilization & Ethics'; & have come to the conclusion that it is his incidental excursion's, & *not* his main positions, that are really valuable. The latter are built on foundations too sceptical to allow of the *mystical* beliefs which he rather timidly suggests in support of his ethical maxims. 'Reverence for *life*' is a sadly indefinite rule of conduct; & yet he would seem to be constrained to this formulation if he is at all to justify the contention (really necessary to give his ethics its religious inspiration) that the key to all life, even that of a plant!, is found in the reverence for the life which we discover in ourselves & in the self-sacrifice & devotion which it demands from us.

On the other hand his estimates both of 18th Century & of present-day ways of thinking, & on many other incidental matters, are so suggestive, fresh, & helpful; & the personality behind it all is so big, sincere & courageous!

I am, my dear Baron, with all good wishes,

Yours ever affectionately,

NORMAN KEMP SMITH.

[247] Francis Herbert Bradley (1846–1924), British philosopher, educated at Cheltenham and Marlborough; Fellow of Merton College, Oxford; his chief publications were: *The Presuppositions of Critical History* (1874), *Ethical Studies* (1876), *The Principles of Logic* (1883), *Appearance and Reality* (1893), *Essays on Truth and Reality* (1914).

13 Vicarage Gate W. 8.
 27th Sept. 1924.
I so much want these lines to catch you before you leave for home on Monday, my Brother's birthday. Alas, you will, I fear, have *not* had a sunny last week! Here we have had rain, rain— much or little—but always that about us. —Still, even so these first 2 weeks of work have not depressed me, for I have found my texts quite tolerable as starting points and my strength quite fit for at least 4, at most 5 full mornings' improvements a week— am now to'rds end of Ch. III. —May Oct. bring us all steady sun- shine at last—getting into the open air for at least 2 hrs a day makes a great difference to me, I find. —I have so loved your being invited on to the titlepage of the 'Kant Studien'—excellent for numbers of reasons; and then that you have now modified yr view of Schweitzer as a thinker. I love the man—a magnificent character and to seek for beams of it in his writings; but the thinker is greatly inferior to the willing, intuitive creature within him—a mixture of scepticism and violent straining. I feel him always in this a bit like Fichte—the Father—he fails to attain to that quiet listening to the heartbeat of real life—there is a violent, vehement pressure within his mind which prevents the genuine, gentle receptivity so lacking in his Jesus-books, the first of which I know so intimately well.

Yr. aff. old Friend,
H.

The Ghyll,
Underskiddaw,
Sept. 28. 1924.   Keswick.
My dear Baron,
    We are leaving for Edinburgh tomorrow morning, having been blessed by some days of sunshine at the last. Yesterday was a gorgeous day, especially in the sunset hours, & we had a won- derful walk of some ten miles right round Skiddaw, over the old packtrails on the mountainside—meeting not a single soul the

whole way, until we got back on to the highway at Bassenthwaite village.

This forenoon we were at the Harvest Festival Service in Crossthwaite Church—a very fine service spoilt, as so often, by a sadly ineffectual sermon. The Dean of Lancaster was preaching, in an ambitious manner, with neither simplicity, directness, continuity or force. It is sad to see such opportunities mishandled.

I have been rereading L'Abbé Huvelin with increasing admiration. The pages that have impressed me most—if I may select —are pp. 97–100, 106, 111, 146, 198, 211, 229–30. The last two sections are especially magnificent.

I had a letter from A. E. Taylor the other day. He has found rooms—until he can receive a house—in Strathearn Rd., some ten minutes walk from Ellerton. Writing from Oriel, he speaks of having been intimate with F. H. Bradley & of missing him from his College. I trust that Taylor is taking trouble over his Inaugural Lecture, & makes a good impression at the start. He is introduced to the Senatus on Oct. 9th. Class start on Oct. 14th.

You will have noted in papers that Professor Darroch's body was washed up on the shore of Jura. It is not known how he met his death. It will be difficult to find a really good holder of the Chair. Really good men almost never specialise in "Education".

I shall write next from Auld Reekie.[248] Meantime, my dear Baron, with all good greetings & best wishes, I am,

Yours ever devotedly,
NORMAN KEMP SMITH.

Ellerton,
Grange Loan,
Edinburgh.

Oct. 5. 1924

My dear Baron,

Here I am settled down again, for another winter's work; & there are the usual many interviews with students & others, &

---

248 A colloquial term for Edinburgh.

some degree examination papers to attend to. Tonight we have three students coming in to supper, one of them the best student that I had at the University of California who has come here for the winter, & one an Instructor from Harvard, & one an Indian from Madras who has submitted a quite excellent thesis for Ph.D. in criticism of J. Dewey's naturalistic ethics.

I enclose the syllabus of courses for our W. E. A. On Friday night we made a somewhat ambitious opening for our W. E. A. Classes. Had a meeting in the Usher Hall addressed by Adamson,[249] the Secretary for Scotland, with Wm Graham,[250] Member for Central Edinburgh, & Parliamentary Secretary to the Treasury in the Chair: the meeting came off very well. About 1500 of an audience. As President I had to speak, in proposing the vote of thanks to the Chairman: Adamson is a very likeable type. Before entering Parliament he was Secretary to the Miners' Trade Union in Fifeshire. He conducts a Bible class every Sunday afternoon in Dunfermline, & misses few Sundays even when Parliament is sitting! The meeting ought to help in increasing interest in our work.

Your card of September 27th found me the morning we left Keswick, & was a most welcome greeting. I am so glad to hear that you have been getting in four to five good mornings each week of work, & are making good progress. The weather this past week—tho' not today, if I may judge by our downpours of rain —will have allowed you afternoons in the open.

This winter I have thus far continued to keep free of outside engagements, save for two lectures (one in Hawick on the 16th) & one in Edinburgh in December, & a talk to the W. E. A. Discussion Club at end of this month on the theme 'that all men are

[249] William Adamson (1863–1936), Scottish politician and son of a miner; Member of Parliament for West Fife, 1910–1931; Chairman, Parliamentary Labour Party, 1917–1921; Secretary for Scotland, January–November 1924, and 1929–1931; received honorary degrees from St. Andrews, 1927, and Glasgow, 1929.

[250] William Graham (1887–1932), Scottish economist and politician, edu-cated at Edinburgh University; Member of Edinburgh Town Council as Labour Representative, and member of many public bodies in Edinburgh; Justice of Peace, Edinburgh; Member of Royal Commission on Income Tax, 1919; Financial Secretary to Treasury, 1924; Lecturer in Economics for the Workers' Educational Association, Edinburgh University, 1915–1918.

equal in intellect, & differ only in character'! So I shall be able to give my energies to my classes, & hope to get some work helpful to myself done in connection with my Honours Class.

I had thought of calling this evening upon Pringle-Pattison, but the rain is too discouraging. Before the end of the week Taylor will have settled in Edinburgh. He is introduced to the Senatus on Thursday. On Friday I had a visit from my old friend Macneile Dixon of Glasgow. He has finished a book on 'Tragedy' & it will be out next month, & should be good. If so, I should like to send you a copy. Meantime, my dear Baron, with all good wishes to yourself & your work, I am

Yours ever affectionately,
Norman Kemp Smith.

Ellerton,
Grange Loan,
Edinburgh.

Oct. 12. 1924.

My dear Baron,

The past week has been a very scattered one—interviewing students, seeing returned colleagues etc. Our first Senatus meeting was on Wednesday, & Taylor was introduced. He gives his Inaugural on Thursday next, on the subject of the 'Freedom of Man'. I understand that he is to discuss the problem of the freedom of the will, in some of its bearings. His most outstanding characteristic so far as the Edinburgh public has yet had opportunity to observe is a tie, the most garish I have ever seen anyone wear, in many colours & large in size! I don't feel that I know him well enough to expostulate. But perhaps the sooner Edinburgh becomes acquainted with his superficial idiosyncrasies, & learns to discount them against his many very remarkable qualities the better.

The Privy Council has approved of Edinburgh's petition to have 70 fixed as the obligatory age of retiral for its professors,

& 75 for its principals—Glasgow being permitted, at the same time, to fix its limits at 65 & 70. But even our high limit does not apply to present incumbents. So I may conceivably continue on in idleness & incapacity in my Chair until 80 or over, & no one be able to enforce the law against me!

Some ten days ago I had a rather painful interview with a former student who came to talk with me about his condition. He was in a state of high excitement, & full of wild schemes, desiring to throw up his teaching post in a school, & to go to London to do journalism. I could not make up my mind about his condition, but happily I managed to quieten him down & to persuade him to continue in his usual work for the present. Now last night his sister came to tell me that he had been behaving strangely & has had to be put under restraint in an institution. He is a quiet, serious-mind fellow of pleasant manners. I trust this is only a passing condition. I find it almost a relief to know that it is *not* an after-effect of the war.

The General Election seems very needless. And it is difficult to see how anything can be settled by it. No one of the three parties seems likely to gain a majority.

James Ward has a very unsympathetic & severe review of my *Prolegomena* in the 'Hibbert'. He says the book shows no lack of ability but that the ability is sadly misplaced. I expected that he would by no means agree with my criticisms of his own views or with my position; but he seems to object even to my attempting to proceed on opposite lines.

Your work is proceeding satisfactorily, I trust—though I have no doubt that, as in all such work, there are unfortunately times when it proceeds less easily or even sadly uphill.

With affectionate greetings,

Yours ever gratefully,

NORMAN KEMP SMITH.

Ellerton,
Grange Loan,
Oct. 19. 1924   Edinburgh.

My dear Baron,

Our Term is now well under way. I met my Degree Class on Tuesday & my Honours Class on Wednesday for the first time; & both promise to afford very congenial opportunities for work.

Wednesday night I lectured at Hawick, & stayed overnight with Mrs Forman, daughter of my predecessor Professor Campbell Fraser.[251] She is a widow, & has a very beautiful house & small estate 6 miles out of Hawick. She gave me some interesting reminiscences of her Father & his friends. She is herself a very able & interesting woman, who does much good with her large means. On Thursday morning, before breakfast, she conducted prayers herself for the whole household, in the good patriarchal fashion.

Thursday afternoon at 5 p.m. Taylor gave his Inaugural to a large audience. Enclosed is the scrappy & disgracefully inaccurate report of it from the 'Scotsman'. It was a very able, & an interesting, address, but not very suited to the audience. However Taylor made, I think, a very good impression, & is well launched. The tie was not in evidence! His main point in what was a defence of freedom of the will as quite vital to all morality was that we are competent to pass a quite impartial judgment as to which of two goods is the better, & that this, & *not* motiveless choice, is what is meant by *libertas arbitrii*; & that freedom is therefore as well authenticated as our capacity for passing impartial intellectual judgments. However his position really depends, I think, on his doctrine of the good; & had he discussed this latter it would have interested his audience more. He says he will not print the Address as written.

At the end of last week I read Schweitzer's 'Quest of the Historical Jesus', & it has set me reading the New Testament, starting with St Mark, then St Matthew, Luke & John. I have just fin-

[251] Alexander Campbell Fraser (1819–1914), Scottish philosopher, educated at Edinburgh University; Professor of Logic, New College, Edinburgh, 1846–1856; Professor of Logic and Metaphysics, Edinburgh University, 1856–1891; Gifford Lecturer, Edinburgh, 1894–1896; his publications were largely concerned with Berkeley and Locke.

ished 'Acts' & mean to read continuously through the Epistles. Then I hope to return to study of Holtzmann.

There are many very striking passages in Schweitzer, as when he denounces the modernisation of Christ's teaching as preventing the true Jesus from acting at all on our times—& as neither being genuinely historical nor truly clear in thought. He is very good in his polemics, as against Renan & others. You will remember his comment on Kalthoff, that "he draws his figure of Christ in red ink on blotting paper", & because it is red in colour & smudgy in outline, wants to make out that it is something "new".

Now I must stop, as some students who are coming to supper are due in a few minutes. Your work makes good progress, I trust, & gives you much happiness in it. I am, my dear Baron,

Yours ever gratefully & affectionately,
NORMAN KEMP SMITH.

Ellerton,
Grange Loan,
Edinburgh.

Oct. 26. 1924.

My dear Baron,

Sir J. G. Frazer commenced his Giffords on Tuesday last—the weariest of discourses, in a strangely old fashioned style of 18th century freethinking. Taylor was wiggling in his chair all the time, restraining himself with difficulty from expostulating in protest. I felt likewise. I may have in courtesy to attend one or two more, but only for that reason. He has a dreary programme, which I enclose. Even our Principal who is responsible mainly for his appointment is disappointed with it. And Frazer also announced that he found the material of his first course had so multiplied that his next year's course would be on the same theme! It *is* just the sort of stuff that *can* go on for ever.

My wife & I met the Frazers at dinner at the Principal's on

Thursday evening. I had talk chiefly with Lady Frazer—quite evidently an able woman with abounding energy. I am told she has written good stories for children—I trust not on the lines of her book of selections from her husband's works. As you probably know, she is French & has translated the 'Golden Bough' into French. Her views are evidently akin to those of her husband: she deplored to me Andrew Lang's attack on Anatole France's 'Joan of Arc'.

Taylor is settling in very well. He was round yesterday, & talked for an hour & a half in the most delightful & interesting way. He thinks that C. D. Broad, whom he saw much of in St Andrews, & who as you know says that he knows only by hearsay that there is any such thing as religion, may very likely have a conversion as complete as St Paul. If so, it would as certainly have to be a work of grace. He spoke too of F. H. Bradley, & of the 'heart of fire' that separates him off from Bosanquet. Another of his (Taylor's) dicta was that Plato & Kant are the two greatest of ethical writers because of their conviction that man is a denizen of *two* orders. And he concluded with a eulogy of James Payne as a novelist. I have omitted the connectives. Tomorrow night I am speaking to the Discussion Club of the W. E. A. on the thesis: 'That all men are equal in intellect, & differ only in character'—in favour of which much can, I think, be said.

In my reading of the 'New Testament' I have today finished the 'Epistle to the Hebrews'. It could be dropped from the Bible without any real loss, don't you agree? The other Epistles I have found much new interest in. Have also been browsing in my volumes of Newman's Oxford Sermons.

Professor Tovey's[252] Sunday night Concerts begin tonight, & my wife & I had thought of going; but it is very wet, & as we are to be out most nights next week have decided not to. The pro-

[252] Sir Donald Francis Tovey (1875–1940), British musician, educated at Balliol College, Oxford, where he held the Lewis Nettleship Memorial Scholarship in Music; first series of chamber music concerts, London, 1900; followed by similar concerts in Berlin and Vienna; gave the Chelsea Concerts, 1906–1912; Reid Professor of Music, Edinburgh University, from 1914; knighted in 1935.

gramme is mainly Chopin. The Scotch Sabbath is abating its terrors, you will observe, with such happenings in Edinburgh. This is the second or third year of the Concerts.

Otto Schlapp, our German Lecturer, had tea with us this afternoon—a very handsome, large built, German of a best type—very artistic & musical. I am sorry that he is due to retire this year. He is one of the picturesque figures of Edinburgh. You may know his book—some 40 years old—on Kant's 'Critique of Judgment'.

Your own work goes well, I trust, my dear Baron. I pray that you may have all the energy,—you will then have the inspiration —needed for your great book.

Yours ever gratefully & affectionately,
NORMAN KEMP SMITH

On Friday night my wife & I heard Masefield[253] give an address on poetry. It was quite superb. I had heard him before when he was more or less ordinary. On Friday he was quite inspired & inspiring. I am glad that I was present: my wife, & indeed all the audience, felt likewise.

Ellerton,
Grange Loan,
Edinburgh.

Nov. 2. 1924.

My dear Baron,

We have all been rather tired out this week-end, recovering from our exertions at a Hallowe'en party of the daughter's. Forty of her friends & schoolmates gave us three of the most strenuous hours I have spent in a long time—very cheerful withal.

On Wednesday I voted for the first time in my life at a Parliamentary Election—having been so tossed around the world be-

---

[253] John Masefield (1878–1967), British poet and Poet Laureate from 1930; received the Order of Merit in 1935.

fore the War, & having changed our house once since we came to Edinburgh. I voted for that lost cause, the Liberal Party. But I am glad there is to be a stable government for a few years: only I do hope that Curzon[254] will not return to do more mischief in the Foreign Office. Ramsay Macdonald seems to have got into a truculent, nervous condition, & to have lost his head & better judgment. It will be interesting to hear what his investigating committee reports on the Russian letter.[255]

I was worried the past fortnight about a Ph.D. thesis, *really good*, submitted by an Indian student, Cornelius by name—a friend of Appasomy's—(the most attractive Indian student I have yet worked with) on John Dewey's 'Naturalistic Theory of Moral Values'. The External Examiner was Prof. Alex More of Liverpool (MacCunn's successor); & he reported unfavourably on it. However I got Taylor to read it, & he entirely agreed with me as to its merits; & between us we have got the Faculty of Arts to grant Cornelius his Ph.D. He would have been broken-hearted otherwise. It is strange how people can honestly differ so greatly in judging a thesis. It was largely I think that More believes more in Dewey's naturalism than either Taylor or I can do.

The students have restarted a dormant Philosophical Society, & it meets here on Thursday night, for its opening meeting— Taylor speaking about his work on the 'Timaeus', of which he is now busy at the proofs.

[254] George Nathaniel Curzon, Marquess Curzon of Kedleston (1859–1925), British statesman, educated at Eton and Balliol College, Oxford; Member of Parliament, Southport division of Lancashire, 1886–1892; traveled extensively in Asia and gained reputation as authority on Asiatic affairs; succeeded Balfour as Foreign Secretary, October 1919; his policies mostly unsuccessful; Lord President of the Council, 1924; created Earl Curzon of Kedleston, 1911, Marquess, 1921; Knight of the Garter, 1916.

[255] On Saturday, 25 October 1924, four days before the national elections in which the Labour Party was already running behind the Conservatives, the British press published a letter purporting to be from Zinoviev, President of the Presidium of the Communist International in Moscow, addressed to the Central Committee of the British Communist Party, urging the mobilization of the British working classes for agitation in favor of the ratification of a pending treaty between Russia and Great Britain. The letter created a "red scare," and the Conservatives won the election by a landslide. On 7 November 1924 Stanley Baldwin formed a Conservative government which lasted until 1929. MacDonald asked for a proper inquiry about the letter and its authenticity. He never got it.

The other day I received an article from G. M. Stratton[256] of University of California—you may know his disappointing 'Psychology of the Religious Life' & *much* better, more recent volume on 'Anger'. In his letter he said he was glad to read Taylor's praise of my 'Commentary' in the new supplementary volumes of the *Encyclopaedia Britannica*. I have looked up Taylor's article there, under title of *Philosophy*, on the philosophical literature of the past ten years—I had not known before of the article; & find it extremely interesting. He is most generous to my own book on Kant. I am glad, however, I did not know of it before fighting for his coming here. I see too that the English translation of Vaihinger's 'Philosophy of the 'As If' ' is out: he refers kindly to my Commentary in his own Preface to the English edition.

Taylor is daily exhibiting his many-coloured tie, & talking perpetually though most interestingly, & I think he will soon be happily regarded as a privileged person, not to be judged by common-place standards like common-place people. I think he will fit in very well.

J. G. Frazer is well launched on his peregrinations among the savage people of the Earth: so far I have deferred my revisit of courtesy to his lecture-room.

Sir Richard Lodge retires from the Chair of History in the Spring & from his Deanship of the Faculty of Arts & Membership of the University Court this month. He & others approached me as to succeeding him in the Deanship, but happily I have been able in honour to decline candidacy for that however, not that I would not have enjoyed the work with the students, but it is a very onerous post, with much letter-writing, interviewing & committee work & would have meant the ruin of my hopes of work. However I have had to agree to nomination for the University Court, & if the Senate elects me, I take office before end of this month. I rather like some business work, as a variety & change from the contemplative life, & the present time is a very Critical

[256] George Malcolm Stratton (1865–1957), American psychologist, educated at the Universities of California, Yale, and Leipzig; Professor of Experimental Psychology, The Johns Hopkins University, 1904–1908; Professor of Psychology, University of California, 1908–1935; he published *The Psychology of the Religious Life* in 1911.

one in many ways. I shall also be interested to get to know, by common work, some of the members of the Court. But the loss of Lodge is very serious. He was quite our *most* effective member both of Senatus & Court.[257]

All this letter has been about my own affairs almost, but you must know that thoughts of you & of your work are continually with me as an inspiration. I am, my dear Baron,

Yours ever devotedly & affectionately,

NORMAN KEMP SMITH.

Nov. 9. 1924.   Ellerton,
                                            Grange Loan,
                                            Edinburgh.

My dear Baron,

The past week has been a very busy one with me, & I trust has meant much good work done by yourself. On Tuesday night I had to speak in welcoming the Freshers at a meeting in the Mc-Ewan Hall—a quite desperate place to speak in—the Principal being unable to attend. On Thursday night the Students' Philosophical Club met here—about 25 in all—in my Study, with a few colleagues & our Philosophy Staff in addition; & Taylor gave a *most interesting* talk on his work on the Timaeus, of which he is now correcting the proofs. With Burnet he maintains that Plato has not given in any of the Dialogues the philosophy that he taught in the Academy—as he himself says in one of his Letters, (is it the 7ᵗʰ) now generally regarded as genuine. This general thesis Taylor proposes to test in the special case of the Timaeus, which is, he says, an historically exact representation of the teaching held in the Pythagorean Schools sometime after Pythagoras' death, being (as also appears in the naturalistic doctrine of the soul as a harmony or attunement of the elements composing the

---

257 For a full account of the personalities and structures of Edinburgh University about which Kemp Smith writes in this and other letters, see *History of the* *University of Edinburgh, 1883–1933,* ed. A. Logan Turner (Edinburgh: Oliver and Boyd, 1933).

body, in the Phaedo) a working out of the Empedoclean physical & medical theories in terms of Pythagorean mathematics, & demonstrably, from contemporary evidence & later Platonic traditions, *not* Platonic at all. Taylor is so full of detailed knowledge, & at the same time so persuasive & suggestive in the use thereof, that the evening was a most delightful one.

Last night I was at a meeting, dinner & discussion, of our Symposium Club. Sampson, our Astronomer, read a paper on 'The Hortus Siccus of Science'—a *not* very well thought out paper on the *unreliability* of science, notwithstanding its successes. It was interesting to find an Astronomer taking such a view of his science; but we all fell upon him, not excepting C. G. Darwin[258] our physicist, & Tovey our musician. I sat next my friend, John Duncan, the artist, who has just returned from a month in an Eng. Church Nunnery at Whitby. But I'll tell you of that another time. He was doing fresco work.

Sir Richard Lodge is resigning the Chair of History next Spring, & meantime is resigning his Deanship of the Faculty of Arts, & his Seat on the University Court. Some friends have been urging me to allow my name to be submitted for succession to the Deanship, & Lodge himself has desired me to. But I have successfully resisted, & with a good conscience as Whittaker, our Prof. of Mathematics, is willing & indeed desirous of serving, & will do the work well. The work is heavy, & I could not have had time for what I regard as much more important, teaching & getting some writing done. However I have had to agree to go on to the Court, & was elected to the Assessorship on the Court, representing the Faculty of Arts, at the meeting of the Senatus on Thursday. This will involve considerable work of some responsibility in the way of getting up considerable business & other detail, & also serving on a number of Committees; but I like to have some work of that kind, & it brings one into contact with quite

---

[258] Sir Charles Galton Darwin (1887–1962), British physicist, educated at Marlborough and Trinity College, Cambridge; Lecturer in Physics, University of Manchester, 1910–1914; Lecturer in Mathematics, Christ College, Cambridge, 1919–1922; Tait Professor of Natural Philosophy, Edinburgh University, 1923–1936; Master of Christ's College, Cambridge, 1936–1938; Director of National Physical Laboratory, 1938–1949; knighted in 1942.

a number of interesting people, & counteracts the dangers to which a teacher of youth, too much with his juniors, is very liable. So I rather look forward to this new experience, the more so as the University will have very critical decisions to come to in the 4 years of my service; & there is a certain zest in being in the thick of the fight.

Then best of all my friend Macneile Dixon, Sir Walter Raleigh's successor in Glasgow sent me a few days ago his book on 'Tragedy'. It is quite excellent—so good that I feel I should like to send you a copy, which please accept & keep by you, in case you may find leisure, say next Summer to enjoy it. Meantime I am sure Lady Mary would enjoy it. It seems to me better than anything Raleigh has done. Dixon is himself personally as attractive as this little book must be found to be. I told you, I think, that I have sent the Sec. of the Kant Gesellschaft copies of all papers I have been able to collect with notices of Kant's Bicentennary. There is also an article in *Dublin Review* for October by M. C. D'Arcy. Can you let me have a card as to who this D'Arcy is? Just a word: Is he a son of the Archbishop? And a private scholar? The article is very intelligent & well written. I would like to ask all sorts of questions about yourself & your work, but must not do so. But I need not say you are much in my thoughts & always with gratitude,

Yours ever affectionately,
NORMAN KEMP SMITH.

Dixon's book is a delightfully effective criticism of *all* the philosophical theories of tragedy yet propounded, & also is much else.

13, Vicarage Gate,
Kensington, W. 8.
Nov. 12 [1924]

My very dear Friend

I wonder whether you realize what you are doing for me. These letters of yours coming in so regularly once a week telling me so unforcedly exactly what I so much care to know with their gentle simplicity, entire spontaneity, kindliness & yet discrimination, they remind me of nothing so much as of the healing waters of Wildbad in the Schwarz Wald, where after you had got into the water, you would in some minutes feel all sorts of usually quite unperceived aches & pains & then this same water would brace them away. I know how sincerely you mean my writing only very rarely & indeed only so would I, alas, accept your kindness, but you have now asked me a definite question the answer to which will, I trust, enable you to do the most solid & valuable kindness to a man whom I much appreciate—M. C. D'Arcy S.J. I, a little wonder at your asking me, since, some 3 or 4 years ago, you knew chiefly through myself I think about as much concerning him as I did & do myself. You remember, don't you, how deeply I appreciated the way in which Charles Plater S.J., now already dead, dear thing, pressed me to accept his hospitality as head of the Jesuit House of Studies in Oxford & how I discovered that this was done, as a deliberate proof to me how thoroughly, in spite of all the Tyrrell affair, the younger English S.J.s trusted me? & how he was royally backed by his group of young students who got me to come out on long walks with them severally & consulted me on one difficult point of my subject matters after the other? Well one of these young men by "young" I mean a Jesuit young man i.e. about 27 or 30, was the man you now find writing so confidently upon Kant. D'Arcy is one of 2 brothers both much distinguished at Oxford, both Jesuits, both Jesuit priests by now. I only know this one. He carried off one big Oxford University prize after the other—I think it was 4 that he so gained. They are certainly not converts, not even—I think—the sons of converts & very certainly not the sons of the present Protestant Bishop D'Arcy[259] that most able but strangely un-balanced & often phantastic thinker. M. C. D'Arcy holds now one of the

[259] Charles Frederick D'Arcy (1859–1938), Church of Ireland ecclesiastic, educated at Trinity College, Dublin; ordained, 1885; held various lectureships and preaching positions at the Universities of Cambridge, Oxford, Glasgow, and Durham; Bishop of Clogher, 1903–1907; Bishop of Ossory, Ferns, and Leighlin, 1907–1911; Bishop of Down and Connor, 1911–1919; Archbishop of Dublin, 1919–1920; Archbishop of Armagh, 1920.

Professorships at the English Theological College of the order from which most of the letters from him to myself, herewith enclosed, as the best helps I know towards your understanding him, are written.

You remember "God & the Supernatural" that they asked me to join in writing & I escaped on the ground of the *Imprimatur* difficulties. Well—the paper on God there is by D'Arcy. Pray read it. It is unfortunately rather obscure, but, surely, a memorable piece of work. I do not doubt that this Kant paper of his must be still better. And I am very sure that anything like a cordial appreciation from you somewhere in print, would deeply gratify & encourage a thoroughly sound sincere mind & nobly laborious life. His Superiors also are sure to be much impressed in his favour by anything you can thus honestly say especially if you so write as to make it plain that you are no agnostic & that you welcome any solid piece of work upon Kant because only thus, by recognition of his great points, can he be abidingly refuted in his weak points.

You will please let me have the enclosed 4 letters back when quite done with.

I write another thing. There is a book of genuine Negro animal stories about to appear at Williams & Norgate's "The Little Wise One" with hundreds of sundry sketches, which I have ordered to present to Janet at Xmas, feeling sure it will be difficult to find out whether she or her mother or her father will more entirely delight in it. I tell you this now so as to get you please to have the way open for me—don't order or get it yourself for her, please.—

How happy the things you tell me about A. E. Taylor make me. Do tell him so please. I hope so much to live and thrive sufficiently still to master his doubtless great Commentary on the *Timaeus*. How wonderful it is the way in which the brilliant emptiness of the 18th century manages to live on, self-complacent, waited upon as a sort of an inverted orthodoxy & yet how along side of such Mummy Lives, we can & do get men in astonishingly close touch with the very saints of God.

And dear old Sir Archibald Geikie[260]—I was just in time carefully to read & reread every word of his long life's work, to write him a long letter about it & about all the joys I owed to him & he was able still to answer in a touching little preliminary note, which promised me, when he had got over his "present little illness" he would answer in full. The "little illness" carried him off on Monday, as of course you will have seen. What a delightfully central mind, what a power of driving recalcitrant horses in joyous obedience to his gentle sympathetic master! —Thanks so much for the tickets to hear Dr. Hogarth[261] on the Kings of the Hittites. They are being excellently placed. I have finished my first careful revision of the Introduction & of the first 3 sections of my book, but I have now carefully to carry out the exclusions, transpositions & additions thus revealed as necessary.

There has been a series of 5 articles in "The Tablet" on St. Catherine of Genoa which have brought me a good deal of distress of mind, because of their revealing some 3 very stupid ignorances or slips of my own & because even so smart & in some ways capable a writer so completely refuses to accept the chief & I still think reasonably irresistible conclusions of those many years of hard work.[262] I have now to make a several days break in my new book work for getting ready for Mr. Dent's insertion in the Mystical Element edition 1923.

Goodbye God bless you

Yr grateful old friend
F. v. Hügel.

[260] Sir Archibald Geikie (1835–1924), Scottish geologist, educated at Edinburgh University; entered Geological Survey, 1855; Director, Geological Survey of Scotland, 1867; first Murchison Professor of Geology and Mineralogy, Edinburgh, 1871–1882; Director-General, Geological Survey of United Kingdom, and Director, Museum of Practical Geology, 1882–1901; among his many publications was his autobiography, *A Long Life's Work* (1924).

[261] David George Hogarth (1862–1927), British archaeologist, educated at Winchester and Magdalen College, Oxford; Director, British School at Athens, 1897–1900; Keeper of the Ashmolean Museum from 1909; President of the Royal Geographical Society from 1925.

[262] Montgomery Carmichael, "St. Catherine of Genoa," *The Tablet*, Vol. 144, Nos. 4401–4405, (13, 20, 27 September, and 4, 11 October 1924), pp. 332–33, 365–66, 396–97, 428–29, and 461–63. The tone of these articles was condescending, and they missed entirely the real genius of von Hügel's *magnum opus* on St. Catherine of Genoa and mysticism.

Ellerton,
Grange Loan,
Edinburgh.

Nov. 16. 1924.

My dear Baron,

I shall often be sorely tempted, but evidently I must refrain from asking a question (the rhetorical ones we agree don't count), even though accompanied by the suggestion that a postcard is the utmost of my expectations. For I will not have you squander your precious energy in dictating—my gratitude to Lady Mary for writing. However great my own delight in receiving a long letter, it is a way of expending your energies that I must heartily—no, I mean *honestly*—deplore.

I have been again reading M. C. D'Arcy's article on Kant in the *Dublin Review*. It is admirably done, from the point of view of a follower of Aquinas; & much of it I can myself endorse, with very hearty sympathy. If Catholic writers would write of Kant with this amount of understanding & insight, however categorical they may also be in their criticisms, they would reach the ear of the general philosophical public in a way they seldom do, on this theme, to the great benefit of the latter.

I well remember you speaking of your visit to the Jesuit House of Studies in Oxford, but I had not remembered, not then knowing anything of M. C. D'Arcy, that he was one of that group of young men. Meantime I am only handing on to the Sec. of the Kant Gesellschaft the English articles, with some short comment, for their independent use in preparing their volume thereon. I shall read D'Arcy's 'God & the Supernatural' at first opportunity. Meantime many thanks for the *3* letters (inadvertently you say *4*: only 3 were in the envelop), which I herewith return.

The daughter, my wife & I all look forward delightedly to your promised Christmas gift: it sounds most delectable.

We are as usual having a Christmas Tree for the daughter, & a Christmas Tree party here for the University settlement children.

This afternoon Mrs Simon Laurie (widow of Scotus Novanticus, author of *Metaphysica Nova et Vetusta*) called with a framed large photo of the portrait of her husband by Fiddes Watt,[263] for which I had asked for my Retiring Room.

Tomorrow we are having an old friend of my wife's visiting us for a few days, with her husband an Italian Opera Singer. Tomorrow night we go to hear Weingartner conducting the Scottish Orchestra (from Glasgow) in a Beethoven programme. My wife used to hear him in Berlin.

Taylor's incredible tie is now in daily wear! However I do think it is helping in the right direction, giving ordinary people that feeling of superiority which makes it the easier for them to recognise those greater merits to which they have never themselves, even to themselves, pretended to lay claim.

Yesterday—this being the daughter's Mid-Term—we all went, with the four-footed Roy, my sister-in-law, with a Fräulein teaching in the German Department of the University, & a small maid, aged 16, who assists in the house, for a picnic on the Pentlands. There we made a fire for lunch, & after lunch the others returned by an early train, while the daughter, the maid, Roy & I climbed to the top of the ridge. Returning by a 4-30 train I had to fulfil a promise to Janet to have tea down town. So we found a very crowded tea-room, & with difficulty secured a portion of a table for ourselves, the dog & paraphernalia. And amidst the crowd the iron kettle broke loose from our string-bag & rolled over the floor to the great delight of Janet & the amusement of the onlookers. But I finally got them all home safely. And Janet's verdict is that it was a well-spent day.

With all good wishes, I am, my dear Baron,

Yours ever gratefully & affectionately,

NORMAN KEMP SMITH.

[263] George Fiddes Watt (1873–1960), Scottish artist, educated at the Royal Scottish Academy, where he won the Chalmers' Bursary for painting; his portraits of statesmen and others hang in Lincoln's Inn, Balliol and All Souls Colleges, Oxford, and in the Tate Gallery.

Nov. 23. 1924   Ellerton,
                                                        Grange Loan,
                                                        Edinburgh.

My dear Baron,

Since tea this afternoon my wife has been playing Christmas carols, to select them for a Christmas party of the University Staff, which is proposed for Dec. 23rd, with children in Tableaux while they are sung. Janet is to be a very large cherub, with a halo!

Most of the week we have had M^r and Mrs Priosi with us, & as they are very musical, we have had to have musical guests to meet them. One night we had Tovey, & another night Dr Schlapp (German Lecturer) & his wife; & very delightful music we had in consequence. Tonight the Taylors & two other friends are coming to supper. The Weingartner concert on Monday last was rather a failure; as he & his orchestra were evidently not at all in harmony.

Tomorrow I have a meeting here at Ellerton to discuss whether a local University Committee can be formed to cooperate with a national "China Universities Com." to further cooperation between the British & Chinese Institutions of Higher Learning. About 25 are coming & a Miss Agatha Harrison from London is to address us on the subject.

On Thursday night the American Club of the University is having a "Thanksgiving" Dinner, & my wife & I are guests of it. It is an annual occasion now in Edinburgh, & always pleasantly cheerful. Among the American students here this year is a *very* picturesque youth, called Rush Rhees—of rather distinguished parentage, on the side both of his mother & of his father. He is quite a picture, like the young Shelley, & rather lives up to it— tho' quite a nice & simple youth—wearing his shirt collar loose & open at the neck. Why he has been sent over to Edinburgh, I can't quite make out: he is taking undergraduate courses, & is in my big class. I cannot help thinking he must have got into some kind of youthful trouble at Syracuse University where he was studying & where his father is President. He came with an introduction, so I feel some responsibility for him. Asking him whether in his work here he wanted discipline or mainly stimulus, he replied, as I expected, very definitely the latter. He aspires to be a poet (I have not yet seen any of his verse) but conceals this high ambition under the very thin disguise of journalism.

Chesterton[264] addressed the students on Friday night on 'The Unusual University'—letting off his usual fireworks. I did not go to hear him. As a writer & thinker he does not seem to mature, as we could have hoped. His 'Napoleon of Notting Hill' & his 'Man Who Was Thursday' are my favourites.

Macneile Dixon's book was sold out at my bookseller's, & a copy only came last week; & I posted it to you on Friday. Some time I hope that you may find leisure to dip into it.

Later   10.30 P.M.

Our guests have gone. Taylor was talking among other matters of Milton to whom he is not evidently very partial,—of Milton's "colossal egotism" & of his denouncing King Charles in unqualified terms for qualities that he calls upon us to admire when practiced by God, etc. We had rather a nice story of F. H. Bradley (who detested Gladstone) as saying when Tennyson was dying that he wished it had rather been the other Old Man: "But the Devil is afraid to come for him."

The Egyptian situation is evidently quite serious. But perhaps the tragic occasion may give opportunity for getting the situation more in hand than it has been recently.[265]

I rejoice to think of your book as making reasonably good progress, & am always, my dear Baron,

Yours ever gratefully & devotedly,
NORMAN KEMP SMITH.

[264] Gilbert Keith Chesterton (1874–1936), British writer and controversalist, educated at St. Paul's School; his conversion to Roman Catholicism led to a series of apologetic lectures and books for that faith; in 1934 he was made Knight Commander with Star, Order of St. Gregory the Great; his *The Man Who Was Thursday* was published in 1907.

[265] On 19 November 1924 the British Governor-General of the Sudan, Sir Lee Stack, had been murdered. Britain insisted on the immediate evacuation of Egyptian troops from the Sudan, and began tightening up her own control there. In 1922 Britain had unilaterally declared its recognition of Egypt's independence. But, among other things, this recognition had been dependent on the continued British administration of the Sudan. Egypt had resisted signing a treaty on these conditions, and the murder was the latest atrocity in this period of unsettlement.

Nov. 30. 1924   University of
                                          Edinburgh

My dear Baron,

This has been a quieter week, but less quiet than I had hoped. The 'China Universities Committee' that I called here, was all right as regards attendance, but the people in London rather let me down by their unbusinesslike procedure. They had not instructed Miss Harrison properly, & indeed she was rather ignorant of the main matters under discussion. I have this evening been writing a letter to the London Office, not blaming her, for she played up manfully but their own careless procedure. However we all did our best, & I was left to name a Provisional Local Committee to explore the matter & to act if & when the Central Committee defines its policy more clearly. I am rather inclined to think that this 'China Universities Committee' has been started by people who hope to raise money thereby, to annex the Boxer Indemnity surplus, for the Missionary Schools & Colleges, & *not* for strictly University purposes at all. I indicate, in my letter, that we are unanimous against any such policy, & will *not* co-operate in it.

On Thursday night my wife & I were guests at the American Thanksgiving Dinner; & I had to prepare a speech for that. The American Consul also spoke. The American students in Edinburgh this winter—some 30 in all—are rather disappointing, with 3 or 4 exceptions.

Then on Friday—we had elected a new Dean on Thursday in place of Lodge at Faculty of Arts meeting—I was looking forward to some leisure for my own work, when a letter came in from a senior colleague, who was in bed, making the very proper suggestion that the Faculty of Arts ought to give a dinner to Sir Richard Lodge before he sails to America on Dec. 13th. So I had to bestir myself, telephone & write letters to the other members of the Faculty; & it looked as if I would have to take on the details of arrangement of dinner. However, yesterday I made the blessed discovery that Whittaker, the new Dean, regards that as his province; & I am my own man again, or relatively so.

The Prince of Wales is to be in Edinburgh on Wednesday,

opening new science buildings & getting an LL.D., & the Hon. Fellowship of the Royal Society (Edin.) The University is having a luncheon in the Upper Library Hall.

My wife has been equally busy. She is arranging a University Christmas party, with the children invited, at the University Union, with children in tableaux & carols. The children taking part are all coming here next Saturday with their Mothers for a rehearsal. It all needs a great deal of arranging. But she is very good at that sort of thing, & enjoys it.

The Scots Philosophical Club has its meeting on January 9th & 10th in Glasgow, & I have got Latta to give the paper at the Saturday forenoon meeting—on Spinoza & Leibnitz: not a particularly good subject for a discussion. But often that is best when least has been anticipated.

Principal Laurie[266]—son of Simon Laurie (Scotus Novanticus) & Principal of the Heriot–Watt Technical College—has been writing to the "Scotsman", advocating what do you think? You would never guess, except from his parentage—that Philosophy be made compulsory for *all* University students, in Medicine & Science as well as in Arts! And that a new Chair be founded in the History & Principles of the Natural Sciences, to complete & strengthen the Philosophical Department. He further argues that Philosophy being made central, some progress would be made towards neutralising the present tendency towards extreme specialism. By all I can learn, it is my Science colleagues who are most dissatisfied with the products of a purely scientific education. Not only has positive science *not* brought the new Heaven & the new Earth so many expected, it cannot, apparently, even give education: some of our Science Lecturers—fortunately so far none of our Science Professors—are positively illiterate, a kind of academic proletariat; & of course, in this respect, it is very much worse in the American Universities.

I have been reading a refreshingly good novel 'Mr Judge

[266] Arthur Pillans Laurie (1861–1949), British educator and chemist, educated at the Universities of Edinburgh and Cambridge; Lecturer in Physics and Chemistry at St. Mary's Hospital Medical School, 1895; Examiner in Chemistry to Royal College of Physicians, London, 1898; Professor of Chemistry, Royal Academy of Art, 1912; Principal, Heriot–Watt College, Edinburgh, 1900–1928.

Driver' by Paul E. Neuman; & a very interesting small volume, unpretentious but really illuminating, on the Russian Revolution as shown on the stage of a small Russian town, called 'A Week' by Iury Liebinsky.

I am, my dear Baron, with all good wishes, Yours ever gratefully & affectionately,

NORMAN KEMP SMITH.

Dec. 8. 1924   Ellerton,
                                            Grange Loan,
                                              Edinburgh.

My dear Baron,

This is Monday: I did not get writing yesterday, owing to visitors. *After* this week, life, I am glad to think, will be more leisurely.

On Tuesday night Principal Irvine[267] of Sᵗ Andrews spoke to our Staff Club on 'The American Universities', & I had to move the vote of thanks to him. Next day the Prince of Wales opened the new Chemistry Laboratory, got capped 'LL.D.' by Earl Balfour, made a pleasant little speech, & the University gave a luncheon at which the Principal was able to announce donations to the amount of £75,000—a *very* welcome announcement as it almost wipes out our deficit of £95,000, that has been an incubus on the University, necessitating all sorts of petty economies. The release from this situation will also make work on the Court pleasanter. £50,000 is from Sir Alex. Grant[268] who some

267 Sir James Colquhoun Irvine (1877–1952), Scottish chemist, educated at St. Andrews and Leipzig Universities; received honorary degrees from Glasgow, Aberdeen, Edinburgh, Wales, Toronto, McGill, Columbia, New York, Princeton, Pennsylvania, Yale, Liverpool, and Cambridge Universities; from Professor of Science, St. Andrews University, he became Principal and Vice-Chancellor of the University in 1921; his many publications were mainly concerned with the chemistry of sugars.

268 Sir Alexander Grant (1864–1937), Scottish businessman; Chairman and Managing Director of McVitie and Price, Ltd; purchased on behalf of Scotland the Advocates Library, Edinburgh, renamed the Scottish National Library; generous benefactor of Edinburgh University and other civic and national institutions. A boyhood friend of Ramsay MacDonald's, Grant gave MacDonald a Daimler automobile and a number of shares in McVitie and Price; subsequently Grant received a baronetcy. The result was a loud public outcry, and much pressure on MacDonald.

18 months ago gave £100,000 towards a Scottish National Library—in which the Advocates Library is to be merged. It was Grant too who gave his old friend Ramsay Macdonald the motor car. He is chief partner in McVitie & Grant—the firm of bakers & biscuitmakers, having himself risen from a very humble position in the employ of the firm. He lives very simply, & spends his wealth as the best American millionaires so often do.

On Saturday I went through to Glasgow to make out examination papers with Latta—we are examiners for the Shaw Fellowship this month, the chief Scottish Philosophical Scholarship, worth £200 a year for five years. One of my pupils is in for it, & two from Glasgow. In Glasgow I had time to see a few old friends & had dinner with Macneile Dixon, who is to be staying with us over Thursday night when he lectures to a Joint Meeting of the Classical & English Associations. There is a very stupid & stuffy review of his 'Tragedy' in the current 'Times Literary Supplement.'

On Saturday meantime my wife was very busy here, with a crowd of children & their Mothers, arranging for the Tableaux & Carols. She is out this evening hearing Weingartner & the Scottish Orchestra.

All around me on the floor & desk are essays—some 170 of them—all on the same theme, & nearly all *very* poor—on 'The Sophistic Movement & Socrates'. Fortunately a first reading of them is done for me, but I have to read a proportion of them— all the best. But lectures stop this week. Tomorrow night our Fac. of Arts is giving the dinner to Sir Richard Lodge on his resigning the Deanship. But this is a dull chronicle & written in more haste than I like. When life becomes a whirl I steady myself by thinking of your steady & quiet labours at your great book. All progress to it. I am, my dear Baron,

Yours ever affectionately,
Norman Kemp Smith.

P.S. Last night I read some of Newman's wonderful sermons.

13, Vicarage Gate,
Kensington,
W. 8.
17th December 1924

My very dear friend,

I find that the [*sic*] by far the easiest of my various means of communication are now simple dictations to my unhappy Secretary who cannot thus escape the infliction of even my remoter feelings and affections. So let me now write you a little Christmas letter—to you friend of friends who have been making my life for many months now into simply a different thing; this is literally true; for if I ask myself, What is it that keeps up, in a way with such ease, my sense of persistent growth and of persistent applications of this growth to its self-expression— What is it that makes me feel, with such comfortable ease, that I have somehow got an audience and that provided only I can add to the knowledge and experience of my great subject-matter I might even in the Calvinist University of Edinburgh disport myself as an Anglo-Catholic with ever so strange a tie: I know again from whom I get that; God bless you then for it. You see it has this oft ready utility about it that your letters, since first I got to know you at all, have all been kept just little fixing of dates of meeting etc. excepted. So it might really turn out some day to be of use to your biographer thus to have ready to his hand a quite comfortable and pleasant weekly review of what he has been doing, thinking and feeling.

I do, indeed, agree with you as to importance of little holidays and may we both have good ones just now. I intend to continue you [*sic*] my little labours through this week but to do nothing in the next and as to the week after to make it by some sort of happy device merely part and parcel of the preceding week.

This last fortnight my physical condition, I am well aware of it myself, has somehow been different to what it had been ever since mid-March last and both Doctor and Nurse are each very proud at one moment of themselves and the other moment of each other without I think always being quite clear in their own minds as to where precisely lies the gain. I think myself it lies in this that if they really succeed I shall be greatly eased in the matter of what troubles me now still, though much less at night.

I think that my difficulties as regards my dear book are at this moment really rather intrinsic than extrinsic—I mean that they come chiefly from a pretty severe bout of depression caused by, what I think is a highlander and this certainly a member of his Brittanic Majesty's Consular Service. Mr Montgomery Carmichael[269] has lived many years in Leghorn and since he is only five years my junior he has had plenty of time to do this much, he writes as far as I can judge with a certain point of plausibility; but I find to my relief that so fine and cautious a scholar as my dear friend Prof. Edmund Gardner finds his self-assurance a thing of most trying dimension—he says he tried to read all the five articles as they appeared in September and October in the Tablet but found that he really could not stand more than one of them. I doubt whether we ever really know exactly why this and that criticism of us depresses us specially but in this case I really think it was two things which arrested me which otherwise would hardly have stopped me at all. For one thing there was the very elaborate and I think very demonstrable matter of the authorship of St Catherine Fiesca Adorno's *Dialogo*. Was this very long, very characteristic piece abounding in all sorts of traceable and comparable details written by Catherine or not? I quite see that even now this is not directly a first rate question; and yet for people of my sort who must have history history—who cannot live without religion and without a religion full of history and yet again cannot live unless you allow them to retain and to utilize the test of downright history, must be a depression. For though it does not really much matter whether such types of mind express themselves to their own comfort amongst such people as I here feel myself to be one myself yet it does matter, so I feel, though I daresay really only for the most part in a subjective way

---

[269] Montgomery Carmichael (1857–1936), British civil servant and writer, educated at Bonn and Munich; employed in Consular Service, 1890; British Vice-Consul at Leghorn, 1892, Consul, 1908– 1922; Consul-General to the Republic of San Marino, and H.M. Consul for Tuscany (except Florence), Umbria, and the Marches, 1912–1922.

that such people should not appear too preposterous through such a very cocksure mind, since in this latter case one finds oneself within the Church where Moses was when the candle went out.

The second reason why I found Mr. Carmichael so very trying has been that he really did find out, very cleverly I think, what was the poorest bit of my entire performance—the sentence of eight lines all intended to honour and glorify my fine scholar friend Dom Cuthbert Butler O.S.B.[270] into which, I somehow, managed to pack certainly the most amazing Collection of apocrypha, of wildly impossible dates, of the queerest of 'possibilities' and the like—a sentence which I withdrew all right in 1923 but unfortunately then too late not to give the impression, to those who might care to take it up, of the real standard of work traceable in the toils of this man's many ups and downs of clumsy English leading to so little of any kind of usefulness. I minded this much because Dom Butler is one of the most thorough Scholars I have ever known amongst living R. C.s; and because, unfortunately, I see myself how impossible it is to say anything worse of this sentence than the sentence deserves.

I am enclosing for your kind preservation somewhere in my *Mystical Element* the two little papers—the one a postscript November 1924 to the 1923 Edition, to the Preface of that Edition. And this little affair is permanent. I also enclose a little list of

---

[270] Edward Joseph Aloysius (Dom Cuthbert) Butler (1858–1934), English Benedictine abbot and scholar, educated at Downside School; ordained, 1884; Headmaster, Downside School, 1888–1892; Superior, Benet House, Cambridge, 1896–1904; Abbot of Downside, 1906–1922; careful scholar whose major works include *Benedictine Monachism* (1919), and *Western Mysticism* (1922). Von Hügel, a long-time friend, wrote to him after the appearance of Carmichael's articles offering to correct in the Preface of his new edition of *The Mystical Element of Religion* the incorrect reference to Butler's work which Carmichael had pointed out. Butler gently persuaded von Hügel to forget about the Carmichael articles, telling him: "You cannot be expected in midst of a second edition to meet criticisms made on that second edition. Nor are you called on to give them perpetual life. . . . For myself, I have not, & had not, the feelings & emotions you seem, in your great & generous goodness, to fear. My only feeling was that your great book should be clear of all mistakes. . . . Life is too short, & we all have our own works to be about. So I hope you will understand that not on my account ought you to refer to Carmichael's articles." Butler to von Hügel, 21 December 1924, St. Andrews University Library, von Hügel MS 2373.

printed corrigenda which is temporary and necessary only because Mr Dent has printed off so many copies from the uncorrected plates and since, though he has now corrected these plates, he does not care to run into the expense and trouble of their more thorough correction.

I also send you a little German translation really by myself of part of a letter I wrote to Canon Streeter[271] and Mr Appasomy some years back, just before they finally settled upon the text of their Sâdhu Sundar Singh for publication. I now think looking at this little performance of mine as it stands thus by itself in black and white, that I exaggerate any tendency there may have been in St Teresa to recognise and to welcome as wholesome and holy any convictions not directly expressed or at least easily expressible as part and parcel of a faith in the Roman Catholic Church and Pope. Still I continue to feel that there is some real point in what I say here and that it is no good for the Parkers and their friends to assume that they are straight away comparable with those great Spaniards.

I am sending you also a piece of work in no wise my own but which interests me much for a whole number of personal reasons —I think you might yourself come to be interested in several of these points. You will, I think, readily feel and see how *real*, how psychologically inevitable and yet how difficult to resolve intellectually, is the case as here brought up by Henri Brémond himself an ex-Jesuit and still more the case as here given of Père Charles Smedt, who lived and died a Bollandist and Jesuit. And what adds a touch of piquancy to the whole situation is that the Pope—the present Pope Pius XI before whom with every possible mark of the profoundest respect he argues the case is still after well over a year's delay keeping back the ms of the fourth and last unpublished History of the Early Church of Msgr

---

[271] Burnett Hillman Streeter (1874–1937), British Biblical scholar, educated at King's College School, London, and Queen's College, Oxford; Fellow and Dean, Queen's College, Oxford, 1905, Provost, 1933–1937; ordained, 1899; Canon of Hereford, 1915–1934; his main works include *Studies in the Synoptic Problem* (1911), *The Four Gospels: A Study of Origins* (1924), and *Reality: A New Correlation of Science and Religion* (1926).

Duchesne. The whole situation is like a strange sounding yet as I believe an inevitable survival of the ancient controversies under Erasmus, although Duchesne as I knew him so intimately well always struck me as much more evidently a Catholic at heart, but whether Loisy who was so annoyed with my letter to the Times Literary Supplement precisely because it took this line will be pleased with Henri Brémond because he takes the same line but with considerable greater *aplomb* still remains to be seen.[272]

What a charming looking little volume is Prof. Dixon's publication on 'Tragedy'. I am so glad that you thought of my wife for it. I gave it to her at once and I believe you understand the sort of books that appeal to her, but I have also quite clearly taken in that you want me also to read it and I hope next week to read it all or at least a good part of it.

I am not forgetting the *Little Wise One* the collection of Negro Fables I have had lying beside me ready for that sweet little Janet of yours, but this volume I intend to dispatch next week by itself begging you to put it into her hand only with such other Christmas presents as you may have to give her. I think that with ourselves as children we never got clearly beyond the two dates of Christmas *Eve* any hour still December 24th and Christmas Day, any hour still within December 25th and so I shall be quite happy if you will care to make my little gift wobble with the other great offerings ready for the hands of that sweet little lady.

I had intended to write to you about Mrs Lillie who came back to England just about two years after she had come here and joined the Roman Church, but though I am quite ready to do so in the sense of unbroken esteem and respect for her and indeed also in feeling that her coming to us has been and continues most sincere and shows her to have gained very solidly in the deepest

[272] The issue in this somewhat confusing paragraph is that of Vatican censorship of responsible scholarship by Roman Catholics, especially clerics. The book in question is the final volume of Louis Duchesne's *History of the Early Church*, and the challenge to Vatican policy is a published address by Henri Brémond. The letter to the *TLS* which von Hügel mentions is a lengthy obituary appraisal of Duchesne which he published at the time of Duchesne's death. See Friedrich von Hügel, "Louis Duchesne," *The Times Literary Supplement*, No. 1062, 25 May 1922, p. 342.

of ways, I do not feel somehow that I have enough to say, yet she certainly leads a very useful and devoted life and before I pass away from this earthly scene I may find it quite easy to point out where I can trace the very definite gain in her . . .[273]

27th Dec. 1924   13 Vicarage Gate,
                                                            Kensington,
                                                                W. 8.

My very dear Friend,

I am slowly getting through my Christmas holiday, which my little Secretary and I have fixed—perhaps over grandly for this week and the next, so as to begin work again not before Jan. 5th. The Dr has just been here and is much pleased at certain reconstitutions wanted in the system and which, even now, it is responding to very nicely, he says—that I am markedly better with regard to various salts etc. than I have been recently, or indeed for many years. I shall indeed be grateful if he thus brings me back a working power unknown to me for long. I think I really can already trace something of the kind though all formal tests stands adjourned, as just described.

Your charming little-big book, *Schweitzer's early Memoirs*, arrived on Christmas morning—therefore exactly right; and I have been living, breathing, growing in and with it most happily and very gratefully. That is certainly a truely large soul, a genial welcomer of all things true and good. His address is simplicity itself—given to me, very proudly as thus sufficient at any time, in his astonishingly small, spidery writing: Günsbach, Alsace Supérieure, France. —By all means write to him. But we will—won't we?—take care to keep going within us the distinction you brought out so well in one of your letters to me the other day—a certain co-natural greatness of soul that adorns all he thinks and proposes; and the question, never identical with this fact, never itself answered by this greatness, as to the adequacy and

[273] The manuscript of this letter breaks off in mid-sentence.

grip of the explanations sought by him in such big, complex sub-ject-matters as the central convictions of Jesus and as to the es-sence of Civilisation. I should be very sorry to be restricted, in either of these subjects, to his final solutions of them. And yet it is certainly very difficult I find, to appreciate the man sufficiently and not to exceed in one's estimate of his views, since the views, in his case, are so exceptionably closely the children of his own nature, and since this nature is not only rarely noble but unusual unto excentricity. Without being a crank himself he lives not far from them.

I did not, Friend, make myself clear as to St Catherine's *Dialogo*: I was not rendered sad by any doubt arising within me, that the saint did not write one word of the D.—that *Battista* wrote it all. My depression came merely from being brought up, bump, against one more, one other fellow creature, who, in such matters, would be quite incorrigible—beyond all arguments whatsover; and to feel that most men will think this quite enough.

The charmingly brought out little book on Tragedy is to be read by me most carefully as soon as ever possible; but I [*sic*] the same troubles dog me now which used so to limit my brain activity in the past: the need that the books read by my [*sic*] during composition weeks only requiring a sort of secondary at-tention. Trollope has been exactly right for this; even now I have still some 400 pages of vol. II of the 'Last Chronicle of Barset', to read

. . .

Here, Friend, is Henri Brémond's *Dèscours*, as new French Academician in honour of Mgr Louis Duchesne. I do not know whether it will produce upon you the impression of rare un-worldliness that it does upon myself; for, tho' I do not know what were his chances before of becoming *persona grata* with the leading—determining—Roman authorities before, he surely has spoilt such chances thoroughly. I do not remember any Church situation quite like this one in the past; its interest is doubtless largely caused by the Bollandists who cannot fail to have been consulted by B. and to have desired him thus to underline the solidarity between their *Society* and Duchesne.

Your very grateful, devoted Friend, F. v. H.

The Feast of Christmas is entirely the work of the (local) Roman Church. I am much interested in Mrs K. S.'s feeling for it.

H.

> Ellerton,
> Grange Loan,
> Edinburgh.

Dec. 28. 1924

My dear Baron,

All good wishes to you for the coming year, & may it lead to splendid progress in your work! The volume of negro stories is being a great delight to Janet. She has already read all of them, & some I have been rereading to her, with equal enjoyment. They are most delightful in their simplicity & directness: The inscription too will make the volume a treasured heirloom in the family.

The week has been a pleasantly busy one. The University Children's tableaux-carols went off quite well, the many difficulties of place etc. notwithstanding, to the great credit of my wife. On Christmas evening we had forty homeless students & others here—22 of them Americans together with the American Consul. Last night we had the Christmas Tree lit again for some 25 little urchins from the University Settlement. And this afternoon our Reader in German, Dr Otto Schlapp & his family have been with us, singing old-time Carols, English & German. Last night too my friend Wm Menzies turned up unexpectedly for the weekend, & we have put him in the last vacant bed, my eldest sister & her daughter being likewise with us.

On Tuesday I had a conference with Prof. Latta from Glasgow on the Shaw Fellowship examination papers, & have awarded the Fellowship to a student of mine who is adopting the teaching of Philosophy as his profession. I am very glad he has won it against the candidates from Glasgow. I think I told you that the Fellowship was founded at Edinburgh by a former Lord Mayor of London, & is of the considerable value of £220 a year for five years. A. J. D. Porteous[274] who has been awarded it, was first in my Degree Class my first year here—the best class I have ever had, being the senior men back from the War.

Menzies being here, I cannot write more at length. Tomorrow morning I go to join a golfing party at St Andrews for a couple of nights, & then to my people for a couple of nights at Dundee, Amy going meantime South for a fortnight to friends & the daughter with an Aunt to Windermere. My wife & daughter join me in all good wishes of the season to Lady Mary, to Baroness Hildegarde & to yourself. I am, my dear Baron,

Yours ever gratefully & devotedly,
NORMAN KEMP SMITH.

13 Vicarage Gate, W. 8.
　Dec. 30 1924.
My very dear, ever kind Friend,

I wrote you quite a long letter some days back—alas, I cannot lay my hands on it! —But one thing it contained you ought to have had from me long ago—the address of Prof. Schweitzer. In his own astonishingly small yet clear hand-writing that tall, also in various mental and spiritual ways gigantic man, wrote down for me:

'Doctor Albert Schweitzer,
　　Günsbach,
　　　Haute Alsace,
　　　　France.

He added, with a grin that this had been his only safe address since he was quite a little child; and that it would assuredly re-

274 Alexander James Dow Porteous (1896–), Scottish philosopher, educated at Edinburgh and Oxford Universities; Shaw Fellow in Mental Philosophy, Edinburgh, 1924–1929; Assistant Lecturer in Logic and Metaphysics, Edinburgh, 1924–1926; Professor of Philosophy, Smith College, Northampton, Massachusetts, 1926–1930; Associate Professor of Philosophy, McGill University, Montreal, 1930–1931, Professor, 1931–1932; Lecturer in Ancient Philosophy, Edinburgh, 1932–1937; Sydney Jones Professor of Education, University of Liverpool, 1954–1963; Emeritus, 1963.

main so even if he *did* succeed in returning, repeatedly to his beloved African natives. —I have his photo somewhere—a fine, handsome head—but must not worry to find it.—

I am so *very* grateful for the little *Memoirs* book: how genuine and homely, what power of self-expression! And yet how utterly unusual even among extraordinary men—e.g. that having to drop (or at least, dropping) all games whatsoever, as too exciting! Am reading it very slowly, again and again—like a caramel slowly dissolving in the mouth. —Am still at, Trollope—very happy over 'Last Chron. of Barset'—at least, full of admiring sympathy with the fine sides of the finer characters. My eyes do not allow me to read very much; but, never mind, one can thus learn further to deepen one's peace.—

So glad that sweet little Janet likes her African Fables, and that you, too, find pleasure therein. And how good the holidays for us all. Have arranged not to resume till . . .[275]

Jan. 5. 1925.   Ellerton,
                                                    Grange Loan,
                                                       Edinburgh.

My dear Baron,

All good wishes for the new year to you. It has inauspiciously begun for me with a bad cold in the throat & head, but not such as to disable me for work; & it is pleasant to see my desk getting cleared of business letters & other similar impediments. This morning I have completed the making out of examination papers for Durham University. Now I have the more genial & congenial task of writing to yourself & to the little daughter. At present I am alone in the house, save for the maids, my wife being South visiting friends & the daughter being with an Aunt at Windermere.

The two nights & three days at St Andrews went very pleasantly. We were a party of nine—Professor Hugh Macintosh from Edinburgh, Prof. A. B. Macauley from Glasgow, W. D. Ross, the

---

[275] Here the manuscript abruptly breaks off.

deputy-Professor of Moral Philosophy at Oxford, whose edition
of Aristotle's Metaphysics is just out, J. C. Smith one of our Scottish School Inspectors, R. P. Harden our Lecturer in Greek Philosophy, & three youngsters. G. F. Stout joined us one evening.
The weather happily was propitious for golf; & I also enjoyed a
stroll round the little town, renewing many memories.

Stout still speaks of the first volume of his Giffords being out
this year, but is now more shy of giving a precise time. He is still
putting in much work on them.

Many thanks for your welcome letter, with Schweitzer's address, & with a second copy of M. Bremond's *Discours* (for you
sent me one before Christmas). However I shall not return it,
but hand it on to Taylor who will be much interested to have it.
Yes, it is an inspiring document which I am glad to have read. I
especially liked p. 46 ff.

A request has just come in that I write on James Ward's work
for the *Monist*. The editor says Ward complains to him of never
having his work recognised in the *Monist*. So he (the editor) is
asking Stout & Taylor to write special articles. After Ward's onslaught upon me, it would be rather humourous to get in a eulogy
of him: but my other engagements forbid, unfortunately.

Our Scots Philosophical Club meets in Glasgow on 9th & 10th.
Stout is coming, along with his son who is now teaching Philosophy at Bangor, & I presume Taylor will turn up.

Yesterday, on occasion of my Durham papers, I read through
Butler's *Sermons*—the first time in 25 years—with immense enjoyment: must go to his *Analogy*. Butler always shows sound
sense & judgment—a marked contrast in most ways to his otherwise worthy successor, Dean Inge. I find Butler was in Durham,
as Bishop, less than two years. But the University has great pride
in him.[276]

I am, my dear Baron, Yours ever devotedly & gratefully,

NORMAN KEMP SMITH

[276] Joseph Butler (1692–1752) was
Dean of St. Paul's from 1740 to 1746,
and died as Bishop of Durham. His *Fif-*
teen Sermons were published in 1726, and
his famous *Analogy of Religion* in 1736.

Appendices

I

Letter of Norman Kemp Smith
to Lady Mary von Hügel

(von Hügel MS 3066, St. Andrews)

Eira,
Rhoscolyn,
Holyhead, N. Wales.

June 7. 1919.

Dear Baroness von Hügel,

I have been writing the Baron, but I should also like to thank you for the pleasure and privilege of your most kind hospitality. I have seldom spent two such happy days, or days that I shall remember for a great many reasons with livelier gratitude.

I got back very comfortably. Instead of staying overnight at Chester, I reached Holyhead after one a.m. on the Thursday morning, & had a delightful seven mile drive in the semi-darkness to Rhoscolyn.

With kind greetings to the Baroness Hildegarde and to yourself, I am,

Yours ever gratefully,
NORMAN KEMP SMITH.

II

Inaugural Lecture of Norman Kemp Smith as Professor of Logic and Metaphysics,

Delivered in the University of Edinburgh on 16 October 1919
and subsequently printed by the University Publisher

THE PRESENT SITUATION IN
PHILOSOPHY

As I think of the time when, as an undergraduate, I
studied under Professor Pringle-Pattison in St Andrews
University, and consider that I am now called upon to
act as his successor, I feel that I stand much in need
of the kindly consideration you so generously extend
to me. I can but pray that the traditions of this famous
Chair, handed on with added lustre by Professor Pringle-
Pattison, may in some degree support me; and I can
at least promise that I shall not be found wanting through
any failure to appreciate the magnitude of the task and
the greatness of the responsibility which it imposes.

Before this audience, and in Professor Pringle-
Pattison's presence, it would be presumptuous for me
to speak in praise of his great services to the University
and to philosophy, but there are certain matters upon
which I may claim that I am qualified to pronounce
with some authority. It is well when succeeding genera-
tions are bound together by respect and reverence; and
I know that I shall be expressing the feelings of all
Professor Pringle-Pattison's former pupils here present
when I say that there is no one to whom the younger
generation in philosophy looks up with more unqualified
admiration, reverence, and affection. We count it a high
privilege that he will continue in our midst; and we look
to him to give us, as the fruits of his greater leisure, still
more of the inspiration that has meant so much to us in
the past.

3

4

As Professor Pringle-Pattison left St Andrews, to occupy this Chair, while I was only in the third year of what was then the four years' Arts course, I did not have the privilege of his instruction in the Honours classes, but already in the Junior class I had sufficient opportunity of appreciating what I believe has been an outstanding feature of all his teaching; and it is one that I would wish to imitate. The teacher of philosophy stands to his students in a relation of greater delicacy than does the teacher of any other subject in the University curriculum. He deals, and is obliged to deal, with problems that are concerned in the most intimate and searching way with the ultimate issues of life; but since, unlike the workers in the positive sciences, he cannot in so doing appeal to any authoritative and universally accepted body of doctrine, he is by the nature of his subject peculiarly exposed to the temptation of imposing upon his hearers his own merely personal views. The Scottish student is not, indeed, entirely at the mercy of his teachers in any subject, and certainly not in a class of philosophy. But none the less, if a teacher selects his material, and does not press his conclusions until he has prepared the ground beforehand, he can prejudice the issues before they have been squarely faced. He has also under his control the reading prescribed for class and degree examinations; and by its means he can enlist in his support standard works that do not raise in too convincing or too suggestive a form the difficulties which his own philosophy is least capable of meeting; and the books will thus seem, as by independent testimony, to confirm the soundness of the doctrines that he is propounding.

From this particular disadvantage Professor Pringle-Pattison's teaching has always been singularly free; one of its most impressive features has been the faithfulness with which he deals with his hearers, not concealing, and not withholding, the expression of his own convictions, but also at the same time demanding that the problems

5

should be faced in all their difficulty before judgment is passed upon them. None of his students, in looking back, can feel that their introduction to the great and critical problems of philosophy has been unduly biassed, or that the perspective in which they have been presented was other than that which a fair-minded thinker could rightly give to them. I shall endeavour, to the best of my powers, to follow Professor Pringle-Pattison's example in this respect. If the teacher of philosophy can enable his students to appreciate the problems at issue, and the conclusions to which they will in consistency stand committed according as they adopt a philosophy of one or another type, and if, further, he can interpret to them the great historical traditions within which these conflicting philosophies appear, then the Scottish student may generally be relied upon, sooner or later, to acquire a philosophy for himself. What that philosophy will be, is determined, as is only fitting, by wider and more representative influences than can, or should be, brought to bear in the class-room.

On an occasion such as this, however, I shall very rightly be expected to give some indication of my personal sympathies and convictions, and I have therefore chosen as the topic of my remarks the present situation in philosophy.

Though philosophical systems vary indefinitely, they are reducible, broadly considered, to three main types. They are either idealist, or naturalistic, or sceptical. Under one or other of these three rubrics every philosophy can be brought; and at every period in which free discussion has been possible, we find the sum-total of knowledge and experience being interpreted from these divergent points of view. The three types are, it would seem, perennial in the fluctuations of human thought. Each of them every little while finds some new and hitherto unconsidered difficulty cropping up in its path. Fresh additions to knowledge seem at first sight conclusively to favour one of them and to rule out the others.

6

In the end, however, each contrives to reassert itself, and to propound some method, more or less feasible, of reconciling the new knowledge with its own standpoint. Scepticism and naturalism, not to mention idealism, are as much alive to-day as they were in the time of Aristotle. Idealism now, as hitherto, is probably the philosophy of the great majority of men. Naturalism still represents the attitude of those who incline, whether on pragmatic or on scientific grounds, to a secularist reading of human life and destiny. Scepticism still draws its comparatively small band of followers from very various sources. But in nearly all other respects the situation has undergone complete change. Each of the three typical philosophies has developed almost out of recognition. The sceptical and naturalistic philosophies of the present day differ from those in Ancient Greece even more fundamentally than the Hegelian philosophy differs from the idealism of Plato and Aristotle.

Most histories of philosophy have, as it happens, been written by idealists; and we are therefore well acquainted with the idealist's claim that his type of philosophy has progressively deepened, has been fertilised, strengthened, and enriched by the whole progress of human thought throughout the centuries. Have not the natural sciences confirmed idealist teaching as to the rationality of the Universe, and have they not by their magnificent conquests borne striking witness to the capacities of the human spirit? And have not the labours of the sceptics likewise furthered the idealist tradition? Could idealist philosophy have developed its present strength save under the severe and salutary discipline to which the sceptics have so continuously and zealously subjected it ever since the time of Zeno and Protagoras? That is to say, both the results of the positive sciences, the facts to which naturalism makes appeal, and also the arguments upon which the sceptics have reared an agnostic philosophy, have all contributed to the ultimate strengthening of the idealist position. The stream of tendency has been towards idealism.

7

As a matter of fact, however, scepticism and naturalism have undergone a corresponding development. The history of philosophy can be written from the sceptical point of view, and several such histories exist, the best known being the famous biographical history by George Henry Lewes, probably the most widely read history of philosophy ever written. Though now considerably out of date, it is still readable. He wrote it in order to show that the lesson which history teaches is that every idealist system and every naturalistic system, in short every constructive philosophy, inevitably, sooner or later, falls prey to the sceptic. The idealists, he argues, by their ingenious attempts to elude refutation, have so sharpened the wits of their opponents, that largely thanks to these idealists—thanks to Socrates, Plato, Descartes, Kant, and Hegel—the sceptical position has now at last been firmly established. Scepticism, he maintains, can now demonstrate from the very constitution of our faculties, and from the so-called knowledge which we have acquired in the natural sciences, that we know nothing of ultimate reality.

Similar claims may be urged on behalf of naturalism. As Friedrich Lange has shown in his *History of Materialism*, there is as great a difference between ancient and modern materialism as there is between primitive forms of life and the complex organisms which have evolved from them. Naturalism, it may be contended, has kept pace with moral and religious experience as well as with the growth of the positive sciences: so that it can now account, from a naturalistic point of view, not merely for physical, chemical, and physiological processes, but for the development of civilisation and for the misconceived, but none the less indispensable, services rendered by idealist and sceptical thinkers in Greek and modern times.

These three typical philosophies thus stand in a constant relation of interaction and mutual aid. Each in the struggle for self-maintenance compels the competing systems to develop on fresh lines, meeting new objections by modification of their former grounds. But

8

they are so opposed in fundamentals that, with the best will in the world, they can neither compromise on their differences nor convert one another to common conclusions. So that while each main type of philosophy has undergone what may accurately be described (allowing for minor deviations) as a continuous and steady development of its initial principles, this development, astonishingly rich and fruitful as it has undoubtedly been, has not enabled any one of them quite decisively to displace the others. However they may have altered in their methods of argument, and however they may have approximated on this or that particular tenet, in their fundamental principles they remain as antagonistic as at any period in the past. In this address I propose to define the relations in which they stand to one another in present-day controversy.

The idealists, ever since the time of Socrates, have contended that in interpreting man in terms of his physical conditions naturalism rules itself out from answering those questions, moral, social, and religious, that outweigh in human interest and in practical importance the more purely theoretical problems with which a naturalistic philosophy chiefly concerns itself. To such a charge naturalism, even in its least developed stages, has always been able to make weighty reply. Frankly non-religious, it could point to the superstitious, ambiguous character of religious belief and practice; frankly revolutionary, it could trace moral distinctions to social conventions adopted for their beneficial consequences in forwarding the secular welfare of the individual and of society. And regarding happiness as the end of life, it could welcome the fine arts; rejoicing in the lust of the eye and in the pride of life, are they not its natural allies?

For several reasons, however, this naturalistic philosophy has seldom succeeded in obtaining acceptance save in strictly limited circles. But there can, I should say, be no more fatal error than to argue that this must

9

necessarily continue. Though speaking as a convinced idealist, I should like to indicate in what respects the naturalistic position has been strengthened—and it has, I should say, been very greatly strengthened —by the advance of knowledge, especially in the historical sciences, in the nineteenth century. Naturalism can now profess to meet idealism on more equal terms within its own field, that of our specifically human activities.

But let me first define the present situation as regards scepticism. Scepticism must hold a high and worthy place in every history of philosophy, by whomsoever written. It has been one of the main agencies of human advance. It is the enemy of fanaticism and of false sentiment in every form. The mind to which it is utterly uncongenial can have no capacity for philosophy, and is little likely to have discrimination in regard to the truth. Professor Paterson has recently said that the Scotch—and we always like to hear ourselves praised—have the most complex character of any people in the world. Is not David Hume one of the greatest figures in the history of philosophy, and does he not represent a national trait? For though we are theologically inclined, and endowed with a Celtic fervour in the convictions we adopt, are we not hard-headedly sceptical in equal degree? To what is the admitted Scottish capacity for philosophy due, if not to this happy combination of caution and tenacity, of circumspection when we are invited to accept a statement, and of readiness to fight for it once we have made it our own?

But while scepticism is valuable as a regulating balance-wheel, it can supply no engine-power. When through the miscarriage of positive efforts at construction error arises, or when beliefs and institutions justified in their day and generation outlive their usefulness and abuses accumulate, the sceptic is indeed in his element. But when his destructive work is completed, and the ground is cleared, he is left without occupation. He is a

10

specialist in the subject of error, and when the community's stock of error gives out, he is faced by the spectre of unemployment, condemned to idleness until a new crop has been grown. If he takes to some more constructive line of life, his creed commits him to the belief that he will himself be adding to the sum of what, as a sceptic, he lives only to condemn.

Thus though scepticism contributes to the history of philosophy some of its most exciting and critical incidents, it has perforce, when it endeavours to represent this history as establishing its own truth, to defer its apotheosis to the close of the drama, leaving the stage free for the more positive creeds. The history of philosophy, quite obviously, is *not* the history of sceptical thinkers. Scepticism is, at most, a kind of Greek chorus, commenting ironically upon the course of the action, and when it closes tragically, in failure and disappointment, summoning the spectator more wisely to be content with the cry of wonder and ignorance that alone befits a creaturely being such as man.

The sceptic, therefore, if he be as keen in his powers of appreciation as he is clear-sighted in the detection of error and illusion, will recognise that the creative forces of civilisation are positive in character. Is not even his own onslaught upon error due to a fastidious insistence, more or less unreasoned, upon intellectual standards?

The better understanding of these positive forces has indeed led, during the past thirty years, to a very remarkable change of attitude in the philosophical world. Scepticism, or to employ the term invented by Huxley, agnosticism, was never probably more favourably regarded or more influential than in the period between 1820 and say 1890. It was developed as a self-sufficing creed by Auguste Comte and Herbert Spencer, by Huxley and Helmholtz; and in the hands of Sir William Hamilton and Mansel was even employed as a buttress to traditional religion. More recently, however, the trend alike of philosophy and of popular opinion, both in the scientific

11

and in the religious spheres, seems to have set very definitely against it. It is now generally recognised that though for certain of our problems we have no sufficient available data, we cannot so far predict the future as to set up a boundary-line between the possibly knowable and the absolutely unknowable. And even granting this could be done, the exigencies of life constrain us to adopt an attitude towards practical, social, and religious problems. The position thus taken, even if only on pragmatic grounds, is what determines our philosophy. Our attitude to these more immediate questions must be either naturalistic or idealist in type and tendency, and consequently it is between these two forms of philosophy that we are called upon to decide.

Before I leave scepticism, allow me to indicate what were the influences that gave it a new lease of life in the nineteenth century, and why, while at first seeming to contribute to the establishment of an agnostic philosophy, they have in the end led away from it.

At the period I refer to, say roughly from about 1820 onwards, the Romantic movement, passing from literature into scholarship and history, awakened a new interest in human life as lived under conditions different from our own, whether in the Far East, in classical, or in primitive times, and so originated the historical study of civilisation in all its manifold forms. This historical method obtained an added prestige from Darwin's application of it in the biological sciences; but it had already borne good fruit prior to the publication of the *Origin of Species*, and very soon thereafter was able to systematise its main results through the creation of the new science of anthropology.

Now anthropology made possible for the first time an understanding of the beginnings in which human thinking takes its rise. It has shown that primitive thinking, among savage peoples in all parts of the earth, invariably bases itself upon a distinction between soul and body, and that it employs this distinction to account for all those

12

phenomena which most attract its attention, especially the facts of disease and death. Animism, as it is called—that is to say, the animistic distinction between the body and a soul supposed to be capable of leaving it in sleep and of surviving it in death—is the cradle of all human thought. It has made possible the first beginnings of religion, and has thereby yielded the necessary sanctions for the moral and social values embodied in custom and in tribal institutions.

The conclusions to which the study of primitive thought thus led were mainly twofold—that animism is false as a theory, and yet profoundly beneficial as an influence. It is false because the data upon which the distinction between soul and body is based have been wrongly interpreted. The asserted facts are either themselves fictitious or, owing to primitive man's ignorance of the forces at work within and without him, have been misunderstood. Thus human thought is cradled not in ignorance, but in positive error and delusion. Its primitive beliefs rest upon foundations which, from a logical point of view, are grotesquely incapable of supporting the superstructure. These beliefs may be re-established on other grounds, but certainly not on the evidence which originally led to their adoption.

But that is only one side of the picture; the other was for its first discoverers even more important. For they were constrained, by the same line of reasoning, to recognise that since animism has not been arbitrarily invented, but has arisen from natural causes among peoples in all parts of the earth, being indeed co-extensive with human thinking in its earliest known periods, it must have performed in a relatively satisfactory manner some useful function. It must have aided in the development of civilisation. They therefore concluded that the justification for the animistic beliefs is to be looked for exclusively in the practical domain. Save in the favouring environment of animistic beliefs, religion, they argued, could never have come into existence; and in the

13

absence of religion, the social and moral codes could never have acquired those terrific sanctions which only the religious emotions (so powerful in primitive societies) could confer, and through which alone the counter-influence of the self-regarding, non-social instincts and passions could be broken down. Religion, that is to say, is on this view a bye-product of evolution. It is simply one of nature's many and strange devices for furtherance of her ends. The communities in which religion appears and takes root acquire all the advantages of unified action, and are therefore favoured by the processes of natural selection. These services, however, are only temporary. Though they have proved indispensable in the earlier stages of man's development, they cannot hope to maintain themselves under the altered conditions of a civilisation that is scientifically organised.

From this point of view, agnosticism proceeded to extend the pragmatic method of explanation to our so-called scientific knowledge. Even science, it was contended, is not a form of theoretical insight; it is merely a means to power. Science, rightly understood, never seeks to explain, but only to simplify. By scrupulously careful observation we verify the ultimate co-existences and sequences among our sensations, and under the guidance of elaborate hypotheses, which have a merely subjective value in directing enquiry, we define the co-existences and sequences in exact quantitative terms. Acquaintance with these relations, when thus precisely defined, enables us to predict the future, to construct machines, and so progressively to gain control over our physical environment; but they yield no insight, it is maintained, into the independently real. What is alone truly characteristic of science is not the obtaining of insight, but the acquisition of power. Thought is an instrument developed through natural processes for the practical purposes of adaptation. Its criteria and values are exclusively determined by the instinctive equipment of the species in its adjustment to environment. They have no independent

14

validity of any kind. The human mind, the argument proceeds, is limited to appearances; to attain knowledge in the absolute sense, that is to say through distinguishing between the true and the false, is impossible. There is a mechanism or economy of human thought; but logic, so-called, is a science with pretensions as excessive and quite as unfounded as those of theology. The distinction between the true and the false claims to be an absolute one; and how can man, a merely natural existence, expect to have dealings with the absolute in any form!

These conclusions made possible a sceptical philosophy immensely more comprehensive in its scope, and much more assured in its methods, than any that had previously been propounded. The history of human thought, when thus taken on its philosophical side, is the record, not of a progressive discovery of truth, but of our gradual emancipation from error. Recognising the misleading character of this, that, and the other belief, we renounce them; and those beliefs that are left we retain, not because they can be demonstrated, but simply because we find them serviceable. Though they cannot be proved, they cannot be refuted; and the probability, it may be argued, is that, like the beliefs which we have come to reject, their usefulness is no criterion as to their truth. They aid us in adapting ourselves to our physical and social environment, but that is no reason for ascribing to them any independent validity. We cannot have dealings with the absolute in the practical any more than in the intellectual domain.

But in proportion as agnosticism developed this position, it overreached itself, and fell into unstable equilibrium. It is easily shown that in drawing an absolute distinction between appearance and reality— and it is upon the absoluteness of the opposition that its scepticism rests—it is simply retaining from meta-physical thinking a belief for which, on a secularist reading of human life, no practical or instrumental justification is or can be offered; while, on the other

15

hand, it is equally clear that all those beliefs of the traditional religions, which agnosticism is so bent upon eliminating, are bound up with it. If the distinction between appearance and reality be retained, then more must be made of it, and justification must be given for our preferential treatment of it. But in that case the agnosticism is undermined, and the way is opened for idealist teaching. This is the line taken by those who employ it in support of religion. If, on the other hand— and this has been the more usual tendency of the School—the distinction between appearance and reality be allowed to be as relative and empirical as any other, agnosticism at once reveals its true affiliations. Agnosticism, in its usual and most influential forms, has really been naturalism in disguise.

Present-day naturalism, if asked to outline the history of philosophy, would therefore reply somewhat as follows. Animism developed through Pythagoras, Socrates, and Plato into spiritualism. This spiritualism was reaffirmed in modern times by Descartes and his successors, and under the disintegrating influence of sceptical enquiry was developed by Locke, Hume, Kant, and others into agnosticism. But agnosticism, naturalism maintains, is itself a compromise between science and animism. The dualism between the phenomenal and the real, upon which agnosticism bases itself, is the last survival of those many dualisms which owe their origin to the primitive distinction between soul and body. With the total elimination of all dualistic distinctions, agnosticism likewise vanishes, and we are then for the first time left with a thoroughgoing and completely consistent creed— the creed which is progressively strengthened by every advance in science, namely, naturalism.

Up to a certain point, in its treatment of animistic beliefs, naturalism argues on lines very similar to those of scepticism, viewing the primitive distinction between soul and body as resting upon a number of false inferences, and as being the ultimate source of all those dualisms—

16

between mind and matter, between the natural and the supernatural—that, as it believes, have hitherto vitiated philosophical thinking. What distinguishes naturalism is its more sympathetic attitude towards animistic beliefs on their practical side. For as I have already suggested, naturalism has ceased to be exclusively interested in physical and cosmological problems. As a *philosophy*, it now rests its main hopes on the medical, psychological, and social sciences; and from the recent developments of these sciences it has, like idealism, learned many lessons, especially as regards the predominant part played in practical life by instinct and the emotions. It recognises that in virtue of our instinctive equipment we have profound idealising tendencies, and that one of our fundamental needs is that of devoting our energies to some end more enduring and wider than our own personal well-being. And it also recognises—what is so abundantly evident in the light of history—that until a social movement takes on an emotional character, and indeed becomes a religious crusade that can regard itself as directed against the powers of darkness, it can never be genuinely popular and secure the adhesion of the masses of men. Accordingly naturalism has in recent times more and more expounded itself in the form of an enthusiastic, humanitarian, and indeed utopian creed, with an ethics emotionally charged by the harsher impulses of hatred and indignation as well as by the softer sentiments of love and pity.

Even of the traditional religions naturalism now speaks in a more sympathetic manner. Having discovered, as it believes, a use for religion, it has a fondness for eulogising the beneficial influence exercised by religious illusions in the past; and may even be heard to express fears that, owing to their merely theoretical falsity, they may be undermined too rapidly, before education and social reform can be sufficiently advanced to allow of the more reliable sanctions of a secularist religion taking their place.

This view of traditional beliefs as illusory and yet temporarily beneficial also enables naturalism to assign an

17

honourable place to poetry and the fine arts. They have strengthened the illusions that are biologically necessary, eliminating what is deleterious in them, and purifying them of all but their quintessential stimulating power. This, it is contended, is the function of the arts so long as we remain at play in nature's nursery. But even in the enlightened society of the future, when nature will no longer be allowed—so it is argued—to treat us like children, deluding us for her own ends, and when nothing, therefore, will be permitted to come between us and reality, to the arts will still belong the task of keeping up man's courage and of allaying his discontentments. They will depict the ideals of a secularist society and the modes of life that most contribute to its consummation.

Thus present-day naturalism has all the more seriously to be reckoned with that it is no longer exclusively intellectualist in its interests and outlook, but endeavours to organise a type of civilisation and of religion in harmony with itself, and can provide a programme that may guide us in the supreme and ultimate choices of our practical life.

Naturalism has also, in the past twenty-five years, made one other very notable change of position, and again in reaction against agnostic teaching. In its most recent expositions it shows an eagerness to come into line with the idealist view that the logical criteria have absolute validity, that knowledge is really knowledge, that is to say a form of genuine insight, revealing to us the independent real. Accordingly what present-day naturalism is now generally most anxious to disavow is any sympathy with the sceptical, subjectivist, pragmatic view of knowledge. It claims to be realistic, and to interpret man, not in the manner of John Stuart Mill or Huxley, as dealing with reality only through the mediation of subjective sensations, but as apprehending it face to face. The distinction between truth and falsity is as absolute a distinction as can well be conceived. When we assert that a proposition is true—for instance the proposition, gravity varies inversely

18

as the square of the distance—we are claiming that it must
be recognised as valid by other minds as well as by our
own. This is the feature whereby the true is distinguished
from the merely advantageous or useful. It holds independently of the needs and special constitution of the
individuals that assert it. Knowledge is objectivist in
character; and its judgments have jurisdiction throughout
reality as a whole.

That naturalism should thus have come to agree with
idealism in rejecting the sceptical, subjectivist view of
knowledge, may at first sight appear to be a comparatively
small matter. Both types of philosophy, it may be said,
are, of course, concerned to maintain the validity of *logical*
distinctions, since otherwise neither can hope to establish
itself as true. What we desire to know is not whether
we can distinguish between truth and falsity—that may
be granted—but in which of the competing systems
truth is to be found. For why, it may be asked, should
the conclusion that science is really science, revealing
to us the independently real, be regarded by idealism
as so vitally important, especially when what science
teaches seems to place so many obstacles in the way
of an idealist philosophy, and seems indeed, if anything,
to favour naturalism?

To these questions there is a twofold reply. In
the first place, the supreme concern of idealism is
to show that the æsthetic and spiritual values have
a more than merely human significance; and there is
apparently not the least hope of so doing if the values
that hold in the intellectual domain cannot be substantiated
as possessing objective validity. If you will pardon the
seeming truism, it is the very purpose of knowledge to
know. If knowledge is itself a deception, and its conclusions are merely practical devices for temporary
adaptation, forcing belief independently of demonstration,
there can be no hope of vindicating for the other values in
life any supra-human significance. The genuineness of
scientific knowledge must therefore be regarded as one of

19

the main supporting pillars of an idealist philosophy. Idealism cannot afford to be obscurantist; it may legitimately in certain circumstances be sceptical as to whether or not a theory has been scientifically established; but should it attack science, it will be undermining its own foundations.

But there is also a second reason why idealism welcomes, as no small advance towards eventual agreement, the recognition by naturalism of the absolute validity of the logical criteria.   If, as idealism maintains, intellectual and spiritual values stand on the same plane of objectivity, and therefore justify parity of treatment, half the battle is won when the human mind, its natural history notwithstanding, is allowed to be capable of transcending not only its subjective but even its planetary limitations.   That the human mind should possess the power of comprehending its own natural origins, and of ranging in what we call thought over the entire material universe, of which, as an animal existence, it is so minor and transitory a product, is, in the view of idealism, a fact of such central and supreme significance that agreement in regard to it must, in consistency, bring other important consequences in its train.   And this, indeed, is why the problem of knowledge—somewhat to the bewilderment of the outsider in philosophy—has always bulked so prominently in idealist systems.   The *specific* results of the natural sciences, taken by themselves and so far as they go, may support naturalism no less than idealism, and perhaps on the whole can be regarded as favouring naturalism—I should myself be willing to make this admission—yet *the fact that science exists at all*, that the human mind has proved capable of acquiring it, *when taken with the other achievements of the human spirit*, in the arts, in the moral, social, and religious life, outweighs in philosophical significance, and sets in a very different perspective, the conclusions reached exclusively through study of man's physical conditions.

If, then, scepticism, though likely to come forward

20

again in the future, is meantime in abeyance; if present-
day thinkers, with very few exceptions, can be classed as
either naturalistic or idealist in tendency; and if, further,
naturalism and idealism have in certain respects come
more into agreement with one another, what are the
issues that still divide them? Obviously this is too
large a question for me to discuss at this time; but the
differences are few and vital, and can be briefly stated.

But before I do so, I must indicate the interpretation
which idealism gives to animistic beliefs. In most
respects it is almost diametrically opposed to that given
by naturalism. Since in the early stages of human
development reflective thinking plays only a very minor
part, what we have to consider is not the *logical* sufficiency
of the causes generating the animistic beliefs, but the
extent to which these beliefs have themselves stood the
test of later experience. And judging them by this
criterion, idealism is prepared to maintain that so far are
the dualisms in which animism has issued from being the
main source of error in philosophy, that on the contrary
only through recognition of the distinctions to which they
direct our attention can human life be rightly understood.
Primitive man's distinction between the body and its
ghostly duplicate is simply the first crude formulation of
that later distinction between the physical and the
psychical which in one form or another we are bound to
accept as fundamental. The particular forms in which
such beliefs first present themselves are largely false. But
how could it have been otherwise? Their crudity stands
in a necessary correlation with the limitations of the
social *milieu* in which they are formed. Their beneficial
consequences are, indeed, dependent upon this correlation;
and to that extent their serviceableness is proportionate
to their falsity. This, however, is not because primitive
beliefs are not travelling upon the path to truth. The
path is long and devious, and can lead to its goal only as
civilisation itself progresses.

But from the point of view of idealism, animism has

21

another and even more important aspect. It embodies
certain values and criteria which reveal the human spirit,
already in the earliest stage in which it is known to us,
as being radically different, in nature and destiny, from
the animal. There may perhaps be no breach of continuity. Upon that we can hardly decide until more is
known. But meantime, as in the distinction between the
living and the lifeless, the differences between the two are,
for philosophy, more significant than any features in
which they agree. For, as we must remember, with
animism is bound up the first emergence, not only of
intellectual curiosity, and therefore of the strictly logical
criteria, but also of the moral, social, religious, and
æsthetic aspects of human life; and the fundamental,
permanently valuable character of the categories which
they involve is sufficiently established by their after-
history. Naturalism, in contradiction of its own earlier
prophecies, has itself been compelled to recognise that
they have a continuing validity, and represent so many
ultimate and irreducible aspects of human existence.

And now I return to the questions at issue between
naturalism and idealism. They are opposed on one
fundamental conviction. According to naturalism, parts
of the Universe are more complex and are more completely unified than is the Universe as a whole.
Certain parts, too, possess higher qualities, such as life
and consciousness, which are not to be found in the wider
reality that includes them. That is to say, when we
sample reality, parts are found to be superior to the
whole. The Universe is, as it were, merely the stage,
and is not itself a centre of interest; what alone

22

signify are the episodes that happen in this or that part of it.

Idealism, on the other hand, is committed to the assertion that the Universe is at once richer and more highly unified than any of its parts. And as man is the most complex existence known to us, it is upon the clues supplied by our specifically human experience that idealism bases its ultimate conclusions. For though man can, indeed, be studied only in his natural setting, for an understanding of his nature and destiny idealism refers us to that wider reality which is depicted in poetry and the arts, and worshipped in religion, and which, though not yet scientifically known, can be philosophically discerned as conferring upon human life its standards and values.

This main cleavage of opinion determines all the other differences between naturalism and idealism. Naturalism finds in matter, or at least in the non-conscious, the ground-work of reality; idealism finds in spiritual values the key to ultimate problems. Naturalism has to treat human values as merely relative; idealism interprets them as disclosing a richer and more comprehensive Universe than can yet be defined in scientific terms.

The picture which naturalism forms of the Universe is decided for it, in its main features, by astronomy. Reality is made up of solar systems scattered throughout infinite space, many of which, presumably, contain planets inhabited by beings more or less similar to the human race. These systems arise and decline, in the manner of plants and animals on the surface of the earth; their life-period is immensely longer, but not otherwise different. Though innumerable civilisations have, we may believe, already made their appearance and vanished in infinite time and infinite space, they do not, like the lives on one planet, form a series or evolution. They are detached episodes that combine to form no cosmic drama. Meaning is to be found only within the parts of the Universe; there is no meaning in the Universe itself.

Idealism cannot, in opposition to this cosmology,

23

profess to offer any definite picture of physical reality as a whole. This, frankly, is the weaker side of idealism. At best, it can only confess its ignorance. But since astronomy makes no claim to finality in these matters, and indeed can already detect traces of a systematic order in the stellar Universe, idealism is not disabled from postulating that on fuller knowledge physical reality will be found to be unified in a manner consistent with all that the facts of the spiritual life may demand. Idealism can venture on this postulate without professing to have the least knowledge how in detail the required unity can be possible, and on what lines, mathematical, astronomical, or other, science may ultimately perhaps be led to its establishment.

Now since the only basis upon which idealism can rest this far-reaching conclusion is the contention that spiritual no less than intellectual criteria have an absolute validity, idealism must stand or fall according to its success or failure in upholding this latter position, in face of the counter-arguments of the naturalistic philosophies.

Present-day naturalism, as I have already stated, is not only willing but eager to recognise all values, spiritual as well as intellectual. As a philosophy, it embraces the whole ambit of human existence, and professes to offer an interpretation adequate to every one of its many aspects. But while doing so, it claims that the intellectual values stand apart by themselves, and that from them no argument applicable to æsthetic and moral values can be obtained. Logical criteria, it is argued, are indeed absolute; scientific judgments are valid through-out reality as a whole. But the æsthetic, spiritual, and social criteria, it contends, are in a very different position. They are so inextricably bound up with the civilisation of our planet, that upon them no judgments having wider jurisdiction can legitimately be based. Our ter-restrial civilisation, in all its main characteristics, is deter-mined by the particular physical, geographical, biological, economic, and other conditions that render it just the kind

24

of civilisation it is; and should we attempt to consider moral or spiritual values in abstraction from the complex contingencies in which alone they are known to us, they lose all definiteness and all meaning. They are so many forms of adaptation, and are as specific as the environment that prescribes and defines them. Anthropomorphic conceptions are meaningless, and therefore useless, in metaphysics.

This is surely obvious, naturalism argues, in the case of the fine arts. They are merely human, being conditioned by physical, physiological, and psychical factors that cannot be conceived to exist with sufficient uniformity beyond this earth. Is it likely that on other planets other animal species should develop senses exactly like those of the human race? And if not, can any of the fine arts have meaning beyond this planet? Is not even the most sublime poetry inseparably bound up with the language in which it is composed, and is not this language accessible only to beings with organs of articulation and of hearing identical with our own? Or, as Spinoza has asked, can we conceive a Divine Being as delighting in music and harmony? Would not that be to picture God as an animal and as having ears?

In respect to moral values the argument may not be so obvious, but can be developed, naturalism teaches, on analogous lines. We cannot distinguish in our civilisation between elements strictly human and elements of a higher order. Our civilisation is all of a piece. It cannot be divided. What is highest in it has meaning only by reference to the detailed contingencies of terrestrial existence. Indeed, if a distinction is to be drawn between higher and lower, it must be to the lower that we assign the wider meaning. The physical elements are more uniform than the chemical, the chemical than the organic, the organic than the psychical. As we rise in the scale we pass from the less to the more organised, and therefore, according to naturalism, depart ever further from the types which alone exist universally. As we rise in the scale,

25

existence, in growing ever more complex, increases in contingency, in uniqueness; it becomes, as naturalism teaches, less and less like what is elsewhere in the Universe, more and more provincial, more and more characterised by the idiosyncrasies of its own peculiar modes of existence.

Idealism, when asked to meet this philosophy, has, it is clear, no easy task. So much of the argument must at once be granted. Man is indeed, in one sense, all of a piece. The products of art, in their æsthetic quality, have no existence save by reference to our specific sense-organs. Only beings with ears exactly like our own can appreciate or even hear the sonatas of Beethoven. The colouring and perspective in a landscape by Turner can have no æsthetic value save in reaction to the human eye. Our moral duties are similarly determined by our social institutions. Looking back on the history of the race, we see how they have varied in correspondence with social customs; and presumably our descendants, looking back upon us after some thousands of years, will discern a similar correlation in our present moral codes.

Idealism does not proceed by evading these facts. On the contrary, it objects that naturalism has inconsistently broken off its argument in mid-career. When naturalism distinguishes between logical and all other values, assigning absoluteness to the one and denying it to the others, by what right does it do so? If man is the most highly organised form of existence known to us, and therefore the most contingently conditioned, and therefore also, as naturalism is constrained to argue, the most provincial, how comes it that he can pass judgments that have universal validity? These judgments depend upon the working of a nervous system that is even more elaborately organised than the eye and the ear. They are expressed in a grammar and through concepts all of which are as complexly conditioned in their historical development as are any of the products of the fine arts. If naturalism replies that at least in its concepts science contrives to abstract from the limiting conditions peculiar to human

26

thought, the sufficient answer is that, by its own teaching, conception is conditioned by imagination, that imagination is conditioned by perception, and that power of perception is as relative to the constitution of our sense-organs as are any of the æsthetic qualities. And lastly, there is no such thing in human experience as thought apart from language, any more than according to naturalism there can be thinking apart from the brain. If all this does not disqualify thought from possessing independent validity; if man, the most complexly conditioned of known existences, can none the less so far rise above his individual and planetary limitations as to apprehend the universal, a more subtle treatment of the allied problems is surely demanded.

That the moral duties imposed by the honour code of the blood-feud are no longer recognised as binding, and would indeed under present social conditions be actively anti-moral, does not prove that these primitive distinctions have no wider or deeper moral significance than that discerned by those who practised them. Meaning is always relatively independent of its embodiments. This is why the same meaning can in some degree, however small, be translated from one art into another, from one language into another. The essential characteristic of meaning is that it carries the mind beyond what is immediately apprehended, disclosing to it something more than is actually presented. Beauty is not in sounds, nor in form and colouring, taken by themselves; it exists only in and for the mind in its reaction to them. Similarly, morality does not consist in this or that act, but in the disposition and the will that find through such acts a mode of expression. And this is equally true of intellectual apprehension. The materials employed are certain sensations and certain articulate sounds, and the psychological mechanism through which they are filled out from past experience. But the outcome, the apprehension of meaning, while made possible by these materials, is distinct from them; it is an act of the mind,

27

and only so is able to transcend subjective contingencies, and to reach to the independently real.

Naturalism, that is to say, cannot explain the fact of knowledge and the employment of logical criteria, save by allowing to the mind a power of transcending its subjective limitations, and of apprehending from subjectively conditioned data, by means of subjective processes, an objective meaning. No more is required in order to render intelligible the objective claims of æsthetics and morals. As possessing *some* kind of absoluteness, they are neither more nor less mysterious than the fact of knowledge. They reveal human existence as being of the same ambiguous texture—rooted in contingency, acting only through the channels provided by its natural setting, and while transmuting itself to ever higher forms, yet still to the end remaining a creaturely existence that finds its salvation not in independence of its animal conditions but in using them as the instruments for the expression of desires and meanings that genuinely transcend them. For, from the point of idealism, once it has been accepted, the chief mystery is not how the human spirit should be able to rise above its natural conditions, but how these conditions should be so amazingly responsive to the demands made upon them—that in sounds, in rhythm, in pigments, in lines and surfaces, that by such a beggarly bag of tricks as constitutes the stock in trade of the poet and the artist, so great a wealth of spiritual meaning can be conveyed. But it is no more wonderful than that man, a being endowed with some few senses, and incapable of thought save through the conventions of language, should be able to discover in science the secrets of the Universe. *A priori* arguments, and analogies drawn from the purely physical, cannot decide the issue. It is not to be dealt with in any merely dialectical fashion. It must involve a first-hand study of the facts to be accounted for.

Bertrand Russell has advocated the limiting of philosophy to the strictly *a priori*; and others, while allowing it a wider range, would assign æsthetic, ethical,

28

and kindred problems to special sciences. These are views which I cannot now discuss. But in any case, it will probably be agreed that the most important and fruitful of the changes that have taken place in the philosophical disciplines since the eighteenth century has been the growing recognition that logical analysis and dialectic, however indispensable, can play only a subordinate part in the solution of the problems traditionally assigned to philosophy. For instance, in theology it is no longer regarded as possible to demonstrate by dialectical argument the existence of God. It is recognised that such so-called proofs are at best merely outline indications of the various directions in which such demonstration can be sought. It is in the highly specific facts of religious experience in the past and in the present, in their co-ordination with the other aspects of life, and through study of them in all the detail of their historical accompaniments, that the evidence—if adequate theoretical evidence there be—is alone to be found.

In philosophy, as in all science and in all art, the fundamental maxim of sound workmanship is that we keep our eye upon the subject. Many opponents of idealism, to judge from their frequent practice, seem to believe that the more they keep their eyes off the human values, or at least away from the great traditions in which they have found expression, the less they will be biassed in passing philosophical judgments upon them. They approach them only through the study of our natural and economic setting, or through analogies derived from the study of animal behaviour. Virtually, the result is that they do not study them at all. In effect, though not in intention, they depict them from hearsay and condemn them *in absentia*. The outcome is not science but pseudo-science, and a violation of all those principles of sound reasoning to which they give their adherence in the fields in which they are more familiarly at home. The more intimate aspects of human existence must be appreciated from the inside; otherwise the distorting

29

preconceptions that are inevitable to an outside spectator will never be detected.

Philosophy, it is admitted, must not presume to compete with the sciences in the fields appropriated by the sciences; but this makes it all the more necessary that it obtain due recognition of those aspects of life for which no sciences have yet been able to make themselves responsible. And for this reason philosophy is more closely bound up with the historical and humanistic disciplines than with those of the deductive and demonstrative type. As Renan has remarked, the modern philosophical school should have as its device: "Let no one enter here who is not acquainted with the human spirit." In Plato's time geometry was a new thing, and few had knowledge of it. Nowadays science is in the ascendant, and is even in danger of encroaching on other legitimate interests.

If, therefore, objection be made that the argument upon which idealism rests its case is merely general, and lacks the detailed evidence that makes science so irresistible, I should reply that in what I have said thus far the evidence proper has not been considered. As I have suggested, it is to be obtained only through careful and exhaustive study of all that the human spirit has brought into existence, in the arts, in the moral, social, and religious spheres, as well as in science. By these activities it has added, as it were, new dimensions to the non-human world which, according to naturalism, alone previously existed, and by which naturalism has allowed the main outlines of its philosophy to be predetermined.

When all is said, it is still, of course, true that philosophy remains philosophy. It is a more precarious enterprise than science. The personal factors cannot be eliminated in the same complete degree; and at the present time, as I have tried to show, we are faced by two alternative ways of thinking, neither of which has been able, quite decisively, to displace the other. Allow me, in conclusion, to restate the opposition in a few sentences. In the view

30

of a naturalistic philosophy, man is a being whose capacities, even in their highest activities, are intelligible only as exercised *exclusively in subordination* to the specific requirements of his *terrestrial* environment. For the student of the humanities, on the other hand, man is adapted, indeed, to his environment, but measures himself against standards for which it cannot account. He is not a piece of nature's mechanism, but himself a microcosm, prefiguring in his art, in his moral codes and social institutions, and in religion, the wider reality to which as a finite being he can have no more direct method of approach. His true self-knowledge is made possible by values and standards that constitute his humanity in distinction from the animals; and it is by their absoluteness that they deliver him from the limitations of strictly animal existence.

Naturalism grants this argument in so far as it applies to our *intellectual* standards. We attain absoluteness, naturalism declares, in the intellectual domain, but never in other fields. That we attain it in the intellectual domain, and likewise in other fields, is the creed of idealism. And if, as must be admitted, idealism has its own difficulties, they are not, I should say, of the same desperate character as those which naturalism is called upon to face.

There is, it appears to me, this difference between naturalism and idealism. The first steps towards naturalism are easy and convincing. Naturalism takes the present results of the positive sciences at what appears to be their face-value, and from them it professes to obtain data sufficient for the establishment of a comprehensive philosophy. When, however, this philosophy is applied in interpretation of the more intimate aspects of human experience, it becomes ever increasingly unsatisfactory. With idealism, on the other hand, the first steps are the most difficult. Its final conclusions exceed the insight yet yielded by the positive sciences, but do not contradict them; and it may be claimed that they are based upon a

31

more thorough study of those features of our experience which have not yet been subjected to scientific treatment.

I did not, however, set out to argue these high matters, but only to present the issues upon which naturalism and idealism are at present divided. Though each of these types of philosophy may be developed in a variety of forms, with subordinate differences, in regard to the main issue they express the two alternatives between which we are called upon to choose. They are, we may say, the summary and expression of opposing types of civilisation; for there is little in human life that will be left unaffected, according as we make our decision for one or the other.

III

Draft of Letter from Norman Kemp Smith
to Samuel Alexander

(von Hügel MS 2999, St. Andrews)

The Lagg,

August 16. 1920   Boat of Garten,

Inverness-shire.

Dear Alexander,

I have just finished a first reading of your 'Space, Time & Deity', & also a second more summary reading of main sections; and before setting to on a further study of special portions should like to send you my first impressions. I have not read anything on the theory of knowledge for *very* many years that has so stirred up my thinking, or made me so keenly conscious of the thin or wooly places in the speculations that I have been entertaining. Taken as a whole it makes a most massive impression; & is likely, I believe, to mark an epoch in British philosophy. And if that is the impression which it makes on me, with my present very different tendencies, this is likely to be felt even more strongly by others.

I was rather afraid, judging from my experience in studying your Gifford summaries, that I should not be able quite to grasp your argument regarding Space–Time; but here, as in your other doctrines, I have found that the difficulties be mainly (apart from novel terminology) in the previously formed assumptions that are brought to the reading of your argument. It is not easy to reverse them or even sometimes to be conscious of them; & hence the bewilderment. Your theory or rather analogy I have found quite fascinating, & especially in its bearing on the meaning of present, past & future. Your distinction too between sections & perspectives is very illuminating. But the doctrine is so revolutionary, carrying with it, apparently the consequence that nothing can exist that is not spatial, & that mind as in time must also be in space, that thus far it disquiets & unsettles me in fundamentals quite as much as it enlightens.

Your discussion of the philosophical significance of the higher geometrics I also welcome. In my *Commentary*, under the influence of my Princeton colleague Veblen (who, I think, has collaborated with the Young, from whom you quote, in a 'Projective Geometry') I accepted non-Euclidean spaces as metaphysically possible. Your criticism is most helpful, & I am very willing to reserve judgment. Indeed I should adopt your standpoint but for two difficulties: (a) that I am far from clear, as I shall indicate below, as to the relation in which conception & intuition stand to one another; & (b) that I cannot altogether away with Euclidean Space–Time viewed as ultimate. But this does not keep me from feeling the force (as I had not before) of your defence of the older standpoint.

Recently I have been rereading Bosanquet's Gifford Lectures—this time with greater profit, & with somewhat the same feelings of constant distroughtness between attraction by and opposition to what I read. Where the argument touches me is that I have been more or less wont to practise the method which Bosanquet (I, p. 278) describes as "fundamentally eristic, proceeding by the juxtaposition of extreme cases in the absence of (or at least with less attention to) the analysis which would exhibit their continuity."

This, I take it, is one of the main points in your own argument, when you insist upon the mind's "alignment with other things", as "the way of the world", & upon accepting only those miracles that *pervade* the world of things.

I recognise the force of this position; but should urge that such a method has its own dangers, leading to an exaggeration of the possibility of a rounded metaphysic for beings situated as we are, & arguing as we must from imperfect data. And in support of this contention I might point to the frequency with which you are constrained to argue deductively from ultimate principles & analogically from the type of existence we know best as embodied in ourselves.

Thus the sections in which you deal with the secondary qualities (apart from your contention of their non-mental character) I still find very difficult, especially your conceiving the secondary qualities as related to their space–time patterns on the *analogy* of the relation of mind and body. And I feel the danger of your general method still more forcibly in the concluding sections of vol. II on Values. You seem to me there in the main to be rounding off your system according to certain deductively applied corrolaries to which you are committed not by direct study of the moral, aesthetic and religious fields but almost exclusively by your Space–Time doctrines. Sorley in his Gifford Lectures distinguishes between the Berkeleian & the Platonic methods of dealing with ethics, & adopts the former. All my sympathies are with the latter. A social ethics, such as you outline, is certainly better than an individualist point of view; but subjectivism in any form, even in your socially conceived form, seems to be as perverting in this field as it is in the field of knowledge. *Tensions*, produced by metaphysical (or better, religious) & not merely social influences, seem to me to be fundamental in accounting for the moral situations. You were saying that you cannot read ethics: I wish none the less you would look some-time into E. Troeltsch's 'Sociallehren der Kirchlichen Sekten u. Grup-pen'.—really a history of Christian ethics: I think you would find there material that would interest you, even tho' his main positions you certainly could not accept.

A further difficulty I have in these Sections in vol. II is in your cor-responding treatment of the truth values. It appears to me hardly in harmonising it with your realism [*sic*]. I can see that opportunities of social intercourse are required to enable the individual to appreciate the nature of truth & to discover it; but does this justify your treatment of truth as intrinsically a *social* product?

Apart from the fundamental Space–Time doctrine, there are (A) two of your doctrines that greatly appeal to me, & (B) two that drive me the other way. *A*. (1) Your assertion of direct intuitional appre-hension of real space & time. Stout's theory of knowledge—the most adequate statement that I know of representationism—involves either the reduplication into mental contents of the characteristics of the world known, or else (as in Ward) a Monadism or pan-psychism that lies open to the criticisms that Bosanquet so admirably states. From a short conversation that I had with Stout in July, I gather that he now inclines to agree with Kant that the mind must have an *apriori* intuition of a pure space-manifold. If so, I fail to see why this intuition should not be, as you contend, the intuition of real space–time. Your criti-cisms of the objections to this latter procedure I find extraordinarily helpful; & especially as regards images & ideas, memory & expectation & the illusions of perception. (2) Your insistence, in agreement with Stout, on the conational character of all consciousness. In writing my *Commentary* I tried, in laying my mind as best I could alongside Kant's, to work out his final position (phenomenalism as distinguished from his subjectivism), but more & more I was forced to the conclusion that it is a sheer *impasse*, & that for two reasons. First, because it makes impossible any proper recognition of the conational character of all consciousness; & secondly (& closely connected therewith), because it lies open to the objection which you state so forcibly (II, p. 111) to Holt's position & to the "searchlight" view generally. I welcome your statement that no one can differ from it "without misgiving", for it very long attracted me, ever since I found it in Malebranche, in Avenarius & in Bergson's 'Matiere et Memoire', & as I had at first thought in your own position. Such a view may take us to "consciousness in general", but not, as you justly contend, to the cognitive situation in which consciousness is always self-consciousness.

B (the doctrines that make me stumble).

(1) Your view as to the relation in which apprehension of the categories stands to the intuition of space–time. The latter you seem to take as in the first place a pure intuition, not involving employment of the categories. The categories, you appear to say, are simply read off from a previous purely intuitional apprehension of space–time. Certainly the categories *as such* can only be known reflectively; but can space–time be intuited save, as Kant argues, in so far as the categories are employed in such intuition? This raises, of course, all the questions involved in the general problem of the relation of perception & conception, of perception & judgment; & I do not feel that I have yet quite got your point of view. I should at least have expected that, as you praise Kant's argument in The Principles of Understanding, you would have introduced some criticism of his contention that only through the categories can space–time be apprehended *at all*, even intuitionally.

In this connection I find your argument regarding the intuitional apprehension of infinity in space particularly difficult to follow, especially as you recognise that Descartes (& Kant) is correct in maintaining that the infinite is known directly & before the finite. The apprehension of this aspect of space (likewise its apprehended continuity, of which infinity is one aspect) seems to be explicable only through the presupposed categorical factors.

When Kant correlates the relational categories with the various aspects of Time, he does so in order to prove that it is only in & through employment of the categories that these aspects can be apprehended at all. The categories, for him, condition apprehension of space–time, not a priori intuition of space–time the consciousness of the categories. Consequently the reason you give in I p. 189 why the categorical characters belong to the self as well as to external things would, on this view, be that as they condition *all* consciousness they also condition self-consciousness. This would also be Kant's reason for agreeing with you that the categories cannot be obtained by reflection on the self. Conditioning *all* consciousness, they make possible reflective consciousness.

(2) Your doctrine of emergences. The better you succeed in establishing your fundamental contention that reality is at first simply & exclusively space–time, the more incredible you seem to make any doctrine of emergence; & I do not see that you can justify your contention by pointing out the empirically undeniable fact of the existence of matter, secondary qualities, life & consciousness. When your argument makes emergence impossible save by a miracle—a conjuring trick of rabbits from a hat that does not contain them—the empirical fact refutes—I am pressing the difficulty as I see it—, & may not, I should say, be employed to supplement your interpretation of the initial reality. Can the "way of the world" be thus brought in, as an *opus operatum*, at every point at which your "realities" give out. You almost seem to me, at times, to appeal to "experience" as Bacon & Descartes were wont to appeal to "Revelation". The two differ of course vastly, since admittedly there can be no appeal from experience, duly analysed; but in the cases at which I stumble you seem to me to be employing an experience that cannot be harmonised with your theories to eek out the shortcomings of your theories. Do not the successive empirically verified emergences thus become so many *supplementary* hypotheses to make good the *defects* of your main hypothesis?

To the views that all truth is *defacto* & that creativeness is universal, I have no objection & indeed welcome them; but that you are prepared to regard creation as pervading all nature surely makes it more & not less necessary that your "reality" be such as to allow of it. Bergson, *in extremis*, is wont to fall back on dualism; is not even that preferable to falling back upon sheer miracle? If philosophy, as I am ready to agree, can never be more than *interpretation* of experience, can your philosophy be said to interpret when it explains the experienced by reference to Space–Time plus a miracle that becomes more & more gorgeously miraculous in proportion as experience becomes more complex—a process to which, on your philosophy, there *can* be no end, since Time is infinite, & can never reverse itself so as to become cyclical or even retrogressive (am I correct in taking this to be your contention?)? Such a Space–Time is indeed big with promise of the Divine! We might well long for a deified immortality, when we think of the 10,000 emergences beyond consciousness, still to come.

The difficulties of your position seem to me to show themselves occasionally in your modes of expression. Thus in II p. 82 you say: "Cognition, then, instead of being a unique relation, is *nothing but* an instance of the simplest & most universal of all relations". Should you not rather be saying: "Cognition then is in certain respects a unique relation, & yet is an instance of the simplest etc.". Again in II p. 103: "Knowing is *nothing but* the empirical form which etc.". Why 'nothing but'? Your whole meaning is still expressed when the 'nothing but' is omitted. Similarly on II. p. 105 (six lines down). "For such a being etc."—I do not see why you insert "only". Also in I p. 26 should not summary at side of paragraph run: 'The relation of compresence involved in cognition not unique'. Otherwise you appear to be arguing from non-uniqueness of the relation of compresence in cognition to the non-uniqueness of the conscious cognition itself.

With your desire to treat the secondary qualities as non-mental I am in entire sympathy, & should incline to finding their conditions in physiological conditions, & so to regard them as transitory *events* that make their appearance when these conditions are completed through action of the physical stimuli. Your criticism of this view is one of the sections that I wish to study more attentively. Such a view is, I should hope, reconcileable with your view that space–time is apprehended intuitionally, in terms of but not through sense.

Pardon this lengthy letter & the general & rather vague character of these remarks. I wish I could try to repay some part of the debt under which your book lays me by writing quite specifically upon parts of it; but my views are still too vague & unformulated to allow of that. I could not meet you in argument on your own ground. And the above remarks, as I reread them, seem to me to dwell too exclusively on my personal difficulties, & by no means to express, as they should, the admiration with which I have followed your close-knit argument. I have got from your Lectures the best that any book can give, the stimulus & aid in moving forwards—indeed much more than I can easily cope with these days, in view of the necessity of writing class-lectures that will be sufficiently definite for lecture purposes, & yet not expound what I feel too great doubts over. Anyways your independence, courage & tenacity are the best of lessons for us youngsters (among whom I still struggle to count myself) in the duties of our profession. I shall keep the volumes at my elbow, & look forward to doing them better justice as time allows.

Yours ever sincerely,
[unsigned]

P.S. I have said nothing directly as to your view of consciousness & cognition. Had I done so, it would only have been to query, how far your treatment involves rejection of the Kantian view that employment of the categories conditions intuitional apprehension—that latter is at present my *main* difficulty.

IV

Part of a Letter from A. A. Bowman
to Norman Kemp Smith

(von Hügel MS 3003, St. Andrews)

27th Dec. 1920.

138 FitzRandolph Road
Princeton, N.J.

My dear Kemp Smith,

One of the disadvantages of distance is the difficulty of conveying greetings with the spontaneity that naturally goes with their seasonal character. When this reaches you Christmas & New Years Day will both be a matter of ancient history. Nevertheless let me wish you & all of yours a very good New Year. The times seem very dark & lowering at home, but I have almost inexhaustible faith in the British, & I think we'll pull thro' this winter as we have done thro' others.— Your letter with all its news was very specially welcome. Many thanks. Von Hügel's paper made a profound impression on my mind—& on Mabel's. There is something galvanizing in the use he makes of the term 'supernatural'. A mind to which this conception, as von Hügel expounds & marvelously illustrates it, is still unintelligible, which cannot recognise the thing by mark of head or thrill to its manifestations everywhere about one in life—is a mind to which one whole aspect of truth, & that the deeper, more illuminating aspect, must remain opaque & undivined. I cannot tell you how much I owe to the simple circumstance that von Hügel has seen the complete appropriateness of this term & has set it up as a name for things otherwise hardly to be designated in words. His closing remarks on the continuity of the natural & the supernatural are very fine & to my mind conclusive. And yet it is just here, if anywhere at all, (& I hate to think that there should be even one jarring note in my total response to a thing that has impressed me so much) that I would join issue with him. My point (or, perhaps I should say, my difficulty) is this: The Natural I know; also the Supernatural; & between the two I divine the necessity of a great & fundamental synthesis. But to my mind, altho' everywhere I detect wisps & shadows of it, & altho' in some phenomena, marriage, for instance, it becomes an embodied Fact, on the whole the Synthesis is not here & now. Especially I cannot, except in fugitive moments of admiration,

335

react positively to the Church. I deeply regret that I cannot, & the matter is perhaps temperamental. Certainly I feel to the full the impoverishment that comes from failure to detect the embodied truth in the world of established institutions—especially in institutions like the church, hoary with age & apparently impregnable to the assaults of time. It is something, however, to have even the bare intellectual conviction that in the end there must be some sort of fundamental unity between the actual & the ideal. The whole question (in one form or another) will form the subject of what I hope will be my first book. For about a year past I have been grappling with the theme, & one conviction is emerging in my mind. Philosophy is the demand for a unified experience, but the thing that matters is the precise nature of the initial plurality for which an underlying unity is sought. Now the point here is that no genuinely *philosophical* progress can be made until the initial plurality is definitely defined as a *duality*. It is possible to begin otherwise, with mere manifoldness; this is the starting-point of science. In philosophy it leads to the fallacies of naturalism. I am prepared to argue the point therefore that the specific function of philosophy, as determined by the total progress of human thought, is the resolution, not of a manifold, but of a dualism. Now in this everything depends upon the formulation of that dualism. I should say, for instance, that modern philosophy made a very bad beginning with the Cartesian dualism—thinking & extended substance being a wretchedly abstract & artificial formulation of the great antithesis of man & nature, or the world & the Kingdom, which lay ready to hand in the Fathers & the general consciousness of mankind. What philosophy must do, & do at the present day, insistently & tirelessly is to clarify the fundamental duality of existence. Out of the duality will emerge the solution. For this reason it behoves the philosopher (so it seems to me) to stand somewhat aloof—not out of the world but with his head slightly above the waters. Otherwise the practical solution which comes with identification with some great movement or institution will threaten his sense of the fundamental dualism. And it seems to me there is comfort & compensation for the pains of isolation in the thought that the deeper the cleavage the nearer we are to a final resolution. What is wrong with humanity is that it has not yet realized the nature & extent of the antithesis upon which all conscious existence rests. Every false or inadequate formulation of the dualism, every premature solution, is a retardation of the end desired. Not that the end could ever be attained without perpetually repeated unsuccessful efforts. For the compromises of history, for the established institutions, even if doomed to final ineffectuality, we cannot be sufficiently thankful; & a wise man will stand by these things even beyond the limits of their complete justification, as the early Christians stood by the Roman Empire & as we all within our spheres & to the extent of our opportunities, stood by our country in the war. But the philosopher must stand above the practical adjustments of his individual life. This seems to me the inexorable law of his existence. He is a specialist in cosmic conflicts, & the end is far off. What has meant so much to me in von Hügel's paper is his magnificent formulation of the antithesis, & if I cannot follow him into the church on earth I feel to the full the exquisiteness of his appeal; & in fact for every one but the philosopher I can conceive nothing comparable to this solution. Compared with this how meretricious & shabby is the shelter of a party or a class, an economic creed or a social code; & from no other standpoint does morality show more thin & insubstantial in the light of a higher spiritualization.

Your news interested me intensely. What a busy man you must be! Also very tired, I have no doubt. I hope to hear from you regularly about the W. E. A. Lots of your friends here are much interested in this. On Christmas night we were at Prospect at a party. There Mrs. Duane Stuart told us she had heard from Mrs. Kemp Smith how hard things are at home. The situation here is easing appreciably. Deflation is in full swing, & hard times ahead—tho' not so hard as with you. — Perhaps you'd like to hear about the salary proposition. Well, I'm afraid the poor faculty has been badly sold. It's too early to say positively, but things look very bad. I get my information exclusively from Fite & in the strictest confidence. The facts as I know them are these. A committee of three (Abbott is one. I forget who the others are) was appointed to go into the matter of each individual man's salary. Having completed their survey, they had to report to the advisory council, consisting of the heads of departments. Fite returned from this meeting in a towering passion. The president, it seems, effectually obstructed all business by refusing to permit any information as to men's salaries to be given. The council was not permitted as a [incomplete].

V

Letter of J. W. Scott
to Norman Kemp Smith

(von Hügel MS 3005, St. Andrews)

University College of South
Wales and Monmouthshire.
Cathays Park
Cardiff.
18 Jan. 1921

My dear Kemp Smith,

I have read the von Hügel pamphlet with the greatest interest and have given a reading of it to J. M. Thorburn my assistant who would like if it were possible to get a copy, for which he would of course send you the shilling. But do not worry about this if you have not more to spare.

It is all surpassingly beautiful. It has exactly the fascination, but more clearly and definitely, which his paper at Oxford had, the peculiar fascination of conveying to you the feeling that he is grappling with a goodness beyond goodness, not as a rhetorical flight but as a definite and (to him) familiar psychological fact. It is as strengthening because so simply convincing in that way.

The root of the fascination is hardly even that, though, I think. It always has a captivating power, when you encounter anyone who can speak or write in this way about the higher reaches of goodness as a thing familiar. I've encountered it once or twice before—the type of mind that has not to spend its strength merely in being good (getting the better of old Adam) but which is, habitually and easily, sublimely good. It is a great thing to meet—not necessarily a man who has achieved that but even—one who has, *indeed and authentically*, known it in another. *But* the root of von Hügel's idea, as I apprehend it, is that this advanced good, this finer bloom upon the ordinarily good life, seems to come of itself, as a kind of divine benediction "all of grace" to a man from the moment he has brought himself to do a heroic action. He (v. H.) seems, so to speak, to have his apprehension of the "supernatural life"; and having described it to us to challenge us to consider certain heroic passages of virtue and say if that be not

339

what is indeed enacting itself there. I feel very much the force of his qualification—that it does not enact itself there *only*.

And he says it is its containing the promise of these higher possibilities (of the change not merely from the bad to the good, but from the merely good to the heroic) that makes the romance of *religion*. There I want I think to disagree—not out of levity or any love of making a difficulty but because the romance of religion (that has gone out of it!) is to me always the overcoming of the Bad. Of course this is not romance exactly—it is something quite as exciting, though. If one speaks of strict *romance* in religion probably it *is* where v. H. is finding it, after all. But then, the machinery is the same—the bad is converted to goodness by the same machinery (horrid word, though) which makes goodness itself sublime. What that is I do not know, nor I think does anybody, perhaps. But this authentic transformation from the merely good to "the supernatural life" seems to me not different in kind from, but entirely of a piece with the great transaction that turns a man from sin and swings him up towards God. Perhaps once I've digested St Augustine's Anti-Pelagian writings I may be a little more articulate. Meanwhile, thanks for putting a stirring and pursuing piece of writing in my way. If you can send a copy to Thorburn, address it to University College, Cathays Park.

Many thanks too for references to Calvin & Augustine and accompanying reflections. Rather glad I told you I wanted the bottom knocked out of 'selfrealisation'—or rather to have some sort of an apology for a foundation put with it!

No. I haven't read *anything*; as you are slowly and inexorably discovering. But I'll wake up one day, D.V. I cd fain go to the Devil over psycho-analysis but I'm not going—mind quite made up!

J.W.S.

VI

Letter by Baron von Hügel
on Ernst Troeltsch
to the Editor of
The Times Literary Supplement

(No. 1106, 29 March 1923, p. 216)

ERNST TROELTSCH.

TO THE EDITOR OF THE TIMES.

Sir.—The shock brought me by the death of Professor Ernst Troeltsch, my junior by thirteen years, has been followed for me by the distress of an enforced delay in here responding to your kind permission to write a little about this great man, my much-loved friend.

It was in 1896 that, at forty-four, I first came across Dr. Troeltsch, at thirty-one, as the writer of articles on "The Autonomy of Religion." In 1899 I was absorbed in his "Metaphysics and History." Already in 1896 I possessed mature and deliberate convictions, but longed to find them similarly acquired by another mind, through slow, severe study, stress and suffering. This I now found, to my surprised delight, in strange plenitude and precision, in this young man's labours, combined, alas! with strangely little insight into the religious greatness of the extant Roman Catholic Church. It was not there that he helped me, but indeed it was not there that I required help. Ten years before I had found more than all I had ever wanted or expected in the said Church. Yet it was not nothing to be confirmed and stimulated as to certain preliminaries, complements and consequences to be described presently.

I wrote and told him all I had found in his writings, and received his first letter in April, 1901. "It is an extraordinary joy to me to meet in you a man who, by his thinking and seeking, has been led along ways similar to my own." And he then "entirely assents" to my adverse judgment on the Ritchlian theologians, Kaftan and, especially, Wilhelm Herrmann, as to their hostility to all philosophy in religion, their (violently Pauline) concentration upon only the Passion in the life of Jesus Christ, and their (more than Pauline) refusal to find God in any degree outside of His revelation in the historic Jesus.

341

I spent a week with him at Heidelberg at the end of that April—
my first and last sight of him. He was married at the end of the May
following. Though happily married to his wife, a woman with full capacity to understand his greatness, they had to suffer much from their
twelve years' childlessness, and from her long ill-health and enforced
absence from home. The only child, a boy, was born in July, 1913,
just a year before the manifold trials of the Great War fell upon us
all. The first letter after the war, January, 1920, reported four family
calamities.

> We all lament dear dead ones. My mother was struck by paralysis
> from terror at the outbreak of the war, and died soon after. My father
> was broken down by this, and lived two years longer without under-
> standing that there was a war. My sister lost her only son after two
> weeks' war service. My brother-in-law was shattered in consequence, and
> died a year later.

I always found him free from all chauvinism. Thus in October,
1905:—

> I have always before me the aim and desire to come to you to London,
> even simply at last to see at close quarters that English world for which
> I have so great an admiration. I need not tell you that I observe the
> present political development, with its increasing hostility to England, with
> pain and deep anxiety. It would be a profound calamity, and, for us,
> even a question of our further existence [as a united nation, should mat-
> ters end in war between us]. May God prevent such a conflict, which
> could bring joy only to very carnal and worldly interests.

His letters since the war all show how profoundly it had shaken his
naturally admirable psychic health and spirits. His widow wrote to me
ten days after his death (February 1, 1923), "Now the burden of the
work, the conflict, the ardent sympathy which he took upon himself
since 1914, has broken this strong heart before its time."

His labours were indeed colossal. Already at Heidelberg he combined theological and philosophical courses with concentrated authorship and membership (by election) of the Baden Upper House; and
in Berlin (when he wrote in January, 1920) he held two separate
courses as professor, laboured at research and authorship, was a
Deputy to the Prussian Landtag and Under-Secretary of State to the
Ministry of Public Worship.

The ultimate support of this storm-tossed, most strenuous life will
appear presently, but I must first indicate more plainly where lay our
chief differences. Already in his first letter, April, 1906, he declared:—

I have before me not things and persons, but principles and the historical development. And there I must admit I think that (despite the greatness of the conception of a universal ecclesiastical spiritual home for all souls) the protective means which were taken from the beginning (*i.e.*, since the Pauline theology and Church) for giving full security to this community against the world and against subjectivity have so ruthlessly elaborated the consequences of a supernaturalism bound to material things (*ein dinglicher Supranaturalismus*)—as to make a reform no more possible.

But in May, 1906, he writes:—

What you say as to my not comprehending Catholicism does not altogether surprise me. I am concerned with practical politics (that is, with immediately tangible realities) and with historical comparisons; and, for these purposes, I go by the *Officials*, as Tyrrell calls them. If I were busy with Catholicism in and by itself, especially with its future, the matter would stand differently; for Catholicism contains very much more than can be gathered thus, and possesses also, to my mind, possibilities for the future which no man can foretell.

Indeed, Dr. Troeltsch himself was thoroughly Catholic in other great matters, and for these I sought him.

I sought him for his most rarely vivid, massive, persistent, all-penetrating perception, application, and indeed living of the following profound facts and truths.

God—a Reality, *the* Reality distinct from the world, which nevertheless springs from, is supported, and is penetrated by Him. He lived this faith with grand directness. Thus in 1905, after nearly five years of childlessness and of his wife's long illness: "I am clearly conscious of the schooling by pain and trials throughout my entire being, and have found opportunity not only to utter my faith but also to live it"; and "There is too much superficiality and pose in the new religious movements, at least here in Germany. People fight shy of serious demands upon them and of definite acceptance of God in the full sense." In 1913, after the birth of his son and his wife's restoration to health and home life:—

It is impossible to express how deep are the thanks I owe to God for this happiness. We have indeed to take all things from His hand, even the heaviest, and can demand nothing, not even what may be most essential to our life. But when, after trouble, the free gift of God reaches the soul and tarries within it, it is easier to resign oneself thus fully into His hand.

And in January, 1920, after recounting the deaths of his dear ones:—

The man is to be accounted happy whom death has released from the madness of this world, and he who tarries on here has to strain his love for his fellows not a little in order to hold out amongst them. Fortunately the love of man is, at bottom, not a love of man but a love of God, which loves what is divine in man and not the poor muddle-headed creature in itself.

Man's earthly life always and everywhere [is] essentially a warfare, yet with a deep peace possible in the very midst of it. In February, 1912:—

> Whatever may happen [to depress us as to our own day], life has at all times consisted in battle and strife. Life remains a compromise between a thousand tendencies and their countless inter-crossings, but the soul can possess its dwelling in an abiding and eternal home, and can take its share of all this battle without losing its interior peace.

Conscience begins, indeed continuously operates within, the ethics of Christianity; but the living difficulty and genuine fruitfulness of all ethics begin only where conscience meets and strives to penetrate the cultural values and the social organisms. This will be grandly brought out in the coming King's College lectures.

Christianity essentially requires and rightly utilizes non-Christian, indeed not directly religious, philosophies; and, quite generally, grace presupposes and requires (innocent) nature, as especially Aquinas has finely seen and shown. This appears most impressively in the "Social Doctrines" (1912).

Christianity, as indeed every at all genuine spirituality, contains a *polarity*: from first to last it is world-fleeing as well as world-seeking; a particularly noble, delicately poised asceticism is part of its very life —the principle of monasticism is eternal. He writes in March, 1913:—

> As concerns Christian ethics, I have long been clear in my own mind that the union of the original eschatological impulse with the ancient world's ethic of cultural values is not only a peculiarity of Catholicism, but that Catholicism, by this combination, has grasped the problem as it lies within the subject-matter itself. Luther's ethics are, of course, only a transposition of the same dualism into the subjective life and the imposition of it upon all men without the escape of monasticism and without the priestly, sacramental mediation. Only the modern Protestant ethics have understood Christian ethics as an immanent ethic of the love of one's neighbor—one of the strangest and most violent misconceptions in existence.

Christianity, as all specific religion, is profoundly historical—without a genuinely historical Person and a nucleus of downright happenednesses it ceases to be itself. So in the separately published lecture "The Significance for Faith of the Historical Credibility of Jesus."

And finally, the great non-Christian world religions are not mere creations of the devil nor the sheer imaginings of the vain heart of man. In them all, though variously less than in Christianity and mingled with much obscuration, can be found some life and some help; God has nowhere left man utterly to himself. So, perhaps even excessively, in the Oxford lecture just delivered in Dr. Troeltsch's place by Professor Webb.

How humble and how homely was this mighty intellect and rich character! In March, 1903, he writes: "I ask myself whether these writings, born so largely of conflict and trouble, these fragments which so clearly betray their hurried origin, are worthy of all the love and care you give to them." And in August, 1921:—

> Pray do not over-estimate me, otherwise I must live in fear of a disillusionment should you come to know me at close quarters. I do my best, and I hope to be a man of good will; but I am painfully aware of the limitations amply set me by my endowments, my nature, and the subject-matter of my labours.

He was a mind without lightness or humour, but full of a common sense which left no room for any fanaticism. His form rarely did justice to its content. His habitual absorption in things greater than himself and others seldom allowed his native kindliness to blossom out into the charming little attentions to others readily paid by less concentrated souls. But he was great if ever man was great: "He was a man, take him for all in all, we shall not look upon his like again."

Yours faithfully,
FRIEDRICH VON HUGEL

Kensington.

INDEX

Grandmaison, Léonce de, 112
Grant, Sir Alexander, 279–80
Green, Thomas Hill, 99
Grierson, Sir Herbert John Clifford, 76, 142
Gurney, Edmund, 156

Haldane, John Scott, 132, 135
Haldane, Richard Burdon (Viscount Haldane of Cloan), 32, 56, 62, 130, 135
Handyside, John, 129, 134, 178
Harden, R. P., 291
Harnack, Adolf von, 208
Harper, George McLean, 193, 203, 230
Harrison, Agatha, 275, 277
Harvard University, 17, 57, 64, 243
Head, Sir Henry, 203
Headlam, Arthur Cayley, 94
Hegel, Georg Wilhelm Friedrich, 99, 104
Hegelianism, 120, 197
Heiler, Friedrich, 120
Hell, 149, 158–59
Heraclitus of Ephesus, 103
Herbert, J. A., 17
Herbert of Lea, Lord and Lady Sidney, 2
Herbert, Sidney, 17
Herford, Charles Harold, 145–46
Herkless, Sir John, 87
Hetherington, Sir Hector James Wright, 238, 240
Hill, J. A., 144
Hocking, William Ernest, 17, 229, 243, 245
Hoernlé, R. F. Alfred, 231
Hogan, Jean-Baptiste, 155
Hogarth, David George, 272
Holtzmann, Heinrich Julius, 5, 33, 34, 38, 40, 63, 64, 66, 73, 74, 79, 92, 99, 101, 123, 136, 161, 262
Hügel, Baron Anatole von, 146n, 164, 171, 256
Hügel, Baron Friedrich von: attempts to bring Troeltsch to England, 139, 163–64, 170–71, 173–74, 184, 189–90, 192; bad health of, 19, 21, 218, 222–23, 227, 281–82; consulted by Mrs. F. R. Lillie, 110–12, 117, 285–86; early and family life, 2–3, 164; friendship for Kemp Smith, 9–10, 43–44, 90, 107, 154–55, 207, 219, 244; Gifford Lecturer appointment at Edinburgh University, 10, 118, 130, 169–70, 172–73, 180, 182–84,

185, 186–88; historical approach to philosophy, 1; importance of spiritual values for, 23–25, 96, 125, 136–38; Jesuit reaction to, 270, 273; offered honorary D.D. by Edinburgh University, 217; on abiding consequences of sin, 158–60; on the Church, 161–62; on church membership, 8–9, 37, 48, 112–14; on the death of his dog Puck, 181; on Einstein, 191–92; on faith-healing, 138–39; on Troeltsch's life, 341–45; on his writing style, 66; participation in Oxford Symposium, 95–96, 99, 101–103, 105n; personal recommendations made by, 54–55, 58, 106–107; publication of Troeltsch's posthumous lectures, 195, 196–98, 199–200, 201–202, 206, 209–11, 213–14, 214–15; quotes letter from Troeltsch, 66–71; reaction to Kemp Smith's Inaugural Address, 44–47; repudiates appellation of "Apologist," 157–58; receives D.D. from Oxford University, 93–94; scholarship attacked by Montgomery Carmichael, 272, 282–84, 287; writings of, 18, 20, 22, 48–49, 54, 81–82, 90–91, 108–10, 172, 191, 205, 207, 245–46, 256
Hügel, Baroness Gertrud von, 9
Hügel, Baroness Hildegard von, 32, 34–35, 36, 42, 43, 49, 53, 58, 114, 146n, 180, 182, 186, 187, 193, 194, 218, 225, 289, 295
Hügel, Lady Mary Catherine von, 32–33, 35, 36, 41, 42, 43, 49, 53, 58, 87, 105–106, 114, 116, 117, 123, 127–28, 130, 133, 135, 146n, 164, 169, 171, 174, 180, 182, 184, 186, 187, 193, 194, 196, 203, 205, 206, 222, 269, 273, 285, 289, 295
Hume, David, 4, 101
Huvelin, Henri, 5, 35, 37, 38, 49, 161, 233, 234, 257
Huxley, Julian, 204–205
Huxley, Thomas, 204–205

Idealism, 5, 50, 51, 299–305, 312–15, 316–17, 319, 323–24
Inge, William Ralph, 7, 29, 200, 210–11, 213, 217, 253, 291
Interdenominational Summer School of Social Service (Swanwick), 136–37, 139, 141–42, 163, 208
Irvine, Sir James Colquhoun, 279